PLAYS AND PLAYWRIGHTS

2009

edited and with an introduction by

Martin Denton

Published by The New York Theatre Experience, Inc.
P.O. Box 1606, Murray Hill Station, New York, NY 10156
www.nyte-inc.org
email: info@nyte.org

ISBN-10: 0-9794852-2-3
ISBN-13: 978-0-9794852-2-0
ISSN 1546-1319

 Plays and Playwrights 2009 is made possible, in part, with public funds from the New York State Council on the Arts, a state agency.

Plays and Playwrights 2009 is made possible, in part, with public funds from the New York City Department of Cultural Affairs.

Plays and Playwrights 2009 is made possible, in part, by support from the Peg Santvoord Foundation.

Book and cover designed by Nita Congress

PERMISSIONS

TABLE OF CONTENTS

FOREWORD

Garth Wingfield

Ten years ago, the stars aligned perfectly at a teeny theatre on Mercer Street in New York City.

As those of us in the theatre know as a frustrating fact of life, the stars almost never align, let alone perfectly. There's always something that's off, something you wish you'd done better, something that went wildly off track. There was this one time a cat walked across the stage during a beach scene in a play I'd written, but I digress.

That afternoon, everything shifted into place.

Martin Denton happened to see my play *Are We There Yet?*, which he was reviewing for his website, nytheatre.com. We'd mounted what I thought was a respectable production, but we were having a hard time getting critics and audiences in to see it. It was late spring, when 874 shows were opening on Broadway just before the Tony cutoff. Off-off-Broadway was on no one's radar. Our short run was winding down, and I remember thinking, All this work by these talented actors and designers and a very gifted director, and it's going to close and it will be like it never happened at all.

And then, snap, snap, snap, right into place: Martin loved it. He raved. And most importantly, he got inspired. He later told me he'd had a thought similar to my own as he was leaving the theatre after the matinee he saw—that this small thing we'd created was going to evaporate after the final curtain and what a shame that was and there must be another way.

Six months later, he decided to publish an anthology of new plays he'd seen and enjoyed in New York City. It was to be called *Plays and Playwrights for the New Millennium.* I'm incredibly honored to say I was the first playwright he asked to be in it.

A lot has changed about the off-off-Broadway theatre scene since 1999. Escalating rents have forced most companies well out of Manhattan. The *New York Times* no longer publishes the extensive listings of far-flung shows it used to print on Sundays (not to mention the fact that it rarely reviews such fare at all).

The company that produced my play is long gone. And the teeny theatre where it was produced (and where we had to hold the curtain one evening because there was a rat in the women's rest room) is now a super-fancy performance space, courtesy of a multimillion-dollar renovation.

True, there are encouraging things happening downtown, like the growth and popularity of the annual New York International Fringe Festival. But there are also so many things that have faded away, like my play almost did.

And that's why what Martin is doing is so tremendously exciting and vital. The words I'm writing will appear in the tenth *Plays and Playwrights* anthology. I repeat: the tenth! He has published 104 new plays so far. And because he's published them, theatre companies around the country and around the world have decided to do them—everywhere from Boston to London.

The plays in this volume represent the very best work that's happening under the radar right now—which is where the most interesting work gets done, to my mind. Read them. Enjoy them. Pass them on.

If the off-off-Broadway theatre movement is going to survive, we need people like Martin Denton. He's passionate. He loves theatre. He loves new plays.

Ten years ago, he sat in a theatre as the lights came up and had hope.

As long as he continues to do what he's doing, so do I.

> *Garth Wingfield is the author of* Flight *(produced by the Melting Pot Theatre Company at the Lucille Lortel),* Are We There Yet? *(produced by New Voices Theatre Ensemble at Synchronicity Space),* Sunday Styles, *and* Adonis. *His evening of one-acts,* 26 Dates and Counting, *has been done in New York and Los Angeles. For television, he has written for* Queer as Folk *and* Clueless.

ACKNOWLEDGMENTS

Plays and Playwrights 2009 is a collaboration involving many people, all of whom contributed to the final product in important ways. I am immeasurably grateful to the eleven playwrights who have entrusted me with their plays; you will meet them in the pages that follow, but here I thank them humbly, in alphabetical order: Eric Bland, Rick Burkhardt, Lenora Champagne, Tim Collins, Colette Freedman, Chris Harcum, Andrew Irons, Carlos Lacámara, Michael Laurence, Nanna "Nick" Mwaluko, and Randy Sharp.

I would not have discovered these plays had it not been for the advice and assistance of a number of colleagues, namely: Ron Lasko, Brian Barnhart, Jessica Davis-Irons, Cat Parker, Terry Schreiber, Katie Rosin, Carol Polcovar, Karen Greco, Michael Gardner, Robert Honeywell, David Gibbs, Robert Lyons, Vanessa Sparling, Mark Sitko, José Zayas, José Antonio Cruz, Carolyn Raship, Erez Ziv, Emily Owens, Elena K. Holy, George Demas, and Marc Palmieri.

Once again this year, Michael Criscuolo lent his energy and talent to craft biographical essays with each of the playwrights, and he also interviewed all of them for our website, www.nytesmallpress.com.

Rochelle Denton, Managing Director of The New York Theatre Experience (NYTE), shepherded this project from conception to completion, performing tasks too numerous to name with her customary excellence and aplomb.

And finally, Nita Congress is due major kudos for her tireless work in making this book as perfect as it can be; she designed the book and its covers and meticulously copy edited this volume. The *Plays and Playwrights* books would not exist without her exceptional efforts.

This is the tenth volume of the *Plays and Playwrights* anthologies, and a few months ago, as we neared this milestone in the history of our small press, we were approached by the members of a young theatre company, No. 11 Productions, who wanted to commemorate this anniversary with a series of staged readings of representative plays among the ninety-three we've included in our books over the past decade. I, along with everyone at NYTE, am very glad that they conceived this retrospective, which is helping the works we've published continue to reach new audiences. *Plays and Playwrights 2009* is dedicated to Julie Congress, Mitchell Conway, and Ryan Emmons, who collectively are No. 11 Productions, with gratitude. The theatre community will be hearing from these young artists in the years to come.

Martin Denton
December 31, 2008

INTRODUCTION

Martin Denton

Plays and Playwrights 2009 contains eleven plays that premiered in New York between September 2007 and September 2008. The presidential election dominated our national attention during this period—an election that was widely felt to be of enormous significance. The eventual triumph of Barack Obama signaled a sea change in the direction of the United States, and the economic crisis that boiled over in the months just before the election portended transformations in every sector of American life. There is much uncertainty ahead, but there is also an undercurrent of optimism.

All of this is reflected in the book you are about to read. *Plays and Playwrights 2009* is the tenth volume in this series of anthologies that now spans the entire first decade of the new millennium. Never before has a single theme so defined one of these collections! This book is about identity—about people coming to terms with who they are as individuals, as artists, and as citizens; about a nation trying to find itself and, perhaps, redefine itself.

Bookending the volume are two powerful works about the process of looking backward and looking ahead, *Hospital 2008* by Randy Sharp and Axis Company and *Krapp, 39* by Michael Laurence. In between these pieces are nine plays that fall into two groups: four whose focus is on personal identity, in which protagonists grapple with the death of loved ones, the limitations of their own imaginations, and gender issues (*Linus & Alora* by Andrew Irons, *Sister Cities* by Colette Freedman, *S/He* by Nanna "Nick" Mwaluko, and *Death at Film Forum* by Eric Bland); and the remaining five that are more outward-directed, exploring specific subjects like

1

immigration policy and torture (*Nowhere on the Border* by Carlos Lacámara and *Conversation Storm* by Rick Burkhardt) or more generally the last eight years of American history and our apparent failure to remember what came before them (*American Badass, or 12 Characters in Search of a National Identity* by Chris Harcum, *A Fire as Bright as Heaven* by Tim Collins, *TRACES/fades* by Lenora Champagne). Together, these new American plays encapsulate a year that felt like no other for most of us who lived through it.

They are reflective, too, of the ever-evolving theatre scene in New York City in which they were incubated and developed. Seven of this year's plays were produced in theatre festivals, which have become perhaps the most nurturing environment for the creation of interesting new drama—on these pages you will find work that premiered at FRIGID New York, the Fresh Fruit Festival, the Brick Theater's annual themed summer festival (this year's theme was Film), Ice Factory '08, and of course the New York International Fringe Festival. The other four had their New York premieres at indie/alternative venues of long standing: the Flea, Repertorio Español, T. Schreiber Studio, and Axis Theatre (which occupies the building that once was home to Charles Ludlam's Ridiculous Theatre Company).

Most of the plays included here incorporate media technologies in ways that wouldn't have been attempted when the *Plays and Playwrights* series began ten years ago. *Linus & Alora* relies on a stream of projected video and images both to set the mood and define the space; *TRACES/fades*, *American Badass*, and *Krapp, 39* use a variety of multimedia techniques, including live video, to enhance their storytelling; and *Hospital 2008* and *Death at Film Forum* have significant prerecorded video components. At the other end of the spectrum, *A Fire as Bright as Heaven* is a solo epic performed literally out of a suitcase, with virtually no props, sets, or costumes called for; *Sister Cities*, *Nowhere on the Border*, *S/He*, and *Conversation Storm*—hugely contemporary pieces in different ways—require only the traditional markings of theatre for successful production.

Plays are living, dynamic things, so please do not just read these eleven—perform them, produce them, put them on the stage to share their brilliance with audiences across the United States and around the world into the future. (Beginning on page i, you will find contact information for all of the playwrights.)

Explore and engage with these plays still further online. Visit the book's official website at www.nytesmallpress.com/pp09, where you will find a variety of useful materials—photos, interviews, and links to resources—that will enhance your appreciation of these new American dramas and perhaps encourage and assist you as you mount them yourself. Check out The Indie Theater Companion (www.indietheatercompanion.com/), another NYTE project, to learn more about the history and latest developments in the vibrant and vital indie theater sector. (Here you'll also find our compendium of New American Plays produced in New York City, which was previously included as an appendix in prior volumes of *Plays and Playwrights* and now is available online.)

❧ ❧ ❧ ❧ ❧

Plays and Playwrights 2009 begins with *Hospital 2008*, a four-part serial play by Randy Sharp and Axis Company. Axis has been presenting new editions of *Hospital* almost every summer since 1999, and looking back I am astonished that I never caught up with this remarkable endeavor of theirs until now. The structure of the work is fundamentally the same each year: the protagonist is always a person in a coma, and his/her sub-/unconscious thoughts are conveyed in four thirty- to forty-minute episodes (performed in succession for two-week runs over the course of two months). Each episode begins with a filmed sequence that provides background about the main character's life and then continues with three live scenes, the first depicting the event that led to the person's accident/illness, the next set in a surreal hospital where a team of strange and bungling physicians and nurses attend to the patient, and finally a dream sequence exploring the thoughts and anxieties of the protagonist. (Only the onstage scenes are presented in this volume.)

Like any serial worth its salt, *Hospital 2008* is filled with surprises and suspense—indeed, the early episodes are deliberately riddled with obscure references and puns to keep audiences off balance while disclosing increasing amounts of information to entice them to return to successive shows. (I know I was hooked to a greater degree after each show!) Axis's presentation is meticulous and detailed, with prodigious research undertaken to support the underlying story. In this case, the protagonist—known to us only as the Traveller—is caught in a catastrophic collapse of an underground water tunnel; Sharp and her collaborators set the stage for *Hospital 2008* with this information in the show's press release:

> New York runs on water. From the steam system that heats and electrifies the five boroughs, to the water that flows from millions of taps, without water there is no city. Currently, only two tunnels provide all this water; Tunnel #1 was completed in 1917 and even the newest sections of Tunnel #2 are at least 73 years old. Begun in 1970, Water Tunnel #3's projected completion

date is in 2020. As far underground as the Chrysler Building is tall, teams of "sandhogs" risk their lives digging the path for this tunnel. Every day, far down beneath the feet of all New Yorkers, below the subway and the sewer, the sandhogs live their days in a dangerous, subterranean universe.

Hospital 2008 tells a compelling, even thrilling story of this unfamiliar world while probing the interior life of its comatose hero, who with each passing moment moves away from what he's known and toward something scary and final. That the piece is somehow dazzlingly life affirming speaks to the ultimate genius of its creation.

❦ ❦ ❦ ❦ ❦

Andrew Irons's play *Linus & Alora* manages something quite similar as it tells the story of a married couple dealing with life-changing events. At the very beginning of the play, Alora learns that she is ill and has nine months to live. (Irons uses the device of a perpetual clock counting back the seconds from 21,772,800 to remind us of her—and our—mortality.) But this is not a play about dying. Instead, it's about learning how to live fully: Alora uses the resources at her command—including, principally, her three imaginary brothers—to teach Linus how to recover his own lost sense of wonder and awe.

This is a gorgeous play, and it was beautifully realized by director Jessica Davis-Irons (who is the playwright's wife) for the premiere by Andhow! Theatre Company at the Flea. At the center of the original production were two extraordinary performances in the title roles by Arthur Aulisi and Melle Powers. (For those who keep track of this sort of thing, Aulisi has now had lead roles in plays published in three different *Plays and Playwrights* volumes, having starred as Karl Marx in Alec Duffy's *The Top Ten People of the Millennium Sing Their Favorite Schubert Lieder* [2006] and as Jay in Margie Stokley's *Elephant* [2005].)

Irons has written vivid, poetic dialogue that brings the situations in the play from the specific to the universal. Here, for example, is an exchange from very early in the play, where Alora is trying to push her husband beyond himself, and he can't see what she's doing:

> LINUS: We should get out of here, you know? Go for a walk, take a vacation from the couch.
>
> ALORA: Where do you want to go?
>
> *(The BROTHERS fade into the background but never leave.)*
>
> LINUS: I don't know…the park? Get some fresh air.
>
> ALORA: In the world…The universe. Where do you want to go?

LINUS: I don't know. You know I'm not so good at this.

ALORA: You can do it.

LINUS: What do you want me to say? I want to go to the stars? Sit on the moon and look at the world below?! I want to go to the park across the street, or the grocery store or to do the laundry…with you. What do you think about that? That's where I want to go.

Linus & Alora offers directors and actors great opportunities for the-sky's-the-limit flight of fancy, and I hope theatre artists will seize them with the same vigor that Alora teaches her husband in this touching and richly human play.

✔ ✔ ✔ ✔ ✔

The inciting incident of Colette Freedman's *Sister Cities* is the suicide of Mary, the tough, self-absorbed, glamorous mother of four grown daughters. These women—each of whom, whimsically, is named after the place where she was born (their names are Carolina, Austin, Dallas, and Baltimore)—have not spent time together or even seen each other for many years, and their rediscovery of one another as adults forms the backbone of the play. At the same time, each comes to terms with her own identity, mortality, and individuality as a natural result of coping with the death of a parent.

This is a wise play, as well as a very funny one; its depth sneaks up on you while you enjoy the very natural banter and backtalk that the sisters engage in:

AUSTIN: Family is my priority. Carolina has the career. I choose the family.

BALTIMORE: Dallas has the husband. So, where does that leave me?

AUSTIN: With the potential. That's the nice thing about still being young. You can do anything.

BALTIMORE: I can't do that many things.

AUSTIN: Yes, but your youth perpetuates the illusion that you're capable of infinite possibilities.

BALTIMORE: I'm getting my master's in sociology. I think my possibilities are pretty finite.

Freedman peppers her script with observations on a variety of pro-vocative and serious subjects, including one that fuels a key twist in the story that I will not reveal here but will instead let you experience and enjoy when you read the play. *Sister Cities* is a socially conscious work that gives audiences room to explore and question aspects of their own lives that they may take for granted.

One of the particular gifts Freedman makes to artists in *Sister Cities* is providing four strong, engaging roles for actresses (there are no men in the play at all; how rare is that?). Each of the women is smart, sympathetic, and self-actualized—I love that none of them, starting with the now-deceased Mary (whom we meet in a flashback halfway through the story) requires a man to define herself.

Certainly the New York premiere, directed by Cat Parker at T. Schreiber Studio, showcased the personalities and talents of a skillful five-woman ensemble. One of the particular charms of that production—thanks to a terrific set design by George Allison and the expert work of the company—was the way that we believed, from the outset, that these women really are members of a not-so-close but very real family. Freedman's characters are quirky and theatrical, but at the same time they feel so authentic and so familiar that they lead us organically into their individual stories.

❧ ❧ ❧ ❧ ❧

Nanna "Nick" Mwaluko's *S/He* is the most inwardly directed exploration of identity in *Plays and Playwrights 2009*. Its subject matter is unusual: the struggle of a young African American who is biologically female to manifest her true gender identity, which is male. Samantha—who bristles when people call her that; she insists on "Sam"—is saving up for an operation that will make her outside match what she knows about her/himself on the inside. *S/He* presents Sam in conflict with schoolmates, her boss, her mother, her father, and her ex-lover. The play is startlingly balanced, presenting not only how others see Sam but how s/he sees her/himself. Its forthright depiction of its pre-op transgender hero/ine makes it a singular work of theatre.

But *S/He* has more going for it than simply a seriously underserved subject. Playwright Mwaluko is a gifted writer with a penchant for highly charged personal dramas. I first became acquainted with his work at the 2006 Fresh Fruit Festival, where his play *Waafrika* premiered. That play is about the severe discrimination leveled against homosexuals in Kenya under the repressive regime of Daniel arap Moi.

In addition to its exploration of gender politics, racism, and homophobia, it shares Mwaluko's often unorthodox approach to playmaking. In *S/He*, scenes drift together impressionistically; characters often speak in a kind of street poetry:

SAM: You're smoking. Thought you quit.

MOM: And now I quit quitting. Cigarette after cigarette after pack after— *(Pause.)* Downed half a bottle of—I don't even know what this shit is *(Lifts the bottle.)* Two a.m. with a bottle, why? My nerves are smashed, why? I should call the police. Why? Because my seventeen-year-old daughter—

SAM: I'm not—

MOM: Where you been? And don't lie to me out working when I know for a fact jobs do not end at two in the morning unless you're a drug dealer, a whore, or a drug-dealing whore. Which one are you, Samantha?

SAM: Call me Sam. My fucken name is—

MOM: What I'd just say about curse words in *my* house, Samantha? I will call you what I want when I want how I want to. This is *my* home. I am *your* mom.

S/He also premiered at the Fresh Fruit Festival, under the precise direction of José Zayas. Mwaluko has made some revisions of his script for publication, and is working on a second act that will turn the piece into a full-length play. In its one-act form, though, it is potent and thought-provoking, and deserves to reach a broad audience.

🖊 🖊 🖊 🖊 🖊

Death at Film Forum, by Eric Bland, marks the first time that a script from one of the Brick Theater's annual themed festivals has appeared in a *Plays and Playwrights* collection. For several years now, the Brick has hosted summertime events focused on such diverse topics as moral values and artistic pretension that have helped make this intimate Williamsburg, Brooklyn, space one of the premier indie theater venues in New York City. Bland, who also directs his work, exemplifies the edgy and often irreverent spirit of the Brick with this piece.

Death at Film Forum takes a look at the personas, modus operandi, anxieties, and dreams of four young filmmakers—would-be (wannabe?) auteurs who are so keenly influenced by cinematic masters like Godard and Fassbinder that their own creative impulses risk being squashed—or are they even there? But lest I make this piece sound either serious or precious or both, I need to add immediately that *Death at Film Forum* is simultaneously a satire of every youthful artistic folly and, most tellingly, of the popular reality TV show *Project Runway*.

Bland riffs on the reality formula by having his four contestants compete for a monetary prize by going through a series of elimination rounds: each week, they must create a new film on a random theme chosen by the program's host (a rabidly Euro-chic sophisticate named Victhoria), who unilaterally votes one of the budding directors out of the contest after the films are screened. The play mimics the techniques of reality TV and of the various cinematic idols who are worshipped by its characters—often at the same time; consider, for example, this excerpt from the opening of the contest between Victhoria and one of the contestants, Scott:

> VICTHORIA: *(To SCOTT.)* So what interests you in Film Forum? In film?
>
> SCOTT: When I was a child my father used to take me to Film Forum …All the other kids got to see *Bambi* and *Back to the Future.* I went to the Rainer Werner Fassbinder retrospective. That's probably why I carry around this little jar of poison. *(He pops it out.)*
>
> VICTHORIA: Did you like it?
>
> SCOTT: I dreamt up all sorts of damaging things after I saw *Beware of a Holy Whore* at the age of seven. It's still my favorite movie but it fucked up Halloween in 1987, when I went as a half-empty glass of Cuba Libre being brutally smashed into the floor …It was an abstract costume.

🎬 🎬 🎬 🎬 🎬

If *Death at Film Forum* holds a mirror up to our current relationship with popular culture, *TRACES/fades* reflects more globally on a societal anomie that feels like collective amnesia. Playwright/director Lenora Champagne calls her work "a meditation on Alzheimer's and our national inability to remember history" and that's so apt that I won't even attempt to improve on it. *TRACES/fades* is a thrilling, touching, adventurous theatrical hybrid that uses multimedia, movement, poetic dialogue, and even Brechtian-style song to explore the mind of a woman suffering from Alzheimer's and the mindset of a country that sometimes seems to be likewise afflicted.

Champagne's deceptively simple work focuses on three generations of women in a family. Ann is the grandmother, once a vibrant and intelligent working woman and now confined to a nursing home where she suffers from Alzheimer's. Rose is her eleven-year-old granddaughter. In the middle is Claire, struggling to balance being mother and daughter to women who require much from her while at the same time being herself a writer and political activist.

In the first part of *TRACES/fades*, Champagne introduces us to this trio and examines their relationships. In the second part, we move to the nursing home where Ann resides and spend a while traveling in her shoes, at least vicariously. Champagne's depiction of this place, which can feel surreal to visitors even in real life, is uncannily on target; she gets right to the heart of what we lose by shuttling away our forebears, with all their wisdom and experience.

The playwright only barely conceals a political agenda here, as in this section of "The Ballad of the Pacifist Grandmother," which is sung by one of the residents of the nursing home:

> I had a son in the war.
> Which war?
> A big war.
> The gooks didn't get him.
> Drug addiction did.
> I had a grandson in the war.
> Which war?
> A big war.
> The Arabs didn't get him.
> Friendly fire did.

Champagne co-directed *TRACES/fades* with her husband and frequent collaborator, Robert Lyons; contributing further to the familial nature of the piece (already so present in the writing) was the casting of their daughter Amelie Champagne Lyons in the role of Rose. Their production, which premiered in Soho Think Tank's invaluable new works festival, Ice Factory '08, was dazzlingly imaginative. Champagne and Lyons cast age-appropriate actors to play the residents of the nursing home, and they were superb, thus bringing home one of the play's key themes of listening to and learning from our elders.

✔ ✔ ✔ ✔ ✔

Nowhere on the Border by Carlos Lacámara was originally produced in California (where Lacámara makes his living, mostly in television). The New York premiere was directed by José Zayas (his second entry in this volume) at Repertorio Español, where it was presented as a bilingual play in Spanish and English: dialogue among the Mexican characters in the play was in Spanish, while the sections set in the United States were spoken in English. Here we publish the play entirely in English, as Lacámara wrote and envisioned it.

The story is of a middle-aged Mexican man, Roberto, who may or may not be an illegal immigrant (significantly, his status is never disclosed in the play). We encounter him in the Cabeza Prieta Wildlife Refuge, in the Sonoran desert of Arizona, a mostly undemarcated no-man's-land near the Mexican border. He is searching for his daughter, who paid a (relatively) small fortune to be smuggled into the United States and has not been heard from for an alarmingly long time. As the play begins, he is guarding the decaying remains of an unidentified woman (he explains, "…is somebody's daughter. And if somebody found my daughter…like this…I would like them to watch out for her until somebody come and take her home."), when he is discovered by Gary, an unemployed man from Kentucky. Roughly the same age as Roberto, he is a volunteer border guard working with a post-9/11 proto-militia called the Homeland Patriot Project.

Lacámara deftly and economically contrasts his characters' mindsets:

> ROBERTO: You really hate Mexican people, don't you?
>
> GARY: I don't hate anybody.
>
> ROBERTO: But if you hated somebody, Mexicans would be at the top of your list, right?
>
> …
>
> GARY: I'm here to help the authorities uphold the law.
>
> ROBERTO: For no money.
>
> GARY: For no money.
>
> ROBERTO: Because you are such a good person?
>
> GARY: Because I love my country.
>
> ROBERTO: You don't find that in Mexico. I mean, we love our country, but not for free.

The play progresses, alternating scenes of Gary and Roberto with flashbacks that tell the story of Roberto's daughter, Pilar. Lacámara keeps the focus on his Mexican characters, providing them a much-needed voice on our stage. Without ever resorting to sentimentality, he suggests a path toward mutual understanding for Gary and Roberto that transforms *Nowhere on the Border* from simple tragedy to something more complex, resonant, and uplifting.

❧ ❧ ❧ ❧ ❧

Chris Harcum's *American Badass, or 12 Characters in Search of a National Identity* is the first of three solo plays included in *Plays and Playwrights 2009*. Perhaps because of the rising costs of producing theatre, this genre is becoming increasing popular on American stages, and the ones contained in this volume exemplify the traditions of solo performance that are blossoming in the early twenty-first century.

Harcum's work represents the monologue play: as its title suggests, *American Badass* consists of a dozen monologues delivered by diverse characters that together provide broad and deep perspective on the state of the nation in 2008. The play begins with a sly nod to Harcum's roots as an actor/creator in the world of downtown New York theatre, disarming us with an "anti-post-hipster" who offers criticism—constructive and otherwise—of the one-man show format:

> Anyway, make sure you make it fun for the audience. You know, like don't be too morose or talk about stuff people avoid thinking about. 'Coz we're just out enough from 9/11 to be okay but not enough to really be doing things about something yet. I mean, you don't have to be fluffy like we had to be right after but you can't, like, do anything that's really about 9/11 because that's so…so…Because right after 9/11 we were all about how we're like each other and all human and shit. But now, NOW, we can say we don't like people so much. New York is back in business. You can tell by all the assholes on the subway and…and…God I hate them!

As you can see, the playwright puts his cards on the table right at the outset. What follows are vignettes that are funny, warm, sad, awe inspiring, and downright frightening, as Harcum introduces us to a Bronx dad, a former Blackwater contractor, a competitive eater, Karl Rove, and our (by the time you read this) former Commander-in-Chief himself. The playwright has included short sketches (that he suggests be fitted out multimedia style) to transition between the twelve main characters. The resulting show is like a cockeyed contemporary vaudeville exploring our collective consciousness.

Harcum is an expert actor, and in the original production of *American Badass*, directed by Bricken Sparacino at the FRIGID New York festival, he performed the show himself. However, the writing here is so pointed and varied that it's easy to imagine each of the characters portrayed by a different actor.

❧ ❧ ❧ ❧ ❧

A Fire as Bright as Heaven, written by Tim Collins, has a good deal in common with *American Badass*, but at the same time these two plays couldn't be more different, which is why both are included here. Collins's piece is overtly autobiographical, and it's presented

as a five-part continuous monologue (the author-performer calls
it an "epic solo," and that sounds about right).

The time frame covered in *A Fire as Bright as Heaven* coincides exactly with that in *American Badass*: the seven years since the start of
the Bush administration. It begins in London, just after the terrorist
attacks on 9/11; Collins was studying abroad at that time, and the
first section of his play captures the odd off-kilter feeling of being
away from home for this landmark historical moment, and also the
range of emotions and reactions that 9/11 prompted.

The successive segments are set in a toy store, right at the time
when Bush declared war on Iraq; in a series of street interviews
about terrorism; at the National Rifle Association's annual convention in St. Louis; and in an American town in early 2008, where a
door-to-door volunteer is calling on random strangers and talking
about the (then) upcoming presidential election.

Collins gets the voices of his many characters exactly right, from a
pompous American professor abroad, inappropriately deconstructing the World Trade Center tragedy:

> Now we've negated the World Trade Center as a symbol, but
> the terrorists—and I'm going to ask you to indulge me on this
> point because I think it might lead to something—interesting—
> the terrorists may have done themselves—one better—if they
> had selected a target with more—symbolic impactfulness? For
> example, just off the top of my head—the Statue of Liberty.

to a double-talking Republican son of hippies:

> Look, I understand where you Liberals are coming from. I am
> surrounded in my life by Liberals. My whole *family* is Liberal. I
> understand where you're coming from, and I respect it— Okay,
> I *don't* respect it—but I understand.

to an ordinary Joe trying hard to do the right thing but unsure
how to figure out what that even means anymore:

> And I blame China! I have nothing against China, I like China,
> I buy their stuff, but, according to NPR, China is the up and
> coming world power, China needs oil, China's where the
> money's going, and—I started to think about it.

With great wit, warmth, intelligence, and—above all—balance,
Collins evokes aspects of our national character in *A Fire as Bright
as Heaven*. He's been touring this show around the United States
since his engagement at the New York International Fringe Festival,
and his performance in the piece is impeccable.

◀ ◀ ◀ ◀ ◀

Rick Burkhardt's play *Conversation Storm* had its New York premiere at the FRIGID New York festival (actually in the same theatre as *American Badass*, exactly one hour earlier). Burkhardt performed in the piece along with his colleagues at The Nonsense Company, Ryan Higgins and Andy Gricevich (and co-directed with Gricevich). *Conversation Storm* was the second half of a double bill that commenced with Burkhardt's extraordinary physical theatre/sound play *Great Hymn of Thanksgiving*, which is a musical work scored for a variety of household objects. Although it's just a half-hour in length, *Conversation Storm* packs a wallop way out of proportion to its size.

Conversation Storm—so aptly titled!—starts out calmly if forebodingly with the actors talking about themselves and about what they're performing (very meta); and then Burkhardt's main thesis is slyly unfurled for us:

> ALEC: *(Suddenly seated at the table, in mid-conversation.)* But listen, while we're talking about torture, let's imagine that a nuclear bomb has been planted in Manhattan.
>
> HUGH: Oh no.
>
> ALEC: And you've got the guy who planted the bomb in a cell, for questioning. And the bomb will go off in half an hour.
>
> HUGH: Stop!
>
> ALEC: And the guy won't talk.
>
> HUGH: STOP!

This, it turns out, is a play about torture, and the rationalizations for torture. And it is, at the same time, itself an act of torture, at least of a kind. Burkhardt understands the power of language, and though *Conversation Storm* consists only of words, it is as brutal and horrifying a theatre experience as any I've encountered.

It is also elegant, almost classically so; darkly funny in places; utterly surprising, yet oh so carefully constructed. Two men have a hypothetical discussion about when it might or might not be justifiable to torture someone in the interest of national security. A third man alternately mediates, participates, and interrupts. Somehow, before the brief single act of this play is finished, everyone onstage has been compromised irreparably. And everyone in the audience has been implicated in the carnage.

Conversation Storm continues to tour as part of The Nonsense Company's small but growing repertory. I hope that its inclusion

here will lead adventurous theatre-goers to check out the work
of this Madison, Wisconsin-based troupe, as well as adventurous
theatre-makers to mount the piece themselves. It's a play that
demands to be put before audiences until the time—if it ever
comes—when torture ceases to exist.

✒ ✒ ✒ ✒ ✒

Krapp, 39 is the last of this year's solo plays and indeed the last
selection in *Plays and Playwrights 2009*. It pays tribute to Samuel
Beckett's seminal one-man drama *Krapp's Last Tape* (in the year of
that play's fiftieth anniversary, in fact), but in every respect *Krapp,
39* is wholly original and surprising.

Actor-playwright Michael Laurence provides a thorough and
engaging account of the play's genesis in his introductory notes.
Suffice to say that the premise of *Krapp, 39* is that an actor decides
to record the monologue from the Beckett play on his thirty-ninth
birthday, with the intention of using this recording in his own
production of *Krapp's Last Tape* when he is sixty-nine (the age of
the character in *Krapp's Last Tape*). This does not actually happen
in *Krapp, 39*, however; instead Laurence's play takes the shape of
an elaborate archivist's birthday ritual, in which said actor looks
back on the artifacts of his life (journals, photos, recordings) and
videotapes himself in the act.

It feels intensely personal and genuine, though in fact it is brim-
ming with artifice and turns out to be startlingly universal. Who,
as middle age approaches and youth vanishes, does not examine his
or her own story so far? Who does not at least suspect that failure
is the only legacy he or she will leave behind?

Laurence captures the doubt and anxiety and optimist's hopefulness
against the odds in a play whose profundity, expansive humor, and
deep humanity belie any assertion of failure on his part. Here, about
two-thirds of the way through *Krapp, 39*, the actor/protagonist
reads from a journal entry about an old birthday present:

> Some weeks ago I told my wife that I felt like I thrived best in
> the role of a student, and it was sad to me that as you get older,
> you run out of opportunities to be a student. I'm thirty-seven.
> You're supposed to be battle-tempered and sage at thirty-seven.
> Thirty-seven is not an age for learning, thirty-seven is an age
> for *teaching*. Thirty-seven is an age for *doing*. *Producing*. What
> have I *produced*?
>
> Anyway, I told her this, so she bought me a class at a continu-
> ing education center. As an early birthday present. *What a*

tender and thoughtful gift, I thought. *My wife listens to me, my wife understands me.* Then she handed me something wrapped in pink tissue paper—a catalogue of courses, I guessed—and I thought about the august and intellectually rigorous class I might choose. Something like "Kierkegaard's Ambivalence: A Lutheran Perspective," or "Privacy and Surveillance: A Global Analysis." Or maybe just something *fun* like "The Vampire in Modernist Cinema and Literature." I *loved* this gift.

At the New York International Fringe Festival, under the direction of George Demas, Laurence starred in the world premiere of *Krapp, 39*. Now he shares this gift with readers and artists everywhere, so that we might benefit from his wisdom as we ponder our own identities.

◀ ◀ ◀ ◀ ◀

As I write these words, fully a month remains before the new administration is sworn in. To borrow from Tony Kushner (as many of my friends did on Facebook on election night), the great work awaits. Who knows what America, or American theatre, will be like when I sit down next year to write the next *Plays and Playwrights* introduction? All I know is that I can take great comfort in the intellect and wit and talent of Randy Sharp and her collaborators at Axis Company, Andrew Irons, Colette Freedman, Nanna "Nick" Mwaluko, Eric Bland, Lenora Champagne, Carlos Lacámara, Chris Harcum, Tim Collins, Rick Burkhardt, and Michael Laurence. Their plays help us reflect back on our personal and national character this year, lead us to a better understanding of how we got to the place we're now at, and remind us of lessons in humanity that may help us navigate more sure-footedly toward a defensible future.

HOSPITAL 2008

Randy Sharp and Axis Company

RANDY SHARP is a director. She was born in New York City in April 1963, and was raised in New York and London. She attended Simon's Rock Early College and earned a degree in theatre and English literature. For the past ten years she has been the Artistic Director of Axis Company, whose production credits include the original works *Frankenstein* (2000), *Oppenheimer* (2002), *In Token of My Admiration* (2004), and *Not Yet Diagnosed (Nervous), 1918* (2005), as well as revivals of *Woyzeck* (2000), *Julius Caesar* (2002), and *A Glance at New York* (2003 and 2007). She is also the writer-director of the independent feature film, *Henry May Long* (2008), which won the Audience Award for Best Drama at the 2008 Independent Features Film Festival, the Best Feature Award at the 2008 Sacramento International Film Festival, and the Best Drama Award at the 2008 Buffalo Niagara Film Festival. She also received the Best Director Award at the 2008 Long Island International Film Expo. She lives in New York City.

Hospital 2008 was first presented by Axis Company (Randy Sharp, Artistic Director; Brian Barnhart, Managing Director) on June 5, 2008, at the Axis Theater with the following cast and credits:

Traveller	Brain Barnhart
Jimmy	Marc Palmieri
Frank	Ian Tooley
Research Physician	David Crabb
Specialist	Paul Marc Barnes
Nurse #2	Laurie Kilmartin
Doctor #1	Joe Fuer
Mad Hatter, Karen	Edgar Oliver
White Rabbit, John Henry, Hades, Shift Boss	George Demas
Queen of Hearts, Nurse #3, Barbara	Britt Genelin
Tunneler #1	Regina Bettancourt
Doctor #3	Tom Pennacchini
Persephone	Lynne Mancinelli
The Carol	Jim Sterling

Director and Original Music: Randy Sharp
Stage Manager: Edward Terhune
Sound Design/Music Production and Arrangements: Steve Fontaine
Light Design: David Zeffren
Set Design: Kyle Chepulis
Costume Design—Stage and Film: Matthew Simonelli
Assistant Costume Design—Stage and Film: Elisa Santiago
Assistant Light Design: Sonia Baidya
Set Construction: Josh Higgason
Properties—Stage and Film: Alexis Weiss
Cinematography: Ben Wolf
Film Editor: Laura Weinberg
Website and Graphic Designer: Ethan Crenson
Publicity/PR: Ron Lasko/Spin Cycle
Photographer: Dixie Sheridan

www.axiscompany.org

THE STRUCTURE OF *HOSPITAL 2008*

At the start of each episode there is the Premise Film. Basically this explains what happened in the tunnel. Ours unfolded in four different edits over the four episodes giving more information as it did so. The story in its barest form is as follows.

- After a cave-in in New York City Water Tunnel #3, three men are trapped.

- Jimmy is injured and cannot move.

- Frank goes to get help.

- The Traveller is left waiting with Jimmy. After an aftershock he panics, steals Jimmy's light, and runs away.

- Later Jimmy is rescued and the Traveller dies in a catastrophic collapse of the tunnel.

- He has lived a solitary life with no friends or interaction of any significance.

It is not necessary to have a Premise Film but I am not sure how you could convey the events that occurred prior to the cave-in without one. Any way you think is successful is fine.

Each episode is broken into three parts.

- *The Event:* The Traveller and his companions are literally figuring out what happened. They are in a dream tunnel, each in his own state. The Heading is death (to the left) the Join is life (to the right).

- *Doctors and Nurses:* Ostensibly the dream-state Hospital.

- *The Dream Sequence:* The Traveller's attempt to unravel his past and future by remembering famous stories all of which happened underground or involve the underground.

The tunnel workers' map prop travels through all episodes. Whenever people read anything or look at rules for instance…it is always the map. It is also the present the Traveller receives from his memories at the end.

NOTES ON CHARACTERS, ETC.
CASTING

The same actor should play the following: the White Rabbit, John Henry, Hades, Shift Boss.

The same actor should play the following: the Queen of Hearts, Nurse #3, Barbara (thereby indicating she is Jimmy's sister—"I was visiting my brother in the hospital…").

The same actor should play the following: the Mad Hatter, Karen.

In Doctors and Nurses

Our Specialist is English. There is some language that reflects this. If your specialist is not English then change it if you like.

The Doctors' Prayer recited at the end of each of their scenes is actually made up of random index entries from an AA book with the word "alcoholic" replaced by "doctor." All gather at the foot of the stage and do this after their scene. Don't ask why. Cut it if you like.

Doctor #1 is referred to by three names on purpose: Barry, Bill, and Bob. Similarly, the Research Physician is referred to as Todd, Tim, and Terry.

In Dream Sequences

The people in these scenes break character. Think of it as part of the fallout from the burden of telling someone's sad story. It's as if they have been conjured up by the Traveller to tell the story but once they are they have free will and feel the heartbreak, loss, and confusion of the story. These character-breaks manifest in many ways, i.e.: quiet asides, whispering out of the Traveller's earshot, just stopping doing the scene for a second and making mistakes.

The Carol

Simply put—The Carol is the Hospital. His first appearance in Doctors and Nurses is comical and seems like a huge, spastic robot or a god that has been forced to take on human form with all the difficulties that would incur. His second appearance is much more somber and natural as he comes to claim the Traveller who has never even been in the hospital in the first place.

The Traveller dies alone in the tunnel.

Good luck.

EPISODE #1
EVENT: UNDERGROUND

The tunnel has collapsed. The darkness is impenetrable. Slowly the myriad noises within the infrastructure begin to filter into the chamber: hydraulic pumps clean air elsewhere, the drills and shovels of a remote location, the distant rolling of mine shaft trains, and the spectral voices of people. Suddenly the emergency lighting flickers on. Sand falls from the ceiling.

TRAVELLER: *(Waking.)* Wait. Wait a second.

(FRANK and JIMMY come from under the earth; JIMMY is holding onto FRANK's belt, then lets go and stands, staring. The emergency lighting goes out. There is dead silence. No one moves. Slowly the lights flicker back on. JIMMY and FRANK are gone.)

TRAVELLER: Hello?…hello?

(The emergency lights fail. A radio tries to find a signal so far underground. It's a communication from up above, difficult to decipher and rough.)

RADIO: Frank? *(Static, etc.)* Frank can you hear me? *(Unintelligible.)* Frank?

(The sound of the emergency locators begins to ring in the dark. The faint image of FRANK and JIMMY moves across the tunnel and the TRAVELLER.)

TRAVELLER: Frank!

RADIO: *(Static.)* Frank? *(Sound of an argument between the people using the radio.)* …go to the—… *(Trails off.)*

(Loud static and then the radio cuts out. The emergency lighting returns. FRANK, JIMMY, and the TRAVELLER are all in the tunnel.)

FRANK: I got to get out of here.

TRAVELLER: Wait, what happened.

FRANK: I should've kept going…

JIMMY: Who's that over there?

TRAVELLER: It's…me.

JIMMY: Oh good. Look Frankie, we're all here still. What time is it?

FRANK: What does that matter?

JIMMY: For the shifts!

FRANK: What shift? I should've kept going. I got to get out of here! I'm not supposed to be down here! I'm not even on the shift! I was just helping out.

JIMMY: Maybe they don't even know I'm down here!

FRANK: But we got the radio and everything. *(To the TRAVELLER.)* Right?

TRAVELLER: …Yeah.

JIMMY: *(Losing track.)* What happened?

(Nobody says anything.)

TRAVELLER: We must've had a blow-out.

FRANK: That was no blow-out! This is a cave-in or something.

TRAVELLER: *(Scared.)* That's ridiculous.

FRANK: Well it's a bump then.

JIMMY: *(Has been thinking.)* Wait now, who's got the map, find out who's got the map.

(They all search themselves for the radio. While they do—)

TRAVELLER: Did you guys come through here a couple times before?

FRANK: I should've kept going.

JIMMY: Do you think they know who's in here?

FRANK: Why would that matter? They'll get us out no matter who we are…Anyways it's not my shift and I did not come through here.

JIMMY: Was it a bump?

FRANK: Yes. A big one.

TRAVELLER: You didn't come in here?

JIMMY: No… *(Looks at FRANK.)* It's not your shift?

FRANK: I got it! I got the radio!

JIMMY: Okay.

FRANK: *(Tries to communicate with the surface.)* Come in! Come in!

(Static.)

FRANK: This is Frank at the heading.

JIMMY: We're not at the heading! We're all still here! Make sure they know I'm in here.

TRAVELLER: We're not at the heading.

FRANK: I was! I have restricted clearance!

TRAVELLER: You were at the heading?… *(To JIMMY.)* Were you?

JIMMY: I was here.

FRANK: Yeah…wait…We all were for a minute. *(Into the radio.)* This is Frank…this is Frank! Come in!

TRAVELLER: We were all where?

(JIMMY grabs the radio.)

FRANK: What are you doing?

JIMMY: *(Into the radio.)* We don't know what time it is so we don't know if you know who's in here! Who's supposed to

be down here…? Who do you THINK is down here?

FRANK: *(He grabs it back.)* What are you talking about? Who cares what time it is? I'll get everybody out. Hello? Can you hear me?

(The faintest sound of a reply.)

FRANK: This is Frank…come in.

(The quietest sound of a reply. Then the radio conks out.)

FRANK: It's all right. They probably went to the E.R.F. You shouldn't grab it like that though.

JIMMY: I didn't break it. They went to the emergency response frequency. They have to figure out who's here so they can come get us.

TRAVELLER: What?

JIMMY: They went to the E.R.F…you know…it means they KNOW we're down here. They just have to cross check the shift records and then they'll know who they're talking to. Then they'll know how many people are in trouble.

FRANK: Why does that matter?

JIMMY: I don't want them to forget about me.

TRAVELLER: What is it? Three fifty-eight??

FRANK: Yeah, what is the E.R.F.?

TRAVELLER: *(To FRANK.)* Do you know?

FRANK: No. I don't look at those things. Do you?

TRAVELLER: No.

FRANK: *(To JIMMY.)* Do you?

JIMMY: I know what it is but I just have to remember. We have a couple minutes while they do that though. It's alright. We're supposed to be here. I just think it's important they know WHO is down here. Then they won't leave anyone behind...wait—what time is it?

TRAVELLER: Why does that matter?

JIMMY: So they know how many people are in trouble.

(They stand there.)

FRANK: I should've kept going.

JIMMY: Shut up...I don't feel so good.

TRAVELLER: Were you guys at the heading?

FRANK: I got to get out of here.

JIMMY: What?...Oh.. I don't know. *(To himself.)* I don't want to be left behind! Maybe they don't know how many people are in trouble...

TRAVELLER: Didn't you say you were at the heading?

FRANK: I was. I was at the heading. So were you.

TRAVELLER: Are you sure?

FRANK: YES! We were all at the heading.

TRAVELLER: Isn't the heading really far from here?

FRANK: I worked at the heading.

JIMMY: I don't think I was at the heading. That's not my shift today. I wasn't at the heading I don't think...but that bump can knock it right out of you...know what I mean?

FRANK: *(To himself.)* I got to get out of here.

TRAVELLER: Hey...guys...are you sure we're still in the tunnel?

FRANK: WHAT?

TRAVELLER: When I left I thought—

JIMMY: Yeah! I think you CAN get knocked through a fissure or something! I heard about that thing that happened once! You CAN get knocked out of the tunnel but it doesn't matter where we are because at least they know we're down here! We're where we're supposed to be or they wouldn't know we were here. They just need to know how many of us there are. Get it?

FRANK: I still don't see why that matters.

JIMMY: ...so they don't forget about me...

TRAVELLER: Are you sure you can get knocked out of—

FRANK: Maybe we DID get blown out of the tunnel or something, Jimmy.

TRAVELLER: Through a fissure.

JIMMY: Yeah through a fissure in the tunnel. That's what happened I bet!

TRAVELLER: But this looks like the tunnel.

JIMMY: Yeah.

FRANK: *(Thinks it through.)* Maybe it's an old part of the tunnel.

JIMMY: Yeah. Maybe it's an old part of the tunnel.

TRAVELLER: An old part of the tunnel that runs parallel to the new one?

JIMMY: That's how they do it!

TRAVELLER: Parallel?

FRANK: That's the whole point of being down here! We're replacing the tunnel. I know! I have restricted clearance!

TRAVELLER: But in the same path?

FRANK: YES!

TRAVELLER: So maybe we got knocked into part of the old tunnel?

JIMMY: Yeah.

TRAVELLER: I guess so.

FRANK: It is. It's an annex chamber in the old tunnel!

TRAVELLER: Oh. Maybe you're right.

FRANK: *(Figures it out.)* So we can follow it back to the join!

JIMMY: *(Not well.)* What do you mean "the join," Frank?

FRANK: Well because I work at the heading, plus I have restricted clearance, I see the join every day. You guys just come down through the middle. Back at the start the two tunnels still touch together!

JIMMY: Oh yeah, I heard about that!

FRANK: So all we have to do is turn around and follow the tunnel back to the join, walk out the new tunnel and into the city!

JIMMY: Okay! Let's do it…

TRAVELLER: Yeah but what do you mean "turn around"?

JIMMY: He means go the other way… man, I don't feel so great.

TRAVELLER: But how do we know which way is the other way?

(EVERYONE looks around.)

JIMMY: I don't know.

FRANK: Bang on the steel! Like I said. While they switch to the E.R.F.—they're listening.

JIMMY: Which way is the other way, Frank?

FRANK: I'm going to find out. *(Starts banging on the steel of the tunnel joists. He bangs forever until faintly there is the sound of banging from very slightly to the left. Sound of them.)*

FRANK: Hear that?

(Faint sound of banging.)

JIMMY: What?

TRAVELLER: Yes.

JIMMY: I don't hear anything.

FRANK: I KNEW they knew we were down here. I KNEW it!

JIMMY: I don't hear anything.

(Sound of them.)

FRANK: They KNOW we're down here!

JIMMY: But Frank, they don't know WHO's down here?

FRANK: WHY does that matter??

TRAVELLER: I guess they're at the join…I can hear them. I think it IS them.

(Sound of them.)

JIMMY: What?

TRAVELLER: Maybe it's an echo.

FRANK: That is no echo!

JIMMY: What??? I don't hear anything!

(Sound of them.)

FRANK: See?

JIMMY: No.

FRANK: It's alright. I know which way it is. It's this way.

JIMMY: *(Feeling bad.)* Okay. How long have we been standing here?

(They stand around for a second.)

FRANK: Okay so let's go. I know which way it is.

JIMMY: Yeah…

TRAVELLER: Okay.

JIMMY: Yeah. Let's go.

TRAVELLER: Wait—are we sure THIS isn't the real tunnel.

FRANK: *(Getting ready.)* Yes.

JIMMY: Are we?

FRANK: Yes.

JIMMY: This is not the right tunnel. We shouldn't wait here.

FRANK: No.

JIMMY: You're sure? Isn't there something about staying where you are?

FRANK: *(Bustling.)* No. Not when you can HEAR the join.

JIMMY: *(To the TRAVELLER.)* Is there something about staying where you are?

TRAVELLER: I don't know.

(The emergency lights flicker.)

JIMMY: *(To FRANK.)* Isn't there something about staying where you are?

(They flicker and go out.)

FRANK: No.

(Nothing happens.)

JIMMY: …hey?

TRAVELLER: Yes?

(Nothing happens.)

JIMMY: Is Frank still in here?

TRAVELLER: I don't know.

JIMMY: …Frank?

(No response.)

JIMMY: …Frank?

TRAVELLER: Hello…?

(The lights barely flicker on. FRANK is not there. There is a seismic bump…sand trickles down onto the floor of the tunnel.)

JIMMY: Frank? Are you there?… Frank?

(A faint sound.)

TRAVELLER: What was that?

JIMMY: Wait a second…when did you come in here?

TRAVELLER: With you…What's the matter with you?

JIMMY: Wait—

(The lights come on again. FRANK is fussing with the radio.)

FRANK: *(Interrupting.)* I don't know why it's taking so long. Well, they know we're down here so it's okay.

JIMMY: Are you sure you were with me because I think I was—

FRANK: She's bumping around pretty good, right?

JIMMY: Are you sure they didn't forget about me?

FRANK: Yeah, I think I passed out a little or something.

TRAVELLER: When?

(The sound of distant tunnel railroad cars.)

FRANK: Listen!!

TRAVELLER: When did you pass out?

FRANK: This is the way! It's alright!

JIMMY: *(Confused.)* Are we going to the join?

FRANK: YES!

JIMMY: Frank…

FRANK: Let's get out of here!

JIMMY: *(Fading.)* Frank, are we going to the join?

FRANK: *(Soldiering on.)* We're going to the join! I promise! Everything's going to be alright.

TRAVELLER: Wait, when did you pass out?

JIMMY: Frank, do they know I'm down here?

(E.R.F. radio sounds… they are gone.)

Doctors and Nurses Sit at a Staff Meeting

The RESEARCH PHYSICIAN, the SPECIALIST, and NURSE #2 have opened a hotel. SPECIALIST sings at the bar. The RESEARCH PHYSICIAN is the maitre d' and the chef… his makeup running, his suit dirty and dishevelled. NURSE #2 waits on the empty tables.

RESEARCH PHYSICIAN: Why don't you ask the gentleman if he wants something

(There's no one there.)

NURSE #2: *(Confused.)* Oh… "Would you like something…" "No thank you" "Are you staying at the hotel?" "No."

"Oh… why not?" "Because it's dirty an—"

RESEARCH PHYSICIAN: ALRIGHT! That's enough… SING—you big son of a bitch! *(Stands around, perhaps remembering a finer hotel… a finer age, then giving up.)* Why doesn't the phone ring? Why doesn't anybody want to stay here? Who knew that Inuits hated hotels??

SPECIALIST: Eskimos… well… they don't know what they want.

NURSE #2: *(Quietly.)* They know they don't want that yucky sauce.

RESEARCH PHYSICIAN: It's a BECHAMEL and it wasn't the sauce… it wasn't the sauce.

NURSE #2: Sure tasted like it was the sauce.

SPECIALIST: It was a bit off.

RESEARCH PHYSICIAN: *(Pulls out the sauce.)* You don't know what you're talking about… bechamel is a GREAT everyday sauce. It goes with everything!! I LOVE IT! What are you? A culinary expert in a white dress!? GET TO WORK!!

(The SPECIALIST plays a Casio keyboard.)

RESEARCH PHYSICIAN: *(Covered in bechamel.)* We never should have opened this hotel… Why did we ever leave that other place to go to this frozen tundra, this empty, arctic, frosty plain??? We should have KNOWN not to go into the hospitality business…

SPECIALIST: It was a good idea, darling… we just… we just didn't know.

NURSE #2: "How about a drink" "No thank you" "Are you staying at the hotel?" "No…"

(Suddenly the doors of the arctic bar open, an icy wind blows through…DOCTOR #1 has returned, his coat collar turned up, his face obscured by his hat and scarf.)

RESEARCH PHYSICIAN: *(To NURSE #2.)* Get over there! *(To the SPECIALIST.)* Sing god damn it!! SING!

NURSE #2: Oh…Hello. *(Gets confused, is helped.)* May I get you something to drink?

(DOCTOR #1 takes off his coat.)

DOCTOR #1: No. No thank you.

NURSE #2: Can I help you?

RESEARCH PHYSICIAN: *(Creeping up.)* Wait a second…

NURSE #2: Can I help you?

RESEARCH PHYSICIAN: …Barry?…

DOCTOR #1: Wait.

RESEARCH PHYSICIAN: Bill?…where have you been, Bob?

DOCTOR #1: *(Trying to regain his composure.)* I…I don't know.

RESEARCH PHYSICIAN: Bill when we left…I didn't know what to do. I opened this place…I…

DOCTOR #1: Yes I know.

RESEARCH PHYSICIAN: Why didn't you come get me?

NURSE #2: Nobody stays here.

RESEARCH PHYSICIAN: NO! That's not true…once we were the gilded bar of the tundra Bill…but now…now it all seems…we're alright though, Bob…we don't need any help.

SPECIALIST: What's he doing here?

RESEARCH PHYSICIAN: Why DID you come Bill? Do you think we're helpless without you and your precious jobs??

DOCTOR #1: What are you, Tim?

RESEARCH PHYSICIAN: Well…I'm a kind of…doctor.

DOCTOR #1: Really? You look like the cook. Oh and who's he? He's a kind of doctor too? Is that it?

RESEARCH PHYSICIAN: Yes.

SPECIALIST: I'm a specialist from England.

RESEARCH PHYSICIAN: Yes…he is…from…Engerland.

DOCTOR #1: Big deal.

NURSE #2: We HAD to do these jobs!

DOCTOR #1: Yeah but now you don't! Have the pluck! Have the moxie, have the nerve!! Or aren't you brave enough to walk out of here with me and…

RESEARCH PHYSICIAN: Let me ask you something, Bob. Is this how you're going to come back into my life? With your back up and your fangs out? With your fists curled to punch and hit?

SPECIALIST: Yeah!

DOCTOR #1: What?

RESEARCH PHYSICIAN: We waited around for quite some time for you to return!

NURSE #2: *(Selling out the RESEARCH PHYSICIAN.)* He told us to open the hotel!

RESEARCH PHYSICIAN: We had to do something, Bob…what did we do before we opened the hotel? Well, we sat in laboratories off of darkened hallways in sad, depression-era buildings, their rooms filled with dusty, half-packed boxes, their lonely, golden, lobbies empty. There's no one there!

SPECIALIST: It's just an empty building!

RESEARCH PHYSICIAN: Yes, it was sad! That's right! Before we came out here I sat peering through the lens of some once-magnificent, busted machine, searching! Looking! Looking for YOU, Barry! *(Clutches at DOCTOR #1.)*

DOCTOR #1: *(Grabbing him back.)* It's time, Terry. It's time to come home, Tim.

RESEARCH PHYSICIAN: *(Weeping.)* I know…I know that now.

DOCTOR #1: *(Comforting him.)* Yes Todd. It's true.

SPECIALIST: What?

RESEARCH PHYSICIAN: What?

SPECIALIST: What's true?

NURSE #2: What he said.

DOCTOR #1: What?

SPECIALIST: What's true?

NURSE #2: What he said.

DOCTOR #1: What do you mean?

SPECIALIST: You just said that. You just said "It's true."

DOCTOR #1: No I didn't.

SPECIALIST: Yes you did.

RESEARCH PHYSICIAN: *(Musing.)* Is it?

DOCTOR #1: What?

SPECIALIST: You just said it.

RESEARCH PHYSICIAN: Is it true?

DOCTOR #1: What?

SPECIALIST: You just said it.

DOCTOR #1: What?

NURSE #2: What he said.

SPECIALIST: "Is it true."

RESEARCH PHYSICIAN: Is it?

DOCTOR #1: What?

SPECIALIST: You just said it.

DOCTOR #1: What?

NURSE #2: What he said.

SPECIALIST: "Is it true."

RESEARCH PHYSICIAN: Is it?

SPECIALIST: What?

NURSE #2: What he said.

DOCTOR #1: WAIT A SECOND! *(Thinks it through.)* YES! It IS true. That IS what I came here to tell you! We work in the…in the—

RESEARCH PHYSICIAN: Hospital.

DOCTOR #1: It's time to work in the Hospital again, Terry.

SPECIALIST: What time IS it?

RESEARCH PHYSICIAN: Why does that matter?

DOCTOR #1: I'm ready! I'm tired of not having anywhere to go.

RESEARCH PHYSICIAN: SO…you weren't working before.

DOCTOR #1: When?

RESEARCH PHYSICIAN: Well! You came in here like you were some kind of big shot to come here and save us!

SPECIALIST: That's a bit out of order!

DOCTOR #1: When?

RESEARCH PHYSICIAN: I mean you're not our big saviour, Barry. We opened this place…we tried to make it!! We—

SPECIALIST: That's right! I mean he's been alone here drinking himself into oblivion every bleeding night…

(The RESEARCH PHYSICIAN tries to refute this.)

SPECIALIST: …waiting for some help!

NURSE #2: I was here too.

SPECIALIST: Yeah but you don't do anything do you? I mean I'm a Specialist and all but I can't be everywhere, can I? I can't watch over him and his research and still get out and try to find work, right? I got to leave him here with his pills and his drink, don't I?

(The RESEARCH PHYSICIAN again tries.)

SPECIALIST: I try to help him run this place but no Eskimo is going to stay in a hotel out here! A thousand nights he's ended up slumped over the front desk, mumbling about his dreams that will never come true! A hundred times he's slept on the kitchen floor in his sauce pots and spoons! He's had no one to help him, no one to stand by him…I mean I do, I really do but he needs some help! He's a Research Physician not a hotelier…he needs…he *(Cries.)*

DOCTOR #1: Jesus christ! What is the matter.

SPECIALIST: You…you wouldn't understand.

DOCTOR #1: *(Trying to figure out a way to make the RESEARCH PHYSICIAN feel better.)* Come on, Tim.

RESEARCH PHYSICIAN: Yes?

DOCTOR #1: Let's get the jobs figured out.

NURSE #2: Figure them out!

DOCTOR #1: That'll make everyone feel better.

RESEARCH PHYSICIAN: Well…

DOCTOR #1: You are going to be the research physician. Right?

RESEARCH PHYSICIAN: Well…yes! Yes I am!

DOCTOR #1: *(To the SPECIALIST.)* You're just the clean-up guy!

SPECIALIST: No.

DOCTOR #1: YES!

SPECIALIST: No. I am The Specialist. I'm from England.

DOCTOR #1: Big deal…Engerland. Well…then now, don't all doctors have those Nursess-ersurers that walk behind them!

RESEARCH PHYSICIAN: They walk behind the doctors! They're Nursesserers!

NURSE #2: NURSES!!! I am a nurse! Not a waitress! I have returned to work. I was wandering around outside for all this time. "What were you doing?" "Oh nothing." "Where were you?" "Here." "Were there Eskimos there?" " No!" " Do you want to come back to the Hospital now?"…"I don't know…" I remember all the things you did now!

DOCTOR #1: No you don't.

NURSE #2: "Yes I do."

DOCTOR #1: No you don't.

NURSE #2: Yes I do.

DOCTOR #1: No you don't!

SPECIALIST: *(Seeing the notice in her pocket.)* What's that then?

(EVERYONE stops.)

DOCTOR #1: What?

RESEARCH PHYSICIAN: What's what?

NURSE #2: What's what then?

SPECIALIST: What's that then.

NURSE #2: What?

SPECIALIST: That.

RESEARCH PHYSICIAN: Where.

SPECIALIST: There!

(NURSE #2 finds the letter.)

DOCTOR #1: *(Quietly.)* I got the heebie…jeebies.

SPECIALIST: What do we do?

RESEARCH PHYSICIAN: You know…I think we should open the envelope.

SPECIALIST: Where did you get it.

NURSE #2: It was in my pocket.

SPECIALIST: No no! Before that.

RESEARCH PHYSICIAN: *(Receives vision.)* She got it on her way over here! She's coming to work! She's got a letter from someone on the other side. Someone who sponsored her passage, or whatever it is—you know ! On that boat with no room or beds but only hammocks that swing around a lot. But on the deck she looked at the statue in

the rain with all the other tired, lonely freedom-longers. She walked through the vaulted building clutching the letter in her smudged and tiny, foreigner's hand, walking through the inspection praying not to get the little chalky mark that would send her right back where she came from!! All through the days and nights of the awful, solitary quarantine she clutched the sweaty papers until finally they opened that big sort of barn door thing, like a big huge door and let her out into the city in her best clothes, the ones she wore on the hillside of her rocky home town built of stones so far away…she clutched the letter, who knows who sent it…who knows where it came from—

NURSE #2: It was in my pocket!

SPECIALIST: Oh my god.

RESEARCH PHYSICIAN: SHE'S AN IMMIGRANT!!! She's LOOSE in the filthy ghetto town…walking in her ten dresses she had to wear because no one had a suitcase…here she comes with it!!! *(Cowers.)*

(NURSE #2 opens the letter. The bottom half of the paper is ripped.)

DOCTOR #1: READ IT!

SPECIALIST: JESUS CHRIST!

RESEARCH PHYSICIAN: *(Forgotten where he is…Blanche DuBois.)* Please don't turn the light on…

NURSE #2: "Dear people working there."

RESEARCH PHYSICIAN: *(Terrified.)* That's us! That's us!

DOCTOR #1: Is it?

SPECIALIST: It'll be alright. Come here.

(He gathers the RESEARCH PHYSICIAN in his arms and they listen…slowly DOCTOR #1 creeps into their circle. They are all afraid.)

SPECIALIST: It'll be alright…

NURSE #2: *(Starting again.)* "Dear people working there. Here is your message starting now. Take care of the guy down the hall. Do your jobs. This is the main thing: don't—"

DOCTOR #1: Oh…I've heard this before…

SPECIALIST: What guy?

NURSE #2: OH! *(Starts to say something.)* Oh…forget it.

SPECIALIST: WHAT guy???

NURSE #2: "this is the main thing: don't—"…huh.

RESEARCH PHYSICIAN: *(Hands covering ears.)* Is it over? Is it over??

SPECIALIST: It's alright now. WHAT GUY!

NURSE #2: "You know."

DOCTOR #1: You know what? Maybe this isn't such a great idea…

SPECIALIST: *(Stands up.)* Well, that's it then. We know the jobs. We know what we've got to do. Let's get on with it.

NURSE #2: So we definitely work there now.

DOCTOR #1: Yeah, but maybe it's not such a great idea…Terry?

NURSE #2: You're from England?

SPECIALIST: We'll talk about that later.

DOCTOR #1: But it's not like they know WHO's supposed to report there,

right? I mean there's no specific names mentioned…?

NURSE #2: "Right."

DOCTOR #1: Good. *(Consults train schedule.)*

RESEARCH PHYSICIAN: We do have jobs?

NURSE #2: Yes.

RESEARCH PHYSICIAN: Good.

SPECIALIST: That's what the letter said?

NURSE #2: Yes.

SPECIALIST: Good.

RESEARCH PHYSICIAN: …How long have we been standing here?

NURSE #2: *(Looking at the letter.)* …hmm…This doesn't seem too hard.

DOCTOR #1: What time is it?

ALL: A doctor takes responsibility for himself. A doctor copes with sexual intimacy. A grown doctor gains freedom. Learning to live in the present. Never too old to change for the better. A very special way.

DREAM SEQUENCE: ADVENTURES UNDERGROUND

JIMMY and the TRAVELLER walk underground. A WHITE RABBIT passes through at great speed a few times; the boys try to follow. Finally it stops.

JIMMY: Where's Frank?

WHITE RABBIT: *(Settling into character.)* What are you doing in here?

JIMMY: We're just going to the join.

TRAVELLER: *(Looking at the WHITE RABBIT.)* …that's not right.

WHITE RABBIT: We're late you know!

JIMMY: What? I'm not late! I'm never late!

TRAVELLER: Just keep walking, Jimmy.

WHITE RABBIT: Well, you're late now, Jimmy! Very very late indeed.

TRAVELLER: What are you talking about?

JIMMY: I've never been late once in my life! I was waiting!

WHITE RABBIT: Why are you late? Were you left behind as well??

TRAVELLER: I'm not late.

WHITE RABBIT: Oh…did you run the wrong way then?

TRAVELLER: What?

JIMMY: Where's Frank?

TRAVELLER: Yeah…where IS Frank.

JIMMY: Christ, I hope he didn't pass out again.

TRAVELLER: Yeah. Maybe he passed out.

WHITE RABBIT: Yeah maybe. *(Looks at JIMMY.)*

TRAVELLER: What are you talking about? *(Tries to get a better look at the thing.)*

JIMMY: What's he doing down here?

WHITE RABBIT: What time is it?… *(Slight hint of a chill for JIMMY.)* I'm late! The queen will have my hat!! I'm late for the trial!!

JIMMY: …no. I'm not late. *(Digging in his pockets.)* Look on the shift list! I was there!

(The MAD HATTER and the QUEEN OF HEARTS enter. The QUEEN comes up and tries to talk in the WHITE RABBIT's ear—he whispers back.)

WHITE RABBIT: No…is that right?! *(To them.)* We don't want to be left behind! We'll miss the trial!! *(To the TRAVELLER.)* It's this way in case you forgot.

TRAVELLER: What?

WHITE RABBIT: Yes, yes! Follow ME to court!!

TRAVELLER: *(Walking past.)* What trial is it?

JIMMY: Maybe it's about the accident?

TRAVELLER: *(Slightly nervous now.)* Oh. Is it about the accident?

WHITE RABBIT: *(Clandestinely to the TRAVELLER.)* They're this way, in case you don't know…Just go along with it.

JIMMY: Hey! Don't forget about me! I want to testify at the trial.

WHITE RABBIT: It IS a trial yes! Follow ME! The queen will have our hats and we'd never get the deposit back! That WOULD be a trial!

TRAVELLER: Just keep walking.

JIMMY: No let's go. We should sue for damages.

(The WHITE RABBIT, the QUEEN OF HEARTS, and the MAD HATTER awkwardly transform the place into court. The QUEEN exits. Then—)

WHITE RABBIT: SIT DOWN! *(Awkwardly blows a trumpet, then also makes noise of trumpet.)* TRA LA! TRA LA!! Here we are at the Very Important Trial! All rise for the Queen!

JIMMY: Why is it so dark in here?

(The QUEEN reenters.)

JIMMY: Is that Frank? I can't see.

WHITE RABBIT: Start!

QUEEN OF HEARTS: My first sentence is light. *(Girds.)* "Where is everybody?"

JIMMY: I want to sue for damages! I was in an accident!

TRAVELLER: *(Interrupting.)* Is this the liability trial for the water tunnel accident?

QUEEN OF HEARTS: Is everybody here?

JIMMY: Our friend went up the road.

WHITE RABBIT: I thought you did.

TRAVELLER: What?

QUEEN OF HEARTS: I will now pass a short sentence: "Begin!"

(Court begins.)

MAD HATTER: The time has come the bailiff said to shout and sometimes sing: of sand and moles and ceiling traps, of pools of mud and things!

QUEEN OF HEARTS: Then will you play a game?

JIMMY: So! When do we testify.

QUEEN OF HEARTS: WILL YOU PLAY???

JIMMY: What?

WHITE RABBIT: Testify now. Don't wait!

TRAVELLER: Where are we?

QUEEN OF HEARTS: Well???

WHITE RABBIT and MAD HATTER: YES!

MAD HATTER: Well-come to the well!

TRAVELLER: It's not a well!

JIMMY: I thought we were testifying at a trial!

MAD HATTER: It is a well indeed! A well in which we try the case!

TRAVELLER: In a well!?

QUEEN OF HEARTS: Well in!

JIMMY: That is definitely not Frank.

QUEEN OF HEARTS: Indeed I am not Frank! But I will do just as well!

MAD HATTER: A justice well, yes.

QUEEN OF HEARTS: Yes! Just as well!

WHITE RABBIT: Legally speaking. What conclusion can you draw from this?

QUEEN OF HEARTS: Water !

TRAVELLER: Listen. Are we in the other tunnel? The old one? Or the new tunnel?

JIMMY: Yeah, were we SUPPOSED to wait where we were?? We're lost, kind of.

QUEEN OF HEARTS: In answer to your question, you are in. Well in. And also yes to the second part. And let's definitely call it a well for now. It's safer than this tunnel you keep on talking about.

MAD HATTER: But children fall in wells.

QUEEN OF HEARTS: And when they do they sue, frankly.

JIMMY: *(Didn't hear.)* Frank was never in a well!

QUEEN OF HEARTS: *(Challenging the TRAVELLER to disagree.)* Frank's not here.

WHITE RABBIT: No Frank is all alone in some other tunnel.

TRAVELLER: So we are in the other tunnel.

MAD HATTER: You are.

QUEEN OF HEARTS: *(Quietly to the TRAVELLER.)* Will you play?

TRAVELLER: Play what?

JIMMY: *(Interrupting.)* Weren't we testifying at a trial?? Isn't that what we were doing??? I'm sick of waiting around!

MAD HATTER: *(Looking at the paper and the TRAVELLER.)* Yes, upon discovery of who is responsible, certain waiting parties will—

WHITE RABBIT: *(Pun on "waiting" versus "wading.")* But only up to their knees.

TRAVELLER: *(Apprehensive.)* What is this?

WHITE RABBIT: Day One of the Damages Trial.

JIMMY: Good!

QUEEN OF HEARTS: During day one of the trial, which we're in, the court will discover: *who* fell in the well.

MAD HATTER: Like kids do.

QUEEN OF HEARTS: Who got out!

WHITE RABBIT: The one with the map of course!

QUEEN OF HEARTS: *Who* ran away! *(She runs back in line.)*

WHITE RABBIT: Question One: Where is everybody?

JIMMY: Frank went to the join.

QUEEN OF HEARTS: Where is everybody else?

TRAVELLER: We're here.

WHITE RABBIT: Excuse me Ma'am, but who is the judge in this matter?

QUEEN OF HEARTS: The judge!?

MAD HATTER: The arbiter?

QUEEN OF HEARTS: Who did!??

MAD HATTER: Arbiter, Ma'am.

QUEEN OF HEARTS: *(Confused with "Arbiter" versus "I bit her.")* Off with his hat!

WHITE RABBIT: Your Majesty, the hatter is crazy from eating lead on paintbrushes or something. He did not mean to bite your grace.

MAD HATTER: AR-BIT-ER!

QUEEN OF HEARTS: Is he going to bite me again?

WHITE RABBIT: Oh dear.

MAD HATTER: *(To the WHITE RABBIT.)* And it's not from paintbrushes. It's the AIR down here!

WHITE RABBIT: *(Agreeing.)* That would make anyone go crazy.

MAD HATTER: I'll say! No wonder they're lost!

JIMMY: *(Pushing through.)* We want to sue for damages! I'm sick of waiting around! I don't want to get blamed for anything.

TRAVELLER: It's not about that.

MAD HATTER: I'll be the judge of that!

WHITE RABBIT: Well! THAT'S settled. *(Puts judge's hat on top of the HATTER's top hat.)* Now onto the second question!

QUEEN OF HEARTS: Question Two: Why didn't you talk to me in the apartment?

TRAVELLER: What?

WHITE RABBIT: *(Looks at paper.)* That's not on there!

QUEEN OF HEARTS: Right! Question Two: Do you feel well?

(The OTHER TWO approach the QUEEN.)

WHITE RABBIT: Excuse me, Ma'am, but of course he feels well, he's in one.

JIMMY: I feel pretty terrible actually. Why is it so dark in here?

QUEEN OF HEARTS: Shine some light on this matter!

MAD HATTER: *(Indicating JIMMY.)* He doesn't have a light. Somebody took it.

TRAVELLER: *(Hastily.)* He's okay. He just got bumped around a little. He'll be fine.

JIMMY: I want to testify! I don't want them to forget about what happened to me! I'm sick of waiting around.

WHITE RABBIT: See? He's waiting in the dark!

QUEEN OF HEARTS: He's sick of it.

JIMMY: I'll tell what happened in the accident.

QUEEN OF HEARTS: Oh—

JIMMY: I work in water tunnel number—

WHITE RABBIT: Objection!

MAD HATTER: No no no the bailiff may not object!

WHITE RABBIT: May I rephrase?

MAD HATTER: As bailiff or barrister.

WHITE RABBIT: The latter!

MAD HATTER: Oh how I wish we had one!

QUEEN OF HEARTS: What?

MAD HATTER: A ladder.

QUEEN OF HEARTS: Who?

MAD HATTER: All of us.

WHITE RABBIT: Exactly. The events occurred in…?

(JIMMY and the TRAVELLER confer.)

JIMMY: In the "water well."

MAD HATTER: *(Compelled to continue.)* Yes, a ladder lit by a single lamp. Its feet stuck in the mud. Where does it poke up to? Ah memories…

QUEEN OF HEARTS: Will you forget the ladder???

WHITE RABBIT: I shall rephrase not using the latter.

QUEEN OF HEARTS: *(Pun on "latter" versus "ladder.")* But how will you get out then?

TRAVELLER: Listen—we were in an accident in the tunnel—

QUEEN OF HEARTS: All three?!

JIMMY: Number three!

TRAVELLER: Yes. Everything's alright. Nobody did anything wrong. We just don't know where we are exactly.

JIMMY: Yeah! We were in a cave-in! Or a bump or something! We don't know WHAT happened! Our friend is up the way a little. I got hurt I think…my friend is…we tried to get out but…I—

TRAVELLER: You got hurt, we all did! We're all just trying to get to the join!

WHITE RABBIT: And…

TRAVELLER: We're walking to the join the way Frank went…I think he came this way

WHITE RABBIT: And?

JIMMY: Where's my flashlight?

TRAVELLER: I came this way because Frank said it was the way out. I think I can get out this way. Is it—

WHITE RABBIT: Yes?

MAD HATTER: Objection! The barrister is leading the witness!

QUEEN OF HEARTS: Where?

MAD HATTER: To the conclusion!

QUEEN OF HEARTS: *(Hastily writing on the paper she has taken.)* Rule number three hundred and fifty-eight: People who work in water tunnels are not allowed to—

JIMMY: What?

QUEEN OF HEARTS: Nothing.

TRAVELLER: Listen, all we want is to go up the road and find our friend and get out of here.

WHITE RABBIT: Query: Why?

TRAVELLER: Because we're trapped in here and apart—

WHITE RABBIT: He's trapped in an apartment!

QUEEN OF HEARTS: My brother took me there.

MAD HATTER: I thought he was in between apartments?

WHITE RABBIT: Is he moving?

JIMMY: Wait—

QUEEN OF HEARTS: *(Writing on the paper.)* Rule number eight hundred and fifty-three! All people trapped in their apartments will have an accident!

JIMMY: Because it's too dark!

TRAVELLER: No she means "in an apartment," not the tunnel. That's not a rule.

QUEEN OF HEARTS: But it's old.

TRAVELLER: You've just written it now.

QUEEN OF HEARTS: No I didn't. *(Stepping forward.)* WILL YOU PLAY?

WHITE RABBIT: *(Quietly.)* I wouldn't play with those rules…

MAD HATTER: You must have rules or there's no game! I will illustrate with cards!!!

(EVERYONE runs around. Elaborate dance. Cards are chucked about.)

TRAVELLER: I don't want to play any game right now.

MAD HATTER: They doesn't want to play. See?

WHITE RABBIT: *(Out of character.)* Why did we throw the cards all over the place.

QUEEN OF HEARTS: *(Whispers.)* Shut up.

MAD HATTER: *(Takes the paper.)* Now I have the aforementioned rules!

TRAVELLER: I'd like to see the rules.

JIMMY: I don't think they're listening. Hey what happened to my light?

TRAVELLER: I'm telling you this is not right.

WHITE RABBIT: "We shall try to keep it light." Write THAT down!

QUEEN OF HEARTS: I will examine the witness. Question Three: Who remains there?

WHITE RABBIT: Whose remains!!?

MAD HATTER: Excuse me, your Majesty.

WHITE RABBIT: I thought I was trying the case!

QUEEN OF HEARTS: You are trying, Hare!

WHITE RABBIT: I am trying here!

MAD HATTER: Well then, do!

WHITE RABBIT: Didn't she ask "whose remains"?

MAD HATTER: Who?

QUEEN OF HEARTS: Who.

MAD HATTER: WHO?

QUEEN OF HEARTS: …who?

WHITE RABBIT: What are you? A couple owls?

JIMMY: I didn't think there was supposed to be other people down here. I thought you had to work here to get in…Do you work here? Are you people from the tunnel?

QUEEN OF HEARTS: So Question Four: Is everybody alright?

TRAVELLER: Yes!

JIMMY: No I don't think so. I don't feel so great. Frank seemed okay but I'm not sure. I mean we were in an accident…I got hurt I think…I need to talk to somebody—

TRAVELLER: *(Hastily interrupting.)* You're fine. Let's get out of here. You don't need anything.

JIMMY: Plus, I'd like to hear the evidence. I mean if these guys work down here, they'd know and then we can get damages.

TRAVELLER: They don't work down here.

WHITE RABBIT: *(To JIMMY.)* I didn't think you'd want any more damages.

QUEEN OF HEARTS: He's waiting in the dark he said?

MAD HATTER: Let's leave off about him sitting in the dark waiting…

QUEEN OF HEARTS: Read back the proceedings!

MAD HATTER: The evidence so far is as follows, fellows. During the trial we discovered the proceedings were: what I am about to say. I begin: He was heard to say "In the end, I was alone."

JIMMY: Who?

MAD HATTER: In terms of the game? No one wanted to play. Regarding their placement? They are lost. Quoted: "In the end we are alone."

WHITE RABBIT: That's all?

JIMMY: I never said that.

WHITE RABBIT: Is that all?

JIMMY: I never said that.

MAD HATTER: *(Looks carefully at the rules.)* ...uh...yes?

QUEEN OF HEARTS: But that's sad! *(She takes the rules from the WHITE RABBIT for a second... looks at them.)*

MAD HATTER: It is...it is sad.

WHITE RABBIT: Let me see the rules please!

(The paper is given.)

TRAVELLER: I'd like to see the rules.

WHITE RABBIT: No you wouldn't.

TRAVELLER: Why?

QUEEN OF HEARTS: No reason.

WHITE RABBIT: What is the verdict?

QUEEN OF HEARTS: It's at the bottom!

MAD HATTER: With them.

(They all cluster around the paper.)

WHITE RABBIT: *(Reading.)* Oh...that's terrible.

QUEEN OF HEARTS: I didn't expect that.

WHITE RABBIT: Why is there all that stuff about him alone in the apartment?

MAD HATTER: *(Clandestinely.)* What do they say we're supposed to do?

TRAVELLER: *(Getting a bad feeling.)* Can I see that?

JIMMY: Are you people from the tunnel?

(They confer.)

QUEEN OF HEARTS: Man, I didn't know it had a sad ending. That's terrible. He just got left behind?

MAD HATTER: Is he still waiting in there?

QUEEN OF HEARTS: *(Scans paper.)* Uh...that's not on there.

WHITE RABBIT: *(Out of character.)* Listen buddy—I would've done the same thing. Your friend there? I don't know what to say about him. Just go! I guess he'll wait here.

JIMMY: No! I don't want to wait here!

TRAVELLER: Is that what it says?

WHITE RABBIT: No...it says something different than that.

TRAVELLER: What? It says something bad about me?

QUEEN OF HEARTS: *(Has taken the rules back.)* No wonder he didn't want to play.

WHITE RABBIT: Now I wish I hadn't come.

TRAVELLER: What is the verdict?

MAD HATTER: Be careful in the dark, Jimmy. Try and make it to the join.

WHITE RABBIT: *(Whispers about the TRAVELLER.)* But he's going to the heading, right?!

TRAVELLER: No I'm not!

QUEEN OF HEARTS: Can we do this somewhere else. I thought it was going to be light hearted...

(They go.)

TRAVELLER: *(Calling out.)* What are we supposed to do??

QUEEN OF HEARTS: This isn't light hearted.

JIMMY: *(Has been staring off.)* Why is it so dark in here?

EPISODE #2
Event: In the Tunnel

JIMMY and the TRAVELLER stand in the tunnel motionless. The radio crackles, sounds of an argument.

TRAVELLER: What's that?

JIMMY: I don't know.

TRAVELLER: Uh…Where is Frank?

JIMMY: I don't know.

(They stand afraid, three hundred feet below the street. Sand falls from the ceiling. Suddenly FRANK appears.)

TRAVELLER: Where'd you go?

FRANK: I found a way out you guys! It's right up there!! It's a shortcut to the join! I'm almost positive.

TRAVELLER: You found a shortcut?

JIMMY: …there's lots of other people down here, Frank.

TRAVELLER: Shut up about that.

FRANK: Well, I walked up ahead of you guys. I think I found a shortcut to the join.

TRAVELLER: That's what you said.

FRANK: Yeah so anyways I spoke to those guys.

JIMMY: What?

FRANK: Yeah, I spoke to those guys!

TRAVELLER: What?

FRANK: They're sending the lines down. They think we're going to be alright!

JIMMY: But do they know I'm down here?

FRANK: Why does that matter?

JIMMY: I can't believe you spoke to those guys.

TRAVELLER: And? what did they say?

FRANK: I don't know! They said they wanted to help us out!! They KNOW we're down here!

JIMMY: Where did you go, Frank?

TRAVELLER: Really?

FRANK: Yeah! They said they knew we were in trouble but they were going to send some guys in to…no…that's not right…they said they—no *(Thinks.)* I had the map…they—I saw the—

JIMMY: What map?

FRANK: Yeah, so I didn't use the radio.

TRAVELLER: What did they say?

JIMMY: What map?

FRANK: They said they were going to send in some help to get us out of here but we should keep walking to the join if we could…I said we could, so they said walk to the join and we'll send someone in there because there might be a problem getting out. It doesn't matter who's down here! Just stick with me!

JIMMY: So we're supposed to keep walking?

FRANK: Yeah.

TRAVELLER: *(Has been thinking.)* Frank?

FRANK: Yes?

TRAVELLER: When you were talking to them…you could hear their voices without the radio or anything? I mean you could hear them outside? From the tunnel?

FRANK: I guess!

TRAVELLER: But then that would mean if we just went to where you heard them it would be so close to the surface they could just pull us out?

FRANK: What?

JIMMY: *(Forlorn.)* Frank?...Where did you go?

TRAVELLER: I mean if you just took us to that spot where you just were...up ahead...then they could just pull us out.

FRANK: Uh...maybe not.

TRAVELLER: Why?

FRANK: Well...I don't like to say...but it's restricted.

TRAVELLER: Restricted in what way?

JIMMY: What do you mean?

FRANK: Well...I didn't want to tell you guys but I know a place that's only on my map...you know restricted to my shift and I went there because I had a feeling it was pretty close, it's in another part of tunnel, but the thing is: the place in the tunnel where I was? It's restricted.

TRAVELLER: Frank, don't you think this is an emergency?

FRANK: What?

TRAVELLER: Us being trapped in here??

FRANK: Yeah but I still can't tell you where I was.

JIMMY: It's restricted.

FRANK: Yes.

JIMMY: From me.

FRANK: Especially from you.

JIMMY: What?

TRAVELLER: What about me?

FRANK: I don't know about you.

(Nothing happens.)

TRAVELLER: So...what do we do?

(They stand there.)

TRAVELLER: Frank?

FRANK: Huh?

TRAVELLER: What do we do?

JIMMY: Restricted to what?

FRANK: What?

JIMMY: The place near the join...where you could talk to them.

FRANK: What I mean is...I don't think we can all go there at once.

JIMMY: Why?

FRANK: *(Thinks.)* I could go there and get out and then tell them I told you guys.

JIMMY: But why would they mind?

FRANK: It's restricted.

TRAVELLER: That's stupid. This is an emergency.

FRANK: I could go there first and then we could all get out later. Just keep walking and you'll be closer to the place where you'll get out. It's in another part of the tunnel. That's all I can tell you. You see, if we go there all at once, it'll get all jammed up. Let me tell them you're coming and then we can all go one at a time. It's not that big. It's in another part of the tunnel. I have to let them know. It's only on my map.

(They stand.)

TRAVELLER: Frank...what section do you work in?

FRANK: What do you mean?

JIMMY: Didn't you say before you worked at the heading?

FRANK: At the heading?

JIMMY: Yeah.

FRANK: Well I've BEEN to the heading, yeah.

TRAVELLER: This restricted area is at the heading?

FRANK: No. It's the OTHER way... closer to the join.

TRAVELLER: How far away did they seem?

FRANK: *(Thinks for a moment.)* Well... pretty close.

JIMMY: Yeah Frank! You should describe it and then if we figure out where it is it's just by luck!

FRANK: No I don't think so. But I got to tell you I could feel them banging on the tunnel and trying to make a hole so they could see me. I couldn't see them of course... but... I could hear them.

(The tunnel shifts.)

JIMMY: What was that?

(The emergency lights go out.)

FRANK: Wait a second.

(The lights flicker back on. FRANK is gone.)

JIMMY: Where'd he go?

TRAVELLER: He went to the restricted area.

JIMMY: Is he going to get us out?

TRAVELLER: I don't know.

(Faint sound of FRANK calling to them.)

TRAVELLER: Listen.

JIMMY: What?

TRAVELLER: That's Frank?

JIMMY: Where?

TRAVELLER: That way... the way he said... the restricted area... listen

(FRANK's spectral voice.)

TRAVELLER: —Maybe he's telling them we're coming to get out.

JIMMY: Really? It should be easy enough, right?

(FRANK's voice, spectral.)

TRAVELLER: I'm going. We should keep walking so we're closer to Frank in case there's a problem getting out like he said.

JIMMY: I want to go too. Frank's going to get us out.

(The lights flicker and go out. FRANK's voice echoes in the tunnel.)

TRAVELLER: *(Bustling.)* Alright. Here's my light.

(TRAVELLER notices JIMMY is hesitating.)

TRAVELLER: What's the matter?

JIMMY: Listen... I got to tell you something... I think something happened to me... before.

TRAVELLER: What do you mean?

JIMMY: I think there's something wrong with me, maybe I should wait here for you. Something happened to me in the accident I think. You go on...

TRAVELLER: You look alright.

JIMMY: Really?

TRAVELLER: *(Looks at him.)* Yes.

JIMMY: I think something happened. I think they forgot about me.

TRAVELLER: So what? It doesn't matter.

JIMMY: I think Frank found out they forgot about us.

TRAVELLER: They did not!

JIMMY: I think that's why we have to go one at a time…Frank has to get back to let them know there's two of us. That's why he left.

TRAVELLER: Why does it matter?

JIMMY: Well it's like if somebody was left behind… *(Thinks it over.)* You know for the rescue effort…it matters who's down here…so they know how many of us there are. Like if somebody left to get help that's different, say if they went over the top, but if somebody just left a guy maybe he'd get there but there might not be any line there to get him out…but I don't think he gets there

TRAVELLER: What are you talking about?

JIMMY: *(Ominous.)* I think you're supposed to stay where you are until they come get you.

TRAVELLER: What?

JIMMY: That's why Frank was surprised to see one of us…he had to go back and let them know.

TRAVELLER: Well, what do you want to do? *(He turns on his flashlight.)*

JIMMY: It's okay now. I want to go too.

TRAVELLER: Here we go.

JIMMY: We're going to the shortcut right?

TRAVELLER: Right… *(Humoring him.)* Frank'll let them know how many lines.

JIMMY: Will he?

TRAVELLER: Yes. Two guys. Two lines.

JIMMY: Two guys. Two lines.

TRAVELLER: Or three, I guess, if you count Frank.

JIMMY: He'll send the line. He's letting them know.

TRAVELLER: Yes.

JIMMY: Hey maybe you'll get a raise.

TRAVELLER: What do you mean?

JIMMY: Well when they find out you helped me out when I was waiting for Frank…you know, by talking to me.

TRAVELLER: Oh…yeah.

JIMMY: *(Walking out.)* I don't feel so great…Are you sure I'm alright?

DOCTORS AND NURSES SIT AT A STAFF MEETING

In the Hospital now.

RESEARCH PHYSICIAN: Well…I'm SO glad that Barry pulled me out of the kitchen and left me here in this place. I mean this isn't even a research facility let alone a hotel.

SPECIALIST: Yeah.

NURSE #2: Where'd he go anyways?

RESEARCH PHYSICIAN: He went his Barry way, Sandy. He blew into our little inn and took off for greener pastures, you might say. In the end, Bill didn't care about me or my research. Bob, NEVER took my cuisine seriously.

NURSE #2: Well…

SPECIALIST: You're a GREAT cook.

DOCTOR #1: Yes, I know.

SPECIALIST: All those sauces and things! They were really good!

NURSE #2: *(Quietly.)* Not the white one.

RESEARCH PHYSICIAN: YES! The white one!

SPECIALIST: The shrimps, the bread, that jelly thing, the chickens and cows… all the bits and bobs…brilliant!

NURSE #2: Not that jelly…that tasted…"bad."

RESEARCH PHYSICIAN: Yeah, I know!

SPECIALIST: NO it didn't!

RESEARCH PHYSICIAN: …We're here! Now what do we do?

NURSE #2: "I don't know."

RESEARCH PHYSICIAN: What do we do? What did the letter say? Take care of some guys we never met? For what reason?

SPECIALIST: Sounds like a lot of work to me, gov.

RESEARCH PHYSICIAN: Yeah! Take care of the guy etcetera. I mean what the hell does that mean? *(Swaggering.)* I'm a big shot research chef/hotelier/physician type thing! I don't have to "take care" of some sad-sack jerk in a back room!

SPECIALIST: That's right.

RESEARCH PHYSICIAN: Get somebody else to do it!

SPECIALIST: YEAH!

RESEARCH PHYSICIAN: *(To NURSE #2.)* Get HER! You do it!

NURSE #2: I can't do it!

RESEARCH PHYSICIAN: Do it! Do it all!

NURSE #2: NO!

RESEARCH PHYSICIAN: YES! I got to get out of here, babe! I'm a big shot chef physician who wears a fur coat—but it's still manly! I got a first-class passage on a clipper ship that cruises all the way across the ocean to…to—

SPECIALIST: To England??!!

RESEARCH PHYSICIAN: *(Disregards…)* Yeah, but I'm not taking you… *(Gets bored.)* Anyways…let's get someone else to do it.

SPECIALIST: Who?

NURSE #2: Yeah, who?

RESEARCH PHYSICIAN: What?

NURSE #2: Who?

SPECIALIST: Who?

RESEARCH PHYSICIAN: What are you a bunch of owls…

(EVERYONE stands around thinking.)

NURSE #2: One time there was another person who worked here. There were two guys and then there was three guys one time and there was also another one of the Fantastic Helpers, like Bill said…he said " Once there were Fantastic Helpers" and I said "Right! A nurse!" and Barry said—

RESEARCH PHYSICIAN: That's it!!!

SPECIALIST: My god! You startled me!

RESEARCH PHYSICIAN: HIRE A SECOND NURSESSERESSES!

NURSE #2: A nurse!

RESEARCH PHYSICIAN: Right, a whatever it is. We'll have to give her some kind of really hard test though! Because the Fantastic Helper is going to have to take care of that guy in the room. Go! Go out in the hall and see if anybody's out there!

NURSE #2: No.

RESEARCH PHYSICIAN: Why are you driving me crazy?!!!

SPECIALIST: What kind of test?

NURSE #2: A really hard test to see if she can do her job.

SPECIALIST: Do I have to take it?

RESEARCH PHYSICIAN: Will you go out in the hall and see if anybody's out there!

NURSE #2: Me?

RESEARCH PHYSICIAN: Yes!

NURSE #2: No way.

SPECIALIST: *(Backing away.)* No... no...not...not...me?

RESEARCH PHYSICIAN: Go!

SPECIALIST: I can't go in the hall!

RESEARCH PHYSICIAN: Go. In. The. Hall. And. Get. A. Person.

NURSE #2: No way.

RESEARCH PHYSICIAN: God damn it! What is the matter with you people. *(Goes in the hall.)*

NURSE #2: He doesn't know what's out there.

RESEARCH PHYSICIAN: *(Backs into the room again.)* There's thousands of them out there!

NURSE #2: See?

RESEARCH PHYSICIAN: My god! It's white and there's all kinds of loud noises! There's beds that roll around on wheels!! No one knows where they're going!! I got in a box with a door, in a shaft sort of thing! The door opened! I got out and saw hundreds of tiny monkeys without any hair screaming in plastic trays! Then I got lost in a mob of people all wearing the same costume who went into rooms and stuck pins and hoses into the openings of some kind of messed-up bed clothes affair! There's chairs that you can drive like a car!

SPECIALIST: You saw all that just now!?

RESEARCH PHYSICIAN: YES! It seems the costume people like to carry different colored bits of paper and talk about the messed-up bed clothes! They stand around them all the time! They stuff the bed clothes with liquids and tiny round foods and then the bed clothes quit bothering them so much!!

SPECIALIST: Really?

RESEARCH PHYSICIAN: YES! I think we'll definitely get some help from that quarter!

NURSE #2: I know all about that kind of thing!

RESEARCH PHYSICIAN: It was...it was—

SPECIALIST: Did you see any nurses...(es)?

NURSE #2: Did you remember?

RESEARCH PHYSICIAN: YES! They were all over the place! I told a good one to come through the hall! She seemed to know what I meant!

SPECIALIST: What did you say then??

NURSE #2: What do you mean "a good one"?

RESEARCH PHYSICIAN: I said "It's job time!" and she said "Where am I?" and I said "I don't know but you're getting a job," then she said "Do I have to take a test?" And I said "YES! A really hard one!"

NURSE #2: What does she look like?

RESEARCH PHYSICIAN: Like us!

SPECIALIST: My god!

NURSE #2: Are you sure she knows where to go?

SPECIALIST: *(Pointing to something in the RESEARCH PHYSICIAN's pocket.)* What's that?

RESEARCH PHYSICIAN: Don't worry about that. Yes! She said she'd be here in a minute. She's a good one!

NURSE #2: Oh dear.

SPECIALIST: What do we do?

NURSE #2: Oh no.

RESEARCH PHYSICIAN: Get the Fantastic Helper Test ready!!!!!

(EVERYONE runs around. In she comes.)

NURSE #2: She looks like a spider.

(The RESEARCH PHYSICIAN and the SPECIALIST have set up for the test.)

SPECIALIST: What are you? Some kind of mouse!

NURSE #2: She looks like a spider!

SPECIALIST: No look! It's some kind of mouse!

NURSE #3: I ain't no kind a mouse!

SPECIALIST: It's a mouse of some kind!

NURSE #3: No! I ain't!!

NURSE #2: It's a spider!

RESEARCH PHYSICIAN: *(Has been shuffling papers, desperately preparing for his role as interlocutor.)* RIGHT! Sit it down for tests!

(NURSE #3 is put into a chair and somewhat restrained.)

NURSE #3: What's this all about! I didn't sign up for this. Get off a me!

RESEARCH PHYSICIAN: *(A little spooked.)* Right! Question ONE!! Why are you talking like that?

SPECIALIST: That's not on there.

NURSE #2: Start the test!

RESEARCH PHYSICIAN: Right! Question One: What is it?

NURSE #2: A spider!

SPECIALIST: A mouse!

RESEARCH PHYSICIAN: NO! Not YOU! HER!

SPECIALIST: But we could answer if we wanted? I mean just to see where we are?

RESEARCH PHYSICIAN: What?

SPECIALIST: Just to see how we're doing?

NURSE #2: I can beat that spider with a shoe!

RESEARCH PHYSICIAN: That's not important! *(To NURSE #3.)* …well? What is it?

NURSE #3: *(Looks around nervously.)* I met you last week in the hall and you told me to come in here and you'd get me some work! I got to get some money to pay for my sick brudda's medicine!

RESEARCH PHYSICIAN: *(To himself.)* Medicine. Ha!

SPECIALIST: …last week?

NURSE #3: Yeah my brudda's sick you know—he got the fever from all the bad water in dere. He been down in de hole too long.

(The RESEARCH PHYSICIAN has been creeping up to get a better look.)

NURSE #2: Don't get too close!

NURSE #3: Too long…too long…HEY! Get me outa this chair you!

NURSE #2: See? It's a poisonous spider!

SPECIALIST: Your brother is sick?

RESEARCH PHYSICIAN: Question Two! Where are we?

SPECIALIST: NO! Don't try and ask that.

RESEARCH PHYSICIAN: *(On the QT.)* Yeah but maybe it knows.

NURSE #2: At work!

NURSE #3: *(Wailing.)* What do I got to do to get this job!

RESEARCH PHYSICIAN: Answer the question! Take the test!

NURSE #3: I don't KNOW where I am!!! That's the problem! My brudda's sick! I went in the fancy hotel—

RESEARCH PHYSICIAN: Hospital.

NURSE #3: Whatever it is, mister! I went in there to try and get some work! I saw a big monkey in a backwards paper dress. He was dragging a metal stick on wheels with a see-through beehive kind of swinging off it…Did you see that, mister?

RESEARCH PHYSICIAN: Yes, yes I did.

NURSE #3: I got to make more than I do sewing them silk flowers! I got to help my brudda!

SPECIALIST: It's got a sick brother!!!

NURSE #3: That's why I go to them parties. I got to make more money to help my brudda. He's been in de hole too long and now he's got that

NURSE #2: *(Inspecting her.)* I didn't know spiders wore clothes.

RESEARCH PHYSICIAN: Well I can help your brother! But only if you work here! I don't just hand out help to sad-sacks in back rooms, you know! I mean THAT'S the whole reason YOU'RE here! So! Question Two! Where are we?

NURSE #2: *(Triumphantly repeats.)* At work!

SPECIALIST: Standing in a room!

NURSE #3: At a party?

RESEARCH PHYSICIAN: HOSPITAL! That is correct! *(Takes out the instrument from his pocket that he picked up "in the hall.")* Now! YOU! *(To NURSE #2.)* Stick this in the ear!

NURSE #3: What? I don't want that in my ear! I don't want the typhus, mister! I'm just a flower sewer!

RESEARCH PHYSICIAN: In. The. Ear.

NURSE #2: That doesn't seem right.

RESEARCH PHYSICIAN: It's right. It is part of the test. Do you want your brother to get that medicine or not.

NURSE #3: YEAH!

SPECIALIST: I REALLY think this is some kind of mouse.

RESEARCH PHYSICIAN: Well then… let me ask you something…are you some kind of mouse that wants a job in here?

NURSE #3: Yes. For my brudda!

RESEARCH PHYSICIAN: *(To NURSE #2.)* In.

(The SPECIALIST holds NURSE #3's head, NURSE #2 clumsily pushes the instrument into her ear…it stays sticking out.)

NURSE #3: *(After a moment and slowly losing the former accent.)* What…about my brudda?

RESEARCH PHYSICIAN: *(Trying to seem nonchalant.)* Question Three: Who is the guy down the hall?

SPECIALIST: My god! You shouldn't ask that!! We're supposed to know that!!

RESEARCH PHYSICIAN: Shut up! There's no one around here.

NURSE #3: I got a bee in my head.

NURSE #2: Oh…no…

RESEARCH PHYSICIAN: Sandy!

NURSE #2: What?!

RESEARCH PHYSICIAN: Ask her in the other ear.

NURSE #2: *(Slowly going to do so.)* Who are the guys down the hall?

RESEARCH PHYSICIAN: …wait is it "guy" or guys"?

SPECIALIST: It's got a sick brother! I mean maybe we should leave it alone?

NURSE #2: It didn't say anything.

NURSE #3: Who's in the apartment?

RESEARCH PHYSICIAN: *(Notes response.)* Right…on to the next question. Number Four. Are you a good Nursesseresses?

NURSE #2: YES!

RESEARCH PHYSICIAN: Not you. There!

SPECIALIST: Your brother is sick, Barbara?

RESEARCH PHYSICIAN: Are you a good nurses?

NURSE #3: Oh my god…what is this?

RESEARCH PHYSICIAN: Close enough! Now the last question! *(Consults lists and papers deeply, then—)* Number Five: What…happened…to me?

NURSE #2: What?

RESEARCH PHYSICIAN: What…happened to me?

SPECIALIST: That's too hard! I'll never get that one!

RESEARCH PHYSICIAN: What happened?…to…me…?

NURSE #2: I got lost…I got lost in here.

RESEARCH PHYSICIAN: I failed… yes…putting it simply…that's right…I am filled with regret…I have failed. Is there a brighter horizon coming because of what I am doing now? Maybe…but it don't change my failure…my regret… my Loss. What happened to me? Answer: I have failed.

RESEARCH PHYSICIAN: I emigrated.

NURSE #3: I was in an apartment. Now I work in the—

(They unstrap her. After a false start—)

ALL: A doctor takes responsibility for himself. A doctor copes with sexual intimacy. A grown doctor gains freedom. Learning to live in the present. Never too old to change for the better. A very special way.

DREAM SEQUENCE: TERRORISTS?

In come the Old-Time Tunnelers…JOHN HENRY out in front. Song: "John Henry."

TRAVELLER: Wait a second!

JIMMY: I didn't think anybody was supposed to be down here!

TRAVELLER: *(Scared.)* Who are you guys?

TUNNELER #1: Boss!

JOHN HENRY: *(Desperately to JIMMY.)* You got your map!?

JIMMY: Do you mean the shift pass? Frank's got the map.

(TRAVELLER shows his pass. JIMMY sees something on it.)

JIMMY: Hey! Let me see that!

TUNNELER #1: Whatta we need the map for, Boss?

TRAVELLER: *(Moving out of the way.)* We're looking for our friend. Jimmy: don't show them anything.

TUNNELER #1: Ha! No map! Just "pass-ing" through!

(JOHN HENRY and the TUNNELER confer, decide "two for one" is alright and proceed.)

JOHN HENRY: *(Violently reverting to character.)* Now what we got here? Somebody lost in the mountain now?

TRAVELLER: Mountain?

JOHN HENRY: Somebody getting in the way of Old John Henry pick hammering his way through? Somebody lost?

JIMMY: Sorry, we don't have the map. Frank has it.

TRAVELLER: You don't have to tell them anything.

JOHN HENRY: I keep my eye on everybody! I keep them all working! That's my job!

JIMMY: Are you John Henry?

TUNNELER #1: *(Points to the boss man.)* John Henry is racing the drill, boys! So we can keep our jobs!

JOHN HENRY: *(Races drill.)* That's right! The big boss man up top, he say: John Henry too slow! He can't beat the drill! He say go on in, John! I bet you a quarter you can't go on in and dig through that mountain! Bet you can't come out the other side!

TRAVELLER: What?

JIMMY: Are you the shift boss, John? Do they know we're down here?

JOHN HENRY: *(Uncomfortably.)* I'm John Henry! I ain't no shift boss! I takes care of everybody!

JIMMY: But at the join? Do they know WHO's down here.

TRAVELLER: We don't know who these people are.

JIMMY: At the join do they know?

JOHN HENRY: *Where?*

TUNNELER #1: At the join Bss, Boss!

TRAVELLER: Wait…how did you get in here?

JIMMY: Yeah! Where'd you come from?

TUNNELER #1: *(Tries to sell it, not sure if it's right.)* Uh—the other way…?

(Momentary loss of thread, JOHN HENRY whispers his thoughts to the TUNNELER…then—)

TUNNELER #1: We came from the other side!! We're behind John Henry!!

JIMMY: Which way?

JOHN HENRY: That a way!!

JIMMY: *(Tentatively.)* Where are we?

TRAVELLER: *(Thinks it through.)* But that means you came from the heading.

JOHN HENRY: Heading? What's the heading? *(Quietly to the TUNNELER.)* Is "the heading" part of the tunnel?

JIMMY: What are you doing down here exactly?

TRAVELLER: The heading is where the tunnel stops…it's the front part.

JOHN HENRY: No, that's not right, then! We came from the other side of this mountain! I'm John Henry! I'm racing the drill!

TRAVELLER: What mountain?

JOHN HENRY: The mountain that we're racing through! The only "start" is the other side! We're UNDER the mountain, the buildings and street!!! I'm John Henry and I can't be beat!!!

TRAVELLER: But how can you dig back from the heading? That doesn't make sense.

TUNNELER #1: The boss man bet him a quarter!

JOHN HENRY: …wait a second.

JIMMY: What are you doing in here? You're just a kid.

TUNNELER #1: I ain't no kid, mister!

JOHN HENRY: *(Back in.)* He ain't no kid. He knows ALL the rules!

TUNNELER #1: Yeah!

JIMMY: What rules?

JOHN HENRY and TUNNELER #1: Tunnel rules!

JOHN HENRY: *(Takes out the rules/map.)* Everybody gather round! No questions until the end. GO!

JIMMY: *(Sees the map!)* Hey that's—!

TUNNELER #1: No whistling! No women! No flowers!

TRAVELLER: No flowers?

TUNNELER #1: No flowers in the tunnel!

JIMMY: Why?

JOHN HENRY: Bad luck! Save your questions for later!

JIMMY: What?

JOHN HENRY: No questions! B-B-B-ad luck!

TUNNELER #1: Don't call animals by the right name! Don't be mean to a tunneler on his way to work!

JOHN HENRY: That's right!

TUNNELER #1: Always feed the snails.

JIMMY: *(Caught up.)* Oh yeah! We see lots of snails!

JOHN HENRY: We feeds them with candle wax!

TUNNELER #1: Avoid black dogs!

JOHN HENRY: If you see a pig on your way to work—

TRAVELLER: What?

TUNNELER #1: No questions until the end!

JOHN HENRY: You must not say what it is!

JIMMY: Oh. You mean say "It's a pig."

JOHN HENRY: NO! DON'T say that!

TUNNELER #1: No matter how scared you are—if your friend's in trouble don't run away and leave him!

TRAVELLER: Who do you mean?

JOHN HENRY: If you see a pile of quarters don't go to work that day! Something bad'll happen to you.

TRAVELLER: *(To the TUNNELER.)* What did you say before?

TUNNELER #1: Always look pretty if you go to a party.

JOHN HENRY: *(Trying to direct them in the direction of the join.)* Bet John Henry a washington coin! Bet you can beat him from the heading to the join!

TRAVELLER: What did you say?

TUNNELER #1: About the heading?

TRAVELLER: No not about the heading.

JIMMY: You guys aren't down here trying to do something are you?

TUNNELER #1: Like what?

JOHN HENRY: We dig and we hammer and we race the drill!— This way! *(Points to join.)*

TUNNELER #1: Under the river, the buildings and street! He's John Henry and he can't be beat!!

(Song: "John Henry"…Disintegrates.)

JIMMY: Uh…hey you know what? We had a friend with us…maybe you saw him?

(This is uncomfortable for them.)

JOHN HENRY: What friend? I'm John Henry!

JIMMY: Yeah…we were following our friend. He said he found a place in the tunnel where he could hear the guys outside.

TUNNELER #1: Oh yeah he—

JOHN HENRY: *(Suddenly whispers violently.)* Shut up…

TRAVELLER: What?

JIMMY: I don't want to be left behind.

JOHN HENRY: Listen—we never saw him.

JIMMY: Oh, because it seemed like maybe you did.

JOHN HENRY: *(Trying to make it exciting again.)* Don't you want to race John Henry to the join? It's this way. *(To the TRAVELLER.)* Don't worry I would have done the same thing!

JIMMY: You know…I don't like the looks of this guy. I mean maybe they're down here messing around, you know what I mean?

TRAVELLER: Yeah, what ARE you doing down here?

JIMMY: Yeah! Maybe they're trying to blow the place up!

JOHN HENRY: I don't need no bomb to dig! All I need is my hammer and pick!

TRAVELLER: Maybe that was an explosion before. Maybe they ARE digging…

JOHN HENRY: I don't need no bomb to dig! I'm the fastest man in here! I can race half a mile a day! Follow me to get out this way!

TUNNELER #1: I bet you a quarter you can't beat John Henry!

JOHN HENRY: Shut up!

TUNNELER #1: I bet you a quarter!!

JOHN HENRY: *(On the down low.)* We're not supposed to mention that.

TUNNELER #1: *(Fiercely aside.)* But these are the same guys, no? Aren't quarters part of the story?

JOHN HENRY: *(Fiercely whispering.)* We just got to get them to the join! Anyways it's the OTHER guy who gets the quarters!

JIMMY: *(Stepping in forcefully.)* Prove you're supposed to be down here!

TUNNELER #1: Well, for one, we know the rules!

JOHN HENRY: Didn't we already do that?

TUNNELER #1: *(Awkwardly.)* Well… for one we know the rules!

JOHN HENRY: Avoid black dogs.

TUNNELER #1: Call a bucket a battleship! And other strange things like:

JOHN HENRY: Avoid black dogs.

TUNNELER #1: Call a jackhammer a jack-leg! And because it's so loud down here—use a lot of sign language: like this!

(They do so.)

JIMMY: *(Bewildered.)* I guess they're not trying to blow it up?

(They do more sign language, and sing the second part of "John Henry" song.)

TRAVELLER: Wait a second…what are you doing?

JOHN HENRY: *(Suddenly honest.)* I don't know.

TRAVELLER: Listen— My friend and I are stuck down here. We think maybe we got blown into another part of the tunnel…maybe an old part of the tunnel. We don't have the map. We just want to know which way our friend went so we can get closer to where they're going to pull me out.

JIMMY: I don't want to be left behind.

JOHN HENRY: They're going to pull you BOTH out?

JIMMY: Yes.

TUNNELER #1: Boss?

JOHN HENRY: You're not BOTH stuck down here.

JIMMY: They're going to pull both of us out!

TRAVELLER: *(To himself.)* Yes, both of us.

(JOHN HENRY and the TUNNELER look at each other and speak quietly; then—)

JOHN HENRY: *(Points.)* Listen—your friend did go that way.

TRAVELLER: Okay. Thanks. That's all we wanted to know.

JOHN HENRY: But I don't think you'll get any help from that quarter.

TRAVELLER: What?

JOHN HENRY: I don't think they're going to pull you out.

TRAVELLER: Why?

JOHN HENRY: We're pretty far under here…there's nobody else down here, buddy.

JIMMY: But you said Frank went this way.

JOHN HENRY: Yeah but that was another time.

TUNNELER #1: Before this.

JOHN HENRY: Another time… *(Looks at them.)* You know? I don't want to do this anymore.

TRAVELLER: *(Feeling apprehensive.)* Well…we'll just go this way until we meet up with him or find the join.

JOHN HENRY: Alright. Okay.

TUNNELER #1: You're all alone down here.

JIMMY: *(Getting excited to proceed.)* That's not right. Frank wouldn't leave us!

TUNNELER #1: There's nobody else down here.

JIMMY: I think I know where they are! I remember! Frank wouldn't leave us!

JOHN HENRY: *(To JIMMY.)* Frank came over the top, remember?…he's coming back. *(To the TRAVELLER.)* Don't worry. I would have done the same thing.

TUNNELER #1: *(Sees they are running out of time.)* Why don't you let your friend go first, mister!? He knows the way.

(JIMMY walks out of the area. The TUNNELER and JOHN HENRY edge away.)

JOHN HENRY: Let your friend go first, he knows what he's doing.

TUNNELER #1: Don't run!

JIMMY: I can't! *(Realizes.)* Oh—

TUNNELER #1: Not you!

TRAVELLER: What do you mean there's no one down here?…We're down here…right?

EPISODE #3
THE OPENING

The TRAVELLER and JIMMY walk along in the tunnel. The lights flicker, go out, come on, etc. Sand pours from the ceiling…distant seismic activity is faintly heard.

TRAVELLER: Sounds like she's bumping around pretty good.

JIMMY: Maybe it's them.

TRAVELLER: It's not them.

JIMMY: *(Tired.)* Maybe they're coming to get us out.

TRAVELLER: I don't think so. That's the tunnel…not them.

JIMMY: What tunnel?

TRAVELLER: *(Tired of it.)* Come on, Jimmy.

JIMMY: Oh yeah. I know…Maybe a big shift's coming. *(Slows.)*

TRAVELLER: What's the matter?

JIMMY: …I don't feel so great. Can we wait here for a second.

TRAVELLER: We don't know where we are! We don't know how far it is to the opening or anything.

JIMMY: I just need to stand here for a second.

(Distant sound of voices. The Hospital is far away.)

TRAVELLER: What's that.

JIMMY: What?

TRAVELLER: Did you hear that?

JIMMY: No.

(Sound of voices.)

TRAVELLER: I think it is them.

JIMMY: Really?

TRAVELLER: Hello?

(Nothing.)

JIMMY: Are they there?

TRAVELLER: Hello?

JIMMY: *(Thinking.)* Hey, don't you think they'd send the line? I mean if they knew where we were…why wouldn't they just send the line down?

TRAVELLER: Maybe it's blocked. But remember: Frank said there was an opening between the two tunnels…where he heard them.

JIMMY: …whatever happened to Frank anyways?

TRAVELLER: He must have gone through. We must be at the opening.

(Sounds of people talking.)

JIMMY: Frank wouldn't leave us…

TRAVELLER: HELLO???

JIMMY: What?

TRAVELLER: How can you not hear that?

JIMMY: What?

(Clear sound of FRANK's voice.)

TRAVELLER: Frank?!

JIMMY: Is that Frank? Where?

TRAVELLER: Frank! *(Starts banging on the tunnel.)* Frank!!!

JIMMY: Where's Frank? I didn't hear him.

(Sounds of a seal being broken…FRANK's hands come through an opening in the tunnel wall…up high.)

TRAVELLER: Jesus christ.

JIMMY: It's Frank! I KNEW he wouldn't leave us!!!

FRANK: *(Just his voice still.)* Hello? Jimmy! Are you guys still in there?

TRAVELLER: Frank!

FRANK: *(Comes partially through the opening.)* HI!

TRAVELLER: Jesus, Frank! Where'd you go?

FRANK: I went up already! Everything's alright!

JIMMY: Hi Frank! Everybody said you left us down here but I knew it wasn't true!

FRANK: I wouldn't leave you!

TRAVELLER: Nobody said that.

FRANK: Here I am!

TRAVELLER: Can you come down?

FRANK: I better stay like this. I'm on some kind of line to come and get you guys. I don't know how long it is.

TRAVELLER: Oh.

JIMMY: Is this the restricted area?

TRAVELLER: Frank? Is this the opening? Is this the restricted area?

FRANK: I can't tell you that. Hold on a second.

(FRANK disappears. There is silence in the tunnel.)

TRAVELLER: …Frank?

FRANK: *(Reappearing.)* Yeah?

TRAVELLER: Can we get out?

FRANK: That's what I'm trying to do! *(Disappears again.)*

JIMMY: I KNEW he wouldn't leave us.

TRAVELLER: Stop saying that.

JIMMY: Frank! Get us up!

FRANK: *(Appears.)* I'm on some kind of line. I don't know how long it is. I'm trying to ask them if we can get a couple more lines in.

JIMMY: Do we need a line to get out?

FRANK: …oh…I don't know.

TRAVELLER: But you're on a line now?

FRANK: Yes definitely. I can feel it.

JIMMY: Frank where'd you go?

FRANK: I went up already! Everything's alright!

TRAVELLER: What did they say about the rescue lines?

FRANK: When?

TRAVELLER: Just now when you asked them.

FRANK: *(Confused.)* What?

TRAVELLER: When you asked them about getting us a line.

FRANK: When?

TRAVELLER: Just now.

FRANK: Oh…hold on a second. They're saying something to me.

(FRANK disappears. The sound of him being spoken to in the Hospital.)

JIMMY: What's happening.

TRAVELLER: I think he's asking about the lines.

(Nothing happens. The voices fade.)

JIMMY: What's happening now?

TRAVELLER: I don't know.

JIMMY: What's he doing?

TRAVELLER: I don't know. I can't see.

(FRANK comes back.)

FRANK: Hand up your passes.

TRAVELLER: What?

FRANK: Let me have your passes. Oh no wait… *(Disappears.)*

JIMMY: I can't find mine.

FRANK: *(Reappears.)* I don't need them. I just need to ask you a couple questions.

TRAVELLER: Why?

FRANK: Well I'm on some kind of line and I can't get to you to get the passes so I just have to make sure we get everybody out…you know…I need to ask you a couple things while they're getting the lines…so we can make sure we didn't leave anybody.

TRAVELLER: You know we didn't leave anybody! You were with us!

FRANK: *(Lying.)* Well that's what they want! They want to talk to you for a minute. Or for me to talk to you. It makes sense, right?

TRAVELLER: Not really.

JIMMY: Frank? I don't feel so great. I think I should just grab a line and come out.

TRAVELLER: Wait—

JIMMY: Frank?

FRANK: They're getting the line. Listen though. It's more than what I said.

TRAVELLER: What?

FRANK: You've been down there a long time. They don't want to make any trouble. I mean if you need to decompress or something.

TRAVELLER: It's not that kind of tunnel.

JIMMY: It isn't?

TRAVELLER: No.

JIMMY: I had to decompress a couple times.

TRAVELLER: It's not that kind of tunnel.

JIMMY: In the beginning it was.

TRAVELLER: What do you mean?

FRANK: Or when it passed under the river.

JIMMY: Hey! My brother worked on the bridge! He had to decompress!

FRANK: Well if you have to decompress they can take you out right away. So I need to ask you some things…to make sure you're alright to come out.

TRAVELLER: What are you talking about.

FRANK: I have to ask you a couple questions to see if you're alright. They gave me the questions. It's not hard.

JIMMY: I can do it.

FRANK: Okay.

TRAVELLER: I don't have to decompress. This is ridiculous.

FRANK: Don't say that…Alright. How long have you been down there.

TRAVELLER: I don't know.

JIMMY: A couple hours?

TRAVELLER: Maybe more.

JIMMY: Maybe a day?

TRAVELLER: It's hard to answer that.

JIMMY: A week? Two weeks?

FRANK: Alright.

(Sounds of papers.)

FRANK: Alright.

TRAVELLER: We can come out now. We don't need to decompress.

JIMMY: Right.

TRAVELLER: I'm fine!

FRANK: Settle down. They're getting the lines, I can hear them.

JIMMY: Did you say you were on a line Frank?

FRANK: Yes. I can feel it.

JIMMY: Does it hurt?

FRANK: Kind of.

JIMMY: Did you have to decompress?

FRANK: No.

JIMMY: Well we've only been in here a little longer than you.

FRANK: I don't know about that.

TRAVELLER: We've only been in here a little longer than you Frank! You know that!

FRANK: *(Looks behind him.)* Yeah… yeah…they're getting the lines. It's just part of the emergency rescue procedure.

Don't worry. *(Turns his head...slightly hard to decipher.)* You'll get out, Jimmy.

TRAVELLER: What?

FRANK: Okay. Where do you work?

TRAVELLER: That's stupid.

JIMMY: We work in the tunnel Frank! In the water tunnel!

TRAVELLER: Come on, Frank!

JIMMY: It's just part of the rescue effort. They're getting us the lines. They don't want any trouble.

FRANK: You work in the water tunnel. Good. They heard that.

JIMMY: Right! *(Shouting towards the opening.)* I WORK IN THE WATER TUNNEL!

FRANK: That's good, Jimmy. Now: How do you feel?

JIMMY: I don't feel so good!

TRAVELLER: I feel fine! Frank! Get the line!

(Sand falls from the ceiling... a small seismic bump occurs.)

JIMMY: FRANK!!! She's bumping again! You got to get us out of here! I don't feel so good! Frank! You got to get us out of here!! There's a big shift coming!

TRAVELLER: It's not stable down here, you MUST know that! We need you to send down a line immediately.

FRANK: I'm not authorized to send the line! I'm just seeing if you're okay for the line! THEY send the line! I have one! I know! I can feel it!

TRAVELLER: Of course we're okay.

FRANK: No I mean if you got to the opening alright.

TRAVELLER: Frank, we're talking to you, right? So we got to the opening!

(Another small shift. FRANK disappears... the lights flicker.)

JIMMY: Frank...I think there's a big one coming.

TRAVELLER: *(Scared.)* Shut up.

JIMMY: What if Frank can't get us out.

(FRANK reappears.)

TRAVELLER: There he is.

FRANK: *(Seems slightly off.)* Okay so Jimmy. You're not feeling so great. You come here and go through first. But listen. If a big shift comes...get away from the opening. It's a weak spot in the wall. It could cause a cave-in.

TRAVELLER: What about this decompression thing.

FRANK: Jimmy doesn't need to he just doesn't feel great but he's going to be okay. They told me...The line is here waiting for you. All you have to do is come up one at a time. But if a big shift comes, get away from the opening.

TRAVELLER: Okay. Jimmy you should go first. You're not feeling great.

JIMMY: Thanks. *(He sets a small ladder up against the wall.)* This is like what that guy said before! Remember? About the ladder?

TRAVELLER: Jimmy don't talk about that stuff or they won't take you up.

JIMMY: Yeah. You're probably right. *(Smiles, tries to laugh.)* Well...see you soon.

TRAVELLER: Yeah.

(The big shift begins as JIMMY disappears. A massive earthquake begins to rumble through the tunnel.)

TRAVELLER: Wait!—

DOCTORS AND NURSES SIT AT A STAFF MEETING

NURSE #3: *(Still has the pick protruding from her ear.)* What happened?

RESEARCH PHYSICIAN: *(Scrambles through all his papers…then—)* Here's the thing, kids. Let's start at the top and work our way down…A. You used to work in a hotel.

SPECIALIST: That's right. A hotel with a great chef!

NURSE #2: No one ever ate there…or stayed there.

RESEARCH PHYSICIAN: REGARD-LESS you worked within the confines of said hotel, correct?

NURSE #2: You don't have to yell. Jeeze.

RESEARCH PHYSICIAN: Alright! So! Beginning again, as usual. A. You worked in a hotel. B. The hotel's excellent chef failed only in not comprehending there was so little need for a fine dining establishment in the frozen tundra.

SPECIALIST: *(Almost to himself.)* Eskimos don't like it.

RESEARCH PHYSICIAN: No. It's not that they "don't like it," it's that they don't understand it.

SPECIALIST: No, no that's right.

RESEARCH PHYSICIAN: Exactly! I didn't even consider that anyone in the entire world would NOT like that sort of thing.

NURSE #2: Well "they didn't."

NURSE #3: *(Terrorized.)* Can I please leave so I can visit my brother? He's sick in the—

NURSE #2: *(On the QT.)* Shut up.

NURSE #3: *(Desperately trying to communicate with the SPECIALIST.)* When we were in the back, she stuck me with a pin!

NURSE #2: No I didn't.

NURSE #3: *(Hysterical.)* She DID and all kinds of other things happened too! He—

RESEARCH PHYSICIAN: ALRIGHT! If we are going to get anywhere, I need to finish talking!

NURSE #2: You're always talking…

SPECIALIST: Go ahead, go ahead, gov.

RESEARCH PHYSICIAN: C. She sewed flowers, or "so" she claims. I met her in the hallway…near the…room where the "guy" is…she came in, passed the test… *(He fiddles with the ear pick absently.)* And now she is working here.

SPECIALIST: That's all right.

NURSE #2: Kind of working here.

RESEARCH PHYSICIAN: Yes…yes it is. *(Suddenly points at NURSE #2.)* D. SHE! She had a letter that said some things. You know…a few things like— *(Trying to be nonchalant.)* "Take care of the guy," etcetera.

NURSE #2: It also said: This is the main thing: don't.

RESEARCH PHYSICIAN: Well, EVERYBODY knows that.

NURSE #3: This is the main thing. Don't.

ALL: RIGHT!

RESEARCH PHYSICIAN: Okay. So if we're going to take care of the guy—as if—we need to know what's wrong with him, right? We need to perform certain diagnostic efforts. Isn't that what doctors do? "Diagnostic efforts," etcetera?

SPECIALIST: I don't know how to do that!!

RESEARCH PHYSICIAN: Calm down. Calm down, little man. YES! Even I, the research physician/chef, admit I need some nominal training in order that I…"don't."

SPECIALIST: What.

RESEARCH PHYSICIAN: Well, that's the main thing.

NURSE #2: What?

RESEARCH PHYSICIAN: "Don't."

NURSE #3: What?

RESEARCH PHYSICIAN: That's the main thing.

NURSE #2: What?

RESEARCH PHYSICIAN: "Don't."

SPECIALIST: What?

RESEARCH PHYSICIAN: You know! It's the MAIN thing.

NURSE #2: What?

RESEARCH PHYSICIAN: Don't you start with me!

NURSE #2: (Under her breath.) You need more than "nominal training," buddy.

NURSE #3: (Triumphant.) I'm going to take care of the guy down the hall!!

SPECIALIST: Yeah but HOW??

NURSE #2: You can't do anything… you're just the—

SPECIALIST: How?

RESEARCH PHYSICIAN: That's what I'm saying, idiot.

SPECIALIST: Oh.

NURSE #3: You shouldn't talk to him like that, mister! He could knock your block off! He's a big fella! You don't want to go twelve rounds with him! He'd beat you all the way to kingdom come! BANG!!

NURSE #2: (Threateningly.) Stop talking all the time.

SPECIALIST: I'd…I'd never do that.

NURSE #3: (Appealing to the SPECIALIST.) You got to help me out of here, mister!

NURSE #2: If we don't do our jobs…you KNOW what will happen!

RESEARCH PHYSICIAN: SHUT UP. I don't want to go in there…I don't know what's wrong with him. I don't know anything about this kind of thing!!! I mean, what if he looks weird??

NURSE #2: We'll get fired! We'll have to leave here again and go away to scary hotels and not work. We'll sit in the empty lobby and look at the board full of hooks and keys, wondering: where did we go wrong? I am a nurse! I WANT to take care of this guy! I want—

RESEARCH PHYSICIAN: SHUT UP!…

(Nothing happens. They begin advancing ominously on the RESEARCH PHYSICIAN.)

NURSE #3: Doctor! I got a bee in my head. Get me out a here!

SPECIALIST: How are we going to do it.

NURSE #3: *(Goes to the RESEARCH PHYSICIAN.)* Doctor.

RESEARCH PHYSICIAN: Get off!

SPECIALIST: *(Advancing on the RESEARCH PHYSICIAN.)* How are we going to know what to do?

RESEARCH PHYSICIAN: No! Stay away!

NURSE #2: *(Also advancing.)* I'm a nurse. I want to take care of the guy! I don't want to get fired!

NURSE #3: I got a bee! Get me out a here!

RESEARCH PHYSICIAN: *(Panics.)* HELP!! HELP!!! Help the physician!!! HELP!!

(A massive explosion heralds the appearance of DOCTOR #3…returned to train the medical staff.)

DOCTOR #3: Holy cow!

SPECIALIST: Oh no!

NURSE #3: *(Facing away.)* What was that noise??

DOCTOR #3: Right. Let's get down to it!

SPECIALIST: Oh great!

NURSE #2: *(Presenting her position to DOCTOR #3.)* I want to take care of the guy!

SPECIALIST: Why don't I just leave now. Go back to England. You know, call it a day.

RESEARCH PHYSICIAN: Shut up! Hello! I believe we once worked together in the—

DOCTOR #3: Yeah yeah yeah. That was a long time ago, buddy. Things have moved on! Time and tide doesn't stop for no man, you know! Now! What's your problem here?

RESEARCH PHYSICIAN: Hello! I believe we once worked together in the—

SPECIALIST: *(Showing off.)* He's a chef AND a doctor.

DOCTOR #3: Whatever you say, Jumbo.

NURSE #2: Look! We got this letter!

DOCTOR #3: *(Reads letter.)* That last part's pretty bad. I mean, you know that, right?

NURSE #2: I want to do what it says in the letter.

SPECIALIST: Me too!

NURSE #3: I do too!

RESEARCH PHYSICIAN: Hello! I believe we once worked together in the.

DOCTOR #3: That's right. How the hell are you, buddy!

(General hand shaking.)

DOCTOR #3: Listen: you don't want to draw too much attention to yourselves over here. Remember what happened last time? You don't want that kind of thing happening again, do you.

RESEARCH PHYSICIAN: No…

NURSE #2: The Carol!

(General mayhem.)

RESEARCH PHYSICIAN: Listen! I need you to tell these folks how to take care of the guy down the hall! I, of course, already know how. However, I will "tag along" as it were, though, just to make sure THEY are paying attention!

NURSE #2: Right.

RESEARCH PHYSICIAN: Exactly.

DOCTOR #3: Alright! Not too hard! *(Writes down.)* Take care of guy! Needs a little training—

RESEARCH PHYSICIAN: But not me! I don't need training.

DOCTOR #3: Needs a little training—

RESEARCH PHYSICIAN: Not me though.

DOCTOR #3: Get subject and start practice diagnostic efforts!

RESEARCH PHYSICIAN: YEAH! That's EXACTLY what I said.

NURSE #2: No it isn't.

SPECIALIST: Yes it is!

NURSE #2: We're going to "practice" taking care of the guy?

DOCTOR #3: Yes!

NURSE #2: Practice on who?

NURSE #3: Not me.

RESEARCH PHYSICIAN: On anybody! It doesn't matter!

NURSE #3: But not me.

NURSE #2: That does not seem right.

DOCTOR #3: You got to do practice diagnostic stuff! I mean especially if the guy is really you know…especially if the guy is *(Can't say the word "sick.")* If he's you know…not feel—

SPECIALIST: Practice makes perfect we say!

DOCTOR #3: Right!

RESEARCH PHYSICIAN: Right!

SPECIALIST: *(About himself and the RESEARCH PHYSICIAN.)* That's what we say.

DOCTOR #3: SO…who's it going to be?

NURSE #3: *(Thinks he said "bee.")* I GOT A BEE!!

(They all grab her and begin securing her to the chair.)

DOCTOR #3: Right—you! *(To the SPECIALIST.)* You're a Specialist right?

SPECIALIST: I'm from England.

DOCTOR #3: Well, go get my stuff!

SPECIALIST: What are you talking about "get your stuff"?

DOCTOR #3: Can't you see I got my hands full here!

RESEARCH PHYSICIAN: Go get his stuff!

SPECIALIST: Jesus christ! *(Stalks off.)*

RESEARCH PHYSICIAN: Now what?

DOCTOR #3: Get her on that…hold on. *(Screams off into the hallway.)* WHAT IS THE HOLDUP???

NURSE #3: I don't want anybody doing anything! I just want to work! Don't hurt me! I just came to work! Wait! Leave me alone! *(Etc.)*

SPECIALIST: *(Comes in with the bag.)* Here's your stupid things. *(Shoves them.)*

(They secure her to the chair. DOCTOR #3 takes out the Stereotactile Headframing Cage Box.)

NURSE #2: Oh no.

RESEARCH PHYSICIAN: What the hell is that!

DOCTOR #3: *(Holding the Cage on display.)* This!? This is the Stereotactile Headframing Cage Box. An excellent diagnostic effort or start of one. Yes…the Stereotactile Headframing Cage…Box or something.

NURSE #2: That doesn't sound like a real name.

DOCTOR #3: Well, it is.

SPECIALIST: What do you do with it?

DOCTOR #3: I think you screw it on. Look!

(He puts the head frame on and screws it into position.)

NURSE #3: Wow! That really hurts

DOCTOR #3: *(Speaking to NURSE #3.)* Hello! If you move while we're doing this you're gonna die!

NURSE #3: What?

DOCTOR #3: Tighten it! We need RIGID fixation!!!!

RESEARCH PHYSICIAN: Me?

DOCTOR #3: Yes!

RESEARCH PHYSICIAN: I'm just an observer!

NURSE #3: It's TIGHT!!!

SPECIALIST: Is this the kind of thing we'll do to the guy?

DOCTOR #3: YES!

(The SPECIALIST turns the screws.)

RESEARCH PHYSICIAN: *(Has gone into a daze…thinks it's a cooking show.)* And what temperature are you turning that to?

SPECIALIST: What?

NURSE #3: Can I move now?

NURSE #2: No! You can't move! We're going to try and learn how to take care of the guy! You want us to learn that, don't you???

NURSE #3: YES!

DOCTOR #3: Alright! Everybody step back. *(He takes out the drill.)*

NURSE #3: Whaddya going to do?? It's rigid! It's rigid, already!!

DOCTOR #3: I'm going to make the initial crack!

(He goes in and cuts out a piece of her skull, throws it on the floor.)

RESEARCH PHYSICIAN: Clean as you go I always say!!! Now how long did you leave that before you cut into it? *(He picks up the piece while he's speaking and samples the smell, possibly the taste.)* Oh, this is delightful! It's smoky!

SPECIALIST: Is this what we'll be doing to the guy?

DOCTOR #3: YES! *(To NURSE #2.)* YOU! Come here! Talk to her!

NURSE #2: No.

DOCTOR #3: Christ! You have to talk to her, it's PART of it! YOU! *(To the SPECIALIST.)* Get the thing! The big thing in the bag! GET IT!!!

SPECIALIST: What am I? Your butler!? I'm from England!! Remember???

DOCTOR #3: Exactly!

SPECIALIST: *(Under his breath.)* Sic transit Gloria, asshole.

RESEARCH PHYSICIAN: Just get it!

(The SPECIALIST gets the tool.)

NURSE #2: Why'd you leave all your stuff out there?

DOCTOR #3: Oh…I don't know.

RESEARCH PHYSICIAN: Don't pester him!

(The tool is fetched.)

DOCTOR #3: *(A little scared of the tool.)* Now! You really got to get in there! Remember?

RESEARCH PHYSICIAN: *(Teaching a class.)* But don't overwork it or it will separate or "split" as we say! Just a light whissssssk!

(They jam the tool in and out of her head.)

DOCTOR #3: TALK TO HER!

NURSE #2: "Hello, how are you"

NURSE #3: You…you killed the bee! They don't got no stinger no more! I feel like I did a long time ago. Wait a second! Why am I wearing this hat? Is it cold outside? Why can't I go for a drive?

NURSE #2: "I am fine."

DOCTOR #3: Good. Okay now get the thing under that little flap there.

SPECIALIST: *(Dazed, participating.)* I'm from England.

RESEARCH PHYSICIAN: Yes and just fold that in until it's well distributed… *(Peering into the hole.)* Perfect! See how easy that is. Good surgery doesn't have to be "slow" surgery…good surgery—fast! It's EASY!!

SPECIALIST: Oh god.

(She lurches to the side, some brains come out.)

RESEARCH PHYSICIAN: *(Picking up the brain fragment…a truffle?)* Come

on now! I mean pigs take months to find these things!! You can't just throw it on the ground. *(Pops the brain in his mouth.)* There! Now, what smells like chocolate?

NURSE #3: I promise I won't be back after dark! He never laid a hand on me! Why can't I go for a drive! I don't want to go to the barbecue! *(Looks around… Scarlett O'Hara?)* I think…I think YOU may get my dessert!

DOCTOR #3: *(Charmed.)* Me?

NURSE #2: *(To NURSE #3.)* Stop talking to everybody!

SPECIALIST: Are you sure this is what we'll be doing to the guy?

NURSE #2: Just go along with it. I don't want to lose another job. I can't go back there! I got to be a nurse! I can't do this anymore. Just do what he says!!

NURSE #3: *(For real.)* Please…please let me go for a drive…

DOCTOR #3: Right. YOU! *(To the RESEARCH PHYSICIAN.)* Come here now!

RESEARCH PHYSICIAN: *(Sidling up.)* Hello! I believe we once worked together in the.

DOCTOR #3: Exactly. Take a look!

RESEARCH PHYSICIAN: Ahhhhh… perfect distribution of color and that expert aroma—I can tell from fifty paces you've far surpassed your reputation. And…now let's see! *(He dips a spoon into the brain.)* Simple yet with a complex clarity. I could not have done better myself.

SPECIALIST: Oh, great!

DOCTOR #3: Now THAT'S what you'll be doing to the guy!!!

NURSE #3: *(Reaching up, poking around.)* What kind of hat is this?

RESEARCH PHYSICIAN: I can't wait for next week's program!

NURSE #2: I don't think I can do this anymore.

NURSE #3: Why are there balled-up paper towels all over the place? *(Throws some brains out of her head.)* They're all over me!

RESEARCH PHYSICIAN: I'm not nervous anymore! I know exactly what we're doing to the guy!

DOCTOR #3: *(Doesn't know.)* Really?

NURSE #2: That's it, man. There's got to be something out there for me. I'm not afraid anymore. This is terrible. You people are hacks. I'm leaving. Forget you ever saw me.

SPECIALIST: Sandy?

ALL: A doctor takes responsibility for himself. A doctor copes with sexual intimacy. A grown doctor gains freedom. Learning to live in the present. Never too old to change for the better. A very special way.

DREAM SEQUENCE:
ADVENTURES IN THE UNDERWORLD

The River Styx.

TRAVELLER: Wait—

(KAREN comes in on the ferry. Song.)

KAREN: I am Karen, Ferryman of the Underworld.

TRAVELLER: Karen?

KAREN: Yes, Karen, Person!

TRAVELLER: What do you mean.

KAREN: Pay me a quarter and I'll take you further on. Oh no wait—

(KAREN thinks there might be something wrong with the TRAVELLER and looks him over carefully. The TRAVELLER digs around for some money.)

TRAVELLER: Hey listen—my friend just got rescued through the shortcut, you know. Do you think you could cart me back to there? Or, if that's blocked, could you take me to the join maybe? I THINK it's this way?

KAREN: I don't have any cart, Person.

TRAVELLER: Train then.

KAREN: No train. Only boat… *(Looking him over more.)* What's the matter with you?

TRAVELLER: Nothing.

KAREN: Huh. Well, no trains. Boat.

TRAVELLER: *(Thinks the guy is giving him a problem.)* Yeah yeah, boat then. I don't have any money, but I am on the shift list and you won't get any trouble for taking me to the join. I need to find my friend. I think he went this way.

KAREN: Oh, I know you're on the shift list.

TRAVELLER: Right. I need to see if he went through here.

KAREN: Show me your pass and you can owe me for the ride.

TRAVELLER: *(Looks for his pass… can't find it.)* I know I had it.

KAREN: Alright. So you want me to take you across to look for your friend. But the thing is, you see, if your friend is passed me he's probably already gone.

TRAVELLER: Gone where?

KAREN: …Gone on.

(Nothing happens.)

TRAVELLER: Could I come in to look?

KAREN: No.

TRAVELLER: Why?

KAREN: The Mister doesn't like "drop-ins"…and there's something "wrong" with you.

TRAVELLER: What?

KAREN: Hold on a second.

(KAREN leaves for a moment. The distant sound of dogs barking. The TRAVELLER stands there.)

KAREN: I was wrong. It seem there's something wrong with the other guy. Not you. You won't bother the Mister, will you? While you're looking for your friend?

TRAVELLER: So he did come through here.

KAREN: Yeah, but apparently he just wants to pass through and go out the other side…at the…whatever it is you called it.

TRAVELLER: The join.

KAREN: Yeah, the join.

TRAVELLER: Wait…the join is through here?

KAREN: It's this way…kind of.

TRAVELLER: Can I see him?

KAREN: Who? The Mister???!!!

TRAVELLER: No—Jimmy. Who we were just talking about.

KAREN: Oh. Uh… (With a flourish.) This way please.

TRAVELLER: Alright. (He steps forward.)

KAREN: Got the pass?

TRAVELLER: No.

KAREN: We'll forget about the pass now. Got the quarter?

TRAVELLER: No.

KAREN: (Looks around.) Lost them all, eh? Well get on. Don't tell the Mister though. I do feel bad for your type, you know. Just "passing through."

(A massive earthquake as HADES and PERSEPHONE appear. Here comes the Mister!!)

HADES: JE SUIS PRINCE OF THE UNDERWORLD!

(Massive divertissement.)

KAREN: That's his wife.

PERSEPHONE: Right! So what is it you would ask of us!!??

HADES: (Conspiratorially upon seeing the TRAVELLER; looking at his wife.) Do you know how we met? Huh? I grabbed her out of the harvest-y fields out there and dragged her down here in some kind of odds bodkin chariot, what! THAT part wasn't my idea. She was in a right state upon arrival, I can tell you.

PERSEPHONE: My mother was REALLY upset!

TRAVELLER: I am looking for a friend who may have passed through here.

PERSEPHONE: A "man" friend?

TRAVELLER: Yes.

PERSEPHONE: Because you know we've had quite the array of "things" as it were, popping in and out, don't you know. There was that fellow who was quite a good musician. OH! Is that YOU? *(She pulls out a monocle.)* Oh no, sadly, it "haint."

TRAVELLER: Uh. No. My friend passed through. He's on his way to the join? I was wondering if I could get through?

(Whispered, serious conference.)

HADES: Well! That's rather more serious. You see our friends from up "yonder," as they say En Amerique, know all about this predicament you're in up to your neck, as it were. Your friend, you see, has indeed, well…he's gone! *(He shakes his two-pronged stick.)*

PERSEPHONE: Oh that's lovely! Do do that again!

HADES: *(Does so.)* Quite regal wouldn't you say?

TRAVELLER: I'm sorry. What?

PERSEPHONE: Yes quite!

TRAVELLER: What did you say?

HADES: Yes, well, your friend? He's gone "up."

TRAVELLER: Up?

PERSEPHONE: Or he's "on his way"!

HADES: Well! *(Awkward standing, starts calling out.)* KAREN!!! KAREN!!

TRAVELLER: Can I see him before he leaves?

PERSEPHONE: He's already gone!

HADES: *(Whispers.)* Shut up dear. *(Then—)* Yes, well, I just want to check with Karen as to why you're here! *(Edging away.)* KAREN!

KAREN: *(Appearing.)* Yes, sir?

HADES: This fellow here! What's his business?

TRAVELLER: I TOLD you!! I'm here to find my friend and get to the join! I don't want to be left behind! This is wasting my time!

KAREN: Oh yeah, this is the one who said he had to see you or he'd rough me up!

TRAVELLER: I did not!

KAREN: Yeah, He had some kind of plan to "get in." He doesn't have a pass OR any money. Honestly, I felt sort of sorry for him. *(Whispers.)* He's an "middle class."

PERSEPHONE: Oh dear! Well, you can't keep them all out, now can you?

HADES: I'm just as liberal as the next chap, but I mean one has to draw the line somewhere.

PERSEPHONE: Yes! Certainly! Soon they'll all want to just drop by for a visit without any money! I mean! Can you imagine?

KAREN: See? They don't like "drop-ins."

HADES: NO, well, I suppose one must let the occasional one…wait a moment…come here!

TRAVELLER: Why?

HADES: Come here! I think I may have mistaken you for someone else!

(The TRAVELLER walks up apprehensively.)

HADES: *(Looking him over.)* Yes…yes… aha…well. Karen! This man will make an excellent fourth for bridge.

KAREN: *(Understands that the TRAVELLER will die…and stay.)* Oh…I see.

TRAVELLER: No, I need to get to Jimmy. I got to get out of here! I don't want to play any game right now!

HADES: Yes! I think you do! *(Finished looking at him.)* Get out the table! P, dear!! we finally have a decent fourth for bridge!

TRAVELLER: No! I don't belong here! I don't know how to play bridge!

HADES: Right! First bet!

PERSEPHONE: Contract bridge! My favorite!

HADES: North!

PERSEPHONE: South!

KAREN: East!

(Nothing happens.)

KAREN: EAST!

TRAVELLER: …west?

HADES: Correct! Right Bridge and tunnel rules! Yes?

TRAVELLER: What?

HADES: Tunnel rules included in the first call yes!

PERSEPHONE: YES!

KAREN: YES! That's the best way to play!

HADES: Right! Deal and declare, dear!

(She deals, as do they all, by simply throwing a bunch of cards around.)

PERSEPHONE: Trump and no-trump. Declared. Down as deep as you go! And if it's deeper than a grave we dug it! Yes?

HADES: Yes! The tunnel rules for bridge!! Defenders?

KAREN: *(Looks at the TRAVELLER.)* Well?

TRAVELLER: I don't know how to play.

KAREN: Yes you do.

TRAVELLER: I don't know how to play.

HADES: Right! So first bid and auction down. Defender?

PERSEPHONE: Going once, going twice and—

KAREN: No defense.

HADES: SOLD to the person in the tunnel. K'you!

PERSEPHONE: Well done, dear.

(They have won the first hand.)

HADES: *(Dealing.)* Auction down and deep as you go—if it's deeper than a grave we dug it…and—dummy is the declarer!

KAREN: *(Points at the TRAVELLER.)* DECLARE!

HADES: DECLARE!

PERSEPHONE: DECLARE, DUMMY!

TRAVELLER: What?

ALL: PASS!

(Redeal.)

TRAVELLER: No wait. I want to declare.

HADES: Too late, dear. Do try to keep up.

TRAVELLER: Alright. I think I get it now.

PERSEPHONE: *(To her husband.)* Hardly!

KAREN: Right! Second sequence.

PERSEPHONE: Second sequence and East has the invitational.

KAREN: East has invitation to declare!

(The TRAVELLER is confused.)

PERSEPHONE: Dear?

HADES: *(Hasn't been listening.)* What?

PERSEPHONE: Why won't it answer?

HADES: Oh, he's been down here too long.

KAREN: *(To the TRAVELLER.)* Just declare it. Or maybe you don't want to play?

TRAVELLER: No I want to play. I want to declare.

PERSEPHONE: *(Quietly.)* It doesn't know the rules.

HADES: *(Speaking to the TRAVELLER as if to an idiot.)* Bridge and tunnel rules, dear. You must declare your shift and bid. Do you understand?

TRAVELLER: Yes!! I'm on the shift! I'm supposed to be down here!

HADES: Oh dear…no shouting.

KAREN: Perhaps he doesn't want to play tunnel-bridge?

PERSEPHONE: You know in the old days the bridge players were the same as the tunnel players.

HADES: Well certainly it's played in the tunnel style no?

KAREN: Same union regardless.

HADES: Yes, well no talk of unions and other bleeding-heart nonsense!

PERSEPHONE: Sorry, H.

TRAVELLER: I declare that I want to find my friend and go wherever he went.

(Nothing happens.)

HADES: *(After some time.)* Is…is that a trump, a trick, or a sign-off?

TRAVELLER: I just want to go wherever he went.

KAREN: Sounds like a sign ON to me.

(They all laugh at the impossibility of the TRAVELLER "signing on" to life again.)

TRAVELLER: Where. Is. Jimmy?

HADES: Oh dear oh dear. That's rather unfortunate now isn't it. *(Loudly and clearly.)* Your friend's gone on, as it were. Let's play tunnel rules and you'll forget all about it. Yes? *(Big smile.)* It's not so bad down here.

KAREN: He doesn't understand.

PERSEPHONE: I'M BORED! Does it want to play tunnel rules or not??

(They all talk quietly for a moment.)

HADES: Do excuse me, whatever you are, but do you understand the rules of bridge and tunnel?

KAREN: The real rules?

PERSEPHONE: Why would it know the rules, darling? It's like talking to a brick wall!

HADES: Well it's down here! It's playing.

KAREN: You want to go wherever he went, do you?

TRAVELLER: Yes.

KAREN: Well, I don't think you can. Can he? I mean he can't play THAT card now, right?

HADES: *(Was off again somewhere.)* What?

KAREN: Not with tunnel rules, can he?

PERSEPHONE: I mean this is tedious! I'm going upstairs to see my mother. *(She disappears.)*

HADES: Oh…well, now it's no fun at all, is it?

KAREN: It didn't declare and now it has to stay till the end of the game.

HADES: Especially with only three.

KAREN: That's interesting. What a funny coincidence.

TRAVELLER: *(Desperate.)* I declare. I don't want to stay down here.

HADES: Oh dear, oh dear. That won't do. *(To a child.)* You can't play that card, dear.

KAREN: Perhaps I can help, sir? I would be willing to try and explain to him.

HADES: What do you know. You're just the guy who drives the boat.

KAREN: True.

HADES: Oh…go ahead. I feel a bit out of sorts now my wife has gone back to her stupid, fecund mother. In fact, I am rather angry this early departure was precipitated by your unwillingness to play!

TRAVELLER: I wanted to play. Can we start again?

(A moment of reflective silence from the KING OF THE UNDERWORLD and his FERRYMAN.)

HADES: Ah…yes. That's what they all say, in the end.

(They speak to each other.)

HADES: *(Waving.)* Right, yes. Well… Good luck!

TRAVELLER: Wait! Where's he going?

KAREN: Person, there is no more game. We are no longer playing. You can't declare. You cannot bid. You can't play that card and we can't "start again." You can only wait…which is what you've been doing this whole time anyway…and then—

(KAREN is backing away. There is the beginning of a massive earthquake again.)

TRAVELLER: Uh oh.

KAREN: Yes…This whole time.

EPISODE #4
REDUNDANCY

There is a phone on the wall. The TRAVELLER sees it. The phone rings. The TRAVELLER goes to pick it up and it stops ringing. He hears the distant sound of FRANK and JIMMY.

TRAVELLER: Frank?

(They speak to each other far away. The phone rings once.)

TRAVELLER: Okay…

(There is a distant rumble. Far away in the Real Hospital JIMMY's family tries to help him come into consciousness…their voices fade away. JIMMY walks back from the join. They stand.)

TRAVELLER: Where'd you go?

JIMMY: What?

TRAVELLER: *(Is scared to ask.)* Where'd you go.

JIMMY: I don't know. Up there. Out the thing. Somewhere that way.

TRAVELLER: Oh.

JIMMY: Listen I keep forgetting to tell you. I think something really did happen to me!

TRAVELLER: *(A little distracted.)* No no you did say that.

JIMMY: I can't get it straight in my head. I haven't been feeling so great...I got...confused.

TRAVELLER: Me too.

JIMMY: Yeah all that time we were trying to get out and find Frank I knew there was something in there that I couldn't remember.

TRAVELLER: *(Doesn't want to hear... knows what it is, kind of.)* You don't have to tell me. Let's just go up the road. I want to get out of here.

JIMMY: I know what you mean. I wouldn't want to get buried down here either.

TRAVELLER: *(Taken aback slightly.)* What do you mean.

JIMMY: They sent the line for me before so all you have to do is wait.

TRAVELLER: Yeah.

JIMMY: Also the boss is coming down.

TRAVELLER: Alright. You're sure he's coming?

JIMMY: Yeah.

TRAVELLER: Alright. Why?

(They stand.)

JIMMY: *(Jovially remembers.)* We were at work in the water tunnel.

TRAVELLER: Yes—

JIMMY: You, me, and Frank.

TRAVELLER: Yes all three of us and—

JIMMY: Man! That seems like a long time ago.

TRAVELLER: I don't know. Does it?

JIMMY: I was...oh...forget it.

TRAVELLER: What?

JIMMY: Hold on a second. Let me make sure he's coming. *(Goes to the phone and dials out.)*

TRAVELLER: Who are you calling.

JIMMY: *(On phone.)* Yes...Yeah he's right here. I am. I am doing it. But now—. What? No. No. Yes it is. Why would you ask me that? Listen...listen... *(Laughs.)* Don't forget about me! Yes we will. Yes yes I will. Okay. Thanks. Bye.

TRAVELLER: Who did you call.

JIMMY: The shift boss.

TRAVELLER: Oh.

JIMMY: *(Antsy.)* Hey, remember when Frank said they had to ask us questions to make sure...oh no...that's not right.

TRAVELLER: It was something about decompressing but it's not that kind of tunnel.

JIMMY: *(Stares at the TRAVELLER.)* It's not about decompressing.

TRAVELLER: *(Getting a bad feeling.)* I know.

JIMMY: That's not what he's going to ask you about. It's like they need to do a sort of interview.

TRAVELLER: Why?

JIMMY: Well you've been down here a long time and—

TRAVELLER: Have I?

JIMMY: Uh…yeah. And there've been a few cutbacks and things…so..

TRAVELLER: Oh. I get it.

JIMMY: Yeah.

(The SHIFT BOSS comes in.)

SHIFT BOSS: Alright. Here we are.

JIMMY: See you.

SHIFT BOSS: See you, Jimmy.

TRAVELLER: *(Suddenly scared.)* Where are you going?

JIMMY: *(Laughingly.)* What do you mean where am I going!?! I'm going back up!

(He leaves. They stand.)

TRAVELLER: Alright.

SHIFT BOSS: So, you understand that there might be a redundancy here.

TRAVELLER: That's what Jimmy said. Have I really been gone that long?

SHIFT BOSS: Yes.

TRAVELLER: Somebody else took my job?

SHIFT BOSS: Well, I don't even know if your job exists anymore.

TRAVELLER: My job in the tunnel.

SHIFT BOSS: Yeah. So, that's what I'm here to find out. It's a normal interview, sort of like an evaluation. If there is no redundancy you will be able to come out and go back to work. No cutback.

TRAVELLER: But I get to come out anyway even if I don't pass the interview.

SHIFT BOSS: Oh…yeah…right.

TRAVELLER: Okay.

SHIFT BOSS: Question One: What do you think is happening up there?

TRAVELLER: How do you mean?

SHIFT BOSS: Just answer as best you can even if it seems weird. There are all kinds of double blinds and procedures in the interview. You can't make a mistake. We'll know the right answer.

TRAVELLER: Okay.

SHIFT BOSS: What do you think is happening up there?

TRAVELLER: People are going to work. They're blasting the tunnel.

SHIFT BOSS: And?

TRAVELLER: *(Hesitates.)* They… they—

SHIFT BOSS: What do you think is happening.

TRAVELLER: Uh…uh…People are looking at maps and eating lunch in the tunnel. Is that right?

SHIFT BOSS: It's not that kind of test. I'm telling you it's a double blind.

TRAVELLER: Okay. I've never had to do one of these before.

SHIFT BOSS: It's alright. Question Two: What did you do the last day you were at work?

TRAVELLER: I can't remember.

SHIFT BOSS: Is that your answer?

TRAVELLER: I don't know what I did.

SHIFT BOSS: Did you have a coffee or a piece of fruit?

TRAVELLER: I don't—

SHIFT BOSS: Did you read the paper and walk to the docks to look at the water and feel that sad, crazy feeling that everybody's just floating by on the same lonely river?

TRAVELLER: Is that part of the test.

SHIFT BOSS: *(Looks at paper.)* Yes.

TRAVELLER: No. I didn't think that. I just walked up and down the street, out of my house and into the tunnel. I didn't talk to anybody. I didn't notice anything unusual. I—

SHIFT BOSS: You didn't notice anything?

TRAVELLER: No.

SHIFT BOSS: …hmm…okay.

TRAVELLER: Why, is that wrong?

SHIFT BOSS: You did not notice anything. Why? Were you tired?

TRAVELLER: No.

SHIFT BOSS: Were you busy?

TRAVELLER: No.

SHIFT BOSS: Huh.

TRAVELLER: *(Suspicious.)* Are you the shift boss?

SHIFT BOSS: Why do you ask that.

TRAVELLER: Well, I feel like I've seen you down here when I was with Jimmy waiting.

SHIFT BOSS: I am the shift boss. I was in charge of the rescue effort.

TRAVELLER: Okay.

SHIFT BOSS: What are your feelings about…oh no, that's not right. If you had the chance, what would you have done differently?

TRAVELLER: Do you mean at work?

SHIFT BOSS: It doesn't specify.

TRAVELLER: What would I have done differently? Maybe…I would have…I think…

SHIFT BOSS: Remember: you can't make a mistake. We'll know the right answer.

TRAVELLER: I…if I was…

SHIFT BOSS: Yes?

TRAVELLER: I would do it all.

SHIFT BOSS: Start again you mean?

TRAVELLER: Yes.

SHIFT BOSS: Do you know that's the most common answer?

(The TRAVELLER doesn't answer.)

SHIFT BOSS: Okay, just two more. Which do you prefer: iron, paper, gold or…oh no, wait— *(Cross references.)* Wait…because of number two that's not needed. Sorry. Forget that one.

TRAVELLER: Are you sure.

SHIFT BOSS: Yes. Okay: Last one. What happens after… *(Looks around the paper.)* Let's see—"what happens after"…wait that can't be the whole thing. "What happens after"…is that the whole question? Huh. I guess so.

TRAVELLER: Listen—

SHIFT BOSS: Okay so: What happens after?

TRAVELLER: I don't know. I don't know what that means.

SHIFT BOSS: Try to think. Remember it's a double blind.

TRAVELLER: I know.

SHIFT BOSS: I mean there's been a lot of redundancies, a lot of cutbacks…make sure you think it through.

TRAVELLER: What happens after…after what.

SHIFT BOSS: It doesn't say. It's part of how the test works I guess.

TRAVELLER: Nothing.

SHIFT BOSS: Nothing.

TRAVELLER: *(Smiles…thinks he's made a joke.)* Nothing happens after.

SHIFT BOSS: Oh. Maybe you think it's a trick question?

TRAVELLER: Is it?

SHIFT BOSS: *(Looking over papers.)* No.

TRAVELLER: It's not?

SHIFT BOSS: No.

TRAVELLER: Well then I take my answer back.

SHIFT BOSS: You can't. It'll mess up the control.

TRAVELLER: But—

SHIFT BOSS: Let's review: People are going to work. I can't remember. Alternate: I don't know what I did. I didn't notice anything. I would start again. Nothing happens after. *(Looks at the TRAVELLER.)*

TRAVELLER: What?

SHIFT BOSS: Nothing. Happens. After.

TRAVELLER: Nothing?

SHIFT BOSS: Nothing.

TRAVELLER: Oh.

DOCTORS AND NURSES SIT AT A STAFF MEETING

The RESEARCH PHYSICIAN comes in. He picks up the phone and pushes the button.

RESEARCH PHYSICIAN: Hello…? Hello? Hello?…Yes…Five…I don't know…what? Why? I don't want to! Why do I gotta?! Wh— *(He starts crying, takes a pill, suddenly goes blank and obeys.)* Okay. *(He hangs up.)*

(The MEDICAL STAFF comes in. They lounge about watching. Defeated. Deflated.)

RESEARCH PHYSICIAN: Where…did she go?

SPECIALIST: What are we going to do without Sandy?

DOCTOR #3: I don't know.

RESEARCH PHYSICIAN: Where…did she go?

SPECIALIST: What are we going to do!

DOCTOR #3: It's tough, man. It's tough all over.

SPECIALIST: Yeah. It is. It really is.

(The phone makes the off-the-hook signal.)

SPECIALIST: Hang it up for god's sake.

RESEARCH PHYSICIAN: Why are you all bossing me around? I didn't do anything wrong! None of you knew what we were supposed to be doing!

DOCTOR #3: He's right. I mean if you work somewhere, you're supposed to know what the job is. But who were we kidding, man? We didn't have the slightest idea what we were doing! This was all a sham! A flim-flam! A scam perpetrated by hokum peddlers trying to pull one over on the man. A hatched-up, dangerous, and cockamamie plan.

SPECIALIST: Yeah…

RESEARCH PHYSICIAN: *(Musing to himself.)* I knew. I knew what to do to the guy.

SPECIALIST: No you didn't.

RESEARCH PHYSICIAN: Yes I did.

SPECIALIST: No…You. Did. Not.

DOCTOR #3: Quit fighting boys! We got to figure something out or that cat's going to come back here and cashier us permanent like.

SPECIALIST: Sacked for not knowing what to do.

DOCTOR #3: Yeah, man.

RESEARCH PHYSICIAN: Do you really think that he would close the hotel—

DOCTOR #3: Hospital.

RESEARCH PHYSICIAN: That he would close the Hospital and fire us again?

DOCTOR #3: You know what's incredible? It's incredible that we keep making the same mistakes over and over again. It's incredible that we work in hotels year—

SPECIALIST: Hospitals.

DOCTOR #3: Hospitals year after year and we can't get it together to figure out what we're supposed to be doing. I mean Sandy left. You killed that girl—

RESEARCH PHYSICIAN: No I did not. She passed away for an ordinary reason!

DOCTOR #3: What do you mean "passed away"? She died, man! Because of what we did!

RESEARCH PHYSICIAN: NO! It was an ordinary reason. Anyways she's alright!! She…she went to Wichita! That's right! After she "passed away" she went to Wichita! A place where nothing bad would ever happen again, where she could see her friends and relatives that had "passed away" before her and be welcomed and forgiven in their loving arms again…In Wichita there's a benevolent energy-being-thing ensuring her eternal happiness. It's true! Something cares about her and it's never too busy to listen! Yes!…yes! Wichita really does exist.

SPECIALIST: Did she die?

RESEARCH PHYSICIAN: NO!

DOCTOR #3: Yes. But maybe she's alright like you said.

RESEARCH PHYSICIAN: *(Wistfully.)* Yeah…maybe she is.

SPECIALIST: So are we just waiting here to get sacked?

DOCTOR #3: Yeah, buddy. Like I said we didn't figure it out again.

SPECIALIST: But if we're just sitting here shouldn't we go to Wichita? I mean leave before we get fired? It sounds pretty good!

DOCTOR #3: You can't just "walk into Wichita," brother. You got to be invited.

SPECIALIST: Oh.

RESEARCH PHYSICIAN: Plus nobody knows the way.

SPECIALIST: She does.

RESEARCH PHYSICIAN: Who? Sandy?

DOCTOR #3: Sandy's not in Wichita.

RESEARCH PHYSICIAN: Oh... right.

DOCTOR #3: Who do you mean.

SPECIALIST: She! She! The one with the thing! *(Indicating ear.)*

DOCTOR #3: *(Thinks it over.)* I Iuh. Do you think she could get us in?

SPECIALIST: Wait, do you need a reservation or something?

DOCTOR #3: Don't ask ME! He's the one who knows all about it!

RESEARCH PHYSICIAN: You don't need a reservation but there IS a guest list. Wichita is pretty exclusive.

DOCTOR #3: Maybe she could get us on the guest list?

RESEARCH PHYSICIAN: Maybe.

DOCTOR #3: Maybe she knows the guy at the door?

RESEARCH PHYSICIAN: Maybe.

SPECIALIST: How do we contact her?

DOCTOR #3: Yeah we got to try and get out of here before "you know who" comes. Maybe we could get into Wichita and start a little business venture.

SPECIALIST: Yeah, but how do we do it?

DOCTOR #3: Can't we call her up?

SPECIALIST: Yeah!

RESEARCH PHYSICIAN: Nobody knows the number there!

SPECIALIST: We got to do it!

RESEARCH PHYSICIAN: Wait a second! There is a way to talk to people in Wichita! I saw it on the TV!

DOCTOR #3: What! What is it, man!

RESEARCH PHYSICIAN: Well we all gather round in a circle and turn the lights out. Then we yell to the people in Wichita and sometimes they'll talk to you...sometimes they won't. The guys on the TV thought about their friends in Wichita as hard as they could and they got to talk to them...just for a second.

SPECIALIST: Why do you have to turn the lights out?

DOCTOR #3: Are you talking about some kind of telecommunication thing here?

RESEARCH PHYSICIAN: Yes it WAS on the TV!

SPECIALIST: Why do the lights have to be out?

DOCTOR #3: Yeah! Why DO the lights have to be out.

RESEARCH PHYSICIAN: Well, gather round and I'll tell you.

(The environment becomes creepier.)

RESEARCH PHYSICIAN: The people in Wichita only like to come out when it's really dark and there aren't a lot of people around.

DOCTOR #3: He really knows what he's talking about.

RESEARCH PHYSICIAN: Yeah yeah I do. They only come out when it's really dark and there's not a lot of people. They don't ever come out in a normal place and just talk to you. They want to tell you how great it is in Wichita but it has to be a secret.

SPECIALIST: That doesn't really make any sense though. I mean wouldn't they WANT to tell you how great it is in Wichita?

RESEARCH PHYSICIAN: NO! You have to sit in a scary room and think really hard about them…like…like this… *(Begins his trance.)*

DOCTOR #3: Let's do it! "What's his name" won't be able to find us to deliver the old pink slip plus we could start a little business.

SPECIALIST: I still don't understand why it's such a big secret.

(The seance.)

RESEARCH PHYSICIAN: I am calling all you guys in Wichita!

SPECIALIST: *(Under his breath.)* Or why the lights have to be out.

RESEARCH PHYSICIAN: Shut up. I am calling all you guys in Wichita! Wichita! Wichita!

DOCTOR #3: This is creepy man!

SPECIALIST: How do we know he's not just doing a voice?

RESEARCH PHYSICIAN: *(In a "trance.")* Wichita respond! Wichita! Wichita! Is that you? Is that you, Wichita?

SPECIALIST: Who? There's nobody there.

DOCTOR #3: He's talking to them, man! It's a special communication thing!

SPECIALIST: But that's stupid. There's no way to prove that!

RESEARCH PHYSICIAN: *(Coming out of the trance and under his breath.)* Shut up! *(Going back in.)* Yes? No. What?

SPECIALIST: Just ask how we get in.

DOCTOR #3: It's more subtle than that, man! Have a little sensitivity!

RESEARCH PHYSICIAN: Salad! Please don't turn the light on! Yes! Yes! A ladder lit by a single lamp…its feet stuck in the mud…where does it poke up to…

(The TV screens flicker to life. It's BARBARA in Wichita. She is waving. The RESEARCH PHYSICIAN moans in his trance.)

DOCTOR #3: Is she here?

SPECIALIST: Who?

RESEARCH PHYSICIAN: Yes! Yes! I'm…I'm speaking to her now. She's saying…"Goodbye! Goodbye! You cannot come to Wichita!"

SPECIALIST: There's no one there.

RESEARCH PHYSICIAN: She's saying something else…she's saying: "You are in big trouble."

SPECIALIST: Oh, for christ's sake.

(There is a noise. A flash.)

DOCTOR #3: What was that?

SPECIALIST: This is ridiculous. We know what to do. Forget Wichita! Let's just take care of the guy! We know how to do it! Just be nice to him!

DOCTOR #3: Jesus, is it that simple?

RESEARCH PHYSICIAN: She's gone.

(The lights come up. DOCTOR #1 is there.)

RESEARCH PHYSICIAN: BOB!

SPECIALIST: Oh great!

RESEARCH PHYSICIAN: BILL!

SPECIALIST: Fantastic.

RESEARCH PHYSICIAN: Barry!

DOCTOR #3: Who's THIS cat?

DOCTOR #1: Wait.

RESEARCH PHYSICIAN: I KNEW you'd come back!

DOCTOR #1: I'm here for one reason.

RESEARCH PHYSICIAN: What BILL??? WHAT?

DOCTOR #1: I'm here to make a little proposition to you…a little business venture!

DOCTOR #3: Look! That's what I said! That's exactly my bag, man!

DOCTOR #1: *(Looking around a lot.)* But you got to make your minds up fast. Listen—there's no more work here…it's all gone to the immigrants and the hard-luck cases—

RESEARCH PHYSICIAN: Oh…yeah! I know all about that kind of thing.

DOCTOR #1: And…well…On account of you killed that girl—

SPECIALIST: SEE?

RESEARCH PHYSICIAN: I DID NOT! HE did!

DOCTOR #3: It was all for the best, man.

DOCTOR #1: On account you killed that girl AND there's no more work you have about fifteen seconds to make up your mind whether or not you want to do what I propose.

DOCTOR #3: WHAT? WHAT IS IT?

DOCTOR #1: You won't have a lot of time to think it out—

SPECIALIST: Jesus christ man! What is it?

DOCTOR #1: In a few seconds you'll have to decide this complicated issue.

RESEARCH PHYSICIAN: *(Is so traumatized he begins drinking.)* Yes Barry. I'm with you. Bill would you like a little drink, Bob?

DOCTOR #3: Don't distract him! He's got an idea!

DOCTOR #1: I found a little shop in the corner of a quiet street.

RESEARCH PHYSICIAN: That sounds delightful.

DOCTOR #1: We can sell buttons and things.

SPECIALIST: What? A haberdasher's?

DOCTOR #1: Come to the store boys! You're out of time! I already got the place!

(Huge noise…THE CAROL arrives.)

DOCTOR #3: Holy crap!

SPECIALIST: Oh. My. God.

RESEARCH PHYSICIAN: A "sayonara sling"…

DOCTOR #1: Too late…this is it…

RESEARCH PHYSICIAN: *(Is so out of it he does not notice.)* It also has some nice other things in the store! It has bourbon and those crackers you might want. It has pickles and cute little packets of things… you know it's—

THE CAROL: I am The Carol. So know I am The Carol.

DOCTOR #1: Carol we were just leaving! There's no need to fire us. *(On the down low.)* I'm on your side, Carol, I don't even work here really. *(Back up.)* They don't need any firing! They were leaving!

THE CAROL: The next thing you will hear will be The Carol talking.

RESEARCH PHYSICIAN: *(Sees him.)* Oh! Hello! We were just leaving to open our little shop on the corner of a quiet street. It's not a liquor store.

SPECIALIST: I cannot be fired! It would ruin my resume.

DOCTOR #1: That is the truth.

DOCTOR #3: You don't understand, buddy. If you get fired from here? If they close the Hospital? You go nowheres. No. Wheres, man. Nowheres.

DOCTOR #1: Also true.

THE CAROL: You did not do your jobs. The Carol noticed you also wrecked a person.

RESEARCH PHYSICIAN: What person?

THE CAROL: A person who was visiting her brother.

DOCTOR #3: HE got better! I mean that's something isn't it, sir?

DOCTOR #1: I was not here at that time!

RESEARCH PHYSICIAN: No you weren't. You'd LEFT! That's what you ALWAYS DO. That's what you're good at!

SPECIALIST: It was the infection that killed her…

THE CAROL: Leave. Your jobs are over although you did not do them in the first place. The Hospital is closing. You do not work here anymore.

SPECIALIST: Excuse me, sir. What about the guy down the hall?

THE CAROL: Don't worry, I said, about that guy. He's the only one left and he was never down the hall.

DOCTOR #3: Who was?

THE CAROL: Two other guys. They got better and left.

DOCTOR #3: See? We did THAT?!

RESEARCH PHYSICIAN: No we didn't.

DOCTOR #3: Yes we did.

RESEARCH PHYSICIAN: No we didn't.

SPECIALIST: Did we?

RESEARCH PHYSICIAN: *(Drunk and lucid.)* No. No we didn't.

THE CAROL: You cared for no guys. The guy is down in the thing. He was always there. He never even came to the Hospital. If he did you would not have cared for him as you did not care for any guys. At any time. Anywhere. In the Hospital. Leave. Your jobs are over.

DOCTOR #1: That little shop's looking pretty good right about now right?

RESEARCH PHYSICIAN: Hello! May I help you! Yes we do have crackers!

SPECIALIST: I'm going back to England. This really upset me. My God…why can't I learn to do anything right?

DOCTOR #3: It's this place, man. I think I'll go to Engerlund with you, guy.

DOCTOR #1: Come on, Terry. Let's get out of here!

RESEARCH PHYSICIAN: Yes! I DO have the time to talk things over at the front of the shop! I KNOW! Bill planted them! Oh we usually order lunch from a little café! Those are one of a kind! I do! I do love cheese!

DOCTOR #1: Come on Tim. I'll take care of you.

THE CAROL: The Hospital is closed.

DOCTOR #1: Here we go. *(Itching to get out of there.)*

SPECIALIST: We can stay at my dad's for a bit.

DOCTOR #3: That's cool man, that's cool.

SPECIALIST: I'm not working in any haberdashery.

DOCTOR #3: Ditto.

DOCTOR #1: *(Is swept away.)* Goodbye, Tim!

(EVERYONE has left…)

RESEARCH PHYSICIAN: A doctor takes responsibility for himself. A doctor copes with sexual intimacy. A grown doctor gains freedom. Learning to live in the present. Never too old to change for the better. A very special way.

DIVERTISSEMENT

The TRAVELLER is walking in the tunnel. BARBARA comes towards him.

TRAVELLER: *(Sees BARBARA.)* Oh… Hey.

BARBARA: Hi.

TRAVELLER: What are you doing down here?

BARBARA: I came to see you!

TRAVELLER: Really.

BARBARA: I wanted to see where you worked. It does seem pretty unusual!

TRAVELLER: You mean down here?

BARBARA: In the tunnel. What you told me about?

TRAVELLER: Yes. Yes, it is pretty unusual I guess. *(Strangely suspicious for a moment.)* Uh… How'd you get in here?

BARBARA: *(Looks around.)* Don't you get scared down here?

TRAVELLER: Not really.

BARBARA: Oh. I'm scared of the dark.

TRAVELLER: Why would you be scared of the dark?

BARBARA: I'm just scared of the dark, that's all. I always have been.

TRAVELLER: Well… just think of the place where you are with the lights on. It's the exact same place… only the lights are off!

(They laugh. It's a sweet meeting.)

BARBARA: But I'm still scared of the dark.

TRAVELLER: It's not so dark down here. Look. You can see me, right?

BARBARA: Yes.

TRAVELLER: You can see me? You can see the conduit and the rock wall. Look!

BARBARA: Do you get scared down here?

TRAVELLER: I don't get scared down here. I've been here for years.

BARBARA: I know.

TRAVELLER: *(Gets excited.)* We're building the water tunnel that will bring all the water to the city! They're going to shut down the other two, the older ones. This'll be the ONLY one!

BARBARA: It'll bring all the water to the city? For all the houses?

TRAVELLER: *(Warming.)* Yeah! To all the houses and people! It'll fill up the fountain at the museum! It'll come out of diner coffee machines and everything. Do you know how much steam power the city uses?

BARBARA: No!

TRAVELLER: A lot! That'll use this water too!

BARBARA: Wow. I'm so glad Jimmy introduced us.

TRAVELLER: Me too…so…what kind of stuff do you like doing.

BARBARA: Well, I like coming down here to see you!

TRAVELLER: Maybe we could go out sometime? I go down to the shipping docks all the time. It's an interesting way to see the city! Remember it used to be a big port.

BARBARA: Yeah but no so much anymore!

TRAVELLER: No, but you can still see all the boats coming in and they've planted some beautiful stuff down there. It's great to see all the people walking around. Maybe we could go.

BARBARA: Yes. I'd like that.

TRAVELLER: *(Somewhat realizing this might be near the end.)* Yeah! If you like walking this is the greatest place! Wasn't it beautiful today? Isn't it nice out?

BARBARA: Yes.

(They dance to a sad song.)

TRAVELLER: *(Feels so sad.)* I feel great! Let me show you something. *(Takes something out of his pocket.)* Look at this! I found this down here! It's a snail!

BARBARA: Look at that!

TRAVELLER: Your brother feeds them with candle wax!

BARBARA: He says it's good luck!

TRAVELLER: He needs all the luck he can get!

BARBARA: Not like Frank!

TRAVELLER: No Frank's lucky. Look how he won all those quarters. Frank always wins.

BARBARA: I saw him a couple times when I was visiting my brother!

TRAVELLER: Yeah…Once an owl flew into the tunnel!

BARBARA: Really?

TRAVELLER: Yeah I guess it flew down the shaft! Maybe it thought there were mice down here.

BARBARA: There must be!…a mouse of some kind down here.

TRAVELLER: He just flew right in! We never figured out where he went. We lost sight of him.

BARBARA: You mean he could still be in here?

TRAVELLER: *(Slight desperation?)* Probably not! He probably turned around in the dark and flew out the join…yeah he probably did that.

BARBARA: But maybe he's still in here.

TRAVELLER: Maybe he's still in here but I bet he flew right out!

BARBARA: Yeah.

TRAVELLER: I bet he flew out. Did you know— ...come here.

(She moves closer... he's doing well.)

TRAVELLER: There's an amazing story about a guy who got stuck down here! It's pretty interesting.

BARBARA: Really? Maybe we can go for that walk and you can tell me it.

TRAVELLER: Don't worry it has a happy ending!

BARBARA: Good.

TRAVELLER: Yeah, we'll go to the pier. Isn't it great out? I like talking to you like this! We could go look at the boats or we could walk around in the tunnel and look for the snails your brother feeds with candle wax or we could see if we can find that poor owl who flew down here. We could do a lot of things maybe we could...maybe...we...

BARBARA: You said nobody ever found that owl.

TRAVELLER: No they didn't. Maybe he's still down there.

BARBARA: Maybe.

TRAVELLER: I know...I know.

(FRANK comes in.)

FRANK: Listen...people just went on doing things...nobody's mad at you or anything.

TRAVELLER: Frank!

FRANK: I probably would've run too. Maybe you thought we were that way? I ran with you too.

TRAVELLER: Where's Jimmy? Is he alright?

FRANK: Jimmy's fine! I came and got him out a little after you left!

TRAVELLER: Really? Can I see him again?

FRANK: He's coming in a minute.

TRAVELLER: Everybody's alright.

FRANK: Yeah. I know why you ran. It was a good idea. It just happened to be the wrong time. You know...by accident.

TRAVELLER: By accident.

(JIMMY walks over.)

FRANK: Yeah, look!

JIMMY: Hey buddy...how are you?

TRAVELLER: Jimmy...Jimmy I'm sorry. I'm sorry.

JIMMY: That's alright. I got out okay. I don't even think about it anymore.

FRANK: Yeah, nobody thinks about it.

TRAVELLER: We all got out? We're all okay?

JIMMY: *(Exchanging glances with the TRAVELLER.)* Listen though...it's more than what we said.

TRAVELLER: What?

JIMMY: The thing is...

FRANK: It's kind of hard to say.

TRAVELLER: Yes?

FRANK: Well when you ran...you—

TRAVELLER: *(Growing hysteria.)* I did what you would have done. Now we can go talk and maybe get a drink and—and—Jimmy! I can meet your sister and make a better impression! I promise we'll talk. I promise I'll be there! I swear I won't forget the—

FRANK: No…no listen..

TRAVELLER: Yes?

JIMMY: You're still down here, buddy.

FRANK: You're all alone.

JIMMY: You're still here.

(Cavalcade of his memories begins.)

TUNNELER #1: There's nobody down there but you.

FRANK: Yeah. Plus we don't even think about you. It's as if it never happened.

JIMMY: Somebody lives in that apartment already.

BARBARA: Somebody took me on a date.

PERSEPHONE: Me too! Somebody picked up their check…maybe I had a funny talk with them.

KAREN: Somebody else looks out over the river.

SHIFT BOSS: Somebody else climbs down that ladder every day.

KAREN: *(Reciting.)* A ladder lit by a single lamp. Its feet stuck in the mud. Where does it poke up to? Ah memories.

(Gentle appreciation from the CROWD.)

SHIFT BOSS: Yeah…that's right. Hey look! *(Puts on the WHITE RABBIT's ears.)* Doesn't that seem like a long time ago. It all does. It all does. Hey you know what? Oh…forget it.

TRAVELLER: What about the evaluation.

SHIFT BOSS: Oh.

TRAVELLER: Am I…did I

SHIFT BOSS: Your spot was taken. You're redundant. Sorry buddy. It happens to all of us. Cutback. Redundant.

KAREN: Washed up.

TRAVELLER: That's what I was thinking was going to happen.

SHIFT BOSS: Well…it did.

BARBARA/QUEEN OF HEARTS: *(Trying to cheer him up.)* Remember me?

TRAVELLER: Yes. Of course I do.

BARBARA/QUEEN OF HEARTS: Hello! *(Curtsies.)* Maybe we can talk some more…down…here now..

TUNNELER #1: But not for long…

BARBARA/QUEEN OF HEARTS: *(Realizes.)* Oh…right.

KAREN: I am the ferryman with the dogs. The one they wrote the story about. The one who takes people across to the…

BARBARA/QUEEN OF HEARTS: *(Protecting.)* He doesn't need to hear about that. He knows the story.

KAREN: Well, obviously I'm not taking him. That's just a story.

PERSEPHONE: Nobody goes anywhere in the end. Nothing happens after.

SHIFT BOSS/JOHN HENRY: I'm John Henry I ain't no shift boss!…remember that??

FRANK: But you are the shift boss.

SHIFT BOSS/JOHN HENRY: *(Deflated.)* Yeah…yeah I am the shift boss.

TRAVELLER: You remember me, right? It's not that long ago? I haven't been down here that long?

SHIFT BOSS/JOHN HENRY: Yeah. I remember you. Some other guy's coming down the ladder. Right…right now…sorry.

JIMMY: And later somebody else will.

TUNNELER #1: And then somebody else.

FRANK: And somebody else.

KAREN: And someone else.

BARBARA/QUEEN OF HEARTS: And then someone else.

TRAVELLER: I know.

BARBARA/QUEEN OF HEARTS: So here we are.

TRAVELLER: Down here.

BARBARA/QUEEN OF HEARTS: Just us.

TUNNELER #1: Just me.

KAREN: Just me.

SHIFT BOSS: Just me.

JIMMY: And me.

FRANK: And me.

TRAVELLER: Just…me.

BARBARA/QUEEN OF HEARTS: That's right. Just you.

(THE CAROL comes in. DOCTORS and NURSES slowly assemble.)

ALL: Carol…carol.

THE CAROL: All these people came here to see you. We want to tell you something.

BARBARA/QUEEN OF HEARTS: Can't we just pretend we're at a party and not talk about it?

SHIFT BOSS: There's no party here.

THE CAROL: No there is no party down here.

TRAVELLER: I know.

THE CAROL: You've been down here a long time.

TRAVELLER: I know.

THE CAROL: These other guys already woke up. But you remembered them and they came and said interesting things… right?

TUNNELER #1: We tried to be interesting!

BARBARA/QUEEN OF HEARTS: The stories were!

KAREN: We were here the whole time.

SHIFT BOSS: Like you.

THE CAROL: So we brought you something…to commemorate the day.

KAREN: Plus, we got you a card.

TRAVELLER: *(Opens his heart-breaking card.)* Thanks.

TUNNELER #1: Wasn't he going to tell him something?

KAREN: It's alright The Carol knows when to tell him.

BARBARA/QUEEN OF HEARTS: *(So lovingly.)* Don't be afraid.

TUNNELER #1: Although we might be.

FRANK: There's nothing you can do about it now.

JIMMY: Those guys? Those guys from the tunnel…the shift boss?…they don't even think about you anymore.

BARBARA/QUEEN OF HEARTS: But we do!

FRANK: Yeah we do!

JIMMY: Don't be afraid.

TUNNELER #1: Don't be afraid.

SHIFT BOSS: Don't be afraid.

THE CAROL: Don't you want to see what we got you?

TRAVELLER: Is this it?

THE CAROL: Here is your present to commemorate the day. Look at me. Everything is going to be alright. Disappear. It's not so bad down here.

TRAVELLER: *(He opens his present.)* I want to say...I want...Once a guy got stuck down here. He didn't know what time it was. He missed his friends although...he didn't really have any. He kept to himself. He didn't make an impression. He didn't notice anything. If you mentioned him you might say:...Too bad he blew it! You might say: I don't really remember him or oh yeah...that's right...he never...or...you might say: maybe he's still down there...maybe he's still down there...maybe he's still...

LINUS & ALORA

Andrew Irons

ANDREW IRONS is a playwright and teaching artist. He was born on December 26, 1974, in El Paso, Texas, and grew up in Oklahoma City. He studied theatre at the American Conservatory Theater's Young Conservatory and the National Theater Institute before receiving bachelor's degrees in theatre and English from Skidmore College and an MFA from Sarah Lawrence College. He is a founding member and former producing director of Andhow! Theater Company, which has produced his plays *Tunnel, Paschal Full Moon, Non-D, Little Suckers,* and the toy theatre piece, *And Away!* His plays *Yakima Man* and *Iris* received readings/workshops at Blue Heron Arts Center and Starbright Floral, respectively. As an actor and playwright, Irons has worked with adobe theatre company, New Dramatists, Gilgamesh Theatre Group, New Georges, and Turnip Theatre Company. He has been a teaching artist at the Hudson River Academy, Sarah Lawrence College's Summer Writing Intensive, Westchester Community College, the Allen-Stevenson School, and Penobscot Theatre Company. From 2006 to 2008, he was Program Director for Falconworks Artists Group's "Off the Hook," a playwriting-to-performance program in Red Hook, Brooklyn. He won the *Backstage* 2003–2004 STIMY Award for Most Powerful Production for *Non-D.* Irons is currently developing *Purple Creek*, a play with puppets, and an untitled toy theatre prequel to *And Away!* He is a high school English teacher in Bushwick, Brooklyn, and is working toward a master's degree in teaching from Brooklyn College. He lives in Bay Ridge, Brooklyn, with his wife, Jessica Davis-Irons, and their son, Jacob.

Linus & Alora was first presented by Andhow! Theater Company (Jessica Davis-Irons, Artistic Director) on September 5, 2008, at the Flea Theater (Jim Simpson, Artistic Director; Carol Ostrow, Producing Director) with the following cast and credits:

Alora	Melle Powers
Doctor	Maria Cellario
Sam, Sunshine	Alex Smith
Samantha, Noodle	Gamze Ceylan
Owen	B. Brian Argotsinger
Arthur	Tim Cain
Neal	Noah Trepanier
Linus	Arthur Aulisi

Director: Jessica Davis-Irons
Stage Manager: Kelly Shaffer
Choreographer: Jesse Hawley
Associate Director: Brendan Kennedy
Scenic and Video Design: Dustin O'Neill
Lighting Design: Owen Hughes
Costume Design: Becky Lasky
Sound Design and Original Music: Jill BC DuBoff
Technical Director: Andrew Pape
Master Electrician: Jared Welch
Electricians: Wavetek Productions
Postcard Design: Gabrielle Gerwitz
Web Design: Starving Artist Web Design

www.andhowtheater.com

Linus & Alora is dedicated to Andhow! and its limitless imagination and to the loving memory of my wife, Jessica, who is still alive.

Special thanks to: Jessica Davis-Irons, Andhow! Theater Company, Martin Denton, Rochelle Denton, the Irons Family, the Davis Family, Margie Stokley, Clayton Dowty, Neal Wilkinson, Danya Haber, the Flea Theater, Jim Simpson, Carol Ostrow, Beth Dembrow, Zack Tinkelman, Sherri Kronfeld, Lilian Meredith, Marlon Hurt, The Monkey, the Church Street Theater, Arts OMI, Josh Higgason, and, of course, the interns: Joshua Lipman, Rikki Bahar, Marissa Bea, Mariah MacCarthy, David Soblick, and Pete Wallace.

THE WORLD

The play takes place in a pediatrician's office, the street, the home of Linus and Alora, the night sky, and the street again. A large digital time clock up center. There should be projection surfaces throughout and the ability to see a projected image become three dimensional.

THE CHARACTERS IN ORDER OF APPEARANCE

ALORA	SAM
DOCTOR	LINUS
LITTLE ALORA (animated)	OWEN
OLD CUBAN MAN	NEAL
OLD CUBAN WOMAN	ARTHUR
HOMELESS MAN	SUNSHINE
CON MAN	NOODLE
MAN WITH MEGAPHONE	SAMANTHA

ALORA waits under a ceiling of fluorescent lights. She sits on a chair that is too small for her in a pediatrician's waiting room. She pulls saltine crackers from a box as the fluorescents hum. One light flickers and pops. She picks up a magazine. Highlights. *A door opens bringing a breath of warm light. The kindest DOCTOR in the world enters through the door. She is seventy years old.*

DOCTOR: They just told me you were here. I told them it had to be a mistake.

ALORA: *(Falsely enthusiastic.)* Surprise!

DOCTOR: They told me you've been waiting a long…

ALORA: What's a few hours in the grand scheme of things?

DOCTOR: You look beautiful. All grown up. I didn't think I would see you again.

ALORA: It's good to see your face. It's exactly like I remember it.

DOCTOR: Oh god bless you.

ALORA: You know I've never been able to trust anyone else. Not really.

(They stand for a moment in silence.)

DOCTOR: What is it, Alora?

(ALORA pulls a large medical file from her bag. The DOCTOR is paralyzed. Then…)

DOCTOR: I can't look/at those.

ALORA: Please. You're my doctor.

DOCTOR: I haven't been for twenty-five years…

ALORA: For me.

(The DOCTOR opens the cover of the file. One of the many fluorescent lights flickers.)

DOCTOR: Oh, I can't help you with this.

ALORA: You have to.

DOCTOR: I'm sorry, this is outside my area of expertise.

ALORA: You're the only one who can help me.

DOCTOR: I see children.

ALORA: You are a doctor.

DOCTOR: I'm a pediatric/oncologist…

ALORA: You're my doctor. *(Pause.)* I can't trust anyone else. Please.

DOCTOR: *(Opens the folder and flips through it. Barely—IF—audible.)* No. *(After a minute, the DOCTOR pushes it closed and does not speak.)*

ALORA: You said you would never look at me like that again. *(Pause.)* They were wrong, right? Tell me they were wrong.

(Sound of a heartbeat…so incredibly low.)

ALORA: No. You're wrong. Doctors…all of you. *(A longish pause.)* It's positive?

(The DOCTOR nods.)

ALORA: You're positive?

DOCTOR: *(She nods and holds a piece of paper out for her.)* He's the best.

ALORA: It's back?

(The DOCTOR nods.)

ALORA: You're wrong.

DOCTOR: Alora, it's back.

(ALORA freezes. A long and loud amplified gasp. The sound of a spotlight clanking on. ALORA looks almost like a little girl standing in the spotlight.)

(Image: A flash of an X-ray of a cancerous abdomen. A radiation target over a belly button. Shattering images of a gurney wheel and syringes drawing blood and pumping toxic medication in. A shunt. A clinical flat light. Another X-ray.)

(The sound of the heartbeat now bangs in ALORA's ears.)

ALORA: I can't breathe.

(Image: Time elapse of ALORA regressing in age to a five-year-old line-drawn girl. This is the animated ALORA who will appear throughout the play on video behind the songs.)

(The sound of a gasp.)

(Image: A slow-motion syringe needle coming at the audience. The heartbeat thumps.)

SONG: FLIGHT OF THE WHITE COATS

(Image: A sea of white coats.)

(ALORA sits in a tight-lit spot. Behind her, images dance.)

ALORA: *(Singing with a cool voice that hides the panic of remembrance just below the surface…)*
SHUNT CRY, POKE THIS HERE, PULL THAT
    THERE, REACH UP FOR MOMMY,
"SHE'LL BE ABLE TO SEE YOU SOON."
DROP DEAD GORGEOUS GIRL IS TREADING.
LAB RAT. SHARK BAIT. WORM FOOD.

(Image: Backlit shadows. A mass of people in white coats carrying clipboards. One by one, they step forward into the light in perfect military precision.)

DO YOU REALLY WANT TO KNOW WHAT'S
    UP MY ASS?
IF I PISS IN A CUP WILL YOU TAKE IT HOME
    TO SHOW THE FOLKS?

(Image: Hair in a little girl's hand. Faceless doctors. Eyebrows falling out one by one by one and blowing into the

wind. White coats crashing, faceless giants hovering.)

LAB COATS CRUSHING. FACELESS GIANTS HOVERING.

IF WE DO THIS, THEN THAT, THEN ON TO PHASE FOUR.

INJECT THIS ONE. INJECT THESE TOO.

YOU SAID JUST A LITTLE BIT. LIKE A LITTLE BEE BITE

(Image: Each of the faceless doctors pulls from their coat a different medical device. A swirl of sterile instruments. LITTLE ALORA alone, awake in a dark room. Eyes wide open.)

OH SHIT, A TEAR. NOW NOBODY KNOWS WHAT TO DO.

(Image: A red balloon deflates.)

(Both ALORA and LITTLE ALORA watch it fart across the sky. The music comes to an end. The DOCTOR gently puts her hand to ALORA's face. A gasp.)

ALORA: How long?

DOCTOR: I can't say.

ALORA: How long do I have?

DOCTOR: No more than nine months.

ALORA: Nine months.

(A digital time clock with large red numbers appears. They both look at it for a moment. It says 21,772,800. The time clock ticks down, a tick per second and slowly increases in speed. ALORA can't catch her breath. She throws the file on the table. The DOCTOR's office melts around her.)

ALORA: What? No lollipop?

(She is outside on the street. "One Cup of Coffee" by Bob Marley from Songs of Freedom plays. An OLD CUBAN MAN dances with an OLD CUBAN WOMAN …close…intimate…A horn blares by. The sound of laughter in reverse. The buildings above her start to turn and grow. A HOMELESS MAN leads the charge of a swarm of PEDESTRIANS with fedoras and briefcases. The dialogue is on top of dancing.)

HOMELESS MAN: Help me get something to eat? A payment on my condo in Florida?

(Without looking at the MAN, ALORA unzips her bag and turns it over. Bills scatter into the wind.)

HOMELESS MAN: (Holding up a fist of cash.) Much obliged. (Hands ALORA a piece of paper.) You should give him a call. He's the best.

(Image: A silent mouth in the city behind the HOMELESS MAN. A serene woman floats by in water. ALORA does not say anything.)

HOMELESS MAN: Are you okay?

(ALORA looks at the woman quietly.)

(Image: The mouth behind the HOMELESS MAN screams silently. Laughter of a hundred pedestrians.)

HOMELESS MAN: Don't listen to them. There's a lot you can get done in nine months.

ALORA: What did you say?

(Image: The buildings grow. A tidal wave hits and disappears.)

(The laughter grows. ALORA is swept up in a wave of PEOPLE. A CON MAN plays Three Card Monte on an old cardboard box.)

(Image: Cards shuffle. Two aces and a queen of hearts. Round and round.)

CON MAN: Keep your eyes on the lady. Now you see her now you don't. Put your money down. Will she make it or won't she. Blink for a moment and she'll disappear...

(Image: Three slot machine tumblers roll furiously around and around. They stop one at a time. Tumbler 1: A picture of LITTLE ALORA. Tumbler 2: A picture of LITTLE ALORA. Tumbler 3: A strip across the tumbler saying "Censored.")

(The OLD CUBAN MAN and OLD CUBAN WOMAN stop their intimate dance and turn and walk away from one another. The WOMAN almost runs over ALORA. The PEDESTRIANS dance.)

OLD CUBAN WOMAN: So what is it?

ALORA: What is what?

OLD CUBAN WOMAN: Good news or bad?

ALORA: What?

OLD CUBAN WOMAN: Beginning or end?

(A swarm of PEOPLE walk through.)

ALORA: What do you mean?

(A MAN enters with a megaphone and a book of tickets.)

MAN WITH MEGAPHONE: Anyone taking the 4:15 to Cuba, please get your ticket out and move to track 5-4-1.

ALORA: What do you mean, beginning or end?

MAN WITH MEGAPHONE: If you do not have a ticket, you may purchase one here.

OLD CUBAN WOMAN: There's a lot you can get done in nine months.

MAN WITH MEGAPHONE: Again, anyone taking the 4:15 to Cuba, please get your ticket out and move to track 1-4-5.

(The MAN turns to offer a ticket to ALORA. Crowds of PEOPLE swarm by her, pushing to get to the front of the line. She is bumped around, spinning and turning. ALORA steps away from the MAN WITH MEGAPHONE, shoots her hand in the air, and yells:)

ALORA: TAXI!

(Sound: Bing bong. Subway doors open. The pssht of brakes being released turns to waves crashing and the jerk of the train. An armpit. A crying baby. A sneeze. The smell of piss on a homeless man's coat. The world closes in on ALORA. Darkness to the face. ALORA takes a big gasp in to hold her breath. Heart beats. Voices in the dark:)

VOICE: Yo, look it here, the bitch be fiendin'.

ANOTHER VOICE: Dead-ass.

(Another face contained in a tight spot. This is SAM, a young and innocent-looking man.)

SAM: Are you all right? Can you hear me? If you can hear me, breathe.

(ALORA gasps for breath. Lights return to the stage with every breath. SAM and ALORA find themselves in her home. The two things that stand out in this world are a coat rack and a telephone on a pedestal. Coming off the base of the pedestal is a long pole with a blue siren on top. ALORA and SAM stand opposite one another. SAM is a small child. They are alone.)

ALORA: You're beautiful.

SAM: Thanks. You look like you're feeling better now.

ALORA: My god. You're perfect.

SAM: I don't know about that. I hope so. For a little while anyway. I mean...I might be, I don't know, I could be inherently evil.

ALORA: No. Not you.

SAM: You're pretty. You'll do.

ALORA: Thank you. *(Beat.)* Don't tell anyone, but I thought you were going to have three arms.

(LINUS enters in a rush.)

LINUS: My god, there you are.

(ALORA does not break eye contact with SAM.)

LINUS: The doctor called me and she said you were leaving and I should find you. And then you wouldn't answer your phone and I got scared and I don't know…and I came home, and…She wouldn't tell me anything. Are you okay?

(ALORA turns away from SAM to look at LINUS. ALORA doesn't say anything.)

LINUS: My god. It's not back…

ALORA: I'm pregnant.

LINUS: What?

ALORA: I just found out.

LINUS: Are you sure?

ALORA: Yes.

LINUS: But that's impossible…they said you would never be able to/conceive after…

ALORA: They said it would take a miracle. Didn't you hear me? I'm pregnant.

(It sinks in. LINUS picks her up and spins her around.)

LINUS: You're pregnant!

ALORA: Isn't it amazing. Magical. *(Laughing.)* I met him.

LINUS: I'm sorry?

ALORA: I met him and he helped me and—my god he's beautiful and gentle and kind.

LINUS: Who is?

ALORA: Our son. Our son is perfect.

LINUS: You met him?

ALORA: Of course.

LINUS: What do you mean?

ALORA: It was this voice, Linus. This kind voice and there he was.

LINUS: Inside your head?

ALORA: No…"inside my head"…Of course not…You think I'm…? *(She stops abruptly and looks at LINUS for a moment.)* You think I'm crazy.

LINUS: No.

ALORA: You do. You think I'm insane that I'm walking around talking to…

LINUS: No.

ALORA: …Little made-up babies.

LINUS: Of course not.

(ALORA covers LINUS's eyes and turns him to look in the direction of SAM.)

ALORA: The most beautiful boy you've ever seen in all your life.

SAM: You're embarrassing me.

ALORA: *(Drops her hands.)* Ta-Da!

LINUS: *(Is looking right at SAM, but doesn't see him.)* What's his name?

SAM: Sam.

ALORA: Sammy.

SAM: Just Sam.

LINUS: Sammy.

SAM: I hate that name.

LINUS: I like that. Sammy.

ALORA: Linus, you're being very rude.

LINUS: What?

SAM: It's not that big of a deal.

ALORA: It *is* a big deal. I want this to be perfect.

LINUS: It will be.

ALORA: You aren't even listening.

LINUS: Of course…

ALORA: He clearly said not to call him Sammy.

SAM: I really don't mind.

ALORA: You're not listening to him.

LINUS: I'm sorry, Sam.

(SAM throws a ball in LINUS's direction. He runs after it. LINUS continues to speak in the direction of where SAM was.)

LINUS: It was insensitive of me…and I'm your father. We're going to do some really great things.

SAM: *(Realizes LINUS can't see him.)* He can't see me.

LINUS: *(Still looking where SAM used to be.)* Really…great…

ALORA: Soon.

LINUS: Amazing. Times.

ALORA: He'll see you soon.

LINUS: Great.

SAM: Is everything okay?

ALORA: Everything is fine.

LINUS: Just you wait…son.

SAM: Why can't he see me?

ALORA: *(Breaking a little.)* Please let him be real.

LINUS: He is. I can see him. *(Gives an awkward fake stomach punch to the place where SAM used to be standing.)*

SAM: Look at me.

LINUS: I'm going to teach you everything.

ALORA: I'm afraid.

LINUS: Afraid of what?

ALORA: I want you to be real.

(SAM comes behind her and gives her a hug on her back.)

SAM: I am.   LINUS: He is.

ALORA: *(Almost crying.)* I want him to be real so bad.

(SAM cradles ALORA as she weeps and rocks.)

(Image: A red balloon inflates and is popped.)

LINUS: I'll find him.

(LINUS goes to a shelf and gets a tin can. He puts one end to ALORA's stomach and his ear to the other. He listens. LINUS turns back to ALORA. SAM stands and watches LINUS. The time clock reads somewhere near 19,485,000. SAM turns to go. The blue siren on the phone flashes once, twice, three times. The phone rings. LINUS turns as if to get up to answer the phone.)

ALORA: No. Don't get it.

LINUS: It could be important.

ALORA: Whatever it is, it can wait.

LINUS: But…

ALORA: Just listen.

(The phone rings. It rings again. It rings again. Then nothing.)

LINUS: I'm so proud of you.

ALORA: Oh you are, are you?

LINUS: I don't know…

ALORA: You're proud of me?

LINUS: I don't know what to say…

ALORA: What is this, 1952?

LINUS: I've never done this before.

ALORA: Well in the future you know not to say that.

LINUS: *(Caveman voice.)* Strong woman…make babies…make boy to carry on name. *(Beat.)* You know, I've never held a baby before.

ALORA: *(Disbelieving.)* What?

LINUS: It's true. I've never picked up a person shorter than five feet tall.

ALORA: Of course you have…

LINUS: Nope.

ALORA: You've held plenty of…

LINUS: When?

ALORA: I don't know…

LINUS: Name a time…

ALORA: What's-his-name's kid…

LINUS: I didn't…

ALORA: At that party…

LINUS: You did.

ALORA: I saw you.

LINUS: You didn't.

ALORA: You didn't?

LINUS: Nope.

ALORA: Never?

LINUS: They freak me out. Always have.

ALORA: What?

LINUS: They smell pretty…

ALORA: Yeah.

LINUS: And then they cry.

ALORA: Sometimes.

LINUS: A lot.

ALORA: How do you know.

LINUS: I don't know. I can only imagine.

ALORA: Well we know all about you and your imagination now don't we?

(Silence.)

(Image: Sandwiches with their crusts cut off fall gently in the sky.)

ALORA: I'm so sorry.

LINUS: That was rude.

(She grabs his head and hugs it.)

ALORA: I'm sorry, I'm sorry, I'm sorry.

LINUS: Stop. It's okay. *(Back to what they were talking about, trying to shake the last comment, the sandwiches disappear.)* And I guarantee that the second I touch it…

ALORA: A baby…

LINUS: It…it will freak out and cry hysterically…and I won't know how to stop it, and I don't know how I'm gonna deal with that.

ALORA: Oh, you'll be fine.

LINUS: You don't know that.

ALORA: His chin.

LINUS: Whose?

ALORA: All you have to do is tickle under his chin and he'll stop crying.

LINUS: You're patronizing me.

ALORA: I'm serious.

LINUS: I'm not that gullible.

(She tickles under his chin.)

ALORA: See.

LINUS: Stop.

(She goes after him some more.)

LINUS: Seriously.

(She tackles him and tickles under his chin. He breaks and starts laughing. She wrestles him to the ground.)

LINUS: My god... you want me to torture him.

ALORA: You baby.

LINUS: Shatter his psyche into submission?

(LINUS and ALORA kiss a gentle and meaningful kiss.)

LINUS: A baby, huh?

ALORA: A baby.

LINUS: Holy shit. *(Beat.)* What if he's inherently evil?

ALORA: Stop it. *(Beat.)* I'm proud of you too.

(The blue phone siren flashes. The phone rings and LINUS turns his head to look. He does not see ALORA experience a sharp pain to her abdomen. Sound: A gasp.)

(Image: A red balloon inflates and is popped.)

ALORA: Don't answer that.

(The phone stops ringing. He sees her pain, but pretends he doesn't.)

LINUS: I have to... *(Indicating that he has to leave.)* Reality calls.

ALORA: I know...

(LINUS puts on his fedora and picks up his briefcase. He goes to the door. The time clock counts down to around 17 million.)

(Image: Looking down from a building to a busy street, and a brief flash of the Time-Life photograph of the Empire State Building jumper embedded in a car.)

(LINUS hugs her back and says:)

LINUS: I'm happy.

ALORA: Really?

LINUS: I could drop dead right now and be the happiest man alive.

(LINUS leaves. Silence. ALORA tucks her head into her hands to avoid the world. The time clock speeds forward to 16.5 million-ish. The phone rings. ALORA's face looks to the world. The sound of a balloon squeaking as it is being twisted into an animal.)

SONG: LE BALLOON INSTRUCTION OR DE FAIRE UN BALLON ANIMAUX

(A cool smooth jazz standard. The sound of a balloon squeaking gets louder.)

ALORA: *(In song.)* STEP 1: INFLATE A BALLOON.

(Image: LITTLE ALORA tries to blow up a balloon.)

STEP 2: HAVE SOMEONE INFLATE IT FOR YOU.

(Image: Something indistinguishably red slowly grows in size.)

NEXT: FOLD IT A THIRD OF THE WAY DOWN AND TWIST.

(Image: LITTLE ALORA watches the red take over the world.)

NUMBER 4: DO THE SAME WITH THE OTHER SIDE.
AND VOILÀ. A WEENIE DOG.

(Image: We see that LITTLE ALORA is looking at a giant weenie dog balloon.)

NOW. STEP FIVE. TAKE A PIN. POP THE MIDDLE.

(LITTLE ALORA watches a giant pin pierce the red. The middle deflates.)

WATCH IT SLOWLY DEFLATE. AND LIKE A COOL MIRACLE THE HEAD AND FEET STAY ALIVE.

(The sound of a drum roll and cymbal crash. The phone rings. Pause. The laugh of doctors.)

(Image: A sea of eyes without eyelashes.)

(The phone rings, it rings again. The sound of the inside of an MRI.)

(Image: A flash of a needle. A faceless man in a white coat.)

(The sound of the squeak is amplified.)

(LITTLE ALORA watches as the head and feet slowly deflate into nothing.)

ALORA: Shut up, shut up!

(OWEN, NEAL, and ARTHUR enter as if on roller skates to trumpeting fanfare. ARTHUR picks up the phone and holds it out to the OTHERS who yell into it.)

OWEN and NEAL: We don't want any!

(ARTHUR hangs up the phone.)

ALORA: Thank you.

ARTHUR: Don't mention it.

(An awkward silence.)

NEAL: Well…

OWEN: Umm…

ARTHUR: If there's

OWEN: Nothing else.

NEAL: If there's nothing else I guess…

(The THREE awkwardly begin to walk away.)

ALORA: Please don't go.

(They stop and turn back in unison. Synchronized swimmers.)

ARTHUR: We're listening…

(Image: Neon light turns warm. Hospital curtains open up to reveal gentle sunlight through a window.)

ALORA: I'm going to be a mother.

(Image: ALORA speed-motion aging from present to age two, and back again.)

ARTHUR: *(Dryly.)* Congratulations.

ALORA: Aren't you happy for me?

OWEN: What do you expect.

ALORA: I don't know if I can do this alone.

(LINUS enters, puts his fedora on the rack, takes out a blue elephant, and puts it next to the phone. He takes the hat off the rack and puts it back on his head. He exits again. The time on the time clock whooshes down to 16,250,000.)

OWEN: You have *him*.

NEAL: What can we do?

OWEN: Wait. No. You just expect us to…

ARTHUR: Owen.

OWEN: No. You're thinking it too.

ARTHUR: Owen…

(OWEN cowers in fear.)

ARTHUR: *(To ALORA.)* You understand our reservations.

ALORA: Yes.

ARTHUR: The last time we helped it didn't exactly end very well for us, now did it?

ALORA: No. I guess not.

NEAL: Merry Christmas, by the way. I never got a chance to say it.

ALORA: I'm sorry.

OWEN: *(Aggressively.)* So what makes you think…

(ARTHUR stops OWEN with a look. OWEN is terrified.)

ARTHUR: So, what makes you think we would be willing to risk being thrown away like that again?

ALORA: Because it's not for me. Not really.

OWEN: What exactly are you asking?

ALORA: He only sees things as they are…not how they could be.

ARTHUR: He, who?

OWEN: Don't say it.

ALORA: Linus.

OWEN: There it is.

ARTHUR: Ahh jeeze.

ALORA: He can't even see Sam.

NEAL: Whatever. Let's do it.

OWEN: *(To NEAL.)* You've got a lot of nerve.

NEAL: I do.

OWEN: You do not.

ARTHUR: He does too. We all do.

OWEN: Don't you remember what he did?

ALORA: Linus didn't do anything. I did it.

OWEN: He made us go away.

ALORA: I did.

OWEN: Because of him.

ARTHUR: Because you didn't think you needed us anymore.

ALORA: Yes. Apparently I was wrong.

(ARTHUR touches her cheek, kisses her forehead, and gives her a hug.)

ARTHUR: We missed you, girl.

(LINUS enters. He does not take his coat or hat off. He opens his briefcase and places a blue elephant next to the first one.)

ALORA: *(Whispering so LINUS does not hear.)* Please do this for me.

ARTHUR: Vote.

(ARTHUR's and NEAL's hands go up.)

OWEN: And the idiots have it!

(ALORA secretively smiles gratefully. LINUS pulls a yellow raincoat from his briefcase and holds it up. ALORA turns away.)

OWEN: No "thank you," huh?

NEAL: She can't say anything.

OWEN: Shut up, Neal.

NEAL: Shut up, Owen.

(OWEN bites NEAL on the arm.)

NEAL: It's throw-down time.

(They fight. The time clock reads 15,200,000. LINUS still holds the raincoat to her.)

LINUS: We should get out of here, you know? Go for a walk, take a vacation from the couch.

ALORA: Where do you want to go?

(The BROTHERS fade into the background but never leave.)

LINUS: I don't know…the park? Get some fresh air.

ALORA: In the world…The universe. Where do you want to go?

LINUS: I don't know. You know I'm not so good at this.

ALORA: You can do it.

LINUS: What do you want me to say? I want to go to the stars? Sit on the moon and look at the world below?! I want to go to the park across the street, or the grocery store or to do the laundry…with you. What do you think about that? That's where I want to go.

ALORA: This woman was walking her dog and she stopped on a manhole cover.

LINUS: What are you talking about?

ALORA: And the dog. It was a girl dog. A…a…a…

LINUS: Bitch.

ALORA: A shitzu, and it got charged with like a million volts. And that was it. She was gone.

LINUS: So what? She was a dog.

ALORA: I'm not talking about the dog.

LINUS: Okay.

ALORA: There was a story on the news and one of the newscasters laughed because it was just a dog and you could hear the mocking in their voices and they never stopped to think that the woman behind them…the woman whose dog was torched, was gone.

LINUS: What do you mean she was gone?

ALORA: When the dog died, the woman was a step behind death. Her little shitzu got a billion volts a step ahead of her owner.

LINUS: It was just a dog.

ALORA: Could have been a goldfish. It's not the point.

LINUS: A goldfish walking down the street on a leash.

(Image: A goldfish on a leash in an electric chair.)

ALORA: She was a step away from death.

LINUS: Well, staying in here can't help that.

ALORA: I can't take us away anymore. Don't you get it? I can't do it anymore. You take me to the stars…

LINUS: What's wrong with the park?

ALORA: Take me into the stars.

(Slowly they come together, hold hands, and look like they are about to jump into the night sky. ALORA pulls his hand and puts it on her stomach.)

LINUS: I can't. I'm sorry.

(The blue phone siren flashes.)

LINUS: *(Ashamed.)* I can't.

ALORA: Please.

(Another blue phone siren flash. Time winds down fast with every MRI sound.)

LINUS: *(Flustered.)* Where's my hat? *(Looks for his hat, which he does not realize is on top of his head.)*

(The time clock continues to wind down. It reads 14,515,000, and almost stands still through the next song.)

SONG: WORM FOOD

ALORA: *(In song.)* SIMPLE? REMEMBER HOW TO HOLD ON TO A HAND SO SMALL.

(Image: A thumb pushes a call button again and again. A sideways view to a hospital room door. Big soft white shoes stream by the open door but do not enter.)

FORGET YOUR HEAD IF IT WEREN'T AT-TACHED TO A NERVOUS TICK

(Image: A thumb on a call button franti-cally pushing. Vomit on a little girl's chest. Tear down an emotionless eye.)

WHO SAID PUSHIN' DAISES CAN BE DONE SOLO?

(Image: Blue puffy clouds float on a hospital wall. A bad loop. Goes and stops and goes and stops from the same place.)

IT TAKES A VILLAGE TO PACKAGE AND PREPARE WORM FOOD.

(Image: LITTLE ALORA with vomit on her chin. A red balloon droops on its slack string.)

(LINUS collects his things. ALORA speaks as if nothing has happened...sup-pressing.)

ALORA: Tell me the date.

LINUS: The twenty-fifth.

ALORA: Of what?

LINUS: June.

ALORA: It's been three months.

LINUS: A Christmas baby.

ALORA: Almost here.

LINUS: I guess.

(Beat.)

ALORA: You gave me a macaroni Madonna the first Christmas we lived together.

LINUS: I loved that thing.

ALORA: Did you know that my brother Neal shot himself out of a cannon that very morning. He set it all up in our backyard. He had a tent and he tore down part of the neighbor's fence...he said they wouldn't notice.

NEAL: And they wouldn't have noticed the fence being gone if someone—Arthur—hadn't kidnapped their dog.

ARTHUR: She needed to be taught some manners.

ALORA: Neal stole all the sheets in the house to make the tent.

ARTHUR: It just kept yapping and yapping...

NEAL: The final look was far less dramatic with Owen's Shirley Temple sheets...

OWEN: Those were classics.

NEAL: A six-year-old tap-dancing girl...

OWEN: They were worth a fortune. You ruined them.

ARTHUR: Yap, yap, yap.

NEAL: But hey, if that's how you like to fall asleep at night, who am I to judge?

OWEN: Shut up, Neal.

NEAL: Up yours, Owen.

(OWEN and ALORA sing together the first verse of "On the Good Ship Lollipop." ALORA tap dances to the upbeat melody, while OWEN's version is a painful lament. OWEN continues the deeply tragic rendition behind ARTHUR's following words:)

ARTHUR: Yap, yap, yap…Making the decision to shave the left half of that shitzu, rather than the back end was one of the most difficult—and rewarding—decisions I've ever made.

NEAL: You ruined my cannon!

ARTHUR: Bring it!

(NEAL and ARTHUR attack one another in slow motion. NEAL throws a punch and ARTHUR catches it in mid-air.)

ARTHUR: Now what?

(ARTHUR pulls NEAL into a headlock. OWEN jumps into the fray for no better reason than a challenge. Biting and scratching is the norm.)

ARTHUR: Why are you hitting yourself? Why are you hitting yourself?

(An arm flies.)

OWEN: My lip! My lip!

ALORA: Under that tent Neal had made a cannon. A real live cannon out of trash cans, probably two hundred pounds of duct tape and gunpowder. Was going to bring Christmas morning in with a bang. Neal made it across the sixteen Christmas trees that he had stolen from someplace…

NEAL: I do not steal. I liberate.

ALORA: And landed in a pile of empty, gift-wrapped boxes.

(Suddenly NEAL steps out of the fight and addresses LINUS who can't see or hear him. NEAL raises his shirt and shows a scar that runs from nipple to shoulder blade.)

NEAL: One hundred sixty-four stitches. Running from right here, all the way around back here. Hurt like a mother…

OWEN: Pansy!

(OWEN performs a great leaping tackle, taking NEAL to the ground.)

ALORA: He was a little beat up. I haven't seen them since that Christmas. The one you gave me the macaroni Madonna. Not until…

LINUS: When?

ALORA: They're back.

(The sound of a cannon being shot.)

ALORA: Ta da!

LINUS: Are they back for a reason?

(The BOYS stop fighting.)

ALORA: What's the date?

LINUS: The twenty-fifth.

ALORA: Of what?

LINUS: Are you okay?

ALORA: The twenty-fifth of what?

LINUS: Of June.

ALORA: (Holding her abdomen.) It'll be over by Christmas.

(LINUS takes out the can and holds it to ALORA's abdomen. The sound of an MRI.)

ARTHUR: We'll show him the ropes. Don't worry Linus. You too. We'll show you how do Christmas up right. We're in it together now. For the long haul.

OWEN: He can't hear you.

ARTHUR: I know he can't now. But he can.

LINUS: (His head bolts up from the can.) How do you carry a kid and a tree on a subway?

ARTHUR: We'll be right there…

LINUS: Alora. How do we carry a kid and a tree on a subway?

NEAL: We can rig a little somethin' somthin'.

LINUS: I mean we could barely get through the turnstile, and add to that a…well…the amount of sap that we had in our hair…

(A faint phone ring in the background. The three BROTHERS freeze.)

ALORA: And when the cannon went off smoke poured out and billowed up to the sky. And Neal shot straight through it. He would never admit to it, but I saw something…he was wearing a cape. A baby blue one with white puffs on it. The children's wing was painted like that when I was a little girl. Like the sky…I'm telling you right now he won't admit to it…but I know him. He wears it under his shirt. That cape has been with him wherever he has been since that day…

NEAL: You don't just throw away something that can carry you around the world just like that. (Beat.) I wish you could have seen it.

(The phone begins to ring a bit more loudly. The BROTHERS look at the phone with a jerk.)

ALORA: He flew through that smoke and he shot into the air and across the yard in his baby blue cape. He shot

farther than the eye can see…I haven't seen them since that day…god that Christmas was warm. It was like seventy-five degrees, remember? Nothing could touch me then. I had you. I didn't think I would need them anymore.

(A louder ring…The siren on top of the phone starts flashing. LINUS walks to the phone.)

LINUS: Do you need them now?

ALORA: They're my brothers.

LINUS: And they're back again.

ALORA: That's right. But they're not here for me, not really.

LINUS: I have to go. I have to…Where is my hat?

(LINUS exits. ALORA sits and rocks in a chair. The time clock slows to a halt at 9,873,000.)

SONG: A TARGET ON MY ASS

(A country ditty.)

(Image: Toxic sludge oozing. A grid projected on skin.)

ALORA: (Singing.) GRANDMA CARRIED A
     PIANO OUT OF A BURNING HOUSE
A MOTHER DABBED HER DAUGHTER'S
     MOUTH OF BLOOD

(Image: Sonogram/X-ray. The flat image gains dimension and contour—LITTLE ALORA stands on one of its peaks. Red clouds rush by at hyper-speed.)

AND I WADED THROUGH THE BILE
TO BE CROWNED DROP-DEAD GORGEOUS
     GIRL.

(Image: A pitying face. A laughing boy.)

THEY'RE SADDLING UP CLOSE AGAIN,
     SNEAKING A HOWDY-DO

LO JACKED, TRACKED, THEY HAD ME IN
THEIR SIGHTS.

*(Image: A tattoo gun painting a red 0.
A crowd roars, "Olé!" A balloon floats
into the air. A red-nosed clown throws a
bucket of confetti-water and laughs.)*

AIN'T NOTHIN' THAT'S FOREVER
DROP-DEAD GORGEOUS GIRL AIN'T
READY.

*(Image: The tattoo gun continues. We see
it is drawing a target on young ALORA's
bare back. A red balloon pops above her.
Rubber pieces fall.)*

(SAM appears.)

SAM: Is it time yet?

ALORA: No. I don't think quite yet.

SAM: He still won't be able to see me?

ALORA: I don't think so.

SAM: But he might?

ALORA: I don't think so.

SAM: Are you all right? Do you want
some of my cookie?

ALORA: Ohh…you're so sweet. I'm
okay, honey.

(SAM touches her face.)

SAM: I love you, Mommy.

ALORA: I love you too, Sam.

SAM: Love you too, Mommy. Love you
too, Mommy.

ALORA: You're sweet. I have to go to
sleep now.

*(The world dims. The time clock starts
again at 9,873,000. LINUS enters. He
takes off his coat and pulls a blue elephant
from his briefcase. SAM steps directly in
front of him. LINUS looks around the*

*stage. He does not see SAM, who sadly
exits. LINUS sees ALORA and thinks
the worst.)*

LINUS: No, no, no, no.

*(Image: Sandwiches with their crusts cut
off fall gently in the sky.)*

*(LINUS rushes to ALORA and holds her.
She does not move.)*

LINUS: Hello? Is there anybody out
there? If you are out there, if you
could come now, I could really use you
now. *(Begins singing a slow desperate
"Summertime." He breaks into a laugh or
a cry, we can't tell which.)*

*(Three FIGURES appear behind LINUS.
He can feel them there but does not turn to
see them. The sound of a spotlight clanking
on. ARTHUR is in a sharp pool of light.
Sequins everywhere. OWEN and NEAL
get hit by two more spots. They are The
Pips. OWEN, NEAL, and ARTHUR pick
up singing "Summertime" where LINUS
is unable to continue.)*

LINUS: You're them, aren't you?

ARTHUR: We are they.

LINUS: You're real.

ARTHUR: Real as real can be,
Daddy-O.

LINUS: What's that supposed to
mean?

OWEN: Yeah Arthur…what is that
supposed to mean?

NEAL: I'm curious about that too.

ARTHUR: I don't know. But it's right,
right?

OWEN: Pretty much. NEAL: Yeah.

LINUS: Is she okay?

(Long pause.)

LINUS: Guys!

OWEN: I don't want to talk about it.

LINUS: *(Turns to see the BROTHERS for the first time.)* She's not…

ARTHUR: Nope. Still kickin'.

LINUS: What the hell why are The Pips inside my head?

NEAL: What's that smell?

OWEN: Gears grinding.

ARTHUR: Give the guy a break.

NEAL: Probably feels like he was shot out of a cannon.

LINUS: Was that you?

NEAL: One hundred sixty-four stitches. Running from right here all the way back to here. Hurt like a mother.

OWEN: Pansy.

(OWEN performs a great leaping tackle. They fight.)

ARTHUR: She's getting tired.

LINUS: I know. I can see it too. I'm not blind.

ARTHUR: Take her away from here.

LINUS: I can't. She won't go.

ARTHUR: Take her where she wants to go.

LINUS: I can't get there.

ARTHUR: I know you don't know me— or those two numbskulls. But we know Alora from a time when she needed help more than anything else in the world. She's asked us to come back. She wants us here with you.

LINUS: Why?

(Image: A shooting star.)

ARTHUR: You see that?

LINUS: *(Looks up… too late to see.)* What?

ARTHUR: A shooting…

(Image: Another shooting star across the sky.)

ARTHUR: Look. Another.

LINUS: You don't understand.

ARTHUR: What don't I understand?

LINUS: I don't do that.

ARTHUR: What?

LINUS: I don't go wishing on things.

ARTHUR: Who said anything about wishing?

(LINUS looks up at the time clock overhead. It races downward. He looks at ALORA.)

LINUS: I was little. I was in the backyard and I had a sword and was fighting these goblins. They were like three feet taller than I was, and their breath was almost lethal. Not quite, but almost. It was enough to hit you and knock you off your feet, and then the dark green leather-faced bastards get the upper hand, and you would have to fight them from your back and hope not to get hurt before kicking them off you and shove them all the way back to…

ARTHUR: By the castle?

LINUS: Across the yard by the swing set. And then they would come back in at you, but you'd have your footing back and would meet them halfway running full out and with a roar you'd charge to battle. And just as you were killing one of them off, Mom would come out and announce that sandwiches are ready and into the house you would go. This battle had been going on for over a week. Well, one day I had 'em. I had the fuckers by the short hairs, you know? And they were on the run and I chased them down. Over the hills and through the valley. In and out of cities. When they turned to battle, I slaughtered another one of the pack, and then kept after them running and running until with one last blow I slashed the largest of the goblins and watched him fall to his knees and then slowly sink to the ground. Dead. And that was it. There were no more. I had won the war. That final battle must have taken me hours and covered a good bit of ground. And I looked from the dead face of that last goblin and raised my head to the sky to let out a victory cry, and I saw a sea of shining stars. They were real stars. Not just the imaginary ones floating above that goblin. And when I looked back down, and saw a stick in my hand, and the goblin wasn't there anymore, but I was looking at cobblestone beneath where he just disappeared from...I didn't know where I was. I was four years old. I had never been outside in the dark before by myself. I had never been anywhere alone, ever, unless it was in my backyard. And I remember. Standing there, terrified as I looked around looking for anything I recognized. And as scared as I was...and my god I was. The one thing that still haunts me...I felt my stomach growling. Why didn't my mother call me in for sandwiches? She always called me in.

(The BROTHERS have faded into the background, but never leave the stage. It's dark.)

(Image: A shooting star blazes behind two FIGURES standing above LINUS.)

(SUNSHINE and NOODLE appear. They are two bad-ass motherfuckers. NOODLE caries a foot-long ham sandwich. She does not take a bite of it, but frequently smells it.)

SUNSHINE: But she did call you in for sandwiches. Didn't she?

(The sound of dead air...like the inside of an airplane.)

NOODLE: I've never been big on peanut butter and jelly. How 'bout you?

LINUS: I'm sorry?

NOODLE: Why?

SUNSHINE: You didn't answer my question.

LINUS: Who/are you?

NOODLE: Again...

SUNSHINE: She did call you in, didn't she?

LINUS: I don't know what you're talking about.

SUNSHINE: Uh huh. So anyway. There's this guy.

NOODLE: A few of 'em actually...

SUNSHINE: And they said that there's this thing that we had to do. Can't be sure who these guys are...

NOODLE: Peanut-butter-and-jelly kind of guys.

SUNSHINE: But they tell us that the bell has gone off, you know? That the alarm has been sounded.

LINUS: What kind of alarm?

NOODLE: Ham, now that's a good sandwich.

SUNSHINE: An alarm.

LINUS: What kind?

NOODLE: Honey roasted.

SUNSHINE: I don't know…a really loud one.

LINUS: That's not what I meant.

NOODLE: With a little mayo.

SUNSHINE: A really loud one that carries a great and incredibly painful force when wielded correctly. Got me?

LINUS: Yes.

SUNSHINE: We understand each other?

LINUS: Yes.

SUNSHINE: Yes what?

LINUS: Yes, sir.

SUNSHINE: Better. You believe this guy?

NOODLE: Don't look at me…if it was up to me we'd have packed our bags and left for good 'bout thirty, maybe thirty-five years back…stopped off at a bodega on the way out of Dodge to…

SUNSHINE: Well all right then. Now. Where was I?

LINUS: The alarm.

SUNSHINE: Right. The alarm… *(Beat.)* Christ. I lost it.

NOODLE: You're okay, baby.

SUNSHINE: He interrupted my flow, Noodle.

NOODLE: You'll get it back, Sunshine.

LINUS: If I could just ask. Who are you?

SUNSHINE: You believe this guy?

NOODLE: Did you know that 1.3 billion hogs are slaughtered worldwide every year. For ham sandwiches and pulled pork sandwiches and for pork chop sandwiches.

SUNSHINE: Why do you torture yourself like that?

(A brief, but intense kiss.)

NOODLE: Now this next part I want to make sure you hear, understand me? You listening?

LINUS: Yes.

SUNSHINE: You listening good?

LINUS: I'm listening.

(NOODLE stares him down.)

LINUS: Yes ma'am, I'm listening good.

NOODLE: These guys say…

SUNSHINE: The peanut butter and jelly guys say that if we do this thing for them…

NOODLE: Well, it'll be mutually beneficial.

SUNSHINE: Now you have to understand that this thing…

NOODLE: So this thing that we have to do…

SUNSHINE: Well this thing…

NOODLE: This thing ain't such an easy thing.

LINUS: And what does this thing have to do with me?

SUNSHINE: You're joking, right. Just wanted to interrupt the flow?

NOODLE: You just wanted to see what we would do, right? That's what you were up to?

(SUNSHINE pulls out a large stick…)

NOODLE: You just wanted to see what we would do?

LINUS: No, no. I was kidding. It was a joke.

NOODLE: I'm not big on laughs.

SUNSHINE: No more fucking jokes, got me?

LINUS: Yes.

SUNSHINE: Yes what?

LINUS: Yes, Sunshine.

SUNSHINE: *(Lunges with the stick.)* What?!

LINUS: Yes, sir. I'm sorry, sir. It was a mistake.

SUNSHINE: Hey, relax man. We all make mistakes. *(He holds up the stick.)*

NOODLE: What's that?

LINUS: I don't know.

SUNSHINE: Come on, after all we've been through, there's no need to lie.

LINUS: I wasn't…

NOODLE: Don't lie to me.

LINUS: It's a stick. *(Pause.)* A sword.

NOODLE: Specifics.

SUNSHINE: Just a sword?

LINUS: Uh huh. *(Pause—then inaudible.)* Excalibur.

SUNSHINE: What was that?

NOODLE: I'm sorry?

LINUS: *(Almost audible.)* Excalibur.

SUNSHINE and NOODLE: Speak up, son.

LINUS: *(Loudly.)* Excalibur.

SUNSHINE: When did you find out that your mother had died?

LINUS: What?

NOODLE: You heard her.

LINUS: That's none of your business.

SUNSHINE: 'Cause the way we heard it…

NOODLE: It wasn't really the way anyone else knows it.

LINUS: Who the hell are you?

SUNSHINE and NOODLE: What, don't you recognize us?

LINUS: I don't have to tell you anything.

NOODLE: I heard you did her yourself.

LINUS: What?

SUNSHINE: That's the word.

NOODLE: Heard that you went in there and pushed her down.

LINUS: She didn't die from a fall.

SUNSHINE: You didn't know that.

LINUS: Not at the time. But. I know how it happened.

SUNSHINE: I understand.

NOODLE: It must have been real hard seeing it.

LINUS: I didn't see it! By the time someone found me and took me back home it was all over.

NOODLE: So you didn't see anything?

LINUS: No.

SUNSHINE: You didn't see her body lying there?

LINUS: No.

SUNSHINE: On the floor of the kitchen?

LINUS: No.

NOODLE: Next to the sandwiches.

(LINUS sees ALORA folded on the floor. LINUS speaking more to ALORA.)

(Image: Sandwiches slowly falling like rain.)

LINUS: I was battling. And it was time. She always came to get me after a little while. Every day she would come out and she would call, "Lunch time, Linus." And I would play for another five minutes just so I could hear her come out again and call for me. And then I'd run to the sliding door and she would hug me and say, "I was about to give up on you" and then I'd go in and sit at the table and she would tell me to go wash my hands and I would go in and wash them and sit back down and then she would kiss me on the top of my head and put the plate in front of me and tell me not to eat too fast, but never tell me to stop when I was and with my mouth still full I would jump off my chair, hug her leg and run out the door to find my sword.

NOODLE: But she never called you in that day.

LINUS: She did too. "Lunch time, Liney." She calls me. *(Pause.)* But she never comes back out. I wait for her to come back out to call for me again. I wait for almost an hour before going

back into the kitchen. I take my sword, even though I know it isn't allowed in the house. And she is there. I can't see her face. Her hair is pushed over it. And the sandwiches are...all over the ground, and she doesn't stand up to give me a hug, but I give her one anyway. I have to get on my knees, but I give her one, and then I wash my hands without even being told and I sit and wait for her to give me the sandwiches, but she doesn't. She doesn't move...I climb down onto the floor and lie down next to her and I hug her leg, and I push open the sliding door and I fight an epic battle that pushes the goblins out of the yard forever.

SUNSHINE: And that was the last time...

LINUS: That I imagined.

NOODLE: That's right.

SUNSHINE: It's wake up time, baby.

(The phone siren flashes blue.)

SUNSHINE: It would be a shame to lose her forever.

(The phone siren flashes blue.)

LINUS: I have to ask you to leave now.

SUNSHINE: There sure are some beautiful stars out there, aren't there?

NOODLE: There sure are, Sunshine.

(SUNSHINE and NOODLE stroll off stage. LINUS gets down on the floor next to ALORA and hugs her leg. The BROTHERS emerge from the background.)

ARTHUR: There sure are.

OWEN: Oh. Did you see that one?

ARTHUR: Sweet fancy Moses.

NEAL: Careful Owen, don't get hit by it.

(ARTHUR laughs at OWEN.)

OWEN: Shut up Neal.

NEAL: Watch out! Here it comes!!!

NEAL and ARTHUR: AHHHH!!!

LINUS: I don't want them in my head, do you understand me? Take them back. I don't want them here anymore. I need you to listen to me.

(Image: Shooting stars chase the BROTHERS off stage.)

ALORA: What do you see when you close your eyes?

LINUS: Nothing.

(Image: A faceless doctor hangs a pruney red balloon over a bed.)

ALORA: I can still hear my mother's voice from when I was two. It was supposed to be happy. And the sounds of her muffled cries at the side of the crib. Dissonant shrinking sounds muffled into the folds of a blanket. When no one could help, and the doctors hung those sad red balloons that only reminded you you couldn't move. In the middle of the night…they came.

LINUS: Why are they with me now?

ALORA: Chemistry equations.

LINUS: I'm sorry?

ALORA: Do you know how to balance chemistry equations? Like add methane and oxygen and that comes up with carbon dioxide and steam?

LINUS: What?

ALORA: I had an exam in chemistry and I didn't get it. It was like this mental block. But these three idiots show up ten minutes into class. Just walk in and pick up an exam at the front of the room and sit down right beside me and don't say a word until there were like five minutes left. And then one by one I heard it.

OWEN'S VOICE: Hydrogen chloride

NEAL'S VOICE: Sulfuric acid

NEAL'S and OWEN'S VOICES: *(Overlapping.)* Hydrochloric acid, nitrate, magnesium oxide, sodium sulphate

OWEN'S VOICE: Etcetera.

ALORA: And then they were gone…

LINUS: Just like that?

ALORA: They come when we need help.

LINUS: You're not telling me something.

(Image: The stars melt like teardrops.)

LINUS: What's happening?

(A distant cry from a baby—the essence of a whimper. He puts his hand on her stomach. She winces in pain. The siren on the phone flashes blue once. Long pause. It flashes again.)

LINUS: Look at me.

(She does.)

LINUS: It's back isn't it?

ALORA: Take me away from here.

(LINUS puts the tin cup to his ear. There is no sound. A smile.)

LINUS: I just kill goblins.

ALORA: Take me away.

(LINUS runs to his briefcase and pulls a yellow raincoat from it. His eye is caught by something else in the case. He drops the coat, reaches in, and pulls a blue cape with white clouds. He shows it to ALORA.)

LINUS: We can go anywhere you want.

(Image: Clouds and blue sky appear.)

ALORA: You really do see them. You'll never be alone.

LINUS: I could never be alone…I have you. You're always going to be here.

(The whoosh of a heartbeat, or maybe space sounds, we can't tell which.)

(Image: A shooting star traces across the sky behind him.)

LINUS: Flight 4-1-5 departing beta alpha zulu.

(Sound: The crackling response from the other side of the moon.)

(Image: Hundreds of shooting stars light up the sky.)

(LINUS closes his eyes and makes a wish. ALORA leaps on to LINUS's back and laughs.)

ALORA: Come here.

LINUS: *(Laughing.)* Somebody help me! A squidapus from the planet Bletch.

ALORA: I got you.

(ALORA lets out a small gasp of pain and they stop.)

LINUS: Oh my god, are you okay?

ALORA: *(Pain on ALORA's face turns to a smile.)* I think I felt it move.

(He puts his hand to her stomach.)

(Image: The stars swim around them. They are floating in the night sky.)

ALORA: It's so quiet…

LINUS: Why don't more people investigate the possibility of space travel?

ALORA: That's a good question.

LINUS: It's clean. It's safe.

ALORA: A little cool.

LINUS: Sure. A little cool, but bring a light jacket for when you fall into a planet's shadow.

ALORA: Not so much oxygen…

LINUS: But the views!

ALORA: And the peace. I could stay up here forever…with you.

LINUS: Right back at ya. I'll race you!

ALORA: You're getting cocky. Use that thing upstairs once and…

LINUS: To that star!

ALORA: I don't know if I can.

LINUS: All the way to Polaris and back again.

ALORA: What do I get?

LINUS: Excuse me?

ALORA: When I win, what are you gonna give me?

LINUS: What do you want? *(Beat.)* Do you believe what they say about dogs and their owners?

ALORA: That they absolutely look alike?

LINUS: You think the same is true about…you know. *(Indicating her stomach.)*

ALORA: It better not be an insurance adjuster!

LINUS: Ha. Ha. Will it like to, you know…travel?

ALORA: I don't know.

LINUS: I think so. I think it'll like it up here, don't you?

ALORA: Yeah. I do. It's amazing what can happen in nine months, isn't it?

LINUS: Come on. Up to Polaris and back.

ALORA: I need to lay down now. I'm sorry. It's beautiful up here, but I need to lay down.

(LINUS helps ALORA over to a place where she can lie down. He stays with her a moment and strokes her arm and back. He stands and grabs his hat and briefcase. He walks to leave, but does not go out. He stands for a moment before returning into the room. The phone siren flashes blue. He kisses ALORA on the head.)

LINUS: Are you okay?

ALORA: I just need to sleep.

LINUS: Okay. I'll see you soon. *(To the BROTHERS.)* Gentlemen!

(ARTHUR speedwalks across the stage, his shoes steaming, and exits. OWEN enters with a stopwatch. NEAL follows.)

NEAL: He doesn't have a chance.

OWEN: The numbers do not lie.

(ARTHUR returns with a large diaper. Shoes still steaming.)

ARTHUR: TIME.

OWEN: Eight minutes fifty-six seconds.

NEAL: No!

ARTHUR: Yes! That's a new land speed record ladies and gentlemen. Forty-eight states. Eight minutes fifty-six seconds.

NEAL: Hah! You missed two.

ARTHUR: What the hell are you talking about, I missed two?

NEAL: I mean what I said. Hawaii and Alaska.

ARTHUR: You said contiguous.

NEAL: I did not!

OWEN: You did too.

NEAL: I would NEVER have said consipuous...what's the point? Anyone can run around and touch each of the congenius states in ten minutes. TEN minutes...

ARTHUR: You lost. What can I say?

NEAL: I did not lose.

LINUS: Gentlemen. You're never going to believe this...I'm gonna have a kid.

OWEN: We're way ahead of you.

ARTHUR: How much time do we have?

(They all look to the time clock which reads somewhere around 7,257,600.)

OWEN: Talk about a land speed record.

ARTHUR: You might need my shoes for this.

(He takes one off and steam pours out of it.)

LINUS: That's okay. Thank you.

ARTHUR: Your choice. But the offer stands.

LINUS: Thank...

OWEN: Litmus test...

NEAL: Litmus!

ARTHUR: Litmus! Neal...you're up.

NEAL: What?

ARTHUR: Neal.

NEAL: No way.

ARTHUR: You lost.

NEAL: I did not.

ARTHUR: So then you concede?

NEAL: Absolutely!

ARTHUR: Good.

NEAL: What?

OWEN: *(Opens a diaper for NEAL to step in.)* Get in.

NEAL: Never!

ARTHUR: So then you concede?

NEAL: Absolutely.

ARTHUR: Right.

OWEN: *(Opens a diaper for NEAL to step in.)* Get in.

NEAL: But...

ARTHUR: You concede.

NEAL: I concede! I concede!

(OWEN opens a diaper for NEAL to step in.)

ARTHUR and OWEN: We're waiting...

NEAL: I know the truth, man. *(Gets into the diaper.)*

ARTHUR: Okay. So here's the deal. That man right there. That boob in the diaper. That's your kid.

LINUS: That's my...

OWEN: Your kid. Your little bundle of joy... Your little ankle biter... Your lawn-ape... Your... I don't know. Your kid.

NEAL: Waaah.

LINUS: This is a joke right.

ARTHUR: And there you are. Go give your sweet little boy a hug.

OWEN: But you haven't slept in a year so you can't see straight.

(OWEN blindfolds him.)

LINUS: Wait... wait what am I doing?

ARTHUR: Go and give baby a hug.

NEAL: I want Mommy!

LINUS: It's okay baby. *(He starts trying to find NEAL.)* Come here baby.

NEAL: In your dreams old man.

OWEN: Use your instincts.

ARTHUR: Just feel the direction your baby has gone. Find your baby. Remember. You're disoriented. You haven't slept. This is new. You're doing very well.

NEAL: Waaah.

LINUS: I'm coming after you!

NEAL: Come and get me you fuckin' pussy!

ARTHUR: Language!

LINUS: *(Flailing about.)* You just better watch out, 'cause when I catch up with you mister... you... you're... well... you got another think comin'...

NEAL: I want Mommy!

OWEN: Make him more disoriented...

(NEAL swiftly gives him a kick to the groin. LINUS falls to the ground. He lies beside ALORA in pain. ALL are silent.)

ARTHUR: Okay.

(Long pause.)

ARTHUR: So that was…Right then…

(The time clock winds down: 4,000,000.)

(Image: LINUS and ALORA side by side in real time as seen from above.)

LINUS: He said that it was either move to Wisconsin or turn down the extra cash. And I told him you know. I told him. That. Well I told him we were expecting and well, he caved!

ALORA: You told them?

LINUS: I did.

ALORA: It's real.

(The phone rings…siren flashes.)

LINUS: Don't answer that.

ALORA: Did you just say that?

LINUS: Yeah.

ALORA: *(Mocking.)* It could be important.

LINUS: It probably is.

ALORA: It's moving.

LINUS: Is she?

ALORA: Ahh…feel that?

LINUS: She's right here.

ALORA: Ahh… *(Beat.)* I saw her Linus.

LINUS: Little Samantha.

(Image: Raindrops fall up.)

ALORA: Little Samantha with her striped jeans under her princess dress kicking dirt at the little boys on the playground. And I'm with her and I make a big show of telling her not to

be mean to the little boys and pull her aside and give her the gentlest little hug of approval when none of the nannies are looking.

LINUS: And she'll come to me when I'm on the couch and she'll crawl up on my chest and push her head in and say I love you Daddy.

ALORA: And she won't ever get sick.

LINUS: And she'll take trips right here in the living room and I'll look at her and be happy to see your smile on her face.

ALORA: And even happier to see your frown, because she will be ours.

(ARTHUR and NEAL gently hum the "Battle Hymn of the Republic" as a lullaby. OWEN tells a story.)

OWEN: And Hansel and Gretel walked back to their mother and father's house. Back to the house of the parents who twice abandoned them in the woods. Left them for dead. Put them into the mouth of a horrible (yet kinda stupid) witch who wanted nothing else than to kill the little kids and eat them for dinner.

(Lights up on SAMANTHA. She sits on a scooter, TERRIFIED! Silence… EVERYBODY is perfectly still looking at the LITTLE GIRL. Pause.)

SAMANTHA: What the fuck! Ahhh!!!! *(She cries hysterically.)*

(The BROTHERS run into SAMANTHA's face and beg for her to be quiet.)

ARTHUR, NEAL, and OWEN: No, no, no, no, no…

SAMANTHA: *(Through her tears.)* You guys…you guys…you guys suck at this…

(A chorus robustly sings… "Glory, glory hallelujah." No lullaby…a call to arms.)

OWEN: I'm going to do it you hear me. I'm going to swim from here to Cape Verde to Sydney to San Fran around Gibraltar and into the mouth of the Keys. She shall have it. She will behold the comfort due unto her!

NEAL: I got a hundred bucks says he loses an arm to a great white.

ARTHUR: A thousand says a leg and nut.

SAMANTHA: A nut?

OWEN: Laugh… Laugh my good friends, but I shall prevail!

NEAL: I could do it.

ARTHUR: No one can.

SAMANTHA: I bet my dad could do it.

OWEN: You're both pathetic excuses for role models.

(He smacks them both with a swift smack. Three Stooges style. OWEN dashes off.)

NEAL: Wiseguy.

ARTHUR: Hey Moe.

SAMANTHA: *(Laughing hysterically.)* You guys are stupid.

(More Three Stooges business.)

SAMANTHA: *(Suddenly very grumpy.)* Too loud. *(A deep breath before a great scream.)*

ARTHUR: Please no.

NEAL: Sshhhh.

(A scream.)

NEAL: Wiseguy.

ARTHUR: Hey Moe.

NEAL: Wiseguy.

ARTHUR: Hey Moe.

SAMANTHA: Gentlemen please!

ARTHUR: Don't blame me.

NEAL: He started it!

SAMANTHA: Waaaah!

(ARTHUR and NEAL desperately perform a painful Three Stooges routine. OWEN enters with scuba mask and a one-piece bathing suit from the 1930s. He is sopping wet.)

OWEN: I swam all the way around the world for this.

(OWEN holds a golden, shining pacifier high above his head. A heavenly, "Ahhhh." SAMANTHA takes it and throws it. She stops crying and begins riding her scooter. She rides around and around and around. White tires and pink frame. A piece of paper is stuck to one of its wheels. It flaps with every rotation of the wheel.)

SAMANTHA: And then, and then, and then. When it comes. And then when the rain comes and then the water comes down and it comes up and there's like a foot of water or something like a foot of water so that everybody there's covered all the way up to their chins the water…gonna be real cold like it was ice cubes in it. Gonna be that cold. And I'm gonna have my boots on. It's gonna protect me. Keep me safe from the water that's gonna come down and be like up to everyone's nose. The water is gonna be so high, but I have my boots on so…so nothing is going to touch me. 'Cause I have my boots on.

LINUS: Maybe I should have some of those.

SAMANTHA: No you can't.

LINUS: I can't?

SAMANTHA: No.

LINUS: Why not?

SAMANTHA: 'Cause I have 'em.

LINUS: Maybe I could get another pair?

SAMANTHA: Nah…

LINUS: Why not?

SAMANTHA: 'Cause this is the only pair.

LINUS: In the world?

SAMANTHA: In the whole world.

LINUS: Wow. Those must be some boots.

SAMANTHA: They are…they were made by a whole team of people. They got them all together, the parts and stuff, and then made them all magical, and then put them all together, and then made them so no water could get in.

LINUS: They did, did they?

SAMANTHA: Yep, they do that a lot. Yep.

LINUS: They do, huh?

SAMANTHA: They prepare for the things to come. That's what I know from my…Oh sugar! *(Pause, as if caught.)* I didn't put it there.

(SAMANTHA gets off the scooter, looks at the piece of paper stuck to the wheel, gently peels it away, throws it as far as she can…about three feet away. Straight in the hand of LINUS.)

LINUS: When did you get this?

SAMANTHA: I don't know.

LINUS: Who are you?

SAMANTHA: You're scaring me.

LINUS: I'm sorry, but you need to leave now.

SAMANTHA: But Daddy!

LINUS: What did you say?

SAMANTHA: That's not very nice. Not very nice at all. She would never say anything like that.

LINUS: I'm sorry Samantha.

SAMANTHA: Mommy would never have done anything like that.

LINUS: Please forgive me.

(SAMANTHA rides into the darkness. LINUS has the paper in his hand. He looks to ALORA. She is passed out on the ground. He pushes to her and cradles her in his arms. Time clock: 300,000.)

LINUS: Alora, baby, are you here? Come on.

(Image: A spinning gurney wheel. A mother weeping. A door opening. Shining white light. A red balloon…it bursts…red balloon…it bursts…red balloon…it bursts…red balloon…it bursts.)

(Static. LINUS walks to the telephone. He looks at the paper SAMANTHA gave him. He cautiously picks up the phone and dials.)

SONG: THE GREAT ESCAPE

(A ballad.)

(Image: The negative of a woman floating in water. It flashes to a positive image.)

(Sound: A giant gasp of air.)

ALORA: *(Singing.)* DROP-DEAD GOR-
GEOUS GIRL IS READY FOR HER CAPE.

*(Image: LITTLE ALORA is inside a giant
red balloon.)*

CATCH THE FIRST BREATH OF THE YEAR.
OH CATCH THAT BREATH.

(The sound of a gasp.)

*(Image: A little girl hand holds an
enormous pin.)*

PUSH THE DIRT BACK INTO THE EMPTY
HOLE—CAREFUL NOT TO GET DIRTY.

*(Image: Little girl feet jumping on
a bed.)*

I CAN RUN FASTER THAN A MIDDLE-AGED
PONCH.

*(Image: A pin bounces close to a bal-
loon.)*

STICK YOUR HEAD IN DOO-DOO.

*(Image: A big bounce, and the walls of
the hospital shatter and fall in bits of
rubbery pieces around ALORA.)*

LINUS: I understand. Thank you, doctor. *(Pause—to the world.)* You knew.
(Beat.) Me too.

*(The time clock winds down exception-
ally fast to 60,480. LINUS sits beside
ALORA.)*

LINUS: I saw her. I saw our little girl.

*(A gasp coming from under water. ALORA
gasps.)*

LINUS: There you are.

ALORA: You saw her?

LINUS: She was just like you.

(Image: Sharp/pain.)

(A pain doubles ALORA over.)

*(Image: A small trickle of red. Blindfold.
Thick smoke.)*

*(The blue phone siren flashes. She reaches
a hand out. He takes it.)*

ALORA: It's coming for me. Can't you
see? Right on the other side of that song.
I guess it comes to everyone—but I beat
it once before. I don't imagine that's ever
going to happen twice, do you?

LINUS: I can take you away now. I can
if you tell me where to go.

ALORA: It's too late for that now. Hold
my hand. It's time.

LINUS: Where?

ALORA: You think too much.

LINUS: I don't recognize anything.
You're too far away.

ALORA: I'm right with you. Next to
you.

LINUS: I can't see.

ALORA: Stop I'm right here. Open your
eyes. *(Excited.)* I think it's time.

LINUS: Time?

ALORA: It's time.

LINUS: *(A realization.)* No. *(Pause.)* No,
No, No, No, No.

ALORA: Linus.

LINUS: You can hold on.

ALORA: Don't let me go alone.

*(Stillness. LINUS and ALORA face to
face.)*

*(Image: Monitors buzzing, worlds growing
then shrinking.)*

*(LINUS and ALORA are pushing the
world out.)*

LINUS: It's going to be a girl.

ALORA: How do you know?

LINUS: *(Puts his hand on her stomach.)* You don't feel it?

ALORA: A girl.

LINUS: She's going to be the most amazing little girl you ever could see.

ALORA: Samantha.

LINUS: Sammy.

ALORA: Sam.

(Image: The buildings grow.)

(The time clock winds down: 1,000. "One Cup of Coffee" by Bob Marley from Songs of Freedom *plays. ALORA and LINUS dance. Close... Intimate... ARTHUR enters with OWEN and NEAL behind him.)*

ARTHUR: Anyone taking the 4:15 to Cuba, please get your ticket out and move to track 5-4-1. If you do not have a ticket, you may purchase one here. Again, anyone taking the 4:15 to Cuba, please get your ticket out and move to track 1-4-5.

(ARTHUR produces a ticket and hands it to ALORA.)

ARTHUR: Merry Christmas.

(ARTHUR takes ALORA's hand and slowly dances away from LINUS.)

ALORA: It's all real you know. I wasn't making it up.

LINUS: I know. As real as real can be.

ALORA: Daddy-O. Take good care of her.

(ALORA exits with the BROTHERS.)

(Image: A woman floating in water.)

(A distant laughter. An exhale. Time clock: 0,000,000. Stillness. LINUS has a conversation with SAMANTHA, who is not on stage.)

LINUS: You're beautiful. My god. You're perfect. *(Listens.)* No. You're not. You could never be evil. *(Listens.)* Don't tell anyone, but I thought you were gonna have three arms.

(LINUS looks at the audience. Slowly, the time clock starts ticking upwards from 0,000,000. An actual red balloon floats across the sky. Lights down.)

(End of play.)

SISTER CITIES

Colette Freedman

COLETTE FREEDMAN is a playwright, screenwriter, novelist, and actor. She was raised in New York, Wisconsin, and Maryland. She received a BA in English from Haverford College, where she was an All-American lacrosse player and voted Philadelphia Player of the Year in field hockey. She also attended Colgate University, where she earned a master's degree in teaching. She is the author of the plays *Serial Killer Barbie* (Brooklyn Publishers, 2004), *First to the Egg* (Turnip Theatre, New York, 2005), *Bridesmaid #3* (Riant Theatre, New York, 2006), *Deconstructing the Torah* (Odyssey Theatre, Los Angeles, 2005), *Ellipses…* (Elephant Theatre, Los Angeles, 2006), a modern adaptation of *Iphigenia in Aulis* written in iambic pentameter (Hayworth Theatre, Los Angeles, 2006), and the novel *Tennis Dates* (Outskirts Press, 2008). She has won over sixty awards—including the International Summit Award, the Telly, and the Communicator—for her commercial writing and directing. In addition, Freedman was named one of the Dramatists Guild's "50 Playwrights to Watch" in 2007. She was a 2006 finalist for the Eugene O'Neill Playwrights Conference, a first place winner in creative writing at the 2005 Santa Barbara Writer's Conference, and a semifinalist in the 2005 Actors Theatre of Louisville Short Play Festival and the 2004 Riant Play Festival. She is currently working on a stage adaptation of Anna Dillon's novel *The Affair* and has been commissioned to write a new play, *Felix and Fanny*, which will have its world premiere at the Mendelssohn Project. A film version of *Sister Cities* is also in the works. Freedman is a member of the Dramatists Guild. She lives in Los Angeles with her husband, playwright Mark Troy.

Sister Cities was first presented by Circus Theatricals (Jack Stehlin, Artistic Director; Jeannine Stehlin, Managing Director) on May 7, 2006, at the Studio Theatre at the Hayworth, Los Angeles, with the following cast and credits:

Baltimore ....Jade Sealey
Carolina ....Susan Ziegler
Austin ....Colette Freedman
Dallas.. Nickella Moschetti
Mary .... Jill Gascoine

Director: Elise Robertson
Stage Manager: Leah Roobini
Producers: Jeannine Stehlin and Jack Stehlin
Sets/Costumes/Sound: Kitty Rose
Lights: Derrick McDaniel

The New York premiere of *Sister Cities* was presented by T. Schreiber Studio (Terry Schreiber, Artistic Director) on October 18, 2007, at the Gloria Maddox Theatre, with the following cast and credits:

Baltimore .... Jamie Neumann
Carolina ....Ellen Reilly
Austin ....Maeve Yore
Dallas..Emberli Edwards
Mary ....Judith Scarpone

Director: Cat Parker
Stage Manager: Eliza Jane Bowman
Scenic Design: George Allison
Lighting Design: Andrea Boccanfuso
Costume Design: Karen Ann Ledger
Sound Design: Chris Rummel
Assistant Director: Frank Mihelich
Set Decorator: Carolyn Mraz
Technical Director: Rohit Kapoor
Marketing/PR: Katie Rosin
Production Coordinator: Gina Roche

www.curtainrise.com

for Joycie

CHARACTERS

MARY: sixties, tough, self-absorbed, former dancer

CAROLINA: forty, uber thin, A+ personality, lawyer, recently divorced

AUSTIN: thirty-six, athletic, gay, successful writer

DALLAS: thirty, perpetual sorority sister, teacher, uptight, married

BALTIMORE: twenty-six, free-spirited bohemian, Harvard grad student

TIME AND **PLACE**

A modest living room in Poughkeepsie.

Scene 1: Noon
Scene 2: 1 p.m.
Scene 3: 2 p.m.
Scene 4: One week earlier
Scene 5: 3 p.m.

ACT I
SCENE 1

Saturday, noon. The lights go halfway up on a modest living room. One window. A couch. A coffee table. Two side chairs. A small dining table. A television sits on a sizable cabinet. A shelf lined with Russian nesting dolls. An alcove upstage right leads to the kitchen. A hallway upstage left leads to the rest of the house. The front door is downstage. The muted television flickers in the darkness. Framed pictures everywhere. The front door opens. CAROLINA, forty, a tight-laced, too-thin woman in a business suit, enters. She walks with a purpose, rolling an overnight bag. The door remains open. BALTIMORE, twenty-six, an attractive mixture of bohemian student and intellectual do-gooder, replete with knapsack, bolts in.

BALTIMORE: Pee. Gotta pee. Gotta pee.

(She barrels past CAROLINA through the hallway. CAROLINA examines the room. She turns off the television and inspects a pile of unopened letters. AUSTIN, thirty-six, athletic, in a Princeton lacrosse T-shirt and pajama bottoms enters from the kitchen eating a TV dinner macaroni and cheese.)

AUSTIN: Carolina.

(CAROLINA is startled; she loathes being surprised. She acknowledges AUSTIN. There is no love lost between them.)

CAROLINA: No one outside the family calls me that anymore.

AUSTIN: Well, since I'm inside the family, I should be allowed to call you by your Christian name, but, hey, *Carol* works for me…Carol Channing! Carol Burnett…A Christmas Carol. *(Whispers.)* You know who else changed her name, well, not really changed it, more like modified it: CCH Pounder. Her name is like a condensed sneeze. *(Loudly.)* Ha…Cch.

CAROLINA: Are you drunk?

AUSTIN: Not yet. Cch's real name is Carol Christine Hilaria Pounder. What's it been Carolina, three years?

CAROLINA: Two.

AUSTIN: And a half. *(Pecks at the macaroni.)*

CAROLINA: When's the last time you cooked for yourself?

AUSTIN: A few minutes ago.

CAROLINA: When's the last time you cooked for yourself that didn't involve microwaving a box?

AUSTIN: A few years ago.

CAROLINA: If Mother could see you now, she'd be horrified.

AUSTIN: It's good to see you.

CAROLINA: This place looks like a mausoleum.

(She goes to the window and opens it. Light streams in.)

AUSTIN: It *is* a mausoleum. *(Covers her eyes, unhappy with the light.)* Where's Baltimore?

CAROLINA: In the bathroom.

AUSTIN: Is she pregnant?

CAROLINA: No!…Why, is she seeing someone?

AUSTIN: Pregnant people always rush to the bathroom when they get somewhere.

CAROLINA: *(Surveys the room. Examines another picture.)* She's been on the road four and a half hours. She wanted to take the bus the whole way from Boston, but I met her in Albany and we rode the last hour and a half together.

AUSTIN: You took a bus?

CAROLINA: No, Baltimore took the bus. I flew.

AUSTIN: Because you're definitely not a bus person.

CAROLINA: I'm not. I flew…and then rented a car.

AUSTIN: Oh. Did you have scintillating conversation? Baltimore's a scintillating conversationalist.

CAROLINA: I drove. She slept.

AUSTIN: Why didn't you fly into Poughkeepsie?

CAROLINA: It was half the price to fly into a major airport.

AUSTIN: And Albany's a major airport?

CAROLINA: It's more major than Poughkeepsie.

AUSTIN: But, you're rich.

CAROLINA: What does that have to do with it?

AUSTIN: Rich people should be able to fly into whatever airport they choose. That's why we live in a class-based society, to cater to the convenience of the rich.

CAROLINA: Austin, the rich stay rich because they don't spend their disposable income on last-minute airplane tickets flying into Poughkeepsie…and if it makes you happy, I flew first class.

AUSTIN: It does make me happy. *(Beat.)* Did you remember to put in your frequent flyer miles?

CAROLINA: *(Annoyed.)* I remembered. Can we drop it?

AUSTIN: Sure. Dropping it. No worries. Just making scintillating conversation.

(They are silent. There is a sound of a toilet flushing. BALTIMORE bursts into the room.)

BALTIMORE: Mom's in the tub.

AUSTIN: Yeah.

BALTIMORE: Okay, just checking. *(She kisses AUSTIN on the top of her head and flops into a chair. She eats from an open potato chip bag.)*

CAROLINA: Wait. Wait. Wait. Mom's in the bathroom? Our mother's in the bathroom? *(Rushes into the other room.)*

(Silence.)

BALTIMORE: She looks good.

AUSTIN: I thought so.

(They continue to eat in silence.)

BALTIMORE: How've you been?

AUSTIN: I've been better.

CAROLINA: *(Rushes back. She is furious.)* Mom's in the tub.

BALTIMORE: That's what I said.

AUSTIN: That's what she said.

CAROLINA: *(Looks at her SISTERS as if they're crazy. Goes to the phone. Dials. Into phone.)* Can I have the number

for the—*(To her SISTERS.)* Who do I call?

BALTIMORE: Nine-one-one?

AUSTIN: The coroner?

CAROLINA: *(Into phone.)* Hi. Yes. May I please have the number for the police. *(To AUSTIN.)* You are completely inept. *(Into phone.)* Hello, my mother's passed away and I'm not sure who I should talk to about…What? Okay. *(To SISTERS.)* She's transferring me. I thought you could at least take care of this before I got here.

AUSTIN: And miss this drama?

CAROLINA: *(Into phone.)* Hi…Yes. Who do I talk to about getting a body removed?…730 North Diversey Avenue…two blocks west of Greenspring…What? Uh, no, technically, it's not, I mean, I grew up in it, but I don't live here now…it's my mother's house, *was* my mother's house, but it *is* my mother's body…What? No, I found her dead…She slit her wrists…Because her wrists are slit. Yesterday…Because I wasn't here, yesterday. I was in Seattle, litigating a case…Yes, I flew. I took the red-eye. American flight number twenty-two. Obnoxious stewardess—

AUSTIN: Flight attendant.

CAROLINA: *(Glares at AUSTIN. Irritated.)* They showed a Leonardo DiCaprio movie, but I'm not a Leonardo DiCaprio fan so I didn't watch it. Enough details? Can we please focus on my mother's corpse rotting in the tub?…Thank you. *(To SISTERS.)* He's transferring me. Is everyone completely incapable?

AUSTIN: Government worker.

BALTIMORE: Bureaucracy at its best.

CAROLINA: *(Into phone.)* Hello. Hello…Yes. My name is Carol Baxter-Shaw and my dead mother is in the bathtub. I need you to send someone to pick her up…Yesterday…Because I wasn't here. *(Growing irritation.)* …Because I was under the false impression that someone else *had* called yesterday. *(Looks at AUSTIN.)* Because she's mentally unbalanced. *(Losing it.)* CAN YOU PLEASE JUST SEND SOMEONE OVER HERE TO REMOVE THE FUCKING BODY?! *(Composing herself.)* Thank you…Two to three hours?…Yes, I'm certain busy metropolises like Poughkeepsie *are* littered with dead bodies you people need to pick up…730 North Diversey Avenue…D as in David, I.V.E.R.S.E.Y. Thank you. *(Hangs up phone. To AUSTIN.)* Do you have anything to drink?

AUSTIN: It's noon.

CAROLINA: I didn't ask for the time, I asked for a drink.

AUSTIN: There's vodka in the liquor cabinet.

BALTIMORE: Do you think 911 operators are equipped to handle hysteria?

AUSTIN: They must take a course.

CAROLINA: *(Goes to the cabinet. Methodically pulls out bottles of vodka.)* Smirnoff. Absolut. Absolut Pepper. Grey Goose. Stolichnaya. Findlandia. Popov. Absolut Citron. It's a vodka cornucopia. *(Goes to the kitchen.)*

BALTIMORE: *(Surveys the vodka collection.)* That's a lot of vodka.

AUSTIN: Cornucopia?

BALTIMORE: I sent her a word of the day calendar for Christmas.

AUSTIN: That's a thoughtful gift.

BALTIMORE: I thought so.

AUSTIN: 'Cause I would have said melange or potpourri. Even hodgepodge, but cornucopia: That's a mouthful.

BALTIMORE: I didn't know Mom was a boozer.

(CAROLINA returns and pours herself a long shot of Grey Goose.)

AUSTIN: She wasn't. She just liked to "be prepared" in case she had company. Like today.

BALTIMORE: *(Examines the liquor supply.)* Being prepared is having a bottle, maybe two, not a fully stocked liquor emporium. Like this is the set of *Cheers*.

AUSTIN: Where everybody knows your name.

BALTIMORE: Oh my god, the nesting dolls! *(She plays with some of the Russian nesting dolls on the shelf.)*

AUSTIN: Mom took preparedness to a whole new level. Check the closet, there's enough baby powder and Listerine to disinfect a third world country. Once, I was running low on paper, so I asked Mom to pick me up some. Four hours later, she comes home with twenty different varieties. Bright white. Matte white. Print white. Did you know there are actually different colors of white? I'm still using that paper.

BALTIMORE: *That's* prepared.

AUSTIN: That's psychotic. Who needs twenty reams of paper? It's not like we live in the wilderness. There are five Office Depots in walking distance. Plenty of paper.

(BALTIMORE looks at her and shrugs.)

AUSTIN: Never mind.

DALLAS: *Films* don't have titles like *Pretty in Pink*. There's a cliché. Why can't you be pretty in a color other than pink?

AUSTIN: Alliteration. You wouldn't say pretty in maroon or—

DALLAS: Pretty in purple, why couldn't she be pretty in purple?

AUSTIN: Is anybody pretty in purple?

(BALTIMORE gestures to herself. She is wearing purple. Neither of her SISTERS acknowledge this.)

BALTIMORE: So what happens? Do Ilsa and Lazlo make it to America?

AUSTIN: Sure. They move to Darien, Connecticut, and have two point five kids.

DALLAS: —And a white picket fence.

AUSTIN: —And they open a bar. Call it Laszlo's Place. Hire a black piano player.

BALTIMORE: Speaking of which.

AUSTIN: A black piano player?

BALTIMORE: A bar. What's your poison? Vodka or vodka?

DALLAS: I'm going to go with the vodka, thanks.

BALTIMORE: *(Goes to the cabinet.)* Smirnoff. Absolut. Absolut Pepper. Grey Goose. Stolichnaya. Findlandia. Popov. Or Absolut Citron?

DALLAS: I don't usually drink before five…unless it's a Bloody Mary at Neiman Marcus with my mother-in-law on a Sunday afternoon.

AUSTIN: We have tomato juice.

DALLAS: Stoli works for me. *(Looks at the array of bottles.)* God, there's a lot of vodka here.

AUSTIN: A potpourri.

BALTIMORE: A hodgepodge.

AUSTIN: A cor-   BALTIMORE: A
nucopia.   cornucopia.

DALLAS: Tabasco sauce?

AUSTIN: Kitchen.

(DALLAS exits.)

BALTIMORE: I'm starving.

AUSTIN: I have thirty-two varieties of beef in a box.

BALTIMORE: Do you ever cook for yourself?

AUSTIN: Do you?

BALTIMORE: No. That's why I date men who can cook.

AUSTIN: Because why do it yourself when—

BALTIMORE: AUSTIN: Men
Men can do it for   can do it for you.
you.

BALTIMORE: The third commandment in Mom's biblical philosophy.

AUSTIN: Sandwiched in between Marry for love and Divorce for money.

BALTIMORE: And name your children after the cities in which they're born. Dallas is in trouble.

AUSTIN: Why?

BALTIMORE: She'll have to name her kid Philadelphia.

AUSTIN: She's pregnant too?

BALTIMORE: *(Whispers.)* Who else is pregnant?

AUSTIN: *(Whispers.)* You are.

BALTIMORE: I am?

AUSTIN: You're not?

BALTIMORE: No.

AUSTIN: Oh.

BALTIMORE: Dallas is a little puffy. Besides, if she's not, she will be. She and Peter are always going on and on about having a family. Like there aren't enough unwanted children on this planet already. I'm just glad Carolina didn't have kids before the divorce.

AUSTIN: Because she'd be a terrible mother?

BALTIMORE: She's too skinny. Skinny people never have good pregnancies. Carolina and I take after our fathers, whereas you and Dallas both inherited Mom's childbearing hips.

AUSTIN: Thanks?!

BALTIMORE: Was she always this uptight?

AUSTIN: Dallas?

BALTIMORE: I don't think Dallas is uptight. She's fun.

DALLAS: *(Enters with a glass of tomato juice.)* Who's fun?

BALTIMORE: You are.

DALLAS: I know.

BALTIMORE: Austin thinks you're uptight.

AUSTIN: Thanks.

DALLAS: Compared to Austin, a baboon's uptight.

BALTIMORE: We're dissecting Carolina.

DALLAS: Lovely state. Good air quality. Nice beaches.

AUSTIN: And extremely uptight.

DALLAS: *(Makes herself a Bloody Mary.)* Give her a break. Her husband just left her. She puts up this ridiculous veneer of stoicism, but she's really just as confused as the rest of us. She just hides it better.

AUSTIN: I'm not sure she's hiding it.

DALLAS: She works fifty-two hours a day.

BALTIMORE: Yeah. Someone in our family needs to perpetuate Mom's myth that women can have it all. Husband, family, career.

AUSTIN: She doesn't have a family.

DALLAS: Or a husband.

BALTIMORE: Okay. Career. Look, when Mom graduated high school, her two options were to become a secretary or a teacher.

DALLAS: So, she got married. Four times.

BALTIMORE: Yes. Marriage was also an option. But, I'm talking career.

AUSTIN: So, Carolina has made up for Mother's lack of academic fortitude and marital ineptitude by schooling herself through a law degree and ignoring her family in favor of her career.

DALLAS: Is Miss-never-get-uptight tightening?

AUSTIN: Observing. What's the point of a successful career if you can't share your life with someone?

DALLAS: Okay. And I don't mean to be morbid or accuse you of being hypocritical or anything, but who's the one with the successful career still living with her *Mother*?

AUSTIN: Technically, I'm not living with her anymore.

DALLAS: You'd think after your novel came out, you'd, I don't know, move at least NEXT DOOR to Mom, rather than be her roommate.

AUSTIN: *(To BALTIMORE.)* In college when your roommate dies, you get an immediate 4.0.

BALTIMORE: I thought that was just a rumor.

AUSTIN: Fact. Besides, I pay rent. Paid rent.

DALLAS: You and Carolina aren't that different.

AUSTIN: Really? Well, I didn't ignore my family. I've spent countless hours on your couch. I've even visited Baltimore at Harvard.

BALTIMORE: It's true. She has.

AUSTIN: Family is my priority. Carolina has the career. I choose the family.

BALTIMORE: Dallas has the husband. So, where does that leave me?

AUSTIN: With the potential. That's the nice thing about still being young. You can do anything.

BALTIMORE: I can't do that many things.

AUSTIN: Yes, but your youth perpetuates the illusion that you're capable of infinite possibilities.

BALTIMORE: I'm getting my master's in sociology. I think my possibilities are pretty finite.

(CAROLINA enters with a cardboard carrier filled with three large Jamba Juices with straws. She hugs DALLAS.)

CAROLINA: Hey, when did you get here?

DALLAS: I just missed you. Train ran late, surprise. What flavor? *(Picks one up.)*

CAROLINA: Protein with ginseng and echinacea.

DALLAS: *(Puts it back.)* Yum. Enjoy.

CAROLINA: *(Distributes the juices.)* Did the coroner call?

BALTIMORE: Was he supposed to?

AUSTIN: Why do you assume it's a he? Coroners can be shes.

BALTIMORE: Nope, it's a he. Definitely a he. A tall, cute, muscular he.

AUSTIN: Really, how do you know?

BALTIMORE: I was right about Lori Braithwaites's body composition. It's a gift. No, he didn't call. Do coroners call? I thought they just appeared.

CAROLINA: It's been an hour. I wonder if he's running late?

AUSTIN: It's not like Mom's going anywhere.

CAROLINA: WILL YOU PLEASE START TAKING THIS SERIOUSLY.

(EVERYONE is quiet. CAROLINA walks to the vodka bottles and pours a healthy shot of Smirnoff in her Jamba Juice.)

BALTIMORE: Gross.

AUSTIN: You drink a lot for a lawyer. Do all lawyers drink so much?

CAROLINA: Do all writers act with complete disregard for their family in times of crisis?

AUSTIN: I don't disregard my family. I visited Baltimore at Harvard.

BALTIMORE: It's true. She has.

CAROLINA: And you. You just instigate her. Having one of you is bad enough, but two, I think I'm losing my mind.

AUSTIN: Have more vodka, that'll help you find it. *(Exits.)*

CAROLINA: What's her problem?

DALLAS: I think grief hits people differently. *(Beat.)* When's the last time you saw Mom?

CAROLINA: I spoke to her biweekly.

DALLAS: When's the last time you *saw* her?

CAROLINA: I don't know, Christmas?

BALTIMORE: You guys were in Hawaii at Christmas.

CAROLINA: Right. The "maybe-THIS-will-save-the-marriage" vacation. He fell in love with a stewardess, I got shingles. *(She takes a long swig.)* Easter.

DALLAS: You had the O'Hagan case.

CAROLINA: Why do you know more about my career than I do?

DALLAS: You're the second-most famous person to come out of this family, we all have your clippings…Somewhere.

BALTIMORE: I do…Somewhere.

DALLAS: The point is, you haven't seen Mom in over a year. *(She looks at BALTIMORE.)* Have you?

(BALTIMORE shakes her head.)

DALLAS: I haven't since…last Christmas. Wow. Then I guess none of us have really seen her…Except Austin. And we're not the ones who found her.

BALTIMORE: And that whole razor thing. That's really fucked up. *(Beat.)* She obviously really planned this.

CAROLINA: You cannot make me believe that Mother planned this.

BALTIMORE: I'm just saying, we don't know the particulars.

CAROLINA: That's what I'm trying to find out.

BALTIMORE: Did you ever have foreplay before sex?

CAROLINA: That has nothing to do with anything. *(Beat.)* It's none of your business.

BALTIMORE: Says the woman who taught me how to give a blowjob with an unripe banana.

CAROLINA: Yes. I have foreplay. Your point?

BALTIMORE: You can't just barge in and ask what happened. You need to chat, catch up, communicate; enjoy some light banter and witty repartee and then ease into the more intense stuff. A conversational seduction of sorts.

CAROLINA: When did you get so smart?

BALTIMORE: I go to Harvard.

(They sit silent.)

CAROLINA: So, until Austin's ready to open up, we what?

DALLAS: We relax. We try to relax.

CAROLINA: How?

DALLAS: To relax? Take your hair down.

CAROLINA: What?

DALLAS: Take your hair down. Literally. It's not just figurative speech. I want you to take your hair down.

CAROLINA: This is ridiculous.

BALTIMORE: You show me yours, I'll show you mine.

(BALTIMORE swiftly pulls her hair out of its ponytail. She looks at CAROLINA, who sighs and deliberately unpins her hair, one hairpin at a time.)

DALLAS: Now, kick off your heels and take off your panty hose.

CAROLINA: You've got to be kidding.

DALLAS: I don't kid.

BALTIMORE: Panty hose are an anti-quated torture device men invented to give us an equivalent of a tie.

DALLAS: I know you're uncomfortable. Take them off.

(CAROLINA does.)

BALTIMORE: You've got great legs.

CAROLINA: *(Embarrassed.)* Yes. Thank you.

DALLAS: See, don't you feel better? *(She massages her shoulders.)* A little loosey-goosey, free flowing…this is what it feels like to RELAX.

CAROLINA: Okay. I get it. I'm relaxed. *(She clearly is not.)*

BALTIMORE: Hey. Let's play Scrabble and order pizza.

CAROLINA: Now?

BALTIMORE: Why not now?

CAROLINA: Because our mother is in the other—sure why not, I'm relaxed…I can be relaxed. Pizza and Scrabble, sounds delightful.

DALLAS: Remember the tournaments we used to have?

BALTIMORE: You guys never used to let me play.

DALLAS: That's because you were a child.

BALTIMORE: Well I'm gonna kick your butt today. Who has the Harvard degree?

CAROLINA: Technically, you don't have it yet.

BALTIMORE: But I got in. Getting into an Ivy League school is far tougher than staying in. I'll get the degree. Piece of cake.

DALLAS: I still think you should have stayed in New York.

CAROLINA: Not again. *(Goes to the cabinet and pulls out the Scrabble game. Sets it up at the table.)*

BALTIMORE: Right. Cornell is too depressing, NYU is too big, and the rest of the schools are too preppy.

DALLAS: Vassar is not too preppy.

BALTIMORE: You're dressed head to toe in Ann Taylor.

DALLAS: That just means I have impec-cable taste.

BALTIMORE: No. It means that you're conditioned to dress to please others. It's not a big deal, it's learned behavior, Pavlovian. I'm studying it right now. Mom was pseudo-preppy and you wanted to please her so you dressed pseudo-preppy. And the only reason you even went to Vassar, which is a good school, although inferior to fellow sister schools Wellesley and Bryn Mawr, which I happen to know you got into, is because Mom wanted you to stay close to home…And I guarantee your bra and panties match.

DALLAS: What?

BALTIMORE: Your panties. They match your bra. I'll bet money on it. Mom's matched, so my guess is yours match too.

DALLAS: No they don't.

BALTIMORE: Show me.

DALLAS: I'm not going to show you.

BALTIMORE: You just made Carolina take off her panty hose and you won't show me your bra? *(She postures like a lawyer and addresses CAROLINA.)* Counselor? I have just made an accusation. If the defendant pleads the fifth, wouldn't the jury be inclined to sway with my rather convincing indictment?

CAROLINA: She probably would win the argument if you refuse to provide the evidence.

(DALLAS rolls her eyes, unbuttons her shirt, and throws it open. She is wearing a pink bra. She tugs on the corner of her underwear. Pink.)

BALTIMORE: Pretty in pink!

DALLAS: Happy?! You caught me, I match. I've always matched. Take a good look, I'm the Mother-Pleaser whose bra and underwear always match.

BALTIMORE: Don't get your knickers in a twist. I bet you five bucks Carolina's match too. And your tits are better than hers.

CAROLINA: Thanks a lot…don't take the bet. Guilty as charged. How could they not? Remember Mom's sixth commandment?

ALL: *Always match your bra and knickers else the police will give you snickers.*

CAROLINA: That's one of my more disturbing childhood recollections.

DALLAS: I can't believe she was actually mortified at the thought of the police finding our lifeless bodies after whatever catastrophic accident we were in, and judging our poor upbringing by our uncoordinated underwear…Talk about misplaced priorities.

CAROLINA: I was the only person in my gym class whose bra matched her underwear.

DALLAS: Peter makes fun of me. I get completely neurotic if I try to mix it up a little and go blue with red or purple with yellow, or pink with…white. It's pathetic. I can't feel good on the outside unless I feel good on the inside.

BALTIMORE: Mom's ingrained herself in us. Permanently…Ironic that she decided to kill herself in the buff.

CAROLINA: Baltimore.

BALTIMORE: Well, she did. After all these years, I bet she's collected some pretty nice lingerie, but no…We've got to see her distended boobs and gray cootchie.

CAROLINA: Baltimore!

BALTIMORE: What? I'm only saying what you're thinking. And, FYI, I never listened to Mom's dictum. *(She pulls off her jeans. Discards them. She is wearing men's tighty whities.)* I don't give a shit if a cop sees me in matching underwear.

(Imitates cop.) S'cuse me miss. You are in possible vi-o-la-tion of the matching bra and panties act. D'ya mind straddling my car so I can frisk you? *(Sexually, straddles fake car, talks in Southern accent.)* Why yes officer. Forgive me for my possible violation of the law. But, as you can see, it doesn't really matter what the color of my panties are, 'cause I *never* wear a bra *(She lifts up her shirt, no bra.)* ...so, academically speaking, *everything* I wear...matches my underwear. But you can still frisk me if you want. *(She plops down in DALLAS's lap.)*

DALLAS: You are such a slut.

BALTIMORE: If you've got it, flaunt it! Does anyone have a cigarette?

DALLAS: You smoke?

BALTIMORE: No. I'm asking for a cigarette to make conversation. Yes. I smoke. Infrequently. When I'm either drunk or under duress. I am currently under duress. Later, I plan to be drunk. I know all about the death stick lecture so save the sob song.

DALLAS: I think Mom smoked.

CAROLINA: She so didn't seem the type.

BALTIMORE: Really, what's the *type*?

CAROLINA: There are three *types* of people who smoke. One: prepubescent children who think that smoking will elevate them to the unattainable echelon of cool. Two: Fucked-up twenty-somethings without a clue who use cigarettes like procrastination props, hoping the five to seven minutes of ingested cancer will give them some remarkable insight into their unfocused lives.

(BALTIMORE gives CAROLINA the finger.)

CAROLINA: And three: lonely older women.

DALLAS: My students definitely fit into the first category. And I have to say it Baltimore, you're a classic number two. But Mom, she didn't strike me as a lonely woman. I mean, she had Austin around all the time and she had her men.

(They are quiet. They all know about "the men.")

BALTIMORE: Do you think they'll start coming out of the woodwork now that she's dead?

DALLAS: My father won't. He's dead too. Mommy and Daddy are dead. Sounds like a country western song. *(To CAROLINA.)* Is yours still in Vancouver?

CAROLINA: No, I just moved him to Spokane. Alzheimer's. I'll tell him about Mom, but he won't remember her. Shit, he barely remembers me.

DALLAS: I guess on the Richter scale, you're worse off. I mean, I'd rather my parent be dead than suffering in silence.

CAROLINA: He's not exactly silent. He has visions, which I don't think he likes because he's always yelling at them. At first, I thought it was personal, but when he started screaming at me about cheating him out of forty bucks at a celebrity poker game in Vegas, I realized that it was one of his imaginary friends. That, and the fact that he called me Mikey.

DALLAS: Who's Mikey?

CAROLINA: No clue. He had a cat once called Mike. Maybe he thinks I'm the cat...Hopefully, he'll get pneumonia and die before he realizes what his life has dissolved into.

DALLAS: That's cold.

CAROLINA: That's fact. I don't wish it on anyone. Watching a strong, vibrant intellect waste away. First his mind, then his body. Terrifies me. It's hereditary, you know. I've memorized the statistics.

DALLAS: You'll be fine.

CAROLINA: Easy for you to say. We all have the same mother, and she's not sick, just suicidal, which is sick in its own right. Your father died in a car accident. That's not hereditary.

DALLAS: He died because his blood alcohol content was point twenty-two and he thought hitting a tree was the same as hitting the brakes. *(She pours more vodka in her glass. Toasts.)* Alcoholism. Hereditary.

CAROLINA: Austin's father is around somewhere. The city, I think. I wonder if they still see each other.

BALTIMORE: Well, I'm not dying of Alzheimer's or slitting my wrists in a bathroom. And I only drink on special occasions, so alcoholism's out of the question. When my time comes, I'm going to a leper colony to help sick children.

DALLAS: Do they still have leper colonies?

BALTIMORE: I'm going to help the kids.

DALLAS: You can do that before you die.

BALTIMORE: But then I might catch it. I'm still young. And virile.

DALLAS: That's terrible.

BALTIMORE: That's fact. I can do a lot more good work from my desk in Boston than in the middle of a leper colony.

DALLAS: You're being ridiculous. That's like saying a teacher can teach better outside of the classroom away from the students.

BALTIMORE: So you're comparing your students to lepers?

DALLAS: Lepers is politically incorrect.

BALTIMORE: How do you know?

DALLAS: Because it's not appropriate. It's like the N word or the F word.

BALTIMORE: You're comparing the word fuck to the word leper?

DALLAS: You know how much I hate that language. Why do you insist on using it around me?

BALTIMORE: Are you going to wash my mouth out with soap and send me to the principal's office?

DALLAS: I just don't think people use that word anymore.

BALTIMORE: Fuck?

DALLAS: If you google lepers, the last reference will be sometime in the Middle Ages. People just don't get leprosy anymore.

(CAROLINA pulls a BlackBerry out of her purse.)

BALTIMORE: Don't you teach history?

DALLAS: Social Studies. They're fifth graders.

BALTIMORE: Then they should be socially conscious. Recycling, global warming, lepers.

DALLAS: They're studying the presidents.

BALTIMORE: Reagan never mentioned the word AIDS in his eight years as president. Are you teaching them that?

CAROLINA: I'm so glad you can make a joke about this.

AUSTIN: You've only had a minute to digest it. I've had almost two years.

DALLAS: Mom was sick that long? She didn't seem sick last Christmas.

AUSTIN: Did you ever see her get up from her chair?

DALLAS: I thought she was tired.

AUSTIN: She still had it together then, but she went downhill. Yesterday, she was having trouble breathing.

BALTIMORE: *(Realizing.)* God, Mom was alive yesterday.

AUSTIN: If you call it alive.

CAROLINA: It still doesn't give you the right to do what you did.

AUSTIN: Had you been here…Had you seen her…you would have done the same thing.

CAROLINA: Don't you dare tell me what I would have done. You don't know me. You don't know anything about me. *(Beat.)* Right. Well, I'm screwed. I was planning to be a judge one day. Not with these skeletons out of the closet.

AUSTIN: I'm not planning to go public with this, I was telling you guys as a courtesy.

CAROLINA: Assisted suicide is illegal—

BALTIMORE: Not in Oregon.

CAROLINA: We're not in Oregon.

BALTIMORE: I hate our government.

CAROLINA: What you did was morally wrong. It was reprehensible, it was—

DALLAS: How did you do it?

CAROLINA: What?

DALLAS: *(Walks over to AUSTIN and stands in front of her.)* Show me how you did it, exactly. I want to know.

AUSTIN: No.

DALLAS: She was our mother too, Austin, I want to know what her last few minutes were like. *(Grabs AUSTIN's hand and places it on her wrist.)* I want you to show me!

AUSTIN: *(Starts to lose it. This is not what she was expecting.)* I'm not going to show you. You think I enjoyed it? You think I wanted to kill my own mother? I don't wish my last week on anyone…FUCK. You have no clue what's been going on in this house. None of you do. Carolina, you haven't been home in three years. Dallas, you refuse to deal with the slightest hint of dysfunction; hey, Mom started dying right in front of your eyes and YOU DIDN'T NOTICE. And Baltimore, you're so fucking self-absorbed, you can't see past your own terribly oppressive life fraught with important collegiate decisions.

BALTIMORE: What? Me? I'm on your side.

AUSTIN: There are no sides here. There is only reality. Mom was dying and wanted to expedite the process. She gave me no choice but to help her. I have to live with this, okay. The three of you are uninvolved, personae non gratae, not culpable. So go be a judge Carolina, you're off the hook.

CAROLINA: *(Quietly.)* But you're not.

BALTIMORE: What are you talking about?

CAROLINA: She killed our mother. That is a punishable offense.

BALTIMORE: By who?

CAROLINA: Any court of law. It's our obligation to report you.

BALTIMORE: You're crazy.

CAROLINA: Am I? I think the crazy person is one who can get within inches of the woman who bore her, slit her wrists, and watch her die. That is the crazy person.

AUSTIN: You have no idea what you're talking about.

CAROLINA: Don't I? You killed my mother.

AUSTIN: *Our* mother. You don't have proprietary rights.

CAROLINA: Neither do you.

(They glare at each other. Nose to nose. AUSTIN breaks the lock with an easy laugh, attempting to diffuse the tension.)

AUSTIN: I need a drink. You definitely need a drink. *(Goes to the bar and pulls out four glasses. She pours the shots.)* We should all be drinking. Technically, this is a wake, right? So let's drink. And toast. To Mom, this is what she would have wanted.

(AUSTIN hands EVERYONE a drink and toasts. They reluctantly join her.)

AUSTIN: To our mom.

(They all drink.)

CAROLINA: What you did was illegal.

AUSTIN: What I did was compassionate. Do you have any idea what it feels like to lose control? Of course you don't. You've been in control your entire life. Straight A's from the second you left the womb. We all admit it, Carolina, you're

the best. The one sister everyone should try to emulate. Hey, your marriage is the only thing you've ever failed in your entire life.

CAROLINA: Your point?

AUSTIN: You want to be a judge? Don't judge a person's actions until you've walked a mile in her shoes. How's that for an appropriate cliché? You would have done the same thing.

CAROLINA: That's bullshit, and you know it. Help me out here. Baltimore, Dallas, would you have killed your mother?

(They are silent.)

CAROLINA: I'm living in an asylum. You people are nuts. Austin committed a felony… *(She blinks her eyes, hard.)* I don't feel so good.

DALLAS: You've had a lot to drink.

CAROLINA: No. It's not that. *(She stumbles to the chair.)* I can't feel my fucking legs. *(She opens her mouth wide.)* What's happening to me. My arms—

(CAROLINA's body slowly becomes rigid. Only her eyes vividly express anguish. BALTIMORE and DALLAS rush to her.)

BALTIMORE: Carolina? Carol? What's the matter with her?

DALLAS: Carolina!

BALTIMORE: Carol!

AUSTIN: I guess the game's over. *(Starts to clear up.)*

BALTIMORE: What's happening?

DALLAS: Carolina, can you hear me?

AUSTIN: She can hear you perfectly. She can see you perfectly. She just can't do anything else…perfectly.

DALLAS: What did you do to her?

AUSTIN: You can't judge someone unless you walk a mile in their shoes, right?

BALTIMORE: What are you talking about?

AUSTIN: I knew she wouldn't understand. She's too clinical. She had to be shown. It was the only way. *(Pulls a small envelope with white powder in it from her pocket.)* Don't worry, it's not permanent. Doxycyclinal. Clinically speaking, it causes progressive supranuclear palsy. In layman's terms, it causes temporary paralysis of all muscular functions. The brain works, the body doesn't. *Carol* can now walk a mile in Mom's shoes.

DALLAS: You poisoned her?

AUSTIN: I'm educating her.

(CAROLINA murmurs inaudibly. Lights fade with spotlight on CAROLINA's pained eyes.)

ACT II
SCENE 4

One week earlier. Lights up on AUSTIN, sitting on the couch, eating potato chips. In CAROLINA's seat is now MARY, an attractive woman in her sixties. They watch TV in silence.

MARY: I wish you wouldn't eat junk food.

AUSTIN: I like junk food.

MARY: We need to talk about it.

AUSTIN: No, we don't.

MARY: Austin, I'm going to die. Sooner, not later, and I need your help.

AUSTIN: They'll find a cure.

MARY: If they couldn't find a cure for a Hall of Fame baseball player, I don't think they're going to find a cure for a four-time divorcée.

AUSTIN: Four?

MARY: The papers from Baltimore's father just came through. I wanted to take care of business before I took care of business.

AUSTIN: You're not funny.

MARY: I'm not laughing. *(Tries to move. It is too much for her. Relaxes back into her seat.)*

AUSTIN: Can I get you a pillow, or something?

MARY: Why, do I look uncomfortable?

AUSTIN: Are you enjoying yourself? This is not why I came back.

MARY: Why did you come back?

(AUSTIN doesn't answer.)

MARY: A famous novelist. Touring the country. You had your pick, Austin. Fellowships from California, a grant in England, offers from universities. Why did you come back?

AUSTIN: I missed you.

MARY: Fine, don't tell me. *(Beckons to AUSTIN.)* Come here.

(AUSTIN sits at MARY's feet.)

MARY: Do you know why you're so special?

AUSTIN: I have no idea.

MARY: Life is strange, Austin. There are so few things in it that you can plan out…because while you're busy planning, some higher power up there is just going to fuck up your plans. There's this theatre in Palm Springs that only hires dancers in their eighties. I read about it in my thirties and spent the next three decades planning my retirement as an octogenarian burlesque dancer in Palm Springs.

(AUSTIN laughs.)

MARY: What? You don't think I could make it? With these gams? I was born for it. Now I can barely move my legs. See, someone up there is fucking with me. So, you know what I'm gonna do? I'm gonna take control. I'm not gonna wait until a breathing tube is shoved down my throat and some strange nurse is wiping up my shit. I want out. I've had a good life. No, I've had a great life. And I have my four girls to show for it.

AUSTIN: I hate to burst your bubble, Mom, but we're not that impressive.

MARY: Are you kidding? A big-shot lawyer, a teacher, a writer and a...what is Baltimore these days?

AUSTIN: Psychology? Anthropology? Something "ology."

MARY: She'll figure it out. You switched majors three times.

AUSTIN: You switched husbands four.

MARY: Life is too short to spend with one person. How is your father?

AUSTIN: I thought you still spoke to him.

MARY: I do. I was wondering if you did.

AUSTIN: You're not going to do this. *(Goes back to the couch and grabs the remote, changing channels.)*

MARY: What?

AUSTIN: Pick an argument to get me riled up so I feel bad and placate you by doing what you want.

MARY: I would do that?

AUSTIN: You're manipulative, Mother.

MARY: How can I be manipulative? I can't even get up.

AUSTIN: You're doing it right now.

MARY: What?

AUSTIN: Making me feel guilty. I'm not buying into it.

MARY: I'm not asking you to. I'm just asking you to help kill me. *(Beat.)* What? You're the only one who can do it. Carolina will come up with some legality as to why it's ethically wrong to prematurely end my life. Dallas can't handle blood and Baltimore's too young, it would scar her.

AUSTIN: You're worried about scarring Baltimore and not completely fucking me up?

MARY: You're different, you're my Austin. Four daughters. Four cities. Well, technically Carolina's a state, two states; but she was my first and I hadn't made the city decision yet. Poor girl. I think she always felt left out in a way. That's why she pretends to be Carol. Carol, hmmpft. What a stupid name. But you...you're my Austin. My radical. You wrote progressive plays that almost got you kicked out of Princeton. Your father wrote articles for the *Times* which teetered between slander and Pulitzer. You're the only one of my girls who has the cojones to do this.

AUSTIN: Cojones?

MARY: I slept with a Mexican gardener last year. Picked up a few things.

AUSTIN: How many men have you slept with, Mother?

MARY: How many have you?

(AUSTIN looks away.)

MARY: Never? *(Beat.)* Not even one? *(Beat.)* How can you be gay, you're so much like me!

(AUSTIN glares at her.)

MARY: I just wonder if there's something I could have done. *(Beat.)* You know, it's not legal in the eyes of God.

AUSTIN: Says the woman who is asking me to kill her. Look at the commandments, Mother. I don't think Thou Shalt Not Be Gay is one of them, but I'm pretty sure Thou Shalt Not Kill is somewhere in the top ten.

MARY: You were named after the best city in the world. A democratic, liberal, artistic community thrust dead center in a repressed, Republican mess. You're a paradox…and you have no choice. I'm not strong enough to do it. If I do it, I'll do it badly. And it's rather awkward to *almost* kill yourself. Best if it's done right the first time. One never lives down that kind of embarrassment. *(Struggles to catch her breath.)*

AUSTIN: Mom?

MARY: I can't feel my legs anymore. It was okay when I was just stiff, but my body's crumbling. It's going to happen anyway, a prisoner trapped in her own body. I'm just sorry I can't say goodbye. But it's for the best. Carolina wouldn't understand. None of them would.

(MARY coughs. AUSTIN quickly jumps and brings her a glass of water, with a straw.)

AUSTIN: Mom.

MARY: My first mistake with Carolina was not really naming her after a city. She's not even really one state. Carolina, but is she North or South? I could have easily gone with Charlotte, but I couldn't get that song out of my mind. *Carolina in My Mind.* I inspired James Taylor you know. Slept with him. Twice. Bastard. Never gave me credit. Carolina's driven, but she's not happy. Gotta be happy, Austin. *(Beat.)* Now Dallas, she's happy. Didn't plan to have two of my girls in Texas. Ironic. Wanted to make it up to Taos, but the water broke a week early. Still, there are worse places to give birth. My Dallas. She's a good girl. She plays it safe, but that's what Dallas is; a planned community of safe players.

AUSTIN: Mom, maybe it's time for bed.

MARY: Your old mother's on a roll. Besides, there's only Baltimore left, unless I have any more girls out there I don't know about. Baltimore's my free spirit. She's too young to quite figure out what she wants, but she's special. All my girls are special, they were born in the best cities in the world.

AUSTIN: Technically, Paris is the best city in the world.

MARY: Not such a fan of the French. *(Beat.)* So, I was thinking Friday.

AUSTIN: This Friday?

MARY: This Friday.

AUSTIN: This Friday doesn't work for me.

MARY: There's nothing wrong with this Friday, Austin. You have no plans. It's also convenient. You can call your sisters Friday afternoon and they can come in for the weekend. That way Carolina won't miss work and Baltimore won't miss class. But no funeral, I want you to scatter my ashes. You have to promise me that.

AUSTIN: I'm not promising you anything.

MARY: I was in labor with you for seventeen hours.

AUSTIN: You're using guilt to get me to kill you?

MARY: Why, you almost killed me then, why not again?

AUSTIN: Stop making jokes!

MARY: Look, I've already come to terms with this, and I need you to understand. I'm taking control. It's not going to get better from here. I can try to fool myself or use my last few months to "find" myself, but I don't have to…I'm not lost. I've enjoyed the journey…and now, I'm ready for it to end. Help me, Austin.

(No response.)

MARY: Okay. Get me a spider from the garden.

AUSTIN: Why?

MARY: Get me a spider. There are plenty hanging around the tomatoes. Go on, I'll still be here when you get back, I'm not going anywhere.

(AUSTIN exits. MARY talks to the audience.)

MARY: What I miss the most is the sex. No one ever thinks about senior citizens having sex, but we do. And we like it. We like it a lot. It's…slower than it was when we were younger. But the hormones are still active. Even after my men dried up, I didn't. I guess that's why God created masturbation. I can't even move my fingers that well anymore…You can't

imagine what it's like to be trapped in your own body. Maybe, if I were a couch potato my whole life, I would have been used to this sitting thing, but I was a dancer. I had…the most beautiful legs. I'd sometimes dance sixteen hours a day. My feet were bloody until I was twenty…And I used to complain…Imagine that. I used to complain that my feet hurt. It's funny the things you complain about which really don't seem that serious in retrospect. Once, I was on a cruise with husband number three, Dallas's father. That man loved the water. Wonderful cruise. Too much food. Crappy ports, but, overall, pretty wonderful. Quite luxurious. So, the day comes when we return to the States and for some reason the crew hadn't anticipated that everyone would want to leave the ship at once, so the lines to get off went around the ship, twice. You've never seen people so angry. It was like the entire previous fifteen days were negated by the two hours of inconvenience these people had to experience. I even felt myself getting antsy, and I'm not that antsy of a person. With four daughters, how can you be? The guy behind me…tall, balding, with extremely kind eyes said, very quietly, "We could be waiting in a line for bread and water." Wow. Now, there's a perspective…I'm not angry anymore. I was. Boy, was I. When I started to feel the stiffness, I cursed my body for getting older. When I started to have trouble breathing I cursed the scientists for not finding a cure. When my body shut down around me, I cursed God for…just for. He's an easy target, you know. But He's also comforting. Someone who listens, unconditionally…I've had an amazing life. I saw the world. I had four successful daughters. And I don't want to die in a hospice with tubes down my throat. I don't want to wait in line for bread and water. I'm ready.

AUSTIN: *(Enters with a small Tupperware container.)* Mom?

MARY: *(Looks at her, manages a smile.)* Are you afraid of spiders?

AUSTIN: What do you want, Mother?

MARY: I want you to do exactly what I say. No deviations, no permutations. Promise?

(AUSTIN glares at her.)

MARY: Don't make a dying woman beg.

AUSTIN: Fine. I promise.

MARY: Pull two legs off of the spider.

AUSTIN: Ew.

MARY: Just do it.

(AUSTIN dumps the spider on the table and gingerly pulls off two legs, grimacing.)

MARY: What's it doing?

AUSTIN: Nothing. It's not moving. *(Stares at the spider.)*

MARY: That's because you've taken away its mobility. Now, that spider is completely alive and, if spiders can hear or think, she's listening to this. And she's trapped. She'll die because she has no one to feed her, unless you want to take that task upon yourself. *(Beat.)* If she could talk, she would beg you to end her life. What kind of existence is this for a spider? Her friends and family are in the garden. They were happy there. They could go wherever they wanted. Eat whatever they pleased. Now, she's trapped. She can't move. She's going to die. The question is, how long will she have to live in pain before she's put out of her misery? *(Beat.)* What are you going to do Austin? She's waiting.

(Suddenly, AUSTIN smashes the spider with a book. She starts crying and looks up at MARY.)

MARY: I'm ready to go, darling. Please, let me go.

(Blackout.)

SCENE 5

Saturday, 3:00 p.m. Lights up on CAROLINA, who is sitting in the same spot we last saw her. BALTIMORE and DALLAS watch her, vigilantly. AUSTIN paces upstage.

DALLAS: It's been forty-five minutes.

BALTIMORE: How long is this thing supposed to last?

AUSTIN: I don't know.

BALTIMORE: How long?

AUSTIN: I don't know.

BALTIMORE: Take a guess, Dr. Kevorkian.

AUSTIN: Fifteen minutes.

(The SISTERS look at each other.)

DALLAS: Austin!

AUSTIN: She promised it would work.

DALLAS: Who?

BALTIMORE: Who promised?

AUSTIN: It doesn't matter.

DALLAS: It absolutely matters. Who promised?

BALTIMORE: Who promised?…Mom?! I bet she made you do it too.

DALLAS: Did she? Did she make you do this? Did you drink the oxy-whatever-it's-called? Answer me.

AUSTIN: Yes.

DALLAS: Oh, Austin.

BALTIMORE: How long were you under?

AUSTIN: Fifteen, maybe twenty minutes.

BALTIMORE: Then why has she been under almost an hour?

AUSTIN: *(Goes to CAROLINA, helpless.)* I don't know. She's had a lot to drink. Maybe that somehow increases the potency or slows down the poison. I don't know. Look, I'm sure she'll be fine.

BALTIMORE: *(Follows.)* Really? In your vast experience of killing people, you're batting what? A thousand?! You killed Mom. *(Beat.)* You're like a professional killer.

AUSTIN: Shut up.

BALTIMORE: Double O Austin, licensed to kill.

AUSTIN: I said shut up.

BALTIMORE: I am so sick and tired of people telling me what to do. I will not shut up. I have a voice.

AUSTIN: Fine.

BALTIMORE: Fine.

DALLAS: What are we supposed to do?

AUSTIN: We should let her sleep it off.

DALLAS: She's not sleeping.

AUSTIN: It's an expression. It has to go through her system.

DALLAS: Well how fucking long is that going to take?

AUSTIN: Is fuck your new favorite word?

DALLAS: Fuck off.

BALTIMORE: I guess it is.

AUSTIN: She's going to be fine. It's like one minute you can't move and the next, you're…fine.

DALLAS: That's a comforting word… fine.

AUSTIN: What do you want me to say?

DALLAS: Uninjured. Undamaged. Intact.

AUSTIN: *Fine.* She's going to be *intact.*

DALLAS: We should call someone.

AUSTIN: No, we shouldn't.

BALTIMORE: Yeah, could you get me the number of the I-Just-Poisoned-My-Sister hotline?

DALLAS: A doctor. We should call a doctor.

AUSTIN: So he can find Carolina in the chair and Mom in the tub?

DALLAS: I don't care. This is too dangerous. I'm calling someone.

(DALLAS goes to the phone. AUSTIN stops her, wrestles it from her. They glare at each other.)

AUSTIN: I'm stronger than you are, Dallas.

DALLAS: You're psychotic.

(AUSTIN puts down the phone. DALLAS returns to CAROLINA.)

BALTIMORE: Give me a break. If someone wanted to call someone, I'd pull out my cell phone. We're not gonna call anyone.

AUSTIN: Thank you. Someone else who's thinking logically.

BALTIMORE: Oh please. You're not scaring anyone, Austin, you're just pathetic. *(She looks down the hall.)* I'm going to sit with Mom. *(Grabs a vodka bottle and exits.)*

DALLAS: *(Begins to lose it.)* Why am I here? I don't belong here. I don't fit into this family reunion. This is not the family I signed up for. I have my family. Peter's my family. *(Takes a deep breath. Tries to calm herself with a mantra.)* I got away from this madhouse. I have created my own life. I've established my own routine. I have my own boundaries. Why did I come back? I don't even know you people anymore.

AUSTIN: You never knew us.

DALLAS: Why? Because I was the outsider? Mom never cared about me. I didn't make *sense* in our family of overachievers. I could never color outside of the lines or connect the dots into my own pattern. I followed the rules. I was a follower, not a leader. I fit the mold.

AUSTIN: So now that Mom's dead, you've decided to have a pity party for yourself? You have a good life, Dallas. Mom raised you well, so don't start biting the hand that fed you.

DALLAS: You are just filled with lovely little metaphors aren't you?

AUSTIN: Look, if you really think you're ready to open your eyes to the reality of life, be my guest. But you can't handle ugly.

DALLAS: I can handle as much ugliness as you can.

AUSTIN: No. You can't. You created this perfect little world far away from your severely dysfunctional family. You live in your surreal utopia with your perfectly manicured lawns and your perfectly pristine buildings. Your perfect little suburban Garden of Eden where nothing evil ever happens.

DALLAS: Is that what you think? I teach at a private school so I'm inured to the problems of society? I can't feel anything? That's priceless. You've elected to isolate yourself in your house with your mother…what do you know about what I deal with on a daily basis?

AUSTIN: "Your mother?"

DALLAS: What?

AUSTIN: You just called her "*your* mother." Isn't she *your* mother too?

DALLAS: It's just an expression.

AUSTIN: More like a Freudian slip.

DALLAS: You're impossible to talk to, you just keep twisting things around.

AUSTIN: I'm just saying that maybe you'd feel more culpable if you had used the expression "our mother." She stopped being all of your mothers a long time ago.

DALLAS: You're right.

AUSTIN: I am?

DALLAS: Yes. When mothers are so fucking self-absorbed they put themselves before their children…then they stop being your mother—

AUSTIN: —Dallas

DALLAS: —When I got married, Peter became my family. *(Beat.)* I still remember when Mom married Baltimore's father. I was just a kid, but I remember. Do you? Do you remember? She ignored me. She ignored all of us. It was "Richard" this and "Dickie" that. DICK became her life and we were pushed into the background. She was not the perfect mother, Austin. No one can be. Heck, she didn't even come close. Every week she'd fall deeply in love and ignore us while she pottered about with her latest husband or lover or boy-toy. Nothing like being abandoned in your own home, over and over again.

AUSTIN: You abandoned Mom. You all did.

DALLAS: I had an abortion. *(Breaks down.)* Still think I can't handle the ugliness of life in my perfectly pristine world?

AUSTIN: I thought you guys really wanted kids?

DALLAS: We did. He does...But I don't. I always thought I'd have them, lots of them, and how different it would be for them than it was for me. How I'd take them to field hockey practice and piano lessons and pay attention to them. I guess I had painted this life for myself and it was going right on track...but when it happened, I panicked. I suddenly realized, I don't want kids. I don't want to be a mom. I don't want to be like Mom. She ruined me. I just want to take care of me. Me and Peter.

AUSTIN: You're blaming this on Mom?

DALLAS: At the end of the day, I want to jump into my sweats, pour myself a big glass of red wine, and watch bad reality TV. I want to be selfish.

AUSTIN: What did Peter say?

DALLAS: I didn't tell Peter. I couldn't. I told him I was going for my yearly pap smear and I did it, right in the office. I made him dinner that night. I taught the next day. Life goes on, right?

(BALTIMORE enters with a vodka bottle. She is drunk and barrels past a crying DALLAS to confront AUSTIN.)

BALTIMORE: Why doesn't Mom smell? She should smell. Dead bodies smell.

AUSTIN: Let it go, Baltimore.

BALTIMORE: Who died and left you boss? *(Beat.)* Oh, I guess Mom did. *(Beat.)* This is so fucked up. You know that? I mean I was around. I had vacation time. I wanted to come home, every break I had, but no...You guys were always saying, travel, stay at school, study. How much do you think there really is to study when you're majoring in sociology? *(She grabs a Russian doll off the shelf and opens it, pulling out the dolls inside one by one, setting them down.)* You know the problem with these fucking dolls? The smallest one has absolutely no purpose. See, you've got this big one. The one that holds all the other ones. And you realize that she has a purpose. She's the Mother. She contains all these other dolls inside of her. Protecting them. She's like a kangaroo, and all of these other dolls are like...baby kangaroos safely tucked away inside her pouch. So, you've got the Mother. Then the big one whom everyone revered. The talented one whom everyone worshipped. The perfect one whom everyone admired. *(She has opened four of the dolls, revealing the tiniest doll. She holds up the "baby.")* And then you get to the end and there's this tiny doll, this shitty little piece of wood...with absolutely no purpose. The baby. She doesn't hold anything inside of her. Hell, you can barely see her. I call her...Baltimore.

(BALTIMORE places the tiny doll at the end of the row, turns, and slaps AUSTIN, hard.)

BALTIMORE: You didn't let me say goodbye.

AUSTIN: *(Recoils.)* That really hurt.

BALTIMORE: Then it worked. *(Begins to laugh, uncontrollably.)* Hey, *complete non sequitur*, guess who dropped out of Harvard last semester? Surprise! No point keeping that a secret anymore. Why learn bullshit theories by dead white men when I can be out in the real world creating my own theories? Actualizing my own potential! *(She can't stop laughing.)* I signed up for the Peace Corps three weeks ago. I'm going to Cambodia. I'm going to help lepers. *(Beat.)* I was gonna tell Mom I was spending a semester abroad. I thought I'd have time to tell her, to say goodbye. She would have been proud of me. Taking action. *(Beat.)* I used to envy you, Austin. I wanted to be you.

CAROLINA: *(Suddenly speaks in a hoarse whisper.)* You dropped out of school?

(EVERYONE turns to CAROLINA.)

DALLAS: Carolina.

CAROLINA: *(Clears her throat.)* You dropped out of Harvard?

(BALTIMORE nods meekly.)

CAROLINA: That would have killed Mom.

BALTIMORE: Luckily that's been taken care of. Thanks Austin.

DALLAS: Get her a washcloth. GO.

BALTIMORE: *(Imitates.)* Get her a washcloth. Get her a washcloth. *(She exits.)*

CAROLINA: *(Stretches her body gingerly. To DALLAS.)* I think I finally understand what you meant by relaxed.

DALLAS: How do you feel?

CAROLINA: *(Reaches underneath her.)* Spending an hour with your ass glued to a… *(Pulls out Ken doll.)* Ken doll is not my idea of a fun afternoon, but I'm fine. A little stiff, but I'm fine.

AUSTIN: *(To DALLAS.)* See, I told you. She's fine.

DALLAS: Shut up. *(To CAROLINA.)* Is there anything we can get you?

CAROLINA: *(To AUSTIN.)* You—are in a lot of trouble.

AUSTIN: I know.

CAROLINA: What were you thinking?

AUSTIN: I wasn't.

CAROLINA: You've committed two felonies in the last twenty-four hours.

AUSTIN: I know. I'm sorry.

CAROLINA: I could have you arrested.

AUSTIN: Then you could be my lawyer.

CAROLINA: *(Continues to stretch.)* You took that stuff too?

(AUSTIN nods.)

CAROLINA: I've never felt anything like it. It was unbelievable. I was completely paralyzed. I heard…I saw everything. I felt…hot, cold, itchy…that's what was happening to Mom?

AUSTIN: Only hers wasn't temporary.

CAROLINA: Poor Mom.

AUSTIN: I know.

(They look at each other, hard.)

CAROLINA: I would have killed her too.

DALLAS: Carolina!

CAROLINA: Absolutely. You want to try it? *(She looks at DALLAS.)*

DALLAS: No!

(BALTIMORE enters with a washcloth. She puts it on CAROLINA's head.)

BALTIMORE: Why doesn't Mom smell? She should smell. Her body's been decomposing for over fourteen hours. She should smell. She should stink. So why doesn't she smell? *(Beat.)* What time did you kill her?

AUSTIN: I wish you wouldn't refer to it that way.

BALTIMORE: Sorry, what time did you "assist her suicide"?

AUSTIN: I don't remember.

BALTIMORE: Bullshit. I want you to tell me why doesn't Mom smell? It doesn't make sense. It's impossible. If she died yesterday and we didn't get here till this morning, she should smell. She should smell a lot. SO, WHY DOESN'T SHE SMELL?

(There is a long silence. EVERYONE looks at AUSTIN. CAROLINA realizes first.)

CAROLINA: No.

BALTIMORE: No.

DALLAS: What? What am I missing?

BALTIMORE: Please tell me you didn't.

CAROLINA: You couldn't, could you?

AUSTIN: No.

DALLAS: WHAT AM I MISSING?

CAROLINA: She was alive.

BALTIMORE: That's just sick.

DALLAS: If someone doesn't tell me what's going on, *I'm* going to slit my wrists!

(They all look at her.)

DALLAS: What? *(She suddenly gets it.)* Wait, Mom was still alive when you called us?!

AUSTIN: I couldn't…I tried. I had a drink, or three, she thought I'd be more relaxed. I carried her to the tub…and then I just…froze. Time kept passing and…well, she was worried that Carolina wasn't going to get a flight out…so I called.

DALLAS: While she was still alive.

AUSTIN: It was a lot easier than I thought. She held my hand. *(Looks at CAROLINA.)* I told you Mom was dead while she was holding my hand.

BALTIMORE: Us too?

AUSTIN: It just got easier and easier. It's like, because I told you she was dead, I knew that I could do it. I had…a deadline.

CAROLINA: Poor Austin.

BALTIMORE: Poor Austin? That's bullshit. Mom was alive when you called us. So, when did she die?

AUSTIN: Eleven-thirty.

BALTIMORE: Last night?

AUSTIN: *(Looks at her SISTERS.)* This morning.

BALTIMORE: We got here at twelve.

DALLAS: Oh, Austin.

AUSTIN: That's why Mom doesn't smell.

BALTIMORE: I don't envy you anymore.

(EVERYONE is silent, lost in her own thoughts.)

DALLAS: Shouldn't the coroner be here by now?

CAROLINA: This is Poughkeepsie. It's probably a part-time job.

DALLAS: So. When he comes, won't he know? I mean. Won't he know the body is only a few hours dead?

AUSTIN: You're doing it again.

DALLAS: What?

AUSTIN: The body. It's Mom. Your mother. Our mother. "Body" is so… cold.

DALLAS: I really am not in a mood to argue semantics right now. Besides, shouldn't you be a little concerned?

AUSTIN: Why?

DALLAS: I think the coroner, unless he graduated from the New York public school system, is going to realize that Mom didn't off herself, she had some help. That's a coroner's job, right?

AUSTIN: No. He just takes the body away.

DALLAS: Really, Perry Mason? How do you know?

CAROLINA: A coroner's job is to inquire into the cause of death and decide if a death occurs under natural circumstances or due to accident, homicide, or suicide.

(They look at her.)

CAROLINA: Lawyer. Remember? *(Looks at AUSTIN.)* Are you worried?

AUSTIN: A little. A lot. I don't know what I'm going to say.

BALTIMORE: I'll convince him what he needs to know.

AUSTIN: Really?

BALTIMORE: Look, you can write. Carolina can lawyer. Dallas can teach. I happen to have a gift with the opposite sex. Cause of death will be a definitive suicide. Trust me.

AUSTIN: I guess I'll have to.

BALTIMORE: He'll take the zirconia ceramic razor blade as evidence. I do have a purpose.

AUSTIN: I know you do. *(Beat.)* Well, I don't know about the rest of you, but I guess I'm going to hell so I should go pack.

CAROLINA: You put her out of her misery. That's a mitzvah, not a sin.

DALLAS: Mitzvah?

CAROLINA: What's-his-name was half Jewish, I've picked up a little Yiddish here and there.

(Silence.)

DALLAS: So, what happens now?

CAROLINA: We wait for the coroner. We go back to our lives.

DALLAS: It just feels so…unresolved.

CAROLINA: How are we supposed to resolve it? Austin helped Mom kill herself. Mom had ALS. We all hate each other. Case closed.

DALLAS: I don't hate you. I don't hate any of you. I don't understand you, but I don't hate you.

AUSTIN: Life doesn't resolve itself. It doesn't work like that. It never works like that.

DALLAS: That's seeing the glass half empty.

CAROLINA: You're the only one who sees the glass half full, Dallas. Most of us see it half empty.

AUSTIN: My glass is broken.

BALTIMORE: I don't even have a glass.

CAROLINA: Mom raised a bunch of cynics. *(Beat.)* What a fucking depressing day.

DALLAS: What's the matter with seeing the glass half full? I love my life. I mean, how many people can say that, really say it and mean it? Can you guys?

AUSTIN: Not me.

BALTIMORE: Nope.

CAROLINA: Definitely not.

BALTIMORE: You're just happy because you're in a perfect relationship.

AUSTIN: No she's not.

CAROLINA: Austin.

AUSTIN: What? I mean, Peter's great and everything, but you didn't tell him about the abortion.

BALTIMORE: You had an abortion?

(DALLAS nods.)

BALTIMORE: Oh my god, you're not perfect!

CAROLINA: At least Dallas was only lying to Peter.

AUSTIN: What's that supposed to me?

CAROLINA: Lying to someone else is forgivable, but lying to yourself...

AUSTIN: I don't lie to myself.

CAROLINA: Bullshit. How come you moved back home? Why haven't you written a book in the last five years? You're still resting on your laurels?

AUSTIN: As long as I can. That's what makes me an artist.

CAROLINA: Where's your follow-up?

AUSTIN: In my head. Tucked away comfortably.

CAROLINA: You had your freshman success and you're supposed to follow it up with a sophomore sensation.

AUSTIN: Right. My freshman year at Princeton, I started on the lacrosse team, came out, and won the school's lit contest. Sophomore year I blew out my knee, lost my girlfriend, and gained forty pounds...I don't have such a great track record as a sophomore sensation.

CAROLINA: So, then what? You spend the next fifty years holed up here enjoying the royalties from book one?

AUSTIN: Something like that.

CAROLINA: You're a coward.

AUSTIN: I'm really not in the mood—

CAROLINA: —For someone who almost killed two people in the last five hours, I think you can put yourself in the mood. What's keeping you here? What are you hiding from? If you're a writer, aren't you supposed to get out there and observe life? Seems to me, you've spent the last year observing death.

AUSTIN: I can't write. I write one book which manages to land on the *New York Times* best-seller list and all of a sudden, I'm a fucking celebrity? People expect things from me. I can't figure out my own life and other people, strangers, expect things from me. I have no idea how I wrote that book. I just did it. *(Beat.)* Do you know how many self-help books I own? I've tried *everything*: Yoga, meditation…even Kabbalah—but I didn't *get* the whole red string thing. I mean, if you're gonna find yourself, shouldn't you do it privately…not announce to the whole world "look at me"…I have a red string…I'm Madonna. I'm *not* Madonna…Madonna was the perfect mother, right? Not "*Like* a Virgin" Madonna, the "*Is* a virgin" Madonna— the Virgin Mother. The virgin Mary. Ha. Our Mary was no virgin. She slept with the fucking gardener. So, the original Mary has Jesus, who becomes God, right? So then our Mary has *me* who she chooses to play God, on whom she generously bestows the power of life or death. *(Beat.)* But I have to give her credit. She asked for help. She wasn't afraid to show her weakness. I'm terrified. What happens when people realize I am far less than they expected. I write a book and people think they know me. They don't know me. I don't know me. Mom never knew me. She raised the bar so high, so impossibly out of reach. I could never live up to her expectations.

CAROLINA: It's the burden of being her favorite.

AUSTIN: What?

CAROLINA: You were her favorite. Don't worry, we all know it. Show of hands in favor?

(She raises her hand. DALLAS and BALTIMORE do the same.)

CAROLINA: You were the most like her, Austin. You had the talent. You were the artist. I was too focused and Dallas was too… *(She looks at DALLAS.)* Good. Sorry.

DALLAS: I live with the burden.

BALTIMORE: You're not that good.

CAROLINA: Baltimore always kind of did her own thing, so that left you. I used to be so jealous of what you guys had. It's like you were a conduit for her. She never got to explore her creative side, so she lived vicariously through you. You were like…this vessel that Mom could manipulate to her will.

AUSTIN: Okay. That's just creepy.

CAROLINA: You need to get out of the house, Austin. You need to get on with your life.

AUSTIN: I just want to be happy. Mom was happy.

CAROLINA: Well, I'm fucking miserable. Do you think Mom knew? I mean, do you think she had some inkling that her life was going to end like this?

BALTIMORE: Naked in a bathtub? It's very Sonny von Bülow.

(They are silent.)

AUSTIN: She was ready to go.

CAROLINA: I'm going to miss her.

BALTIMORE: Me too.

AUSTIN: Yeah.

(Silence. They turn and look at DALLAS.)

DALLAS: What? I'm not a monster. Just because she fucked up my self-esteem, sense of self, and identity doesn't mean I won't miss her. She's my mother.

CAROLINA: Parents are supposed to fuck up their kids. It part of the evolutionary cycle.

AUSTIN: What do you do when there are no parents left?

CAROLINA: You work with what you've got. *(She looks at AUSTIN.)* Why don't you come live with me?

AUSTIN: Right. Because we're so close.

CAROLINA: I have a huge old rambling Victorian that's far too big for me...Seattle's pretty. Six days a year.

AUSTIN: *(Looks at her, hard.)* Okay.

CAROLINA: Okay.

AUSTIN: Okay.

BALTIMORE: *(Shocked.)* Okay?

DALLAS: *(Excited.)* Okay! Hey, with Mom gone, all we have left to make us crazy is each other. *(Hands out vodka bottles. Toasts.)* To our mom. This is what she would have wanted, right?

AUSTIN: *(Toasts.)* She lived one hell of a life.

CAROLINA: *(Toasts.)* L'chayim!

(They all look at each other.)

ALL: L'chayim!

BALTIMORE: *(Puts down her glass, frozen.)* What about me?

CAROLINA: What?

BALTIMORE: You guys are going back to Seattle and Dallas has Peter. What am I supposed to do?

CAROLINA: You joined the Peace Corps. You're pretty much screwed for the next two years.

(They laugh.)

BALTIMORE: Oh. But you guys will visit, right?

AUSTIN: No.   CAROLINA: No.

DALLAS: I think I'll stay clear of leper colonies, thanks.

BALTIMORE: *(She toasts.)* Oh. To Mom.

(They look at each other.)

DALLAS: It feels like we're missing something.

AUSTIN: I have an idea. *(Runs out.)*

BALTIMORE: Hey, I just thought of something. This is going to be a really fucked-up Mother's Day.

CAROLINA: Why? Do you usually celebrate Mother's Day?

BALTIMORE: No, no I don't.

(They laugh.)

AUSTIN: *(Enters with a lingerie drawer.)* Her favorites.

DALLAS: Can we?

BALTIMORE: She'd be mortified if we didn't.

DALLAS: She'll be mortified if we do.

(AUSTIN and CAROLINA each hold up a different colored bra and underwear.)

DALLAS: It has to match.

BALTIMORE: *(Holds up a matching pair.)* Pretty in pink!

(They all look at each other.)

AUSTIN: I'll go do it.

BALTIMORE: We'll do it together.

AUSTIN: You sure?

DALLAS: Yeah.

CAROLINA: All of us.

(The doorbell rings. EVERYONE looks up.)

DALLAS: Fuck.

(Blackout. Curtain.)

S/HE

Nanna "Nick" Mwaluko

NANNA "NICK" MWALUKO is a playwright. He was born in Dar-es-Salaam, Tanzania, and grew up in East and Central Africa. He earned a bachelor's degree in writing and French from Columbia University, where he is currently working towards a master's degree. He studied at the Iowa Writer's Workshop. His plays include *Waafrika* (2005 Fresh Fruit Festival) and *Mwena* (Culture Project's 2008 Women Center Stage Festival). His work has been published by the *Huffington Post*, the *Washington Times*, and Reuters News Agency, for which he worked for seven years in both Kenya and New York. He is also a member of The Public Theater's Emerging Writers Group. He was awarded Columbia University's J. R. Humphreys Fellowship from 2000–2003 and the Iowa Writer's Workshop's 2004 Norman Felton Award. He has been commissioned by The Public Theater to write a new play and is currently developing a television series. In addition, he is working on a screenplay and novel. He lives in Manhattan, where he teaches and works for the government.

S/He was first presented by the Fresh Fruit Festival (Carol Polcovar, Artistic Director) on July 23, 2008, at the Algonquin Theater with the following cast and credits:

Sam ....Zainab Jah
Dawn, Jill, Nurse Nancy, Singer .... Sadrina Johnson
Helen, Mom, Dr. Rustein, Singer...................... Maria Silverman

Director: José Zayas

The original title of *S/He* was *Are Women Human?* *S/He* may be performed as a stand-alone one-act, but a two-act version is also available.

I wish to thank my Lord and Savior Jesus Christ, without whom nothing would or could be possible given the thin strength of my fiber spirit: thank You God. On a terrestrial note, I wish to dedicate this publication of *S/He* to Liz Frankel. Her passion for the play from its infancy to its present incarnation, her warrior spirit, hard-core resilience, endurance to prod and provoke remain unparalleled in my collaborative experience. Lisa Timmel and Lisa Kopitsky played a protectively subtle role when nurturing thought to page to script. When handing Mandy Hackett my play *Waafrika*—I'll never forget—she thanked me several times. My first thought? "How can I work in this environment?" These four: my debt to them speaks to the unspeakable truth writers labor hard for, often alone in their seemingly solitary pursuit of something larger than themselves. Life's tools are sufficient to harness the enormity of any artistic task, true, but a troop of tested allies always helps when sculpting. Thanks to my parents and family, especially Helen who fights hard for her artistic vision. Thanks to John Harris, Alicia D. House for her initial suggestions, Judith Aidoo, Austin Flint, José Zayas, Zainab Jah, Jehan Young, Maria Silverman, Jennifer Jospeh, Ahmat Diallo, Cindy Creager, James Dacre, Rebecca Y., Luis Castro for taking time from his busy schedule to see the play, Annie Seaton, Senam, Ken Kaissar, Sadrina Johnson, EWG family, Tamilla Woodard, Jennifer Stromberg, Shelley Fischel, the Point, Amy L S., Rebecca Bishaf, UBF, Vince Garcia, Ishmael Osekre, Andrew Lamb for steadfast prayer and supplication, Gabriel and Joe Lamb, AME and its choir, Pastor Flake, Maria Mileaf, Lisa and Mikaela Rabinowitz, Steven Turner, Casey, Paige, Denis Deno, Mdachi M., Antje Oegel, Martin Denton and his family, Elmo Terry-Morgan, Karen Baxter, Sam Porter, Shterna Wircberg, Nehal El-Kashef. My circle of good friends is counted among my silent support group. Finally, a plug for my play *Waafrika*, adapted as a film now in need of a director should anyone wish to apply. Welcome.

IMPORTANT PRODUCTION NOTES

Casting

All characters except Sam 2 should be PLAYED EXCLUSIVELY BY WOMEN, meaning only anatomical females can play these roles. One actress plays Sam. Two other actresses play all other characters. Those two actresses can also play the singing chorus, or the chorus can be played by a separate actress or by a group/chorus.

Staging

There is a cross-pollination between worlds, meaning scenes bleed into one another, transitions flow fluidly from one world to the next. This structural device is meant to underscore the theme of transitioning, the s/hero transitioning from one body to another. To assist quick structural transitions, no characters should enter or exit the stage. There should be no doors. Ideally, little or no props are needed, nor costume changes except where indicated in the script.

CHARACTERS IN ORDER OF APPEARANCE

DOCTOR: Sam's doctor (played by Actress 1)
NURSE NANCY: Sam's nurse (played by Actress 2)
DAWN: Sam's friend, girl (played by Actress 1)
HELEN: Sam's friend, girl (played by Actress 2)
SAM: S/he; Black woman who wants to be a man
BOSS LESTER: Sam's boss, adult man (played by Actress 2)
MOM: Sam's mom, adult woman (played by Actress 1)
JILL: Sam's ex-girlfriend (played by Actress 2)
GOSPEL ANGELS: Singing chorus/soloists
SAM 2: An anatomical male version of Sam

SCENES

(Note: Scenes are not demarcated in the play's text.)

Scene I: School playground
Scene II: Bakery
Scene III: Mother's home
Scene IV: Cell phone conversation outside in the rain
Scene V: Jill's place
Scene VI: Mother's place
Scene VII: Jill's place
Scene VIII: Transitioning

TIME AND SETTING

Present. An urban world.

In darkness:

DR. RUSTEIN: Needle?

NURSE NANCY: Needle.

DR. RUSTEIN: Shot.

NURSE NANCY: Any surgeries, Sam?

SAM: Before now? No.

NURSE NANCY: None whatsoever? How 'bout cuts, bleeding, lacerations? Any scars?

MOM: C'mon Samantha. Tell the truth, you're in pain.

SAM: Mom, that you?

NURSE NANCY: So, no pain? You're free from pain is what you're saying? Good, breathe in.

ENTIRE CAST: Huh huh huh huh huh huh huh huh

NURSE NANCY: And breathe out.

(A school bell goes off. Lights up. Two girls, HELEN and DAWN, are in the school-yard playing their favorite hand game.)

HELEN and DAWN: *(Sing.)* Patty—

(Freeze. Both girls have their hands frozen in mid-air for a long, long time. Unfreeze.)

HELEN and DAWN: Patty-cake—

(Freeze. Both girls have their hands frozen in mid-air for a long, long time. Unfreeze.)

HELEN and DAWN: Patty-cake, patty-
  cake
Baker's dough
Make me a cake so I can grow
Patty-cake, patty-cake
Baker's dough
Make me a—

(SAM enters the yard.)

DAWN: Hey Sam?

SAM: What?

HELEN: Wanna play?

SAM: Nope.

DAWN: How come?

SAM: Girl game.

HELEN: So?

SAM: I look like a girl to you?

DAWN: Hell yeah.

SAM: *(To DAWN.)* Stupid!

DAWN: *(To SAM.)* Stupid!

HELEN: *(To DAWN.)* Stupid! *(To SAM.)* See, Dawn is stupid but she's my best friend so I can say she's stupid but you can't 'cause she's not your best friend. Plus, you're the stupidest.

SAM: Am not.

DAWN: Yeah you are Samantha.

SAM: Don't call me that.

HELEN: *(To DAWN.)* 'Cause she's a boy remember?

SAM: I'm not no "she."

HELEN: Then prove it.

SAM: Look. *(Rolls up his/her sleeve.)* Muscles.

HELEN: Big deal. Mine are way bigger. *(Rolls up her sleeve.)* Look.

SAM: Bet you don't have a cock.

DAWN: A what?

HELEN: Penis.

DAWN: Nahuh, you're lying.

SAM: Wanna see?

DAWN: Nahuh, you're lying.

SAM: Kneel down.

DAWN: For what?

HELEN: Do it, Dawn.

(HELEN and DAWN kneel down on the floor.)

SAM: Now close your eyes.

(HELEN and DAWN close their eyes.)

SAM: And open your mouth.

DAWN: What for?

HELEN: To slip his cock inside, dumb-dumb. My mouth's open Sam.

SAM: Ready?

(HELEN and DAWN nod "yes.")

SAM: My cock is monster big. Promise you won't choke when it goes inside, 'kay? *(Opens his/her zipper, digs in. When his/her hand comes out there is fresh menstrual blood on it.)* Shit! Blood downstairs. Oh God, not again.

HELEN: What?

SAM: Nothing.

DAWN: Where's your cock?

SAM: Keep your eyes closed.

HELEN: But I'm waiting.

DAWN: Forget it, Helen. She's a liar.

SAM: How many times I gotta tell you I'm not no "she"?

DAWN: Where is it then? We're wait-ing.

BOSS LESTER: Late yet again.

SAM: Sorry.

BOSS LESTER: What's that sign say?

SAM: *(Pointing.)* Over there? "Lester's Bakery."

BOSS LESTER: That's right. I'm the boss.

SAM: I'm real sorry I'm late, Lester.

BOSS LESTER: Should I give a shit? Why should I give a shit? Give me one good shitty reason why I should give a shit? Then give me another good shitty reason why I shouldn't fire your ass? Put you out on the street. Hire me one of them Sudanese immigrants fresh off the boat. Work my bakery two cents an hour, huh?

SAM: Lester, like I said, I'm real sorry. You're a great boss. I need this great job. I need the great pay. See, I'm going for an operation—

BOSS LESTER: Hooo—you sick? Tired? Think I give a shit you sick 'n' tired? I don't give a shit you sick 'n' tired. Who ain't sick 'n' tired? *I'm* sick 'n' tired but *I* come here every day. On time. Seven days a week, fourteen fucken back-breaking hours working nonstop. Shove bread in oven. Wrap bread in plastic. Hand bread to customer. Customer smiles. That's aaaalll I'm asking. Come in on time. Do your damn job.

SAM: I'll try.

BOSS LESTER: You'll do better than try or I'll see your ass at unemployment.

SAM: Yessir.

BOSS LESTER: Where you going?

SAM: Downstairs.

BOSS LESTER: What for?

SAM: My apron.

BOSS LESTER: Turn.

SAM: Where?

BOSS LESTER: Around.

SAM: [What the] fuck for?

BOSS LESTER: You arguing? Aw, kid, you look twelve. Them weedy muscles couldn't carry a paper bag without help from the wind. You in school?

(SAM mumbles something inaudible under his/her breath.)

BOSS LESTER: So how come you dress like that?

SAM: Like what?

BOSS LESTER: Hat.

SAM: Huh?

BOSS LESTER: Off.

SAM: Lester this don't feel right.

BOSS LESTER: Mmm-hmm, tha's it, come closer. Closer than that or I can't hear you. Now, I didn't get you that first time: No parents? That how come you dress so poor?

SAM: I got paren—

BOSS LESTER: Sssssssssh-sssh-sssh.

SAM: Mom.

BOSS LESTER: Ain't you got parents?

SAM: Mom!

MOM: Late again.

SAM: Sorry.

MOM: As usual.

SAM: My creepy boss fucken Lester—

MOM: Watch that filthy mouth of yours when you come into *my* home. Mouth full of filth won't make you any more manly. Understand, young lady?

SAM: Please don't call me "young lady." That's not how I see myse—

MOM: Where you been? Look at me. Look at what you're doing to your poor mother.

SAM: You're smoking. Thought you quit.

MOM: And now I quit quitting. Cigarette after cigarette after pack after— (Pause.) Downed half a bottle of—I don't even know what this shit is (Lifts the bottle.) Two a.m. with a bottle, why? My nerves are smashed, why? I should call the police. Why? Because my seventeen-year-old daughter—

SAM: I'm not—

MOM: Where you been? And don't lie to me out working when I know for a fact jobs do not end at two in the morning unless you're a drug dealer, a whore, or a drug-dealing whore. Which one are you, Samantha?

SAM: Call me Sam. My fucken name is—

MOM: What I'd just say about curse words in *my* house, Samantha? I will call you what I want when I want how I want to. This is *my* home. I am *your* mom. At least that's what it says here. (MOM shows an envelope.)

SAM: What's that?

MOM: What's it look like?

SAM: Envelope.

MOM: From school. Open it.

SAM: (Nervous.) Why, what's it say?

MOM: You drop out?

SAM: Of school?

MOM: *(Genuine concern.)* Tell me the truth.

SAM: They beat me up.

MOM: *(Genuine concern.)* Who does?

SAM: Everyone. They pound me at lunchtime when—

MOM: So? We switch schools.

SAM: That's not the point. The point is—

MOM: Girls your age have problems, Sama—

SAM: Wrong. The point is—

MOM: Samantha, I do not appreciate—

SAM: Are you kidding me? "Samantha?" That's not my name! It's a time bomb strapped to my body that goes off without ticking. "Sama"—I look like a girl to you? Do I? When I pee standing up, pants down, face the fucken toilet like a man then leave the door half open so you can *see me* Mom. T-shirts, baggy. Twenty-four seven, hunch my shoulders to hide my chest so no one knows what's underneath. Spit on *(Spits.)* all over sidewalks. "Samantha," Check my hair, here, Mom: bald here, here, over on this side, bald. Don't pretend you don't— My name— Mom? Mom! Can we talk? Please.

MOM: Go—back—to—school.

SAM: Don't do that Mom. Please, don't— Where you going? Not for a drink. Don't go to—

MOM: I'm going to bed.

SAM: Look at me.

MOM: First thing tomorrow morning you will…

SAM: Why can't you look at me? Why can't—

MOM: I what? What else do you want besides curse words and "no school"? Tell me. What else is there?

SAM: I'm not going to school.

MOM: You will go.

SAM: I have to work.

MOM: After school.

SAM: To save money.

MOM: For what?

SAM: For my operation.

(Pause. MOM eyes that liquor cabinet like a hawk.)

SAM: Do you love me?

MOM: I want you to listen and listen to me good or—

SAM: Do you?

MOM: What does that have to do with—

SAM: Do you love me?

MOM: Do you love me?

SAM: YES, God YES.

MOM: Then go to school Then go to college Then find a job Then help with bills Then save some money Then buy a house Then get married Then have kids Then get fat Then get angry Then get fatter Then jog Then he cheats So you separate Then divorce Then sit pretty with your feet propped up on a pillow next to a bag of potato chips watching rich people live your dream life on late night TV Then die. Understand? I am old, too old. I cannot afford to work the way I do and not expect my body to collapse right here on this living room floor. Is that where you plan to bury me? That what you want for our family?

SAM: No I—

MOM: So *if* you love me, *since* you love me, HELP ME OUT HERE!

SAM: How do I—

MOM: Quit dreaming! Stop throwing it away!

SAM: What am I—

MOM: My plans for you! For—

SAM: Mom, listen—

MOM: Still think it's funny? While I'm on all fours at back of the line for this family you laugh? Bruises, look—

SAM: Mom, please—

MOM: *(Showing bruises.)* Here—

SAM: Wait—

MOM: Here—

SAM: Sorry. I'm so—

MOM: Here—

SAM: Hold on. If you—

MOM: Here from the ironing board while I was— *(To herself.)* Why am I doing this?

SAM: I'm sorry. Sorry you feel—

MOM: How old are you? Eighteen? Then why am I negotiating with a chi—

SAM: I promise, I'll—

MOM: What? Take care of me? Like who?, your punk-ass, no-good fucken father does?

SAM: ME—NOT HIM. I'm—sorry, I shouldn't yell. Mom, this isn't about Dad. When I become a—

MOM: Shut up. I don't need more empty promises. I need—

SAM: I know what you—

MOM: Stupidity of this child is beyond me. She doesn't understand all I went through for her to be where she is. The sacrifices I made so she could come home, stare me in the face, give me this bullshit time and time again.

SAM: I know. It's scary, me being a man. It makes no sense. But you have to trust me. You give a lot to this family. I know that. I won't forget you. When I'm a man, just trust me. Okay? I'll make life better for us, okay?

THE WHOLE CAST: *(Breathing/gasping.)* Huh huh huh huh huh huh huh huh huh huh huh huh huh

(Pause.)

SAM: Mom?

MOM: Go back to school. Okay?

SAM: Are you kidding me?

MOM: Switch.

SAM: What?

MOM: I come home half-dead you think, "Hooo-wee, life sure is tough for a Black woman. Don't want that. So maybe I should *switch*. Become a Black man. Might be easier."

SAM: Is that what you think this is?

MOM: Know what this is? This is a Black man with no high school diploma in this country in this day and age. So, let me ask you: How far do you honestly think you can get in life?

(SAM is silent.)

MOM: Silence. What, no words of wisdom—Brother?

SAM: Make fun of me all you want but—

MOM: I'm tired. I am. So decide: school?

SAM: Mom, after everything we just—

MOM: School?

SAM: No.

MOM: Get out.

SAM: What do you mean "get out"? I can't, Mom. Where will I go?

MOM: Don't know. Don't care. Go to your father.

SAM: *(To Dad on phone.)* Dad, yeah, hi. Guess who?...Your one and only—Sam! Sam, your [child] —yeah, hi. How's everything? *(Beat.)* Oh yeah? *(Beat.)* Sorry to call so late but could we talk? It's important, kinda...yeah, sorta like an emergency...No no no, everything's fine. Yeah, everything—Mom, me, the house, everything, we're— yeah sure thanks, I'll tell her. Dad? Could you stop rambling for a sec 'n' listen to—No...I'm not crying. It's raining outside.

(Umbrellas suddenly pop, showering the stage as the TWO ACTRESSES walk slowly from one end of the stage to the other during this call, open umbrellas in hand.)

Phone booth... *(Pause.)* Yeah but Dad could— Congratulations...Why? Do I sound upset?...I'm happy for you, terrific news. How long you been married Dad?...Let's hope it lasts...I said I hope she makes you very happy...That is what I said. That is what I said. Nope, I'm not lying, that's exactly what— Know what? I don't wanna argue, okay?...'Cause it's always this mind game with you when— Fine, you're right, I'm wrong, but Da— uh huh— *(Pause.)* A place to stay, Dad, could you help me with...?

(Pause.) Why not?, forget it, how 'bout money?...I'm not asking for— No, not much, just a few...enough to hold me over for— Why marry a woman with eight kids?...It's a question Dad, a legitimate...yeah, right, stupid me for asking. I should shut my...I am happy for you. I do mean it...Sure, not a problem, take the next call. Sure, go ahead. Put me on hold. Dad.

(Lights shift. Umbrellas fold.)

SAM: Dad?

(JILL appears. SAM and JILL are silent, face to face for the longest time. Suddenly, JILL opens her arms.)

JILL: *(Arms wide open.)* Come.

(SAM doesn't move.)

JILL: It's okay.

(SAM still doesn't move.)

JILL: It's okay. I won't hurt you. Come.

(SAM collapses in JILL's arms. They embrace for the longest time. When SAM tries to pull away, JILL goes:)

JILL: Don't. Stay.

SAM: Oh, God, you feel so good Jill...so...

JILL: It's okay.

(They gradually pull apart.)

JILL: It's not your fault.

SAM: *(Looking at the ground.)* I know.

JILL: Look at me.

(SAM looks.)

JILL: It's not. With your parents, it's not your fault.

SAM: I know, it's cool. It's all good. It's— *(Pause.)*

JILL: But Sam, I can't.

SAM: Why not?

JILL: Because.

SAM: Just for a month?

JILL: Sorry.

SAM: A week?

JILL: Nope.

SAM: A day? One—

JILL: Sorry.

SAM: Why not?

JILL: I can't.

SAM: Booh, listen, I'll do the dishes.

JILL: You can't clean.

SAM: We'll split rent.

JILL: With whose money, Sam?

SAM: Put me on the couch. Fine, forget the couch, I'll take the floor.

JILL: I wish you could.

SAM: So make it happen.

JILL: I wish I could.

SAM: You can. It's your apartment.

JILL: Sorry.

SAM: Why not?

JILL: I have friends.

SAM: So?

JILL: They're my community.

SAM: But I'm your ex.

JILL: Since when?

SAM: Eight months ago.

JILL: Nine.

SAM: Fine, nine months ago.

JILL: And three days, and four hours, and twenty minutes.

SAM: And... (Checks his/her wrist.) ...ten seconds to be exact.

JILL: Surprise surprise, looks who's counting.

SAM: Got an even bigger surprise once we hit that couch, Boo-boo.

JILL: Not happening.

SAM: Por que?

JILL: I'm a lesbian.

SAM: Who fucks men.

JILL: Big difference between a woman who loves cock so she sleeps with men and a woman who hates women so she becomes a man.

SAM: What's the biiiiig difference, Jill?

JILL: I cheat; you lie—to women.

SAM: Wait, you saying I'm a fake?

JILL: Depends. Who are you?

SAM: Right now? Someone who doesn't wanna argue. I'm tired. I need a hot shower, some chicken noodle soup, then peace 'n' quiet so I can fall asleep during my foot rub—maybe?

JILL: February. Dead of winter. We're holding hands marching side by side with an army of dykes. Who are you?

SAM: Your lover.

JILL: Man or woman? Who are you?

SAM: Right now or right there and then?

JILL: Who are you Sam?

SAM: A man who looks like a woman in love with a lesbian who cheated on me with a biological man?

JILL: So you're doing this to get back at me?

SAM: *(Ridiculous.)* By "get back at me," do you mean we could process your never-ending appetite for prime cock, man-meat or—

JILL: Don't change the subject.

SAM: Well what are we talking about here?

JILL: Why are you doing this?

SAM: Because—

JILL: You hate women.

(Long pause.)

SAM: No. Jill. For real. I'm serious now, I do not—

JILL: Yeah you do. You have to hate women at some level to do what you're—

SAM: I love women. And I adore women who love women so—

JILL: Your mom?

SAM: STOP.

JILL: Hate that she's weak.

SAM: Weak how? She's loyal—

JILL: But dirt poor. And you hate that struggle.

SAM: Wouldn't you?

JILL: Hate seeing my mom come home half-dead night after night? Hell yeah. So I wouldn't want to be her. And with hormones, I wouldn't have to. I could be someone else. I could be a...Is that what this is? Sam running from the past to try to correct it? Or you wanna be your father?

SAM: Shut up.

JILL: We all think this way, Sam, at some point, once in a while. We wonder what it's like, with the power suit and the tie, the clipped hair. I'm not saying where is this coming from? Sign of the times. Dying embers of the feminist mystique, who knows, who cares? But what I am saying is—

SAM: Jill, that's not what this is about.

JILL: You hate men. You do. That's what's weird when—

SAM: Get off. Don't touch my—

JILL: Hey! Don't gimme your back when I'm talking.

(Frustrated, SAM stares into space.)

JILL: Sam.

(Silence.)

JILL: Look at me. I'm not talking...not 'til you look. Baby? Look at me.

(SAM looks but not at JILL.)

JILL: At me.

(SAM looks at JILL.)

JILL: Are you...crying?

SAM: *(Gentle.)* F off.

JILL: Know who I see?

SAM: Don't.

JILL: A beautiful woman.

SAM: Jill, stop.

JILL: Beautiful wom—

SAM: Please.

JILL: My ebony queen.

SAM: Sssssh.

JILL: No, Sam, I have to say this 'cause they sure as shit don't say it enough while we're growing up. Sam Michelle Stone, you are a beautiful, intelligent, bold, complex, sexy, funny, smart, vulnerable, articulate, impulsive, creative, decadent, sensual, beautifully Black ebony queen. It's true. You are so strong you cry when you get your period.

SAM: Which makes my head spin because I have to sit face front on a toilet seat...

JILL: Which makes you vulnerable and cute...

SAM: Which makes me question my struggle for manhood every second of every day.

JILL: Question how? By trampling on the souls of women who fight so we can stand strong and proud in this Godforsaken country.

SAM: That ain't what this is about, Jill and you know it.

JILL: You're right! This is about you chopping off your breasts. Doctor comes, scrapes off your pussy/vagina, inserts a fake penis where I'll put my mouth to suck you off. Hell mother-fucken no! If you think I'm gonna help you punish yourself just 'cause you don't like who you see.

SAM: What about my freedom? What about my truth?

JILL: Fuck that. What about the slave woman who died so you could have your freedom because of her truth?

SAM: She's dead. And so is her world.

JILL: I believe in it.

SAM: Then let me stay here.

(Pause.)

SAM: Please? Pretty please? With extra crispy cheese?

(Pause.)

SAM: *(Very vulnerable.)* You love me?

(Pause. JILL is torn.)

SAM: *(Recovers quick.)* Guess not. *(Makes for the exit.)*

JILL: Sam!

SAM: If I'm lost it's cause I ain't got community. I ain't got community 'cause nobody wants me.

JILL: Baby.

SAM: If my body don't make no sense it's 'cause the world don't. Not when a cop can shoot fifty-plus bullets at a Black man then go scot-free. Meanwhile the Internet says what? We are aaaaall connected. How? When doctors say I *have* to be a girl because my body says so. Since when is my body my truth? Especially because I'm Black. Naah, not in my world—which is nowhere near the world my parents gave me. Their world had laws. We have no code. And that's what's written right here *(Indicating his/ her body.)* ...on my body. Man, woman, in between, I decide. Not no doctor. In my world? My baby could be a girl on Monday, boy Tuesday, whatever Wednesday.

JILL: That's crazy.

SAM: So don't believe what I believe in, Jill. But give me room to survive. I'll run your bubble bath for you. Back rubs, ear scrubs, honey oil, hot tubs, you name it, I do it. Yo!, maybe we could celebrate when I get my first chest hairs!

JILL: You're so cute.

SAM: Aren't I though? Especially with this haircut. Me and you, double trouble, mega-power couple like in the movies how two—

(JILL goes in hard for a kiss.)

SAM: Do you love me?

JILL: Yeah No Maybe. Aw, fuck.

SAM: Do you?

JILL: Wanna be a real man?

SAM: Jill. Do you love me? Me?

JILL: Go home. *(Disappears.)*

GOSPEL ANGELS: *(Sing.)* I just can't give up now
Gone too far from where I started from
Nobody tol' me
The road would be easy
And I don't believe You brought me this far to leave me.

THE WHOLE CAST: *(Gasping.)* Huh huh huh huh huh huh huh huh huh huh huh huh

(Phone conversation with MOM and JILL.)

MOM: *(On the phone.)* Can you fool Mother Nature? Can anybody—me, the grocery boy—can we fool Nature?

JILL: *(On the phone.)* No.

MOM: Then why try? People she might fool. Someone on the street walking past who can't be bothered to take a close look at her, but Almighty God, He knows. He made her female, am I right?, so female she will stay—forever.

JILL: *(Mumbling.)* Guess so.

MOM: Hello, you there?

JILL: I'm listening.

MOM: Then speak up.

JILL: Sorry.

MOM: I'm sorry for your generation if they define themselves through homosexual activity—

JILL: Sam's not a lesbian, I don't think. I think—

MOM: Selfish. Just like her father, no difference. David won't do nothing, not if he won't get anything out of it, neither will Samantha. She won't help me out. I tell you that?

JILL: Why not?

MOM: Can she cope? Look at her, look at her clothes. How will she get by? She can't cope. How will she get anywhere with those clothes and no place to stay?

JILL: Yeah.

MOM: There you go mumbling to yourself again.

JILL: I WORRY ABOUT THAT TOO.

MOM: Know how intelligent that girl is? Bright bright brighter than sunshine. I'm sitting here staring at—debate trophies, wishing the father would send cards on Christmas, birthdays, shake her hand after winning, "for God's sake do something David to let her know she's special. I would but I'm working God knows how many hours to plop an egg in my mouth." Now there's the tragedy. He gives her nothing—no money, no time, no attention—so she believes she's nothing. Then she acts like nothing. Then she expects me to reward that nothingness in her behavior which I will not or I myself will end up nothing. Now is that fair?

JILL: No.

MOM: It's un-American. That's what it is. And I know, I wasn't born yesterday, I know life's not fair but the father could make it more fair if he shows her love. How? "How do you show love David? Do something for her." Like what? "Well for starters, quit buying your buddy drinks. Spend that time, spend that money on her. There's how you show love. Bring money when you come for a surprise visit."

(There is a knock at MOM's door.)

MOM: *(To door.)* Who is it?

SAM: *(At the door.)* Me!

MOM: Samantha?

SAM: I'm back Mom!

MOM: *(To JILL on the phone.)* Hold on. *(Hangs up the phone.)*

JILL: *(To hung-up phone.)* Hello, you there?

(Lights down on JILL.)

SAM: Hello, I'm here? I'm back home, Mom! Mom? Open up! I'm…! Ma, please open the door, it's freezing cold out here. Look, I don't wanna catch a cold…I wouldn't wanna wake the neighbors—

(The phone rings. MOM picks it up, then puts it down.)

SAM: Mom? I know you're there. The phone clicks when you put the receiver down. Mom?

(MOM is quiet.)

SAM: I got you something, Mom, a surprise. Guess what? Say something. You drunk? *(Beat.)* Guess why I'm here? *(Takes out a white envelope.)* I have a gift

for you. *(Kisses the white envelope, slips it under the door.)* There ya go. White envelope, under the door, take it Mom. It's a gift…from me to you…Nothing fancy but…I think it's as special as you are…Hear that? I said the gift is everything you are to me, Mom. So take it, Mom, please, that way you won't be so angry all the time. *(Beat.)* Look, Mom, I know you don't think much of me and I know why, but it would mean the world if you could get over whatever you're feeling so we could talk…I need to see you tonight, okay Mom? So could you just… *(Beat.)* Please open the door.

MOM: The envelope, what's in it?

SAM: Open it!

MOM: What's in it?

SAM: Surprise!

MOM: I'm not in the mood for your stupid games.

SAM: I'm not playing stupid games. I want—

MOM: Why are you here? To bring an envelope. What's in the envelope? I don't know, you say a surprise. Will I open the envelope? No, not 'til I know what's inside. So what's inside that damn stupid silly envelope?

(Pause.)

SAM: Money.

(MOM immediately opens the door. Long pause.)

MOM: You steal it?

SAM: Could I come in?

MOM: Did you steal that money?

SAM: It's freezing out here.

MOM: I'm not asking again.

SAM: No, I did not steal the money.

MOM: Then where'd you get it from?

SAM: Just take it, Mom.

MOM: Are you lying?

SAM: About stealing?

MOM: You are lying to me.

SAM: No, I'm not.

MOM: Why should I believe you? With your track record, Sam. Give me one good reason why.

SAM: Mom?

MOM: What.

SAM: Did you just call me "Sam"?

MOM: Answer my question. Where'd you get that money from?

SAM: From work.

MOM: *(Very bitter.)* Ah yeah, and what do you do?

SAM: Just take the money, Mom.

MOM: Know how I slave to pay my taxes?

SAM: I know Mom…

MOM: Pay bills on time, my rent. Put food on the table.

SAM: I know Mom…

MOM: Am I looking for trouble? Nooo, I'm not looking for *any* trouble…

SAM: I'm not here to bring you trouble.

MOM: People like you can't help it.

SAM: Could I please come inside?

MOM: People like you do whatever they can to give decent people like me a bad name.

SAM: That's not true.

MOM: It's not? So you're not here to prove me wrong?

SAM: No.

MOM: Then why are you here?

SAM: To see you.

(MOM gives SAM the middle finger.)

SAM: Want me to leave? I'll leave, I will. Just take the money.

MOM: No.

SAM: I want to make sure you're okay.

MOM: I'm okay. I'm perfectly fine, see?

SAM: No, I don't see. I can't see anything through that tiny slit in the door.

MOM: Why should I let you?

SAM: So I don't catch a cold.

MOM: So you can search under my covers for bottles.

SAM: Are you drinking?

MOM: Why are you here?

SAM: To see you, to take care of you, to provide for you

MOM: Provide why? You're not my husband.

SAM: I know I'm not Mom…

MOM: But you are my son.

SAM: What?

MOM: Come.

SAM: What's going…?

(MOM opens her arms for a hug. SAM stares in disbelief.)

SAM: Really? You want…?

(They hug.)

MOM: *(Hugging, whisper.)* This…feels…good…

SAM: …yeah…

MOM: Sssssssh. This, it's … Ssssssshhhhh.

SAM: …uh…

MOM: It's okay…s'okay…don't cry.

SAM: Mom? Is everything okay?

MOM: You look good.

SAM: You wish. I'm all wet 'n' sticky.

MOM: Want a towel?

SAM: What's happening?

MOM: How are you?

SAM: God, this is so—

MOM: Are you eating right, healthy? You look—handsome.

SAM: Think so?

MOM: 'Course I do.

SAM: I look like a man to you?

MOM: We should talk.

SAM: Good idea, that's…

MOM: Your father—

SAM: Forget Dad, I'm here. I can take care of you.

MOM: He has these books on hormones.

SAM: Dad does?

MOM: From now on I want you to wear his clothes.

SAM: Are you drunk? Sorry but this is…

MOM: Confusing? Difficult? Yeah, must be hard for you. Especially since I'm not— Well, we have issues. Trust, communication, honesty is always an issue when two people can't say what's really on their mind. I'll start: I want things to change.

SAM: Between us? I agree.

MOM: I want you to trust me more. How can I make that happen? I'm open.

SAM: To whatever's on my mind?

MOM: Shoot.

SAM: I don't have a home. Could I stay here?

MOM: Again?

SAM: Please?

MOM: I make you like this?

SAM: What do you mean?

MOM: Guess what? I spent all last night stitching Dad's shirts so they'd fit when you put them on.

SAM: Could we please talk about my living situation?

MOM: Put on your father's clothes.

SAM: This is nuts.

MOM: I love you, Samantha. Sorry, Sam. Sam. Your name is Sam now.

SAM: Mom, what is happening?

MOM: To what?

SAM: You. One minute, it's no show at the door. Next minute, well look at us. Heart-to-heart, buddy-buddy. What's going on here Mom?

MOM: Why?

SAM: Because it's strange. It's wonderful, it's fantastic, it's unexpected but bottom line, it is strange.

MOM: Of course it is.

SAM: Doesn't it feel crazy to you?

MOM: How do you mean "crazy"?

SAM: Larger than life.

MOM: That's because I'm not here.

SAM: What do you mean?

MOM: What else could I mean?

SAM: Where are you?

(*MOM recedes into the shadows.*)

SAM: Mom?

JILL: Should I be upset that you leave my place with no word then come back in the middle of the night or that I can't save you no more than you can save your own mom?

SAM: What does that mean?

JILL: It means people suck. It means when you treat them like God they will shit on top of you in your own home. It means you judge them by their actions. It means you should say something quick if you have something to say to me right now Sam, quick.

SAM: Why are you so angry?

JILL: Is there something you wanna say to me?

SAM: Is there something you wanna ask me?

JILL: Are you sorry?

(*Pause.*)

SAM: Oh. Yes. I'm sorry.

JILL: For?

SAM: Stealing.

JILL: What?

SAM: Money.

JILL: From?

(*Pause.*)

SAM: From you.

JILL: Huh.

SAM: Are you upset?

(*Silence.*)

SAM: Are you angry?

(*Silence.*)

SAM: Disappointed?

JILL: Very.

SAM: Are you kicking me out?

JILL: Am I thinking about it?

SAM: I have no place to go.

JILL: Besides a shelter.

SAM: I can't.

JILL: That's right, they'd rape you.

SAM: I'm not a woman.

JILL: You are to them so maybe jail is the answer. Maybe I should call the cops right now seeing as the thief is standing right here in my living room. You'd sleep more peacefully in jail than in a shelter, I think. You'd sleep best in my bed but that's no longer an option, now is it Sam?

SAM: Please.

JILL: Stop.

SAM: Don't kick me out.

JILL: Don't treat me like a jackass—for caring—about you.

SAM: Deal.

JILL: Where you going?

SAM: Bed.

JILL: Not in my room.

SAM: So sleep where, here on the floor?

JILL: Good night.

SAM: Do you love me?

JILL: Can I smack you?

SAM: Good night. *(Falls asleep on the floor.)*

THE WHOLE CAST: *(Gasping.)* Huh huh huh huh huh huh huh huh huh huh huh huh huh

NURSE NANCY: Breathe out.

THE WHOLE CAST: Haaaaaaaaaaaaaaa aaaaaaaaaaaaaaaaaaaaaaaaaaaaaaaaaaaaaaaaa!

NURSE NANCY: Needle?

ANGEL: Needle.

NURSE NANCY: Shot

ANGEL: Sam

DR. RUSTEIN: Nancy?

NURSE NANCY: Doctor?

DR. RUSTEIN: Ad

NUSRE NANCY: Mini

DR. RUSTEIN: Stir

NURSE NANCY: Shot

SAM: Ouch! Aaaaaaaah

DR. RUSTEIN: Patient

NURSE NANCY: Is

TOGETHER: Anesthetic. Sur—ger—y.

NURSE NANCY: Masectomy Nip Slip Cut

DR. RUSTEIN: Off

NURSE NANCY: Breasts

SAM: Ouch! Aaaaaaaah

DAWN and HELEN: Phallioplasty

Patty-cake, patty-cake

Baker's dough

Make her a penis

So she can go

(SAM emerges bandaged at the breasts, blood at the groin.)

NURSE NANCY and DR. RUSTEIN: Operation over

SAM: *(Begins to shake, slight convulsions at first that grow, becoming more and more intense with time.)* I wanna be a man…I wanna be…one…I have to…I…wanna be…a…maaaaa *(Collapses on the floor, the convulsions subsiding as s/he falls asleep. At first, SAM sleeps on his/her back. Later SAM tries to sleep on his/her side. Every time SAM tries sleeping on his/her side, SAM winces from the chest pain because of the surgery. SAM finally falls sound asleep on his/her back, dead to the world.)*

(Swashbuckling sound of ocean water lapping back and forth, back and forth along the shore. It's soothing, a calming sound. Plus the water hints at rebirth, breaking free from the womb. Water underscores the following monologue.)

DR. RUSTEIN: *(Voiceover.)* Who'd you wanna be? Growing up, who? I wanted to be—don't laugh people. Promise me you won't laugh if I tell you the truth. Ignore the thin patch of silver hair near my giant bald spot, that doesn't mean— forget it. I'm not gonna finish that thought. Just promise, no laughing? 'Kay, get this: growing up I, Dr. Rustein with my pot-belly, I wanted to be Elvis Presley. Now ask what a scrawny, pimply-faced Jewish teenager with thick glasses and an even thicker Yid accent living on the Upper East Side saw in Elvis Presley 'n' I'll say *(Sings.)* "I'm all shook up…'cause I don't have a clue." Sex appeal maybe. Style, charisma, a voice so melodic it's a mating call for chicks, I dunno, good looks that fall somewhere between baby-boy pretty and maximum machismo maybe but I dunno for sure. My point is at fifteen when I say, "Ma, I don't wanna be a doctah. I wanna be Elvis Presley" my ma smiles, plants a soft wet kiss on my forehead then case closed, that is the end of that subject. Not so with our patients. Many of them— and remember these are good patients. Most pay in cash, save every cent from menial jobs working well below minimum wage for years to hand every pretty penny over to us, the medical community and we know our history of betrayal don't we? Labeling them as "sick." Suffering from "gender dysphoria" after which they spend many good, long years locked up, that's a good portion of their life in a mental institution on medication they never needed in the first place so they actually *do* end up crazy. My first patient, it's '68, TEN doctors—count 'em people, ten—WOULD NOT PROVIDE MEDICAL CARE because aaaalll TEN swear a lunatic is talking to them, not a human being with a genuine, legitimate problem because they live in the wrong body. Think about that folks. Now think about the privilege we have: born in the right body; everyone sees what you see when you see yourself. Think about the entitlement that comes with that privilege. Living your life free from the anxiety, the terror that comes when someone knows your secret truth. Secret not shameful but shameful because a

secret. Got that? No you don't. If you did you'd use it. How? Control. Rape. Murder. Provoke. Perspective, keep that in mind, especially when that shy, scared individual—shoulders hunched—slips into your private practice with a serious problem they have to talk to you about. Why you? Because you have the cure, you're the doctor with that privilege. So? Do you listen? Or judge them? I'm talking as a doctor with an intimate relationship to suffering, sure, but I am also talking as a Jew with a profound understanding of the stranglehold, the deep power oppression has to shape our world. Our patients, their parents kick them out of the house. They wander the streets homeless, teenage runaways, molested, many of them destitute mumbling to themselves picking food from garbage cans. Some, after years of hormone therapy, look nothing like men but they dream big meaning my job is to nurture their big dreams. So…if they can't make a payment, fine by me. If they need a reference for a job, I go the extra mile with a phone call. Sometimes—I say this in strict confidence—sometimes I boost a patient's shot, add a little extra hormone so their facial hair grows that much faster, that much thicker to make him that much happier. Why? Because hate kills, self-hate worst of all. And we all know the suicide rate in this community…Why? Because I believe in what they want. What do they want? What we all want: to know ourselves. So we can accept others. Worthless, right?—so says a worthless world. Well, I love them, these men. I do. I'm not ashamed to say it. Read my lips: I—love—them. That's why I serve them. They bring meaning to my life. Bestow honor on my profession, medicine. Make no mistake, I am a very very proud man, proud to stand here before you at this medical convention as a servant to this community which I hope to serve 'til the day I breathe my last. 'Cause that's what some of us live for—Service.

(SAM bolts upright. Spotlight on SAM 2, an anatomical male version of SAM. He stands next to SAM. SAM and SAM 2 are side by side.)

SAM: Are you me?

SAM 2: Are you me?

(Blackout.)

DEATH AT FILM FORUM

Eric Bland

ERIC BLAND is a writer, director, performer, and producer. He was born on November 17, 1979, in Richmond, Virginia, where he was also raised. He attended Princeton University, graduating with a bachelor's degree in English with a creative writing concentration. He later earned an MA in writing for performance from Goldsmiths College, University of London. He is the writer-director of *I Felt So Free* (The Brick Theater/Ontological-Hysteric Theater's 2007 Tiny Theater! Festival), *The Children of Truffaut* (The Brick Theater's Pretentious Festival, 2007), *In Big Cities We Are Sentimental*, and *Love Song 1: Faces Like Stalinist Apartment Complexes in Czechoslovakia or Poland, Faces Born under a Fear of Communism in the 80's* (both for the Ontological-Hysteric Theater, 2008). He is also the author of the one-act plays *Mock the Knife* (2003 New York International Fringe Festival) and *Mother Mary Come to Me* (The Brick Theater's Baby Jesus One-Act Jubilee, 2007). As an actor, Bland's credits include *Babylon Babylon* (The Brick Theater/Piper McKenzie Productions, 2008), *Penny Dreadful* (The Brick Theater/Third Lows Productions, 2008), and the 2nd Annual One-Minute Play Festival (TBG Arts Center, 2008), along with roles in his own work. He is the Artistic Director and Co-Founder of the Old Kent Road Theater and was a member of the Princeton Triangle Club for three seasons, serving for two as its writing coordinator. Bland is currently working on two new plays: *The Protestants*, which will premiere at The Brick Theater in January 2009; and *I Stand for Nothing*, which will premiere at the Ontological-Hysteric Theater in July 2009 as part of its Incubator Residency Program. He lives in Prospect Heights, Brooklyn.

Death at Film Forum was first presented by the Old Kent Road Theater as part of The Film Festival: A Theater Festival (Michael Gardner and Robert Honeywell, Artistic Directors) on June 7, 2008, at The Brick Theater with the following cast and credits:

STAGE CAST

Siobhan	Siobhan Doherty
Scott	Scott Eckert
Charlie	Charlie Hewson
Rich	Richard Lovejoy
Victhoria	Victoria Tate
Hollis	Hollis Witherspoon

ADDITIONAL VIDEO AND VOICEOVER CAST

Wurst	Nate Allard
Reinhold	Brian Barrett
Cecile	Iris Blasi
Random Kisser	Grayson Cox
Estranged Girlfriend	Josephine Decker
Vulch	Nicholai Dessypris
Franz Biberkopf	Gavin Starr Kendall
Professor Harrison	Jesse Liebman
Lise	Cara Marsh Sheffler

Directed by: Eric Bland
Technical Director: Scott Eckert
Puppet Designer: Abernathy Bland
Lighting Designer and Board Op: Andy Miyamotto
Video Editors: Eric Bland, Scott Eckert, Charlie Hewson

Special thanks to Peter Hirshfield, Vanessa Baker, Rachel Sorey, Juan @ Café Crest, Brad Raimondo, Diana Morozov, Kent Meister, and the team at The Brick (Michael Gardner, Robert Honeywell, Hope Cartelli, Jeff Lewonczyk, Darren Gardner, Ian W. Hill, Berit Johnson, and Gyda Arber).

The Old Kent Road Theater was founded in 2005 by Eric Bland and Scott Eckert.

www.oldkentroadtheater.com

This play is dedicated to my mother and father who have made trying new things easy.

A NOTE ON THE PLAY

Death at Film Forum is a play with film. It was created for The Brick Theater's 2008 summer theater festival, "The Film Festival: A Theater Festival." Within the play are short films in various genres as well as filmic elements that color and comment on the stage action. The two most prominent uses of film are the monologue/ interview videos, one for each contestant, and the videos created by the contestants as part of the competition. If you visit our company's website, you can find links to all of the films we made for our production.

That being said, a play in this format (and as presented in a book like this) offers the opportunity for independent producers or creative teams to fashion their own videos entirely. In the script, I chose to include a grab-bag of the following information when describing a filmic element: (1) any key text spoken, (2) a rough description of what we did (primarily for the various short films in order to give the reader a sense of completeness with respect to the experience of the play), and (3) notes on what I felt was most vital to convey to an audience by means of a particular film. My primary note is this, however: TAKE IT OR LEAVE IT. And then this: MAKE YOUR OWN MISTAKES. We certainly made plenty, and I number among my favorite moments in the final cuts many of our best mistakes (or, "discoveries"). Part of the original charm of this project was to take a chance with a medium we had only previously dabbled in and to do so in a format that allowed us to do most anything we wanted with it.

Following that note of freedom, one might observe a certain specificity dotting the play, as the characters discuss and wrap themselves around a handful of cinematic auteurs. These are some personal heroes, and Film Forum is an actual repertory cinema in New York's West Village where I caught many of these directors' films during periods of loneliness, happiness, sadness, and, well, whatever-ness. *Death at Film Forum* could just as easily be called *Death at the Westhampton* (after an art house cinema in my native Richmond, Virginia) and all the references to Rainer Werner Fassbinder could be to Alfred Hitchcock or François Truffaut or Martin Scorsese, if only I had been pummeled by their retrospectives four or five years back. Hopefully, these specificities are the idiosyncratic pegs upon which the more general hats of inspiration and apotheosis might be hung.

I think it is worth noting as well that the play traffics in sincerity far more often than parody. For the characters, all that occurs is real and of great consequence. If they seem to ape the speech or attitudes of their idols they do so on account of a common hunger for life and transcendence; there is no overweening commentary. This is especially true when the players all gather together to argue, pontificate, and digress. If the joke is on them—and surely it is at times—it is a cosmic, fatalistic joke, not one forwarded with a smirk by the author.

Finally, forgive all of these notes. They stem from the desire to communicate.

—Eric.

CHARACTERS

CHARLIE: A contestant in a filmmaking competition
SCOTT: A contestant in a filmmaking competition
HOLLIS: A contestant in a filmmaking competition
RICH: A contestant in a filmmaking competition
VICTHORIA: The contest's curator, German
SIOBHAN: Charlie's girlfriend

SET

A means for projecting video. Otherwise, as desired.

TIME AND PLACE

The present. New York City.

SCENE 1
CHARLIE GREETS

An empty stage but for a minimalist table and two chairs center. CHARLIE enters in darkness. He sits in one of the chairs. Suddenly the lights fire up and music (a loud contemporary rock/punk anthem) bursts forth. All of the other characters except SIOBHAN enter the stage and set themselves in cool, disaffected tableau. SIOBHAN enters last and sits at the table with CHARLIE. He hands her a pair of sunglasses, which she dons. He puts on his own pair, staring out towards the audience. CHARLIE now turns to SIOBHAN, cups

her chin in his hand, and gives her a kiss on the forehead. He stares straight out once more. SIOBHAN exits. The OTHER CHARACTERS leave the stage, clearing it for CHARLIE alone. The music builds. He speaks. He must speak over it. He stands up to do so.

CHARLIE: It's out of your hands ... Despite ... it's out of your hands. My hands. But even more so, it's a story ... I can't compete. This is a play, it's a story, about film, how film saved my life. —Well, maybe not completely. It's a play, it's a story ... it's a competition. And I won it, despite...Hands down.

And I fought to the death for it. And that made me special.

(The music fades, a petering out. CHARLIE, glaring into the audience, now turns and exits as the players for scene 2 fill the stage.)

SCENE 2
INTRODUCTION TO THE CONTEST

Music plays underneath this scene, driving it. We are still in an introductory phase of the play. The music should have a sense of mood and story to it, think Leonard Cohen or Bob Dylan. VICTHORIA, SCOTT, HOLLIS, RICH, and CHARLIE are arranged on stage in chairs set on a diagonal across the stage. We are inside the walls of Film Forum in some sort of back room—a space for meeting or working. The characters will speak over the music in fairly quick succession.

VICTHORIA: *(Facing the others in her chair, stands and snakes her way among them, then speaks.)* Congratulations. Out of several applicants, you are the four finalists in Film Forum's first film-making competition. Our mission is to encourage the next generation in American Auteur Cinema. This contest will be sort of like *Project Runway*, but without the television broadcast. Or the wackiness. Or the Heidi Klum. We have a cash reward. Of five thousand dollars ... which seems like an awful lot of money. You probably would've been happy with five hundred ... Or a free Metrocard. *(Beat.)* Can I ask how you heard about this competition?

RICH: I read about it on craigslist.

HOLLIS: Rich sent me the link, from craigslist.

SCOTT: Hollis...and Rich...told me about the craigslist. I picked up a coffee

table and a missed encounter after printing out the application.

CHARLIE: I saw a flyer for it at Film Forum. *(Beat.)* Rich also forwarded me the url, from craigs ... list.

VICTHORIA: So you all know each other?

RICH: Is that okay?

VICTHORIA: Um ...I guess, we didn't really get the word out, huh?

HOLLIS: Maybe you should have run an ad during the Super Bowl.

VICTHORIA: *(To SCOTT.)* So what interests you in Film Forum? In film?

SCOTT: When I was a child my father used to take me to Film Forum ...All the other kids got to see *Bambi* and *Back to the Future*. I went to the Rainer Werner Fassbinder retrospective. That's probably why I carry around this little jar of poison. *(He pops it out.)*

VICTHORIA: Did you like it?

SCOTT: I dreamt up all sorts of damaging things after I saw *Beware of a Holy Whore* at the age of seven. It's still my favorite movie but it fucked up Halloween in 1987, when I went as a half-empty glass of Cuba Libre being brutally smashed into the floor ...It was an abstract costume.

CHARLIE: Yer easily influenced, huh?

SCOTT: I was seven. It's probably why I carry poison around. *(He holds up the plastic container.)* In case the Holy Whore comes. *(To VICTHORIA.)* Are you she? Is she that beautiful?

VICTHORIA: I am not the whore. *(Beat.)* The competition is structured in this way—there will be three meetings after this one, with a week between each, during which time you'll shoot a short film based on a given theme for the week. We'll screen them and someone will be eliminated. In the end there will be a winner. Among you friends.

CHARLIE: It's not like we're in love with each other.

SCOTT: I love you Charlie. Didn't you get that e-card I sent on Valentine's Day? With the hearts and the confession and the homoerotic anime?

VICTHORIA: Next week's theme is "Hope."

CHARLIE: *(To VICTHORIA.)* Thank you. *(To SCOTT.)* I'm not in love with you. *(To ALL.)* See you. *(He exits.)*

VICTHORIA: Why's he not in love with you?

SCOTT: Maybe 'cause he thinks his girlfriend wants to sleep with me.

VICTHORIA: Why?

SCOTT: Maybe she does.

VICTHORIA: Why?

SCOTT: But I doubt it. He's the one who goes around quoting Nietzsche and eating mesclun greens. I mostly just cry in corners and sleep outside.

RICH: He does. He sometimes sleeps outside.

VICTHORIA: Okay—well, see you again here next week, yah? *(She exits.)*

HOLLIS: I should've gone to med school.

RICH: Why didn't you?

HOLLIS: I don't really want to fix people. I want to break them down.

(She turns and exits. SCOTT exits. RICH is alone. His video begins. As it does, he exits, too.)

SCENE 3
RICH

During the course of the show, each of the four CONTESTANTS will appear in a brief monologue/interview video, speaking into the camera about him- or herself. These videos are projected onto the screen.

RICH: I want to be a spiritual being. *(Beat.)* I'm sick though, too. And I know the difference between being sick and being spiritual. At my best, when I am well, or well enough, I feel like Konstantin shouting for new forms. In *The Seagull.* But I'm too sick to accomplish them. I don't know what it is. My asthma. Or my nervous, my nervous disorder. I am very nervous. My gums bleed when I floss, so I don't floss, but once I woke up in the middle of the night and my gums were bleeding on their own, just oozing blood, and I hadn't flossed in years. I was born sickly. Like Proust. Or Toulouse Lautrec. Or Teddy Roosevelt. Maybe I will make something of myself. You know, use my sickness to advantage. Maybe I will make a film about it. I love film. I like the movies of the '30s. I go way back. I wish I had been alive then. For the artistic movies of the '20s and '30s. For the experiments. But I fear that my tooth will fall out, my front tooth. It has a cap on it and it has fallen out three times in my life, and the last time was at the Alligator Lounge in Williamsburg, Brooklyn, when I bit into a slice of pepperoni and onion pizza. See that's the thing about my body. When it's going wrong it's so incredibly all that matters. It just ... it really terrifies me, because if there is such a thing as hell, and I am thought of as bad, and

I go there, oh my God, I can't think of anything worse than creative, eternal, bodily torture…Maybe I should make a film about that …And then I wake up and I am not sick anymore. Something's happened. Maybe I am in love. *(Beat.)* It's time for a revolution. Yes! For a complete overhaul. For New Forms. At least, for me. I see what a stupid idea it is, the idea of change, and yet there are still some who try new things, or engage with the strange things of the past and present. And, for me, it's as if their minds take flight when their bodies are not dragging them down.

SCENE 4
NIGHT IN INWOOD PARK PART I

The next scene takes place in the Inwood neighborhood in the upper-most reaches of Manhattan. CHARLIE and SIOBHAN are walking through the woods. SCOTT, unseen by them, lies along the side of the stage; he is asleep. Projected on the film screen are images of the park which rotate throughout the scene. CHARLIE and SIOBHAN enter, exploring the stage.

SIOBHAN: I love it here.

CHARLIE: I love you here.

SIOBHAN: If you could die would you die here?

CHARLIE: No. *(Beat.)* Yes.

SIOBHAN: I feel like we're upstate. Like this is Nyack or some shit. And Lower Manhattan and Jersey City can just suck my balls.

CHARLIE: I know. And now, because of the trees, the light, light from the moon falls through the trees, the canopy, in splotches. And you can see, that the trees, and the clouds make the light fall in different places, only moments apart.

(Lights play across the stage. Music enters, ethereal, synthetic, ambient. Pause.)

CHARLIE: See if you can get by me.

(They play a game where SIOBHAN tries to run around CHARLIE while he tries to prevent her. She makes it past him at last.)

SIOBHAN: Would you want to be here alone?

CHARLIE: Alone?

(They are together against a wall. They kiss.)

SIOBHAN: Why do you hold my hand like that?

CHARLIE: Like what?

SIOBHAN: So tightly.

CHARLIE: *(Spotting something.)* Oh my God.

SIOBHAN: What?

CHARLIE: It's Scott. *(He looks at SCOTT lying on the ground.)* It's Scott. He's dead.

SIOBHAN: He's dead? Why is he dead?

CHARLIE: *(To SCOTT.)* Why are you dead?

SCOTT: Dead tired…More like it.

SIOBHAN: Someone left your body in the woods to rot. And no one will ever find you.

SCOTT: Who the fuck did that?

CHARLIE: He's alive.

SCOTT: I feel like I'm in heaven. Or Nyack, or some shit.

SIOBHAN: That's what I said.

CHARLIE: No you didn't. No you didn't.

SCOTT: I sleep outside. I like to sleep outside. Here I am. Outside myself. *(Beat.)* Are you gonna kill me?

SIOBHAN: Do you want us to?

SCOTT: With kindness?

SIOBHAN: With laughter.

SCOTT: Hey look, Charlie's got a hard-on.

CHARLIE: What the—how can you tell?

SCOTT: I can see it in the shadows.

CHARLIE: That's fucked up. That's all...that's so fucked up. *(He tries to cover up.)*

SCOTT: I love Charlie. 'Cause he's smart. He knows what the fuck he's doing. He's going to do something. I wish I thought about things like him.

CHARLIE: Yeah right.

SCOTT: Hey, Siobhan, why is it again that you want to sleep with me and stuff?

SIOBHAN: Because you're so hot. Because you're en fuego.

SCOTT: Does it have anything to do with the fact that I terrify Charlie? That when he looks at me he can't see my heart or my soul so he thinks that I'm deeper than him?

CHARLIE: Than *he*.

SCOTT: That since he can't see them they must just be down somewhere deeper?...I wish I was Charlie. Then I wouldn't have to sleep outside. Hey Siobhan, wanna go to the Chelsea Piers and pretend like we could afford to hit their golf balls into the river?

CHARLIE: Get up. I'm serious, get, get up.

SCOTT: Help me. Help me forget everything. All the bad people. Hold my hand. Only you could hold it way too tight.

CHARLIE: Get up. Please...Here. *(He extends his hand.)*

SCOTT: Do you like me? Are there parts of me that you like?

CHARLIE: Yeah I like you, alright? Could you please...it's embarrassing... Get up...Here...

(CHARLIE tries to lift SCOTT, an ordeal; at last SCOTT is on his feet. CHARLIE steps away from SCOTT. He tries to play the game he played with SIOBHAN.)

CHARLIE: See if you can get by me.

(CHARLIE prepares himself. After a beat, SCOTT runs towards CHARLIE, but instead of trying to get past him he simply runs into CHARLIE's body, leaning into him.)

SCENE 5
1st Judgment: "Hope" Videos

We are back in the Film Forum meeting room. However, while the chairs maintain the relation to one another they had previously, as a unit they have shifted in position on the stage, as if this were a different camera angle and we are now gazing on the room from another point of view. SCOTT is the last of the CONTESTANTS to enter.

VICTHORIA: Alright, let's get on with this mishap. The videos. Video number one.

HOLLIS: Slow down Charlie Brown. Take a chill pill.

VICTHORIA: You have good grief but I will not use a sedative. I am happy today.

RICH: I'm happy too. I had a bottle of Pepsi Max on my way here. A whole two-liter bottle. I got here way early. I had a lot of time to kill.

SCOTT: I had a lot of ants to kill crawling around in my kitchen sink. That's why I was late.

CHARLIE: I agree with what you said first. Let's do this maybe.

VICTHORIA: Yes. Yes. I can't wait. Action.

(The films play. Actually only Scott's "Hope" film plays. The others are introduced in teases on title cards, as in "Rich's Hope Video…" [New title card.] "…was shown." "Hollis's Hope Video…" "…appeared." "Charlie's Hope Video…" "…came next." "Scott's Hope Video…" "…is here in full." SCOTT's video then begins.)

SCOTT'S HOPE VIDEO: *In our production, Scott's Hope Video (about seven minutes long) was a largely comic, at times sentimental, homage to the work of Rainer Werner Fassbinder, using such films of Fassbinder's as* Berlin Alexanderplatz, Katzelmacher, *and* Beware of a Holy Whore *as inspiration. In our story, Franz Biberkopf runs into and out of love, danger, and misery. The narrative is fractured, and the overall tone is playful with music entering here and there and a cast of ridiculous characters, most of whom have over-the-top German accents (Franz, however, does not). The film concludes with Franz's death. That being said, what is most important is that SCOTT's film gives us some insight into him as a person—a bit of a loner with a comic bent who tries to balance a sense of absurd tragedy and a general freedom of spirit, etc, etc.*

(The film concludes and the stage lights return. A general pause.)

CHARLIE: *(At last.)* I'm sorry, how does that last one relate to the theme?

SCOTT: What was the theme? *(He rifles through some papers.)* "Hope?" Oh. I thought it was Weimer Germany. *(Beat.)* Of course it's about hope, stupid. It's Fassbinder.

VICTHORIA: Thank you. Nice work. Rich, I think I'll eliminate you. Auf Wiedersehen.

CHARLIE: Why are you eliminating Rich?

VICTHORIA: Look at him. He's so agreeable.

(RICH nods.)

HOLLIS: Are you the kind of person who, at the end of every significant relationship, realizes that the other person never really loved you, and liked you even less?

VICTHORIA: *(Beat.)* Good segue. Next week's theme will be "Love." So bring in your videos on love. I can't wait. *(VICTHORIA exits.)*

HOLLIS: Actually I'm that person. So…pooh.

SCOTT: I don't think you're stupid Charlie. By the way. So. Yeah.

SCENE 6
POST-MEETING BEER

The CONTESTANTS all go out for a beer. CHARLIE, SIOBHAN, HOLLIS, and RICH take the stage. In this scene, you will see various "Ideas" listed here in the script. In the production they were projected during the scene, behind the action, going unacknowledged by the characters. These inner thoughts offer juxtaposition to the naturalistic setting of the bar; this element should be used, disused, or altered as desired.

CHARLIE: *(Out to the audience.)* We went out to this random lounge-type place near Film Forum to grab a drink.

(Music plays, jazzy.)

CHARLIE: *(Pause.)* No I mean this was like a lounge. Seriously.

(Music plays, jazzy with a twist of lounge.)

CHARLIE: So um…everyone was… *(Longer pause, to the person in the booth.)* Alright, I don't mean to obsess here, but, this was a completely weird-ass, airport-y lounge, like, unreal.

(Total lounge-style music plays now and underneath the scene. When this song ends, other music plays beneath the scene as desired.)

CHARLIE: That's—that's where we were.

SIOBHAN: What was it like there?

CHARLIE: You were there. You showed up. You know.

SIOBHAN: Oh yeah, I was playing in the grass.

CHARLIE: The grass?

SIOBHAN: The ground. The floor. Whatever.

CHARLIE: Anyway, Hollis and Rich, oh my God, they were there, really getting along. Hitting it off.

HOLLIS: *(To RICH.)* Sucks to be eliminated, huh loser?

RICH: I knew I'd lose. I have this—I know when I'm going to—look, I was glad just to be nominated. I ended up

fourth in a competition no one but me and my friends apparently entered.

HOLLIS: That's the spirit.

RICH: Do you think that I have spirit? *(Beat.)* Ask me to do something dumb. It impresses people.

HOLLIS: Are you trying to be impressive?

RICH: Why? Is that dumb?

HOLLIS: Yes.

RICH: Perfect.

CHARLIE: Scott came.

(SCOTT enters.)

CHARLIE: And so did our Teutonic curator Victhoria.

(VICTHORIA enters.)

CHARLIE: Rich invited her. Soon everyone felt they had worthwhile ideas and approaches to art and the mysteries of being—of being a body, that thinks, and feels. Our heads were full of scenes of imperfect sex and philosophy. *(Beat.)* It was intense.

(SIOBHAN and CHARLIE are staring at one another, drawing from one another.)

(The first "Idea" appears: SIOBHAN references Walt Whitman's Leaves of Grass. Again, these ideas arise on-screen and fade, unacknowledged by the characters.)

SIOBHAN IDEA: "LOAFE WITH ME ON THE GRASS…" *(After a couple beats this appears under it, in addition to the first line.)* "…I GUESS IT MUST BE THE FLAG OF MY DISPOSITION, OUT OF HOPEFUL GREEN STUFF WOVEN…" *(After a couple more beats, this now appears with the rest.)* "…AND NOW IT SEEMS

TO ME THE BEAUTIFUL UNCUT HAIR OF GRAVES…"

SCOTT: *(To VICTHORIA.)* What do you like about film?

VICTHORIA: I like, I don't like many films. I like television.

SCOTT: Then why work in film?

VICTHORIA: I love, I really love, ten or twenty films.

RICH: *(To HOLLIS.)* What do you like about film?

HOLLIS: *(Beat.)* I can't think of anything dumb for you to do.

RICH: Sometimes I just wanna, do this. I just wanna look for airplanes. *(He lies on top of the table.)*

CHARLIE: Sometimes Rich just wants to look up, and look for airplanes.

SIOBHAN: What do *you* like about film?

CHARLIE: *(Beat.)* What do you like about it?

SIOBHAN: Nothing, really. I liked *Planes, Trains, and Automobiles*, with John Candy. I prefer poetry, because I have an imagination. I like to loaf on the grass. *(She grabs something from the floor and holds it up to CHARLIE.)* The smallest sprout.

SIOBHAN IDEA: "THE SMALLEST SPROUT SHOWS THERE IS REALLY NO DEATH, // AND IF EVER THERE WAS IT LED FORWARD LIFE, AND DOES NOT WAIT AT THE END TO ARREST IT, // …AND TO DIE IS DIFFERENT FROM WHAT ANY ONE SUPPOSED, AND LUCKIER."

RICH: I'll probably just lay here on this table for my entire life.

HOLLIS: *(Correcting him.)* "Lie."

RICH: I was Leonardo DiCaprio's body double in *The Talented Mr. Ripley*.

HOLLIS: What?

RICH: You told me to lie. Remember?

HOLLIS: I was correcting you. You said "lay." And he wasn't in that movie. You have a bad memory.

RICH: I don't. I lied twice. Two lies. So get up here and lie with me.

RICH IDEA: MOVIES, I THINK, ARE THE PREFERRED MEDIUM FOR THE MANIPULATION OF MEMORY. WHEN I MAKE A MOVIE I FEEL THAT IT IS OKAY THAT MY ABILITY TO PLEASE ANOTHER HUMAN BODY IS AN UNKNOWN QUANTITY…QUALITY?

HOLLIS: I'm good.

CHARLIE: *(To SIOBHAN.)* I should get in there, yeah? Do you think I should?

SIOBHAN: Go.

CHARLIE: Bam! I'm in. *(Goes to the table and sits between the conversations. At last, calling to SIOBHAN.)* Gimme a hand. Help me.

SIOBHAN: Do something big. Try.

VICTHORIA: *(To SCOTT.)* You're the one who likes Fassbinder, yeah?

SCOTT: Oh yeah, love him. Love the guy. *(Pause. Leaning back, willfully playing it "profound.")* It's like, all of cinema, you know, I can see all of cinema on this one constant track, this, evolution, born out of the thing before. But then there's Fassbinder. And he's doing something sort of parallel but all the same, something else. Completely, you know? It's radical. It's quite ugly a lot of the time. And brutal. It's like he never saw a movie by Ingmar Bergman or Orson Well-ies *(He pronounces "Welles" with two syllables, as "Well-ies," an unacknowledged joke)*. Or he saw them and was just like, yeah, well I'll do what matters to me. You know?

VICTHORIA: Interesting.

SCOTT IDEA: INTERESTING IS A FUNNY WORD. IT'S AS IF, THERE MUST BE A MORE DESCRIPTIVE WORD TO USE. BUT I'M LIKE YOU—I HAVEN'T SETTLED ON HOW IT ALL MAKES ME FEEL JUST YET, SO I KEEP IT OPEN.

SCOTT: Interesting is a funny word. *(Pause.)* Charlie, now Charlie's the one who likes Nietzsche.

CHARLIE: I'm sort of more into Schopenhauer these days. I'm sort of a pessimist, but finding my own peace with it.

RICH: *(To HOLLIS.)* Hey. Do you like Russian cinema?

HOLLIS: Are you inviting me to a retrospective?

RICH: Should I? You seem like you'd like Russian movies.

HOLLIS: I like to watch movies alone, with a radius of two empty seats tracing a circle around me as the center.

RICH: Yes. Something tells me that you're deep in a sort of funny way. And you're funny in a sort of deep way. Like you're so deep and/or funny that you're funny and/or deep…I could sit three seats to your left, with our jackets between us.

CHARLIE: *(To SIOBHAN.)* I can't talk to them in a normal—in their tone. I'm not—this always happens.

SIOBHAN: Are you okay dude?

CHARLIE: Why do I think about things the way I do?

SIOBHAN: It's just the way you are.

CHARLIE: *(Beat.)* Do you love me? Do you love me babe?

SIOBHAN: I do. I love how I feel about you.

CHARLIE: Keep feeling that way.

SIBOHAN: I will.

SIOBHAN IDEA: "TO ANY ONE DYING…THITHER I SPEED AND TWIST THE KNOB OF THE DOOR, // TURN THE BEDCLOTHES TOWARD THE FOOT OF THE BED, // LET THE PHYSICIAN AND THE PRIEST GO HOME. // I SEIZE THE DESCENDING MAN…I RAISE HIM WITH RESISTLESS WILL."

VICTHORIA: *(To SCOTT.)* I have some good news. Wanna hear my good news? Can I be a bitch and blab about my news?

SCOTT: Are you going to leave us?

VICTHORIA: Am I…why would that be good news?

SCOTT: I don't know. People get happy when they're going somewhere else.

VICTHORIA: I got a grant. A fucking grant finally came through. I'm going to China. To study Cantonese cinema.

SCOTT: Really?

VICTHORIA: Isn't that exciting?

SCOTT: But what if it's all "crouching tiger" this, "hidden dragon" that?

VICTHORIA: I doubt that it is.

CHARLIE: *(Overhearing this and entering.)* Of course it isn't. You read Thomas Mann and all the sudden there's Lao Tzu. And it's like, mind-fuck.

RICH: *(To HOLLIS.)* So what do you really like about film?

HOLLIS: I don't want to get all artsy-fartsy. Okay?

HOLLIS IDEA: IT'S WHERE YOU PLACE THE HUMAN EMOTIONS—LOVE & DEATH—IN THE HUMAN DIMENSIONS—TIME & SPACE.—IS WHAT I LIKE ABOUT FILM.

RICH: You should be artsy-fartsy. You should. I think that you're that way.

HOLLIS: Right. Well, I applied to grad school. University of Perth. In Australia. To study filmmaking.

RICH: That's awesome. That's awesome. We should celebrate. Go to a movie. Right now.

HOLLIS: I don't do that. Boys. I don't do it anymore. I don't have the time. Or space.

RICH: You don't do love?

HOLLIS: Oh I do. I just don't act on it. Because it just gets embarrassing.

VICTHORIA: *(To CHARLIE.)* Why are you so uptight, dude?

CHARLIE: What?

RICH: *(Does a forward roll and pops back up before HOLLIS.)* I'm so embarrassed.

VICTHORIA: Why are you so uptight dude?

CHARLIE: I'm not uptight. At all. No one ever tells me anything. I feel like I never know anything. But I don't know what it is. So it's weird, for me.

VICTHORIA: *(About SIOBHAN.)* Who's this by the way? Dude?

SCOTT: That's Siobhan. Hi Siobhan.

SIOBHAN: I'm Siobhan, dude. I'm Charlie's girlfriend.

SCOTT: Siobhan and I were boyfriend and girlfriend for about a day a few years ago.

CHARLIE: Really? Yeah right. I know—you called yourself—?

SIOBHAN: Dude. Not really.

SCOTT: That's what it felt like to me. Broken heart and a leaking aorta. *(He pretends to die, stumbling over theatrically and falling to the floor.)*

SIOBHAN: Nice.

SCOTT: *("Last breaths.")* You're unlike anyone I ever knew, Siobhan.

CHARLIE: What are you guys talking about?…I'm not uptight.

RICH: *(To HOLLIS.)* You're definitely right. Listen, if you change your mind, though, just post something on craigslist. Like a missed opportunity thing. 'Cause here comes the opportunity…and you're swinging right through it.

HOLLIS: I'm not swinging.

RICH: But it's a strike.

HOLLIS: …I'll post something on craigslist.

RICH: I'll definitely check it out.

HOLLIS: That's where you hang out, right?

SCOTT: *(Into the ether.)* I'm dead tired. I should go up to the park.

RICH: I have a lot of profiles. MySpace, Facebook, Friendster, Blogspot, Twitter,

Splatter, Yelp, WordPress, Hot or Not, RateMyBoobs, SuicideGirls, Netflix, IM, AOL, Microsoft Word, CNN.com, SmartTix, Wachovia online banking, cuteoverload.com…PowerPoint…TI-82…iPod…iTunes…Flickr…oh, right now I'm trying to inscribe my name and password onto your heart.

VICTHORIA: *(To SCOTT.)* Please don't sleep there, dude.

(She tries to lift him up.)

HOLLIS: I'll post it on craigslist.

RICH: Just post it on craigslist.

HOLLIS: Exactly.

RICH: Just slap up a post.

HOLLIS: I'll post it there.

RICH: Just post up like Shaquille O'Neal.

HOLLIS: Like a Post-It note.

RICH: Like the Post Office would.

HOLLIS: Like a poster. Of Jon Bon Jovi on your bedroom wall.

RICH: I love you.

HOLLIS: No you don't.

SCOTT: Charlie could pick me up.

RICH: I love you, asking me all these questions.

HOLLIS: I'm not asking you any questions.

VICTHORIA: Charlie, it's your turn.

RICH: …I love you being present. Right there. Like a fungus on the wet earth.

CHARLIE IDEA: I'VE READ WHAT ANDREI TARKOVSKY HAS TO SAY ABOUT CHARACTER.

HOW CHARACTERS WITH ENORMOUS INTERNAL ENERGIES AND PASSIONS ARE MORE CONVINCING FOR HIM. THAT'S HOW IT IS WITH ME. I HAVE NEVER, IN MY LIFE, REVEALED ANYTHING ABOUT MYSELF SLOWLY OVER FIVE ACTS. MY LIFE HAS NO ARC. JUST AN ENERGY.

VICTHORIA IDEA: I LIKE MOVIES BECAUSE I AM A VOYEUR. I WANT IT ALL NAKED. TO WITNESS IT. THE BODY IN ECSTASY.

HOLLIS: *(To RICH.)* Oh, I have an idea for you. Something dumb to do.

RICH: What?

HOLLIS: Keep coming to these dumb meetings even though you're a loser.

VICTHORIA: *(Overhearing.)* Sorry I eliminated you by the way. There wasn't a tremendously good reason for it. Someone had to go.

RICH: It's okay. I knew I was gonna lose.

VICTHORIA: Really?

RICH: It's weird, it's this thing I have. I always know when I'm going to lose. It's like my Haley Joel Osment.

HOLLIS: Your what?

RICH: My sixth sense. Sorry, sometimes I use a cinematic patois.

SCOTT: That must make things pretty anticlimactic.

RICH: Not really. Thing is, I have absolutely no idea if I'm going to win. It's strange. I never know when I might win. But I always know when I'll lose. It makes gambling weird. I have several bets out right now on a middleweight boxing match I've been scouting. It's tonight.

VICTHORIA: So will you win?

RICH: That's just it—I have no idea. All I can do is dream.

CHARLIE: So will you lose?

RICH: *(Thinks for a bit.)* Yes. I will. *(Beat.)* Oh shit-balls. I gotta cancel some of these— *(He pops out his cell phone.)*

VICTHORIA: *(To SCOTT.)* You should come, you should come to China sometime. Or Germany at least. Get a closer look at what's out there.

SCOTT: I…but why? There are so many movies to watch at home. Alone. Like *Home Alone.*

CHARLIE: I'm so tired. *(Lays his head on SIOBHAN's shoulder.)* I wanna go home.

SCENE 7
CHARLIE

CHARLIE's monologue/interview video.

CHARLIE: I don't know, I know I'm not stupid, I'm not stupid. I mean foolish. Not stupid. I don't feel that I am…I saw *La Chinoise* at Film Forum a while ago. I didn't know how to pronounce it, I said, La Chin-o-ese. Someone I respected had to correct me, very kindly, but that's okay. He didn't make me feel stupid…I didn't *love* it. The movie. I wanted to get popcorn before the thing. But the subway never came, the 1 train, and I was a little late. I was alone. My girlfriend Siobhan didn't, I like her, very much. I think in a way we are obsessed with each other and I like that kind of, behavior…I don't know, you know?…I want to try things. I want to push…I want to try things out. And I know I'm not stupid. *(Beat.)* I read Nietzsche. And, a little bit of, Kant. And Descartes. And…Leibniz. And all the other ones. Spinoza. You

know, all the other ones in that little book. The anthology. See? Now you see what I mean? My self-doubt? Because I'm reading anthologies. Everything, Film Forum, everything in my life is anthologized. But at least I read it. At least I try. Despite. The word I love is "despite." No more spite. Or, even though this is true, also "that," that can exist.

Siobhan likes poetry. Not film. She says she likes to see things for herself. But you can show me one thing and I can see something altogether, despite…

(The image on the camera fuzzes up, static. The rest is relayed in caption as CHARLIE, in the video, mouths the words. Music by Michael Jackson plays underneath.)

I get so angry sometimes. I feel betrayed. I wish I saw things the right way. The wrong…the right wrong way. I would die today if someone just said, "You will, somebody will speak about you the way you speak about your heroes." Like Godard. Godard. Like Andrei Tarkovsky. Or Gertrude Stein. Or even Isaac Newton. Or fucking Michael Jackson. I dig his beats…I'm sorry. I'm not, I'm not trying to be…yeah. Why won't this world work for me? I would so let it. God knows I try.

Despite…

(The video statics again; the following appears in parentheses at the bottom of the screen.) "(The rest of the video was lost. Nothing more could be recovered.)"

SCENE 8
2nd JUDGMENT: "LOVE" VIDEOS

We are back in the Film Forum meeting room again, the room rearranged in another perspective shift. Initially SCOTT and VICTHORIA are alone. SCOTT's face rests in his hands.

VICTHORIA: Don't be so sad to see me.

SCOTT: *(Looking up.)* When my head was down I couldn't see you. Maybe that's why I was sad.

VICTHORIA: What's wrong with you?

SCOTT: Hey, I saw *Rebel Without a Cause* last night with James Dean, by Nicholas Ray. And I thought—it's probably not true—but maybe *Rebel*, and Ray and Dean, link Fassbinder back to, it's a bit of a leap, Sergei Eisenstein's films. His work. I'm looking for a connection, to solve it.

VICTHORIA: To solve what?

(The OTHERS enter.)

VICTHORIA: Tell me later.

SCOTT: I'll try.

VICTHORIA: *(To ALL.)* Guten tag means hello. Alright. First video. *(To the booth.)* Action!

(The films for the remaining three contestants play. The teases occur again for the first two, then Charlie's Love Video is screened in full.)

CHARLIE'S LOVE VIDEO: *In our production, Charlie's Love Video (about five minutes long) told a love-and-loss story between himself and a previous girlfriend. They are shown in scenes of affection and play, then, almost suddenly, we understand that they are no longer together. The bittersweet nature of love pervades the short film. CHARLIE narrates it and a moody yet light pop song weaves through it. Our film was mostly in montage and fairly direct in structure. We also used fewer effects than we did in Scott's Hope Video, providing, perhaps, a less weighty, more organic touch. What is vital, again, is to*

understand more about the filmmaker's character. CHARLIE feels a great deal and infuses his work with sincerity and vigor, placing himself in a vulnerable position, something CHARLIE the non-auteur most likely finds disconcerting.

(The film concludes and the stage lights return. A general pause.)

RICH: Should we offer our ideas?

VICTHORIA: I'm sorry. I just hate "other people's ideas." Having to listen to them. They're all so embarrassing. They're not ideas, they're just drawn-out arguments one explains to oneself to describe one's life experience. No one's paying me to be your shrink. And please stop trying to couch your exhibitionism as genius. *(Beat.)* Sorry, I guess that was sort of an "idea." *(Beat.)* See, to me it was therapeutic. To you it was almost certainly useless.

HOLLIS: So why are you in the arts again?

VICTHORIA: I guess you're old enough to know the secret, dude. At least half the people in the arts are trying to destroy them. *(Beat.)* You're lucky you have me.

HOLLIS: Why is that?

VICTHORIA: At least I can recognize the tendency. And sometimes overcome it. So…go on. Talk about…tell us your ideas.

(A good pause.)

SCOTT: *(Stands.)* I don't believe in societal alienation. I only believe in personal alienation. That's why I'm a pessimist, not a Marxist.

CHARLIE: I'm a pessimist, too.

SCOTT: Hey, Pessy-Pessy-Pessy. Hey, whas-up?

VICTHORIA: Nice. *(Beat.)* Hollis, I'm going to eliminate you.

HOLLIS: That's fine. I'll be filming kangaroos in the Outback this time next year. Care to share why you're so pissy today, though?

VICTHORIA: I'm not pissy.

RICH: You are. You're sort of pissy.

VICTHORIA: I'm not going to China, anymore. I lost the grant. But that happens. I'm not pissy. Next week, the theme is "Death." *(To ALL, but staring at SCOTT.)* Also, a party right here, the night before. To celebrate all this. Be there or be Bavarian…Bavaria is like Germany's West Virginia. *(She exits.)*

RICH: *(To HOLLIS.)* So you wanna catch a movie with me this time next week, loser?

HOLLIS: No. But thanks for being sweet about it. *(She exits.)*

RICH: Totally. Anyone have a tissue? I think I have a nosebleed. *(He tilts his head back and puts his hand to his nose.)* Clean up on nostril two. Clean up—

CHARLIE: Death. Okay. *(He pops up and exits.)*

(SCOTT offers RICH a tissue from his pocket, exits.)

SCENE 9
HOLLIS

HOLLIS's monologue/interview video.

HOLLIS: *(Peeling an orange.)* My life. It's really just a vast rush of synapse and hormones. Head and heart, you know? *(Beat.)* They come for me. Men. I'm not

trying to get anyone's pity vote here. *(Pause.)* But I'm tired of going out to dinners where I'm expected to eat fondue. I don't want to anymore…because it's very boring, while you're letting your entrée sizzle in the oil, and you're wondering if you're doing it long enough not to get salmonella.

I feel sorry for men because they go in the right direction but they cannot stop. Once you finally let them rub your back, very gently, over your shirt, which they do basically well, they're immediately trying to get under your shirt, to touch your back, your bare skin. They're like microwaves, if you don't put a timer on them, they just keep pouring more energy in.

(On the screen a GUY enters, takes the orange she was peeling, and heaves it against the wall where it splatters and drips. He goes in to kiss her; she turns from it but eventually relents, figuring he'll leave after getting it. Indeed, he gets it and goes.)

I've been seeing some lately. Men. Am I mean to them? Men rarely describe me as mean. They're too busy trying, in very gentle and well-meaning ways, to suppress everything I have to say and flatter me into two-dimensionality. It's why I like being behind the camera. I'd rather flatten them out.

Now I *have* heard women, oftentimes, refer to me as an incredible bitch. Which I like. I like it when others recognize you as competition. Otherwise, when you wallop them they get tears in their eyes and start to cry foul. Men.

They're not as interesting as film. But there aren't as many people trying to do them, so if you want to get inside one—a man, not a film—and see it through to its conclusion, you can without selling your soul. If you're able to keep them at bay.

If you say things like, "I don't know whether I'm unhappy because I'm not free, or whether I'm not free because I'm unhappy." *Breathless.* That's from Jean-Luc Godard's *Breathless.* I'm saying it now... well, it's true. For me, right now.

SCENE 10
END OF CONTEST PARTY

The Film Forum room has been rearranged by VICTHORIA to host an end-of-contest party. She is on stage alone setting up a rather meager, bare-bones spread. CHARLIE and SIOBHAN enter, unbeknownst to VICTHORIA.

CHARLIE: *(To SIOBHAN.)* Let's go slow with this one. Let's slow down. Let's play this scene out.

SIOBHAN: Whatever, dude.

CHARLIE: I...I don't wanna give the wrong impression...when I—

VICTHORIA: *(Turns and sees them.)* Willkommen! Have some...Sunkist.

SIOBHAN: I love Sunkist. Do you have any cups?

VICTHORIA: No.

SIOBHAN: Cups are for losers. *(She swigs from the bottle.)*

(RICH enters with soda and corn chips.)

VICTHORIA: Where's Scott? Is Scott coming?

RICH: What?

VICTHORIA: It's not a party—. Do you know if Scott's coming? It's not a party without Scott.

CHARLIE: Why?

SIOBHAN: Right, I know what you mean. He's really bad at intimacy by the way.

VICTHORIA: What? I don't need to know that.

SIOBHAN: I'm not saying you do. I'm just...relaying a really personal fact about Scott, that he'd probably prefer not to be relayed, behind his back.

VICTHORIA: He's really bad at intimacy? What does that even mean?

SIOBHAN: It means he doesn't give very much.

VICTHORIA: A taker?

(HOLLIS enters.)

SIOBHAN: No, he doesn't take anything either. Which is worse. Because people like giving gifts, to build reservoirs of debt.

VICTHORIA: Yes, people are horrible.

RICH: Not Asians. Asians are...good. With their, concepts. Of personal and private space. It's like...bam. They have their very own ways of dealing with the problem of individuality. This is going to be totally racist but Asians make much better hipsters than white people. *(To VICTHORIA.)* You have to find a way to go to China. It's going to be like, bam, welcome to Bedford Avenue. No doubt. South of the Great Wall...it'll be like south of Delancey Street...For miles.

HOLLIS: Bro...

RICH: I pull shit out of my ass. It's all that I have. Is any of it impressing you?

CHARLIE: That's good. The "Problem of Individuality." I get it.

HOLLIS: *(To VICTHORIA.)* I googled you by the way.

VICTHORIA: What?

HOLLIS: I googled your ass. Nervous? 'Cause I know yer like, "Who the fuck are we?" But then I was like, "Who the fuck are you?"

VICTHORIA: You don't like me very much, do you?

HOLLIS: Where do you get that from?

VICTHORIA: I have a hard time reading you.

HOLLIS: Thank you.

VICTHORIA: You're welcome.

HOLLIS: Nice resume, by the way. I didn't get the Ph.D. vibe from you.

VICTHORIA: It's a master's degree.

HOLLIS: It says Ph.D. online.

VICTHORIA: I lie online.

HOLLIS: …Nice boots by the way.

VICTHORIA: Thank you. I got them online.

HOLLIS: Is that a lie? Don't be some giant lying bitch-ass-trick now, okay?

VICTHORIA: Okay. I won't.

HOLLIS: Yeah, don't.

VICTHORIA: No problem boss. *(She gives HOLLIS a goofy salute.)*

HOLLIS: I waver. Between being embarrassed for you, and having a very minor girl-crush on you. *(To the OTHERS.)* Where's Scott? Has he gone missin'?

(VICTHORIA is alone, the OTHERS have clustered together. At this point she will call someone out of the audience—probably a tech person [in our production it was the director]—and speak her private thoughts to him/her. She speaks with an American accent during this, going back to the German one right afterwards.)

VICTHORIA: Where's my friend? *(She sees him in the audience and waves him up. He comes and she speaks with no accent.)* These guys, they are nice. Nice people. I just don't know how to tell them the whole project has been an incredible disappointment. Overall. Why can they not think filmically? Why haven't there been any boats at sea, or bicycle chases, or unbelievable monster costumes? Maybe that's what I implied I didn't want. But it's a film for Christ's sake. There's gotta be something to *watch*. It's all become very…I don't know. Eccentric? Obsessive? Ontological? Hysterical? I don't know about these guys. The girl, overall, is interesting. To me. I understand her. I think like an American girl. When I speak in my head, I speak like an American girl. I have to take on shapes and maneuver quite cleverly to survive, like an American girl. I understand her. Which makes me afraid of her. Maybe that's why I eliminated her. Because, in a way, she reminds me of me. She would vomit—but eventually she'll relent and become me. Moi. And you might think, and you might think I'm about to poop on myself. But I'm not. My life is pretty incredible. I live in theatres and galleries. I'm constantly eating in French restaurants. I have an affinity for German beer, of course, and you don't know how many doors that will open up to you. Try being a woman and sitting alone at a small table in any bar in the city with a slender glass of German pilsner, knock it back in two gulps, and watch the men crawl across the floor to press their dying bodies against yours.

(SCOTT enters. He has a yellow rose in his hand. He approaches slowly. VICTHORIA does not see him but the DIRECTOR does. She continues speaking. During this the DIRECTOR will leave VICTHORIA, stand face to face before SCOTT, shake his hand, and exit.)

VICTHORIA: As they try to make you smell the rot and bacteria buried in their armpits or the odor coming from the tuck of flesh where the scrotum lies against the skin, or the matted scent, the smell like a doormat, that comes off their chests where their wiry hairs thatch to retain all the oozings and olfactions of their various pores and glands. I can't stand a man's perfume, a stupid whiff of cologne—they are so bad at masking themselves. Why pretend tonight? For Calvin Klein or Giorgio Armani? Why shout flowers or citrus in a high-pitched squeal when, once you nestle in beside me or I remove your undershorts or sniff the scruff on the back of your neck, I hear nothing but the undeflectable low-wave frequency that is the bellow and roar of your stank, of your hormonal, fetid stench, of your every desire, you who right now desire little more than a glee-ful-as-a-schoolboy-in-a-bathtub-with-a-photo-of-a-plump-naked-woman-touching-her-giant-areoles bout of sex. *(She sees SCOTT. Back to her German accent.)* Want a whiskey?

SCOTT: *(Holds the rose out to her.)* Want a yellow rose?

VICTHORIA: I do. *(She takes it.)*

RICH: *(Overhearing.)* Yellow rose of Texas.

SCOTT: Hey.

RICH: Hi.

SCOTT: How's it going?

RICH: I hear you have problems with intimacy.

SCOTT: I do. Tread carefully.

RICH: Will do.

SCOTT: *(To VICTHORIA.)* How are you?

VICTHORIA: Good. How are you?

SCOTT: Sorry about your Asian vacation. You seemed like you really wanted to go.

VICTHORIA: Maybe, maybe I should just go on my own. You know, foot the bill.

SCOTT: …What the fuck.

VICTHORIA: Yeah, exactly.

SCOTT: Exactly.

(Pause.)

RICH: Excuse me everyone. Party people. Now that we're all here, I'd like to read something I wrote while I was outside drinking a few Red Bulls when I got here two hours early. It, well… *(Pulls a sheet of paper from his pocket.)* If I break out into a coughing fit it's because I have inflamed bronchial nerves. And if I collapse it's an inner ear problem that makes me fall over whenever I try to do something meaningful. *(Reading from the paper.)* Why do we want different things? Why do we want experimental things? Well for some of us it just isn't enough. The same old stories just aren't enough. If some girl came to me, and I was dating her, and she said, "*The Wizard of Oz* is my favorite movie, let's watch it right now," I think I would kill myself. I mean, I understand maybe, the Proustian recollective quality to it, like maybe that was what her mom and dad tucked her into bed to—but if that's the analysis of life, the moral or dialectical method she uses to negotiate existence, or if it's the extra shot of lifeblood, or profundity, she needs to remind her she's alive, and she is special for being that way, alive—then I guess we simply have our differences. Because for some of us it is not enough. And if, maybe Andrei Tarkovsky, or Ingmar Bergman, or Truffaut or Godard or Welles or Bowes or Ray or Lee or Scorsese or Altman or Kazan or Renoir or Fellini or Antonioni or Fassbinder or Hollis or Chaplin or Wenders or Granovsky or Blogspot or Preminger or Match.com are not enough either, at least I know that they are on their knees with their hands out, reaching like, I don't know, reaching in that direction, where something we don't know might be. Do you catch my drift? I just like to know that someone else is having a tough—or even more so—a complicated time of it as well. And that they are trying. And I feel good. It makes me feel good.

(A few stray claps for his effort. RICH will drift toward the snack table with HOLLIS.)

VICTHORIA: *(To SCOTT.)* So, you like the films of the German New Wave?

SCOTT: I like Fassbinder's films. Because I remember, because my father took me to them. Instead of *Bambi*. So it's like, a Freudian thing, or something.

VICTHORIA: So do you come down on the side of Nietzsche or Schopenhauer?

SCOTT: *(Beat.)* That's more so Charlie's bag.

VICTHORIA: Oh.

SCOTT: Charlie should win this thing. He's the one who, I don't know. He

should win this thing. He'd actually, put the five thousand dollars into buying a good camera, or booking a location or something.

VICTHORIA: Well, listen. Once this contest is over and all. I'm thinking about going to China. On my own dime.

SCOTT: Cool. That's awesome.

VICTHORIA: You should think about going. Too.

SCOTT: Please don't give me the five thousand dollars so I can go to Shanghai with you.

VICTHORIA: I wasn't…I'm just saying I might have some extra money, that I can't spend.

SCOTT: *(Pause.)* You're very pretty. I find you very pretty by the way.

VICTHORIA: *(Places her right foot against the wall that SCOTT leans against, penning him in from the front.)* I've been drinking for a while tonight.

(SCOTT smiles, then walks around behind her until he stands to her right. VICTHORIA remains with her foot on the wall, her right leg extended. She then pivots until she is facing downstage, keeping her right leg in the air, extended, just as it was, but with no wall to support it. She tries to keep her balance.)

VICTHORIA: *(Wobbling.)* Aren't you going to help me?

SCOTT: Aren't you going to help *me*?

VICTHORIA: Help.

(SCOTT reaches out and supports her leg. She turns to him, pulls his face in to hers, and kisses him on the mouth. This lasts for a while. CHARLIE is the only one who

notices this. He whistles at them at last to interrupt it.)

SCOTT: *(To CHARLIE.)* Do you prefer Nietzsche or Schopenhauer? Tell her. That's what she wants to know.

CHARLIE: …Did you and Siobhan ever have sex?

SCOTT: What?

CHARLIE: I'm serious. I want to know.

VICTHORIA: Why don't you ask your girlfriend?

CHARLIE: My girlfriend loves me very much. Why would she want to destroy me?

SCOTT: Charlie only likes virgins. He likes purity.

CHARLIE: That's not true. That's bullshit. You know that's not true.

SCOTT: What do I have? *(Beat.)* How could I be a threat to you? Why do you care?

CHARLIE: How could this guy be threatening? Does this guy even know who he is? *(Turning, calling out to her.)* Siobhan. *(Beat.)* Siobhan. *(Pause.)* Let's go to the park tonight. Let's walk around the park.

SIOBHAN: Sure.

(CHARLIE heads back over to the OTHERS. He snags a beer on his way and also the yellow rose. When he gets to SIOBHAN he offers her the beer. After a moment, HOLLIS and RICH approach VICTHORIA.)

HOLLIS: We're going to check out. 'K?

VICTHORIA: Oh, cool. Thanks for coming.

HOLLIS: Yeah…Oh…for the record, we're not like, "leaving together," or anything.

RICH: Though, we sort of are.

HOLLIS: We're not.

RICH: Nevertheless, essentially we are.

HOLLIS: Nothing's going to happen.

RICH: But it might. You never know.

HOLLIS: Absolutely nothing is going to happen.

RICH: Intercourse.

HOLLIS: What?

RICH: …I said, "of course." Nothing's going to happen. Beyond intercourse.

HOLLIS: Oh, I think you just said "intercourse" again.

RICH: Of course I did. Verbal intercourse.

HOLLIS: Anyway, thanks again—

RICH: And anal.

HOLLIS: *(She smacks him.)* Jesus!

RICH: I'm, I'm sorry…I mixed the Sunkist with the Fresca…

HOLLIS: Are you done?

RICH: Fres-kist.

HOLLIS: So later and stuff.

VICTHORIA: Yeah, totally.

SCOTT: See you guys.

RICH: *(As he and HOLLIS exit, calling after her.)* I don't have halitosis, I don't have cold sores, I'm extremely flexible…

HOLLIS: That's irrelevant.

(They're off.)

VICTHORIA: Is he okay?

SCOTT: Honestly I've never seen him this way before. Happy. Her too. And it's weird, because, they'd be terrible for each other.

(CHARLIE and SIOBHAN head down. They approach SCOTT and VICTHORIA.)

CHARLIE: Hey. So, um, it's getting late.

VICTHORIA: Yeah.

SCOTT: Yeah.

VICTHORIA: Scott found the missing link. To Fassbinder. Through *Rebel Without a Cause*. From Sergei Eisenstein.

SCOTT: Did I tell you that?

VICTHORIA: You had a big idea.

CHARLIE: What's the big idea?

SCOTT: Alright. *(He clears his throat, sort of playfully.)* Okay. Eisenstein's *Alexander Nevsky*. To *Rebel Without a Cause* by Nicholas Ray. To Fassbinder's *Fox & His Friends*. In all of them, the main character just stands there, these histrionic men, being dissected like corpses. As the histrionic women float about like aliens. But the men, the primping they do—how they comb their hair and tilt their faces; the machismo—which fulfills its purpose only when you know it hides a terror; the high energies driving everything towards a homo-eroticism. The jazzy, moody man. It's not true, I'm sure, that one came from the other. But it's not out of thin air to me, anymore, Fassbinder's films.

SIOBHAN: You watch too many movies.

SCOTT: I only see a few. They just become very important to me.

CHARLIE: Yeah so, it's getting very late.

SCOTT: You guys taking off?

SIOBHAN: Yeah. Wanna come with?

CHARLIE: Come with. You know? We're going. You should come with.

SCOTT: Yeah.

CHARLIE: Yeah, you know.

SCOTT: Yeah, I should. *(SCOTT, who has been sitting for a while now, stands up.)* I probably should. I live up near them. I need to get away. From shit…I'll go. *(He sits back down.)*

CHARLIE: Yeah.

SCOTT: Yeah.

VICTHORIA: You sure?

SCOTT: I'm sure.

SIOBHAN: Thanks.

VICTHORIA: What?

SIOBHAN: For the party.

VICTHORIA: Yeah.

SCOTT: Thank you, very much, for everything.

VICTHORIA: I'm sorry you have to go.

(CHARLIE has meandered towards the bowl of popcorn. He flips it over, spilling it on the floor. SCOTT stands up again.)

SCOTT: Yeah I probably do.

(SCOTT sits back down; CHARLIE picks some of the popcorn up.)

CHARLIE: You ready man?

SCOTT: Let's go?

CHARLIE: What's wrong with you?

SCOTT: What?

VICTHORIA: What's wrong with you?

SCOTT: What?

SIOBHAN: We should get a cab. *(Beat.)* We can't afford a cab.

SCOTT: Yeah. *(He gets up to finally exit.)* Okay.

(An "Idea" projects onto the screen, as in the bar room scene.)

THE BIG IDEA: WHAT'S WRONG WITH YOU?

(They exit, leaving VICTHORIA, who exits on her own soon after.)

SCENE 11
Scott

SCOTT's monologue/interview video.

SCOTT: I try not to think too hard about my past; maybe because things happened in my past. Things did happen. I just don't need to think about them right now. Someone once asked me, in church of all places, they said, "Would you rather have a great life but not be able to remember any of it, or have a mediocre, a normal life, and be able to remember everything?" Like any other twelve-year-old I picked the great life I wouldn't remember. I don't think I've ever 180'ed on a question like I have on that. Now I think I'd choose my memories. Even if my memory is the thing I try most often to suppress, I like to know that I have access...to the way it smelled on a baseball field at eight a.m. on a Saturday morning in June. If someone told me that when you die

you just lie in your grave—or in your ash-scatter or whatever—and are able to do nothing but reflect on your life, to remember things and I guess, naturally, extrapolate on them, I think that I would take it. And it would be excruciatingly boring, but wouldn't you rather have boredom than nothing at all? It would comfort me for me right now, and for all those I know who have already died, and are lying there, remembering things and thinking.

But still—I don't want to remember too hard or it drives me crazy. I'm not a great self-regulator...I've heard that I have problems with intimacy too...But bad things happened in my past. Not the kind of bad things you would blame people for, but the kind of bad things you would blame God for. Maybe you'd be surprised that I believe in God. Well I might not say it to your face, if you asked me, but I do...Despite.

And the reason is...Pedro Almodóvar's *All About My Mother.* How do you explain that if there is no God? That scene where she arrives back in Madrid from the train, and she's in the taxi in that circle with all the prostitutes and transvestites, and the music is like—not to be cheesy but it is the sun rising—it's what the noise would be if a sunrise were a sound and not just the incredible gorgeousness of something new yet familiar appearing as a bright yellow in the very light blue, barely chilled sky...Could there be a more unconditional forgiveness for the times I get excited and go just an 'ittle bit too far than that scene of Almodóvar's, with all the color and the love? For those times where yer, "Ehh, I probably shouldn't have done that." You know? That scene of imperfect sex and philosophy? With all the indifferent children of the earth, active, like thinking animals...And I've read Darwin, I read *The Origin of Species* twice, and I agree with Darwin, but there is no reference to *All About My Mother* in it. None. I mean, yeah, it's cool, I've evolved. I used to be five-foot-two. Then I woke up and I was, a rhesus monkey...I believe in God because I believe in myself. And I believe I'm not God, so God must be there as well. *(Pause.)* I'm thinking about what I just said right now and it makes no sense. *(Beat.)* Have you ever heard that British guy James Blunt sing? His voice is godly.

(The video cuts off.)

SCENE 12
A Note about Siobhan

SIOBHAN enters; she speaks to the audience.

SIOBHAN: I'm creepy; I'm weird. Would you like to take my picture?

(SCOTT enters with a video camera. Standing to the side, he'll "tape" SIOBHAN.)

I want to show you the street I was born on.

(A picture of a river appears on screen.)

That's it. Flash flood. Watch out, momma. This is my mother.

(An image of Macaulay Culkin appears on screen, it is rotated ninety degrees to the right.)

That's not her.

(The same image is displayed, this time right side up.)

There she is.

(A map of Asia appears on screen.)

That's my father.

(The screen becomes entirely blue.)

My brother. He's depressed but gentle. He lives where the sky meets a body of water...The girls love him. I don't see it. I call him Smurf...Hey, what do you guys look for, in a person? In a girl? In an actress? *(Beat.)* Yeah, yeah, me too.

(CHARLIE enters.)

Hey, I wonder...I wonder which of you could do the most push-ups. Right now, for me.

(After a beat, a thought, SCOTT exits. As he goes, he places the camera on some surface, aimed towards the middle of the stage. CHARLIE goes down and does one push-up. After this "victory" he awkwardly looks around, waves to the audience, and leaves.)

We decided. To fall in love very hard. Only Charlie, only Charlie is able to meet my needs. To treat love like the gesture of will that it is, because I am so tired of falling, falling, falling out of love. And we agreed not to. We agreed to devour something every time it weakens, to overreact every time it tries to die. *(She runs over to the camera that SCOTT left. She sits in front of it, speaking this part into it, confiding.)* We drink too much coffee. We drink it too fast and we drink too much of it. It is probably destroying some organ inside of us. Good. I hope so. Sometimes we drink so much in the morning we sit around naked all afternoon feeling gassy and farting. Some people think that's gross, but others, after an initial laugh, know what it really is, that that kind of behavior, that it is ideal. My biggest fear...my biggest fear...

(Siobhan's Video plays on the screen.)

SIOBHAN'S VIDEO: *In our produc-*
tion Siobhan's Video (about six minutes
long) was an evocative, fractured profile of
Siobhan, wherein she expressed a number
of her thoughts about love and ruminated
upon the city and her life in general. The
setting for the video was a park in Brooklyn
(McGolrick Park) with images taken from
all perspectives of the park, both with
SIOBHAN in the frame and without her.
What is important is to allow Siobhan a
chance to come alive as a character, and
to highlight the nature of the relationship
she has with Charlie—a highly Romantic,
slightly obsessive, in some ways transcendent
relationship.

(SIOBHAN watched her video play dur-
ing our production. She sat at the foot of
the screen eating popcorn. About halfway
through it, CHARLIE entered and watched
the video as well. At one point there was a
little bit of interaction between the two, with
CHARLIE creating shadows on the screen
over the video and SIOBHAN reacting to
them. But for the most part they remained
separate, and towards the end CHARLIE
exited after approaching SIOBHAN and
giving her a kiss on the back. Music played
over the course of the video, coming in and
out. The music was moody, instrumental,
and mellow. What follows here are sections
of dialogue that SIOBHAN spoke during
the course of her video.)

SIOBHAN: *(On camera.)* My biggest
fear in the world is losing you. That and
skydiving. If I lose you while skydiving,
like if you slip behind a cloud for a second, don't like hang out in the cloud,
but just fall straight through. And when
you land I'll dry the dew off you and
take you to that Ethiopian restaurant on
MacDougal Street.

I like you and me because…listen—
Macbeth is a wonderful love story. And

Macbeth is a brilliant and unnatural man
who screws up almost endlessly; but he
achieves as the result of a ridiculous collaboration. Things come to a bloody end,
yeah, so what. So will all of us; we're only
human, dude. Thing is, they didn't cheat
on one another and you'd be hard pressed
to call their relationship boring.

Plus, implicit in that, is the fact that
I believe in you. I hope you hear that
because I know you often have trouble
sleeping at night and often think very
low things of yourself; that you have
spoken of suicide…That you even worry
about losing me. Sometimes you are
drunk and drooling on your pillow and
you tell me these things. I feed on you.
Your heart. You should go further. We
should go too far.

You know, if you did kill yourself, we
would guarantee our victory. I would
never lose you, you would never lose
me. But I am stopping short of asking that of you…I read poetry—the
American Romantics—for their pan-
theistic worldview. What do you think
of the state of New York City? Its diners?
The Yankees? Of Radio City Music Hall?
Sunset Park? Of Sunnyside, Queens? Of
the Triborough Bridge? Of the Grand
Concourse? Of the seven-foot man you
saw on 24th Street? Of everything all
at once?

(The video continued on for some time
beyond her dialogue. When the video ends
the scene ends.)

INTERMEZZO
HOLLIS ON A TRAIN

HOLLIS enters. She sits in a chair left
of center, on a slight tilt with respect to
the audience. Diagonal from her, largely
facing upstage, sits a puppet (with a string

*tied around its neck that leads backstage)
in a similar chair. A dialogue ensues. It is
entirely prerecorded and played over the
speakers; there is no live speech during
this scene. HOLLIS will, however, react
in her face and body to the scene's drama.
The scene occurs on a commuter train
whereupon HOLLIS has bumped into
an old, favorite professor, PROFESSOR
HARRISON, played throughout by the
still puppet. In our production, various
images of trains (normal, comic, horrific)
were streamed across the screen.*

HOLLIS: Oh my God, Professor
Harrison.

PROFESSOR HARRISON: …Hollis?
Hollis. Hey! It's great to see you. Great
to see you, kid.

HOLLIS: Great to see you too.

PROFESSOR HARRISON: Sure is.

HOLLIS: I…I have to say…I would've
felt silly saying it then but, I really loved
the class, you taught. The directing
class. College seems like forever—I don't
remember anything—but I remember
your class. It was the only thing that
made me feel—I don't know—whatever—I just really got a lot out of it.

PROFESSOR HARRISON: That's
great—that is—I enjoyed that class.
You guys were definitely, an interesting
bunch.

HOLLIS: Tell me about it…Hey, guess
what?

PROFESSOR HARRISON: What's
up?

HOLLIS: You might be excited to
know—I applied to film school. In Perth.
Australia. I really—I really think—you
really influenced me.

PROFESSOR HARRISON: Really?

HOLLIS: I also came in third in this
weird-ass competition thing, too, at Film
Forum, but nobody—I don't know—
sometimes I think I'm just imagining
the whole thing. It has a very insular
feel to it.

PROFESSOR HARRISON: You're
really—you're sort of serious about
this—like in the real world, huh?

HOLLIS: Totally. Hey maybe you could
write me a last-minute bonus recom-
mendation, like a little blurb I can send
in as an addendum—

PROFESSOR HARRISON: Hollis.

HOLLIS: What?

PROFESSOR HARRISON: No, it's
just, well, that's, I'm sort of surprised
actually but no, that's, I hear you.

HOLLIS: What?

PROFESSOR HARRISON: Good luck.
I mean, it's a very hard life.

HOLLIS: Well I figure if it's what I really
want to do—

PROFESSOR HARRISON: Yeah, but
it's also sort of like, get real. I mean, it's
a tough industry, you know?

HOLLIS: Well you always made me,
you always made me feel very special—
I mean, you always said I was very
good—

PROFESSOR HARRISON: I told a lot
of people they were quite good…Wait. I
don't want you to hear me wrong. I did,
I do think you're good.

HOLLIS: Good?

PROFESSOR HARRISON: All I'm saying is—and take what I say with a grain
of salt—I mean who am I?

HOLLIS: My favorite teacher.

PROFESSOR HARRISON: But there's good and then there's great.

HOLLIS: Sure.

PROFESSOR HARRISON: I just, I just don't know why someone would commit that much time and energy—and money—to something unless they were great.

HOLLIS: Maybe I think that I am great.

PROFESSOR HARRISON: Sure. Sure, but I've taught classes like that for five years now and I've seen at least twenty kids who could wipe the floor with you. I don't mean that personally. This is, you might be misunderstanding me. I'm trying to save you a lot of trouble. A lot of time. Listen, are you talented, yes, definitely. Are you inspired? At times. Sure. I remember your work. I have a knack for seeing one piece, actually for seeing just five minutes of a person's work, and being able to size him or her up right there. I can criticize, categorize, and curate a person in the snap of an eye. It's a gift I have. And you, at times you had an inspired moment. But are you exceptional? Are you sufficiently unique or really novel, even, at all? Do you deserve applause from someone who doesn't know you, who isn't just trying to make you feel good about yourself or—pardon my French—to get you off? The answer to that is, well, I'll leave the harsher version of it unsaid and just say that the first part of the milder reply is "Probably," and the second part is "Not."

HOLLIS: Okay. Cool. Glad to know. Good to know that about myself.

PROFESSOR HARRISON: You never seemed like the type who needed it sugar coated or to be coddled. You're going to provide quite a challenge to some lucky guy one day. I'm sure. You'll probably drive him crazy.

HOLLIS: Yeah, I will.

PROFESSOR HARRISON: I haven't upset you, have I?

HOLLIS: No. I guess not. Actually yes.

PROFESSOR HARRISON: I'm soooo busy on this project I'm working on right now for the Italian State Cinemagraphic Institute, in Milan. You have no idea what it's like to create a film over and over in your head and choose which—oh God I must be so OCD. I'm so bipolar these days. The burdens one bears, yeah?

HOLLIS: Right. Sure. Were you always an asshole?

PROFESSOR HARRISON: It takes vision…Were you always such a clever little girl? Person.

HOLLIS: I think I'd like to cut your body open in a way that didn't kill or even hurt you and then take a piece of floss and slowly jerk it along your bones until they're stripped of muscle and fat and ligament…That's my vision. Dickface.

PROFESSOR HARRISON: You should work—you would be a really good doctor. Or I could really see you working in a national park, as a tour guide or a conservationist. You'd be cute in one of those khaki outfits. I have this way of pegging exactly what a person who is not me should do with their life. And I have the bravery to explain to them exactly what their specialty is. To reduce them to the simplest terms. In a constructive way.

HOLLIS: Um, listen…I don't know why I'm even going to ask you this, but, so you really—I mean—I thought you knew—you were very—you really think it would be a mistake to pursue filmmaking? For me?

PROFESSOR HARRISON: Only you can answer that question for yourself, Hollis. But, as a friend, I'll answer for you. The long answer: Do whatever you want. It's your life. Whatever doesn't kill you makes you stronger. Go for your dreams. You only live once. Short answer: It would be a pretty big mistake and you'll regret it. Everything is not for everyone. I'd love to be a sous chef…Or a shepherd. Well, I sort of am.

(A ding is heard.)

PROFESSOR HARRISON: That's my stop. New Fuckerton. Gotta run. See you later dude. Hit me up on my Facebook page if you wanna talk about anything.

(The puppet is dragged offstage by the string.)

SCENE 13
Night in Inwood Park Part II

Post VICTHORIA's party, SIOBHAN, CHARLIE, and SCOTT find themselves in Inwood Park at night. SIOBHAN films this scene from the side. SCOTT sits on the ground with his head in his hands. During this scene, the note "Sound of static, the lights jump, SCOTT and CHARLIE shift position," appears several times. It is almost as if there were a filmic jump cut that occurs on stage. SCOTT and CHARLIE will rearrange themselves and carry on from their new positions, somewhat revived.

SCOTT: What I miss most, about having somebody, like a girlfriend, is being able to be touched.

CHARLIE: What do you mean, being able to be touched?

SCOTT: No one can touch me. And I want to be touched so badly. *(Beat.)* I wish that somebody would come over here and touch me. I mean, I'm practically begging for it. In every way I can.

CHARLIE: Why don't you let Victhoria touch you? Why don't you relax, and just be cool.

SCOTT: Hey, I figured out that James Dean wasn't trying to be cool. He was letting himself be sad. It was never about being cool. It was always, about allowing oneself to be sad. Ryan Philippe is trying to be cool. So is Scarlett Johansson I'm starting to think. But not James Dean. Not Brando. Not Marilyn Monroe. They were all trying, very hard, to be sad. And they pulled it off. Don't you think?

(Sound of static, the lights jump, SCOTT and CHARLIE shift position.)

CHARLIE: Your life is very sad, yeah?

SCOTT: Does that piss you off?

CHARLIE: What?

SCOTT: Sometimes I feel like I piss you off.

CHARLIE: Of course. Of course that doesn't piss me off.

SCOTT: I mean, I sometimes feel like I piss you off.

CHARLIE: You do. Oh, you definitely do.

SCOTT: Why is that again?

CHARLIE: It's not your fault.

SCOTT: Right. That's why.

CHARLIE: What?

SCOTT: It's not my fault. Because nothing's my fault.

CHARLIE: Yes. That's probably it.

SCOTT: And the question is, if it was my fault…—

CHARLIE: If it "were."

SCOTT: If it *were* my fault, would I do anything to change it? *(Beat.)* I don't "feel" her. Victhoria. In my gut. I don't know. She's nice, yeah? She's no Siobhan. I like *you*, Charlie. Yer cool.

CHARLIE: I like, I'd like to kill you.

SCOTT: Wow—it's like you just proposed some weird sex act with me, and I sort of, maybe, want to try it out. But I'm nervous. The ramifications.

CHARLIE: You're not in love with me. You're not in love with anything, yeah?

SCOTT: Siobhan touched my penis. With her whole hand. It was there touching the base of her palm, and her fingers were over top of it. The little lifelines in her palm connected to my veins, my genital veins. Then I kissed her, pulled her hand away, tried to place my hand down her pants—but she stopped it and whispered in my ear, "Don't you find the world very beautiful?" Something very simple, like that.

CHARLIE: I think that she might love me.

SCOTT: I'm almost sure she does.

(Sound of static, the lights jump, SCOTT and CHARLIE shift position. CHARLIE takes a small knife out of his pocket.)

SCOTT: Hey, that's a real grade-A knife.

CHARLIE: I thought maybe we'd come up here, and I would kill you.

SCOTT: Why?

CHARLIE: Death. To transcend the category of death.

SCOTT: Yeah. But is it really you? Or is it, like me and Nietzsche calling all the difficult shots?

CHARLIE: I don't like Nietzsche! I'm not elitist. I want to overturn it. I thought I was pretty brave.

SCOTT: Brave?

CHARLIE: Bold.

SCOTT: A Brutus, a total Brutus.

CHARLIE: Irrational…Definitive.

SCOTT: I think it's a great idea.

CHARLIE: It's not an idea, it's a feeling, a vibe.

SCOTT: It's a great idea. A great plan. An algorithm.

CHARLIE: No, it's impulse. Instinct.

SCOTT: Feeling. I want to feel it. I do. Feeling always conquers thinking.

CHARLIE: I'm not thinking, I'm not thinking at all—don't you see?!

SCOTT: I will destroy you with them. My little feelings. Does that piss you off?

CHARLIE: But you *must* think things through. It's not enough, to emote. You have to think—take responsibility. Even if it's imagined…where's…there must be an element of morality in your life. In your art. But there you are, like Fassbinder, who gets to name his fucking book *The Anarchy of the Imagination* and die early. But you only get to be anarchic because you know that I am responsible, that I am driven by a strong moral force.

SCOTT: Really though, that's not it at all. I get to be the way I am because I am the way I am so much. To the nth. Yeah?

(Pause. CHARLIE drops the knife. Sound of static, the lights jump, SCOTT and CHARLIE shift position.)

SCOTT: I do love you Charlie. I do. I do. You're great. You are every iteration of a human will in defiance. I mean, you'll lose. But you tried. Despite…

CHARLIE: So are you gonna like, go to China with her?

SCOTT: With Siobhan?

CHARLIE: With Victhoria?

SCOTT: I don't think…maybe I'll be there in spirit.

CHARLIE: In spirit?

SCOTT: As a ghost, you know? That's how my three brothers go around with me. Billy. Trevor. Greg. The Billy Goats Gruff. The three little pigs. Winkin', Blinkin', and Nod. They're dead you know.

CHARLIE: I know.

SCOTT: I don't talk about it you know.

CHARLIE: Do you wanna talk about it?

SCOTT: My father. They died because of my father. My father, who took me to see *Love Is Colder Than Death* at the age of nine, sometimes lost track of the world, you know?…Hey, do you wanna go over there and do a film about Siobhan? Like take the camera and do a film about what she's thinking?…I wish I knew more about women. I hope they talk more. Even if—especially if it means I have to shut up.

(Sound of static, the lights jump, SCOTT and CHARLIE shift position.)

CHARLIE: I found Film Forum on my own. I chose to go there, after I broke up with my previous girlfriend. After I moved to the city. This city.

SCOTT: Hey Charlie look. Check it out. *(He pulls out his poison jar.)* It's my poison. Some total Bret Michaels poison. Not even Bret can find true love. I can't believe it took him that long to eliminate Kristy Joe.

CHARLIE: What are you talking about?

SCOTT: *Rock of Love II* on VH1. From very early on I thought Amber should win. Remember when she wore no underwear on their last date and Bret said, "Check please," and "Ka-ching?" I was like, that's what I would've said too. Because I am lame, too. I keep it real, too.

CHARLIE: I don't watch TV.

SCOTT: That's a bad move, dude. It's like ninety-five percent of the world. Why don't you watch the world?

CHARLIE: Godard says once you start you can't stop.

SCOTT: Everyone, the guy who gives me my everything bagel in the morning says that. Why do you need Godard to say it to you?

CHARLIE: Because. You need a moral force, like Godard, to be there through the good and the bad—to lead—and end up somewhere worthwhile. He speaks, he speaks to me like an intelligent human being. He confides, he begins one critical article, I remember: "I do not write to you from a far country. Yet even so everything separates us."

SCOTT: *(Beat.)* I am exhausted. That's lovely. So what the fuck are you waiting for?

(SIOBHAN walks over to the knife and slides it over towards CHARLIE with her foot. He sees it travel but does not go for it.)

SCOTT: I've lost my mind, but you're the one who can't touch anyone.

CHARLIE: ...And who do you touch?

SCOTT: *(Picks up the knife.)* I want to be touched. I want to be touched so badly. *(Beat.)* I wish that somebody would come over here and touch me. I mean, I'm practically begging for it. In every way I can.

CHARLIE: You already said that. You don't...I no longer want to kill you. So you know.

SCOTT: Why not?

CHARLIE: ...I wanted it to be spontaneous.

SCOTT: And it wasn't spontaneous?

CHARLIE: I brought a knife.

(SCOTT fake stabs himself, doubling over, then rising and showing CHARLIE the knife in his opposite hand.)

SCOTT: You're not like most people, you know. You're very unlike most people I know.

CHARLIE: Thank you.

SCOTT: I don't wanna spend a night in Inwood Park with most people I know.

CHARLIE: Thank you. Thank you for saying that. It means more than it should.

SCOTT: It's pretty sad that it does, huh? It's a weird fascination, because, when I

think about it, I don't know why I'd be so obsessed with someone, in a way, so pathetic.

CHARLIE: Yeah? *(Beat.)* What?

SCOTT: Oh, I'm sorry.

CHARLIE: Huh?

(Sound of static, the lights jump, SCOTT and CHARLIE shift position.)

SCOTT: What I—it's that I don't know why I'd be drawn to a coward. To someone so easily convinced he is or is not the way he is.

CHARLIE: What are you, dude, stop playing games.

SCOTT: I'm sorry, I'm just being honest with you. I'm just thinking about you, now I'm imagining how hard it must be to be near you. Like, to exist near you. I sometimes wonder if Siobhan would be happier with me. I'm not saying, I'm not trying to, I'm not trying to break new ground here. I just want what's best for everyone. And I had a thought.

CHARLIE: Please stop thinking. It doesn't, it doesn't work for you. It's not yours.

SCOTT: Maybe I do like Victhoria. Maybe I do. Maybe things are going really well for me. Maybe I should go to Guangzhou and we can make love on the tea leaves. The way Siobhan and I always—

CHARLIE: Jesus Christ!

SCOTT: —Hey you're my first choice! Don't get jealous.

CHARLIE: Come here.

(CHARLIE approaches SCOTT. SCOTT pulls the jar of poison out again.)

SCOTT: Hey dude, look look look, it's my poison.

CHARLIE: What is it?

SCOTT: It's all yer dreams come true. Are you the kind of person who remembers their dreams?

CHARLIE: I have this, I have this overwhelming need to win.

SCOTT: I just wanna feel something new.

CHARLIE: It's not a happy need.

SCOTT: I'm thirsty. I'm a little thirsty. Wanna give it to me?

CHARLIE: Maybe.

SCOTT: Why don't you take your shirt off and give it to me?

CHARLIE: What? *(Beat.)* Why would I take my shirt off?

SCOTT: Last requests. Dying man's… why don't you take your shirt off and give it to me.

CHARLIE: I don't need to.

SCOTT: Yeah well, I want you to. And I get to be dying. So. There.

CHARLIE: …Fine. *(Takes his shirt off.)*

SCOTT: *(Sits on the floor.)* Now, just…

CHARLIE: *(Crouches down.)* Yeah I get it. *(He unscrews the cap.)*

SCOTT: Right. *(Beat.)* This will actually kill me, you know.

CHARLIE: Are you okay with that? Are you cool with that?

SCOTT: Here and there. I'm sort of here and there on it. It's cool. I mean sad. I forgive you, of course. I Pedro

Almodóvar you. You're sort of like an undead brother to me, Charlie.

CHARLIE: I am you. I will be—I like you very much, dude. I wish that I were you.

(CHARLIE places the container to SCOTT's mouth. Both GUYS' hands are around it. SIOBHAN has come down to film this closer. The jar is held there, then tipped back; the poison goes down SCOTT's throat. They look on one another. CHARLIE touches SCOTT; SCOTT's eyes close. CHARLIE looks at SIOBHAN, then exits.)

SCENE 14
3rd JUDGMENT: "DEATH" VIDEOS

We return to the Film Forum room, shifted once more. RICH (with a pair of crutches), CHARLIE, and VICTHORIA sit on stage. After a couple beats, HOLLIS enters. She carries a manila envelope.

VICTHORIA: *(Eventually, to HOLLIS.)* You keep coming.

HOLLIS: Eh, what do I have better to do? I want to make films, you know?

VICTHORIA: What is the package?

HOLLIS: Yeah, I'm going to film school. In Perth. Australia. It's true. I'm going. I'm getting my shit together.

VICTHORIA: Wunderbar. Fantastic.

HOLLIS: Actually, I guess it depends on what this thing says, you know? My letter of notice.

RICH: *(Stands up.)* Listen, I would like to make an announcement. I'll be getting married fifteen months from now, and I'd like you all to be there.

HOLLIS: Oh yeah, to whom?

RICH: To you.

HOLLIS: Oh, sorry dude. My answer is "no."

RICH: No, I'm not asking you to marry me now. I'm just explaining, that I'll be getting married to you, in about fifteen months.

HOLLIS: Well cancel your plans because it's a long shot.

RICH: See, it just went from "no" to a long shot. This is like a scene from a romantic comedy. And we all know how those end. Not with a whimper, but with a bang. *(He sits.)*

HOLLIS: Keep dreaming. I'll be in Perth.

RICH: My love is strong.

HOLLIS: I thought you were weak? You'll fall apart in the next six months.

RICH: *(Bolts up and tosses his crutch to the side.)* It's a lie. It's a crutch. Metaphorically.

HOLLIS: Literally, too.

RICH: I'm okay, look I'm okay. *(He sits back down.)* I'm just saying…I'm ready to seize it.

HOLLIS: The day?

RICH: You.

HOLLIS: Why me?

RICH: *(Beat.)* I don't know. It just seems like we'd be good together…I could totally raise kangaroos. In Perth.

CHARLIE: But what if she doesn't love you?

RICH: She will fall, I will fall so deeply in love, I will give her so much love that she won't be able to absorb it all,

and some of it will be reflected off her body—just how the sun gives things color—and bounce directly back to me, and well, let's be honest, it will have come from her.

CHARLIE: But, you should know. You can tell, right? Whether you'll win or lose her.

RICH: I… —I'm not even gonna think about that. We'll, we'll find out on our own.

HOLLIS: You could save us a lot of time.

RICH: And Hay-Joe Ozmo could have saved us a lot of time had he said Bruce Willis was a dead person in the first frame. But no. Shit-the-fuck no.

(RICH places his hand on HOLLIS's knee. She places her hand on top of his, but only to remove his hand from her knee a beat later.)

VICTHORIA: So where's Scottie? *(Beat.)* I probably…

CHARLIE: What?

VICTHORIA: Nothing.

CHARLIE: He's weak…Maybe he's too…

VICTHORIA: Maybe…It's just, I would've liked to have seen him.

CHARLIE: Should we watch my movie?

HOLLIS: *(Fumbles with her package.)* Why don't we give him a chance?

CHARLIE: …He's not going to come.

HOLLIS: *(Not serious.)* What, did you kill him?

(CHARLIE looks at her.)

HOLLIS: *(Somewhat more seriously.)* You didn't kill him, did you?

(Pause. HOLLIS deflates this pause by opening the seal of the package.)

VICTHORIA: Why did you bring that here?

HOLLIS: It's my sacrifice. To all this. *(Tosses it on the floor without looking inside.)*

CHARLIE: What does it say?

HOLLIS: I don't know. I'm not Rich. I don't know if I lost. And, I'm not going to find out.

CHARLIE: No?

HOLLIS: I'm not looking. I'm not letting them decide if I can do this or not.

VICTHORIA: So you're giving up?

HOLLIS: No, I'm going. To Perth. To the admissions office. Regardless. And ask for a pencil. And some Cinemascope. What the fuck. *(She stands up.)*

RICH: *(Stands.)* I'm going too. I really love Perth.

HOLLIS: No you're not. I'm really sorry, but you're not. And I'm not making a bad decision by saying you're not. Okay? *(She nudges him back down.)* And I'm not being contradictory when I say, that I love a lot of things about you. I could probably love you a lot. But… *(She pauses, then turns and leaves.)*

VICTHORIA: *(To CHARLIE.)* And how do you keep your relationship together?

CHARLIE: We fight very hard for it. It's been an incredible two months.

VICTHORIA: …Two months? I'm sorry it just seemed like a lot longer…Aren't you afraid of losing it?

CHARLIE: I love her very much.

(RICH picks the package up off the floor. He opens it and looks at the cover letter. He reads it and places it down. CHARLIE then does the same. Instead of placing it down though, he looks over to VICTHORIA and offers it to her. She takes it, reads it, and tosses it down. Pause.)

RICH: I would've thought that she was the kind of person they would've wanted.

VICTHORIA: *(Beat.)* Well, we'll see what they say when they get her.

(Pause.)

CHARLIE: Perth. What the fo. Perth.

RICH: G'day mate, which way to Perth? Don't destroy my sense of self-Perth.

VICTHORIA: I'm about to give Perth. To a baby.

(They are giggling right now, not at her expense but at her gumption.)

CHARLIE: Where on Perth, did I leave my one-of-a-kind Hermes Perth. Wouldn't be the Perth time.

RICH: My diet is whack. It's all binge and Perth.

VICTHORIA: Perth. *(Beat.)* Hollis is totally my favorite raging bitch…Where is Scottie?

RICH: He goes missing.

VICTHORIA: *(Beat.)* Well, let's watch the movie. Congratulations, Charlie. You won.

(VICTHORIA stands and goes over to RICH, laying her head on his knee. She adjusts herself over and over on it. CHARLIE's Death Video plays. CHARLIE

will don his sunglasses during the screening and turns upstage to watch the video.)

CHARLIE'S DEATH VIDEO: *Charlie's Death Video is a montage of taped moments from CHARLIE and SCOTT's scene together in Inwood Park (scene 13), from SIOBHAN's point of view (her being the camera-person). In our production we filmed these scenes in Inwood Park itself, in the middle of the woods. The dialogue between CHARLIE and SCOTT was muted and a sad ballad, Stacey Kent's version of Irving Berlin's "Say It Isn't So" played over the images. The video should be fairly brief (no more than three minutes) and lead directly into the credits.*

CHARLIE: *(Over the video, speaks to the audience.)* I won. Despite… *(Pause.)* And I told you, nothing was handed to me.

(SIOBHAN enters after this and crouches downstage of CHARLIE, placing one hand to his back. He hands her a pair of sunglasses. She fumbles with them, trying to put them on with one hand, then flings them against the wall. Just before the credits roll, the following quotation appears on the screen.)

"IN MY LIFE THERE CAME AN IMPORTANT MOMENT WHEN MY BODY SUDDENLY REALIZED IT WAS MORTAL. SINCE THEN LIFE'S BEEN MUCH MORE FUN FOR ME."
—RAINER WERNER FASSBINDER (1945–1982)

(End of play.)

TRACES/FADES

Lenora Champagne

LENORA CHAMPAGNE is a playwright, performer, and director. She was born in 1951 in Opelousas, Louisiana, and was raised in Port Barre, Louisiana. She received a BA in English from Louisiana State University, and both an MA in drama and a Ph.D. in performance studies from New York University. She is the author of *Isabella Dreams the New World* (Ohio Theatre, 1990 and 1994; HERE Arts Center, 1997), *The Best Things in Life* (Downtown Art Co./Ohio Theatre, 1993), *Valentine's Day, 1980* (Ensemble Studio Theatre's 1996 Hell's Kitchen Sink Series), *Flying Home* (Primary Stages' 1996 American Myths Festival), *The Singing: a cyberspace opera* (Dance Theatre Workshop's 1997 Hit & Run Festival), *Wants* (New Georges/Soho Think Tank's Ice Factory 1998), *Coaticook* (Dallas Theatre Center; Soho Think Tank's Ice Factory 2000), *The Mama Dramas* (HERE Arts Center, 2001; Ohio Theatre, 2002), and *Mother's Little Helper* (Soho Think Tank's Ice Factory 2003; Ohio Theatre, 2004). From 1993 to 2000, Champagne was a member playwright at New Dramatists, and she has received numerous fellowships, awards, and commissions from the National Endowment for the Arts, the New York State Council on the Arts, the New York Foundation for the Arts, the Jerome Foundation, Yaddo, and the MacDowell Colony. She edited and contributed to *Out From Under: Texts by Women Performance Artists* (Theatre Communications Group, 1990), and has been published by Smith and Kraus, *Performing Arts Journal*, and *The Iowa Review*. She is currently the head of the Drama Studies Program at Purchase College, and lives in New York City with her husband, playwright, director, and frequent collaborator, Robert Lyons, and her daughter, Amelie Louise Champagne Lyons.

TRACES/fades was first presented by Soho Think Tank (Robert Lyons, Artistic Director; Erich Jungwirth, Producing Director) as part of the Ice Factory 2008 Festival (Vanessa Sparling and Mark Sitko, Festival Producers) on July 16, 2008, at the Ohio Theatre with the following cast and credits:

Delores	Mary Fogarty
Harry	Matthew Lewis
Ann	Joanne Jacobson
Claire	Lenora Champagne
Rose	Amelie Champagne Lyons
Hilda	Judith Greentree
Nettie Harper	Quanda Johnson

Directed by: Lenora Champagne and Robert Lyons
Music and Sound by: Daniel Levy and Lisa Dove
Music Direction by: Eric Walton
Costumes and Curtain by: Liz Prince
Video by: Shaun Irons and Lauren Petty
Stage Manager: Nicole Marconi
Assistant Directors: Tricia Cramer and Janina Santillan

TRACES/fades was developed in the HERE Artists Residency Program (HARP). Work-in-progress performances of excerpts or versions of the work took place at HERE Arts Center and the 3LD Technology and Stage space in November 2005, January 2006, May 2006, August 2006, January 2007, May 2007, and March 2008.

www.sohothinktank.org

Special thanks to everyone at Soho Think Tank, especially Robert Lyons, and at HERE, especially Kristin Marting; Materials for the Arts, New York Theatre Workshop, and New Georges for rehearsal space; to the Corporation of Yaddo, where I wrote Part I; and to all of the artists who participated in developing the work, including Donna Barkman, Lynn Cohen, Ron Cohen, Norman Heidinger, Joseph Keckler, Elaine Barrow Olesker, Molly Powell, Irma St. Paule, Valda Setterfield, Joan Shepard, Dale Soules, Maria Striar, and Jill Melanie Wirth.

AUTHOR'S NOTES

TRACES/fades is a meditation on Alzheimer's and our national inability to remember history. It is an intergenerational reflection on identity.

One of the things that happens with Alzheimer's is confusion about identity—the loss of memory of who other people are, and, eventually, the loss of a sense of one's own identity. In Part I, identity and ideas shift between the generations. Rose, the granddaughter, plays the grandmother (who was once a secretary), as Claire, the mother, tries to compose her presentation. Various thoughts—from her daily life, from the newspaper, from policy statements—come to mind, and she notes them as they pop up. Claire is fond of her mother and daughter, but preoccupied and busy. Ultimately, their roles and identities shift and merge at times, in an exploration of the transmission of ideas and traditions through generations.

Notes on the Set

The stage is covered with seamless white paper (the kind used for photo shoots). The paper hangs straight down from the upstage grid and travels over a long, narrow bench all the way downstage. The effect is of a snowdrift.

Rose's and Ann's "beds," are hung from the grid; they stand upstage so we get a bird's-eye view of them "lying down" in their "beds," as though they are sleeping upright. Claire sleeps on the long bench, covered by newspapers. A manual Royal typewriter and a red Chinese box are placed on stage.

Occasionally or throughout, video projections may play over the performers and the surface of the paper.

Part II, "My Mother's Mind," takes place in the same space, now a nursing home. In Part II, a video monitor on a stand is placed approximately where Rose's bed is in Part I. The images on the television monitor are not identical to the larger projections.

Between Part I and Part II, a floor-to-ceiling white curtain is pulled across the space by Nettie. The prologue to Part II, Delores's intake interview, takes place in front of it.

Notes on the Script

A few lines in the play are from D. D. Lessenberry, T. James Crawford, and Lawrence W. Erickson, *20th Century Typewriting*, 7th ed. (Cincinnati: South-Western Publishing, 1957). The information about a Swiss medical student coining the word "nostalgia" in the seventeenth century is from Richard A. Friedman, M.D., "Traversing the Mystery of Memory," *New York Times*, December 30, 2003.

Notes on the Production

The scenes are continuous, with video projections and music.

The "songs" are sung a cappella in simple, quirky speak-song fashion.

Here is an observation about my work from an anonymous reviewer. I think it helps explain how the script works. "Traditional dramatic structure is discarded to follow the structure of thinking. Focus is removed from the plot and directed toward moment to moment experience. The work operates like a field, where moments are brought forward (similar to the structure of a wave) as if following the way a mind experiences time."

You may stage this work differently. What was important to me was to create a space that was abstract rather than realistic, and that allowed for the imagination to play. What I was after was "the blank page of the stage," which allowed a space for the actors to play out their roles, while images of cursive handwriting, shorthand, and typing (among other things) were projected. In Alzheimer's you lose language, words, which are what the writer works with, and I wanted language and words to be present not only to the audience's ears, but to the spectator's eyes.

CHARACTERS

CLAIRE, a middle-aged political party operative, intelligent, driven.

ROSE, Claire's daughter. A young girl with brightly colored hair, about eleven.

ANN, an elegant older woman (Rose's grandmother, Claire's mother), about seventy.

DELORES, a frail, thin older woman, around eighty.

HILDA, a round, comfortable, more placid older woman, about seventy.

HARRY, an older man, about seventy-five.

NETTIE HARPER, an assisted living/nursing home employee—a guide/orderly/nurse/administrator/activities director. She is in her thirties or forties.

MARIAN, an older woman with brassy hair who plays the piano, over sixty-five.

(It is possible for the actress playing Nettie Harper to also play Marian, perhaps by donning a feather boa and evening gloves.)

PART I.
DOMESTIC DRIFTS

A drift of white comforters in dreamy light, with images of a blizzard or soft snowfall projected. ROSE and the GRAND-MOTHER are in communication, in a kind of dream space. They stretch together. ROSE emerges from the covers.

ROSE: My pillow is lumpy. My leg is asleep. I jiggle it and needles shoot up. It's almost dawn…the light is gray, underwater light.

ANN: *(In another space, another light, lying on white lace.)* Today my lungs are spacious. Earlier they were tight. I had trouble breathing and felt panic and fright. But now they are pink and expansive. There is more space in the gills. Sometimes they're leaky, and the air drifts out. Not enough oxygen to the brain, so I forget things.

ROSE: I'm wearing my grandmother's nightgown; old flannel roses. The cat jumps onto the night stand. She knocks over the water glass and wets the Kleenex. I toss her to the floor and wipe up the mess. My day begins.

ANN: Sometimes my lungs smell stale, and look peaked and greenish and dry. But today they're sufficiently moist. They usually taste like tuna. Today they are more like salmon, pink and sweet. My day begins.

CLAIRE: *(In a third space, light, covered with newspaper. She pops up suddenly.)* Ah, light! Too soon! Too soon! *(Looks ahead and calls out.)* It's a mess outside. The plows are piling it high. *(To herself.)* Something there is doesn't love a wall, fall, call… The snow drifts down, both sharp and soft, and covers us. Makes a clean white blanket of forgetting.

(ROSE and ANN step forward, humming.)

CLAIRE: *(Gathers the newspapers that covered her, stops abruptly, listening.)* What is that humming?

(ANN stops; ROSE leaves.)

CLAIRE: *(Crumples the newspaper into a tight ball.)* My day begins.

ANN: *(Watching CLAIRE crush the paper into a ball.)* She discovers that the discipline of compression gives her pleasure.
She likes to do things with her hands.
She sews sometimes. Simple things, like a wall for the bedroom. A pair of pants. Sheer curtains for the bathroom window.

ROSE: *(Enters.)* Where's the milk?

CLAIRE: There isn't any. I used what was left for my coffee.

ROSE: MOM!!!

(CLAIRE throws the newspaper "ball" to ROSE, who carries it off.)

ANN: The child is contributing herself to the story, her presence to the landscape of language.
There is a story here, but what is it?
Something about words and language and how they constitute us.
Aging, of course, and fading: a consequence.

(Light change. Things are more "real." The GRANDMOTHER heads back to her "bed.")

CLAIRE: *(Calls out.)* It's a mess outside. The plows are piling it high. The snow drifts down and covers us. Makes a clean white blanket of forgetting.

(ROSE enters with that day's newspaper and hands it to her MOTHER. CLAIRE glances at the paper.)

CLAIRE: Our president prefers not to think about yesterday—he's focused on today.
What about tomorrow? Will you even have a future? Will I?
Look at Mom's. It's not what she expected.
She's like that recently dead president in her depth of forgetting.
Out of her element.

ROSE: You don't understand her.

CLAIRE: Don't lecture me, missy.

ROSE: She lives in air and water.

CLAIRE: Like a whale or a dolphin? They found nine whales washed up on a Mexican beach.

ROSE: Dolphins are intelligent creatures.

CLAIRE: So was she.

ROSE: That reminds me, I need to find out about an important historical event in my parent's lifetime.

CLAIRE: How about…racial integration, the women's movement…abortion rights, the AIDS epidemic.

ROSE: *(Makes notes on the paper on stage.)* When did women get the right to vote?

CLAIRE: Around the time of World War I.

ROSE: When did they get the right to choose?

CLAIRE: Near the end of the war in Vietnam.

ROSE: When did they start to lose abortion rights?

CLAIRE: During the war in Iraq.
Look, why don't you get yourself some toast and keep busy. I have to finish my presentation.

(ROSE leaves. Silence.)

CLAIRE: Lately everything seems to be turning into sand. (*Glances at the newspaper and strides forward to address the audience, as though she's presenting her talk.*) We see nostalgia as a negative, a form of memory that keeps us longing for the past. But the word was first coined in the seventeenth century by a Swiss medical student to describe mercenaries who suffered from severe homesickness.
Soldiers who just wanted to go home, get back to where they once belonged.
Get back, get back…

(ROSE, dressed in a late '40s/early '50s get-up, enters, and catches her MOTHER singing, "Get back, get back…" CLAIRE abruptly stops and sits on the bench to make notes as ROSE gestures for her GRANDMOTHER to sit down at the other end of it.)

ROSE: Sit here, Maw Maw. I'll be you, and you be Paw Paw.

ANN: Ahhhh…

(ANN laughs her assent and sits. ROSE takes on her "YOUNG ANN" persona.)

ROSE: I have a good job. I don't want to give it up. The war is over.

ANN: *(As her young husband.)* The war is starting again somewhere else. My job is to go.

ROSE: I have such a good boss. I am using my shorthand. I am useful here.

ANN: *(As her young husband.)* They need me there. I have no choice.

ROSE: You have the bad ear.

ANN: *(As her young husband.)* I don't want anyone saying I shirked my duty.

CLAIRE: What marks us as human is…our bent for making sense of things…While we cannot discern essential truths, we can and must try to make sense of things.

ROSE: All right. I'll give notice.

ANN: *(As her young husband.)* You'll find something where we're going. They need good secretaries everywhere.

ROSE: I've never been anywhere.

ANN: *(As her young husband.)* Hope you like palm trees!

(ANN and ROSE turn their backs to the audience. They take a step together upstage as we hear the sound of a wave. A wave is projected.)

CLAIRE: But the numbers just don't add up. They're off the charts. The justifications are so much mumbo-jumbo. They expect us to buy it, but it's just a shell game. Nothing's where you think you'll find it; when you look for it, you come up empty.

(Sound of palm trees swaying. On video, palm trees sway. ROSE and ANN spin around to face forward.)

ROSE: I got the job!

ANN: *(As her young husband.)* Knew you would.

ROSE: I love living here.

ANN: *(As her young husband.)* Wish I could stay here instead of shipping off overseas.

ROSE: Me, too. Especially since, while you're there, I'll be having a baby!

ANN: *(As her young husband.)* What!?

ROSE: It's the palm trees. They're magical.

(Hurricane footage on video. Storm sounds. ROSE and ANN are buffeted about. Telephone rings. ANN sits back down and looks older and tired.)

CLAIRE: Arghh!! *(Crumples up what she's been working on and does a jerky, anxious dance as she "talks on the phone" to her MOTHER.)* Hello!? What? She's wandering? Put her on the phone. Can you do that for me? Put her on the telephone! Mom? How are you feeling? Are you all right? That's good, Mom. Now listen to me. You have to stay where they put you, all right? You can't go exploring, okay? No, you mustn't go anywhere. I'll get what you need at the store. What do you need? Socks? Black? I can get those for you. You don't need to get them yourself. I'll bring them when I come, all right? I'll come when I can. Soon. I'll come soon, okay? Good. Stay where they put you. Just do what they say. *(All the steam is out of her. She just hangs there in frustration and helplessness.)*

ROSE: *(To ANN, as she leads her back to "bed.")* Behave and take good care of yourself! Stay safe, and come back as soon as you can!

ANN: We'll lick the enemy in no time! I'll be back before you know it!

ROSE: *(Looks after ANN with sympathy. Then, briskly:)* Now I can get to work!

(ROSE places a manual Royal typewriter on the bench, puts a sheet of paper in the carriage, and begins to type as CLAIRE attempts to return to her presentation.)

CLAIRE: Which is why we must work together to amplify the message. At the end of the day, we should be on the same page and think outside the box. *(Looks blankly ahead, crumples a piece of paper, tosses it.)*

(ROSE types. As she types, words are projected on the hanging paper.)

ANN: Dear Children,
We have had the strangest weather lately. First ice, then snow.

CLAIRE: I have to get global warming in here somewhere.
Let's see what I have:
(She rips the page from ROSE's typewriter and reads from it.) A former President convened a panel to study global warming in 1979…? *(She goes back to presentation mode.)*
Storms in the upper Midwest.
Hurricanes expected—

ANN: Hurricanes here!

CLAIRE: —tornadoes,

ANN: Tsunamis!

CLAIRE: —signs that global climate change has arrived. A Bush administration appointee altered the official findings on global warming to downplay conclusive evidence of climate change.

How is it that a president can get away with a snow job, but not a blowjob? *(Crosses this out.)*

(ROSE has continued typing the following text, which appears as a projection as CLAIRE plucks it from ROSE's typewriter and reads it aloud:)

CLAIRE: It is the willingness to step back, stick to someone through thick and thin whether things are going well or badly. That is a fair definition but loyalty is something more.

ROSE: Who was Benedict Arnold?

CLAIRE: Not right now, sweetie. Just a minute.

ROSE: *(Looks up from her typing. She speaks authoritatively.)* I want to feel that my secretary knows and appreciates the part I am playing in my organization. She knows my feelings, but she does not let others know that she knows. She defends me, if necessary, to anyone who questions my motives or methods of working.
What was Nixon's secretary's name again? And what was on the tapes she erased?

CLAIRE: Not now, Rose.

ROSE: What did Sacco and Vanzetti do?

CLAIRE: It's a long story. Things were different then.

ROSE: Did you name me Rose after the Rosenbergs?

CLAIRE: And officials refuse to answer any questions. They claim it's for reasons of "national security." But they're the ones making us feel insecure!

(ROSE has continued typing. CLAIRE plucks another sheet of paper from the typewriter carriage. In frustration, ROSE puts the typewriter away during the following text, which ROSE speaks in its entirety as CLAIRE and ANN echo phrases.)

ROSE, with CLAIRE and a few words from ANN: Loyalty includes a person's attitude and dedication to the job. A person who is really loyal wants the company to succeed and works at all times toward that goal. The loyal secretary "sells" her company, her boss, and her fellow workers.

CLAIRE: Why be a secretary when you can be a boss?

ROSE: She plucks hard

CLAIRE: plucks hard?

ROSE: to help make a better place for everyone.

CLAIRE: *(Lies down on the bench.)* I'm just so tired all the time.

ROSE: You should sleep more, Mama.

CLAIRE: I haven't slept well for some time. I woke up at one and read about the history of the Night.

ROSE: You should try warm milk.

ANN: Of course, they don't have any.

CLAIRE: Did you know that sleep patterns were different before artificial light?…

(ROSE's arm shoots up, like a child who wants to be called on.)

CLAIRE: What?

ROSE: I know how to make a button lamp. You take a button, dip a bit of cloth in oil—any kind, salad oil, old motor oil—wrap it around the button, light it, and there you go!

CLAIRE: I want you with me in a blackout.

ROSE: Then you could sleep more!

(ANN leaves her bed to join CLAIRE and ROSE in singing the Night/Light Song.)

CLAIRE and ROSE:
BEFORE THERE WAS LIGHT
THERE WAS NIGHT
WE ALL SLEPT MORE
AND HAD SHORTER DAYS

ANN: THERE WERE STARS
YOU COULD SEE THEM
YOU COULD SMELL THE COLD AIR
YOU COULD HEAR THE PINES SIGH
AND THE HOOT OWL CALL

CLAIRE and ROSE:
BEFORE THERE WAS LIGHT
THERE WAS NIGHT
WE ALL SLEPT MORE
AND HAD SHORTER DAYS

ANN: THE NIGHT WAS DARK VELVET
SCATTERED WITH GLITTER
A DIFFERENT WORLD
OUTSIDE OF TIME

CLAIRE, ROSE, and ANN:
BEFORE THERE WAS LIGHT
THERE WAS NIGHT
WE ALL SLEPT MORE
AND HAD SHORTER DAYS

ANN: HUDDLED UNDER COVERS
GATHERED ROUND THE FIRE
COOKING AND MENDING
BEFORE THE BLAZE

CLAIRE and ROSE:
BEFORE THERE WAS LIGHT
THERE WAS NIGHT
WE ALL SLEPT MORE
AND HAD SHORTER DAYS

CLAIRE, ROSE, and ANN:
THOUGH A GIRL'S WORK
NEVER ENDED WITH THE DAY
ELECTRIC LIGHT
DID AWAY WITH NIGHT
ELECTRIC LIGHT
NOW WE WORK ALL NIGHT

ANN: TIME FLIES ON LIGHT

CLAIRE: TIME FLIES ON LIGHT

ROSE: TIME FLIES

ANN: TIME FLIES ON LIGHT

CLAIRE: TIME FLIES ON LIGHT

ROSE: TIME FLIES

(The reverie over, CLAIRE breaks away.)

CLAIRE: I don't have time for this. I have to finish my presentation, and do some emails.

Rose, would you go to the store and get some black socks and bring them to your grandmother? I'll drop you off on my way to work.

ROSE: But this is Saturday!

CLAIRE: Exactly! A perfect time to visit your grandmother.

ROSE: Remember Easter?

CLAIRE: Yes. She was better then.

(ROSE gets ANN from her bed and brings her to the bench for the Easter flashback.)

CLAIRE: Why am I so obsessed with facts?
Why am I noting what has already happened, instead of imagining what is possible?

(ROSE gives her GRANDMOTHER a basket with an egg in it.)

ROSE: Here, Grandma, want to decorate an egg?

ANN: Is it Easter already?

ROSE: Almost. We can do it!

ANN: Can we do it?

ROSE: Yes, we can!

ANN: Can I do it?

ROSE: Yes, here are the colors. You can dip the eggs in.

ANN: I can?

ROSE: Or you can make a design. Draw something.

CLAIRE: Why won't it write itself?

ANN: I'll do that.

ROSE: *(Gives her GRANDMOTHER a crayon.)* Here. Use this.

(For the first time—except for the song, which was outside time—CLAIRE can see her MOTHER. At this moment, all three are back at Easter, when ANN was better.)

CLAIRE: Is she doing something?

ROSE: Yes. She's writing on the egg.

CLAIRE: What is she writing?

ROSE: I think she's writing, Boiled Egg.

(CLAIRE and ROSE laugh. ANN joins in.)

CLAIRE: Anchors to the real, please! I am my mother's daughter!

ANN: We can do it!

CLAIRE: Let me see.

ANN: It's for Rose.

ROSE: Thank you, Maw Maw!

CLAIRE: What does it say?

ROSE: It says, "Boiled for You."

CLAIRE: Mother's a wit!

ROSE: It's a gift. Thank you, Maw Maw.

(ANN makes a gesture with her hand, as if to say, it was nothing.)

ROSE: *(To CLAIRE.)* What will you give me?

CLAIRE: We'll see. *(Walks back into her workspace and looks at the red Chinese box.)*

(ROSE picks up the box.)

CLAIRE: Be careful with that!

ROSE: Where did this come from? Was it yours when you were little?

CLAIRE: It was your grandmother's. She won it for writing the best short story in seventh grade.

ROSE: What kind of story?

CLAIRE: Something about an unpopular girl who comes out ahead when a popular girl's nose gets broken. It shows Mum's vindictive side.

ROSE: And the nuns gave her a prize…What did you do in seventh grade?

CLAIRE: I wore a blue corduroy circle skirt and a bright striped top. Whirled round my desk to attract a boy's attention, my face going red as blood rushed to my head.

Do you want that box? You can have it.

ROSE: Thank you.

CLAIRE: Now put it away and let's go.

ROSE: But you haven't finished your presentation. (*Puts the box away and sits next to her GRANDMOTHER, in the center of the bench.*)

CLAIRE: I think I've said enough. (*To ANN.*) And you haven't given birth to me yet.

ANN: I'm waiting for my husband to return from the war.

CLAIRE: A child waits for no man. (*Joins the OTHERS on the bench.*)

ROSE: You mean time, don't you? Time waits for no man. Anyway, we all end up under the earth.

CLAIRE: Only after we've seen the light.

ROSE: Give me time.

ANN: When you're born, I'll name you Claire.

(*Music. Beat. CLAIRE looks off. End of Part I.)*

(*NETTIE HARPER, from Part II, pulls a white curtain across the front of the stage,*

setting the scene for the intake interview, which is the prologue to Part II.)

PART II.
MY MOTHER'S MIND
PROLOGUE: THE INTAKE INTERVIEW.

NETTIE HARPER, a nursing home administrator, and DELORES, a woman of eighty.

NETTIE: I'll say three words. Tell me the first thing that comes into your mind. Ready?

DELORES: Set.

NETTIE: I mean, are you ready?

DELORES: Yes.

NETTIE: All right. Here goes: Black

DELORES: White

NETTIE: In

DELORES: Out

NETTIE: Yesterday

DELORES: Tomorrow?

NETTIE: Very good. Now, I'm going to quote some famous phrases, and you tell me who said them, all right?

DELORES: All right.

NETTIE: "I have a dream."

DELORES: King Arthur?

NETTIE: That's close. It was Martin Luther King. What about this one: "We must make the world safe for democracy."

DELORES: The Bush boy?

NETTIE: Noooo. Woodrow Wilson. That's how he persuaded America to get into World War I.

DELORES: A lot of good it did us. Look what came after.

NETTIE: Just one more. Listen carefully. "We will bury you."

DELORES: That's what I'm afraid of.

NETTIE: No! Who said it? Listen again. "We will bury you."

DELORES: It sounds like that show with the little red-haired girl who drives a hearse.

NETTIE: What? Oh, you mean *Six Feet Under*. No, it was Krushchev!

DELORES: Ahhhh! I thought he was charming!

NETTIE: Sign this, please.

(As DELORES signs her name, her signature is projected. NETTIE ushers DELORES offstage, then efficiently sweeps the curtain open. The space has been altered. There is a wheelchair next to the bench and a television where ROSE's "bed" was. The TV may be on. NETTIE places ANN into the wheelchair. A ball rolls across the space. It is a large, brightly colored exercise ball. ROSE comes running after the ball, laughing. She bats it and chases it off. HILDA and HARRY, with a walker, shuffle out and sit on the bench, joined by DELORES. NETTIE HARPER, as the activities director, leads the exercise class.)

SCENE: MORNING EXERCISE.

NETTIE: Sit up. Keep the feet on the floor. Keep your eyes on the ball.
Strike the ball with a quick, sharp blow.

DELORES: *(Sings.)* AMONG THE RED-
    WOODS
YOU LAY ME DOWN...

ANN: Give me a ladder and I'll bake us a pie.

HILDA: My family runs a newspaper in Summerville, Georgia.

NETTIE: They used to?

HILDA: They still do.

HARRY: What did I do?

NETTIE: Strike the ball.

DELORES: Things rise and fall, you know. Like empires.

HARRY: Napoleon was great.

ANN: And both short and short-lived.

HILDA: Rome wasn't built in a day!

NETTIE: Keep your eyes on the ball.

HARRY: So what? However long you live, you die.

HILDA: That's it.

ANN: What's that?

HILDA: What we leave behind.

HARRY: And that is?

HILDA: A mark. A trace. A sign that we were here.

ANN: In the world?

HILDA: In someone's mind. A child remembers.

DELORES: But does the man?

HARRY: I wake up in a sweat almost every night, when I can get to sleep. We were trained, we were ready. But when the shooting started, the fear took over. We were afraid for our lives. I did what I was trained to do. I survived, and I backed up my buddies. But I'm still a virgin. I haven't killed a man yet.

ANN: Harry has a light.

DELORES: Harry has the right kind of light.

HILDA: Harry fought a hard fight.

HARRY: Shine my boots!

(ANN wheels her chair away.)

DELORES: Harry is a fine chap, but I'm afraid he's no salesman.

(NETTIE ushers in ANN's young grand-daughter, ROSE, to ANN's wheelchair.)

SCENE: CIRCLES.

NETTIE: If you leave the building and wander, you lose the privilege of living here.

ROSE: Maw Maw, don't leave the building, you hear?

NETTIE: We've been finding her in other people's rooms.

ROSE: Stay in your place, all right?

NETTIE: We sometimes put the brakes on.

ROSE: She doesn't get out of the chair on her own.

NETTIE: We're going to use a little restraint.
Don't worry. It's just like wearing a cummerbund!

(NETTIE produces the restraint from a pocket. While ROSE speaks to ANN, NETTIE puts the restraint on the GRANDMOTHER.)

ROSE: You used to sew sometimes. Remember, Maw Maw? You made me a pink polished cotton dress with a pink polished cotton cummerbund. I loved it, but you weren't satisfied. You changed

the sash to pink organdy. When they lined us up, I was last, so I thought I'd lost, but the first was last. I was the winner then.

NETTIE: There! All done!

ROSE: This sash is not pink or organdy, but some stretchy synthetic!

NETTIE: *(Speaks sympathetically to ROSE.)* It's surprising when you're somewhere that's not your home and the embroidery pattern on the dresser scarf matches the embroidery pattern on your grandmother's sewing machine cover. At one time in America, it must have been a popular pattern, a popular pastime, and most of us have forgotten how it was done. *(Addresses the audience.)* The curves in the dresser remind me of cursive. A gesture of self-expression. Today's block letters are bland. No personality there. They're all wearing the same face, like the interchangeable jeans and T-shirts that are all you see in the stores and on the girls and boys alike. When my teenaged niece sends me a letter in block print, I think, doesn't she know anything? Why can't she write? But they don't teach cursive in the schools anymore. You can't assess it, so it's not important. *(To ROSE.)* You'll just use a computer, anyway.

ANN: *(To ROSE.)* I have laundry to do, dishes to wash—you write.

ROSE: I do write. But I'd like to sew. *(To NETTIE.)* You were so lucky. So much happened in your time. The Ramones were still alive, and John Lennon, and Audrey Hepburn. And Martin Luther King. And you wore such cool clothes.

NETTIE: Get your grandmother to teach you how to sew.

ROSE: I think she's forgotten how.

(The following is a dance, all in curves.)

NETTIE: You just go in and out, in and out. Make arabesques in the air. Circle around and hone in. The thread will connect and bind you to one another. You'll have something of her that you can keep for yourself—a skill, not a thing. That's the thing about the domestic arts—they're just another lost tradition.

ROSE: She doesn't remember.

NETTIE: You can always ask. While you're at it, get her to teach you cursive.

SCENE: MENUS/LET US DO.

NETTIE: Want to help me pass out the menus?

(ROSE takes menus and gives one to ANN.)

ANN: We will gain skill in this work if we do it as well as we can each time.

NETTIE: *(Giving DELORES a menu.)* What would you like to eat?

DELORES: None of your business.

(ROSE gives HARRY a menu and exits with NETTIE.)

HARRY: Let us all do big things when we can.
If we do not do big things,
let us do all we do in a big way.

DELORES: Let us. Let us do.

HILDA: Let us do big things.

(EVERYONE sits there. No one does anything. Silence. Pause. Then…)

ANN: My handwriting is prize-winning.

HILDA: Shorthand is a useful skill for secretaries.

Being a secretary or a teacher are good options for women who want a career.

DELORES: Being a nurse is for the more adventurous girl.

HARRY: I was a professor.
My least favorite thing was marking exams.
I hated giving grades.
And faculty meetings. Ugh.

Before that, I was in the Army Air Corps.
I was a captain.
I saw action.
An enlisted man saved my life.
Nothing else ever matched that.

Until I saw the water rising…
It came so fast…

HILDA: Do you remember the flood of '27?
The water was up to the roof.

HARRY: Who was president then?

DELORES: How should I know?

HARRY: Do you remember back in '38?

HILDA: '38?

ANN: Who was president then?
Maybe Roosevelt?

HARRY: The war was over in '45.

HILDA: When did the bomb go off?

ANN: Did Roosevelt do that?

DELORES: Wasn't that Elvis Presley?

HARRY: Was that the fifties?

HILDA: Hippies in the sixties! I'd drive my youngest to the highway to watch the hippies pass.

ANN: Didn't one of them drown in the river?

HILDA: That's right.

ANN: They were against the war then.

HILDA: What else happened in the sixties?

ANN: Who was president then?

DELORES: That Kennedy boy.

HILDA: That's right. He was Catholic.

DELORES: You have a problem with that?

HARRY: I think there was a moon landing somewhere in there.

HILDA: That was a simulation. I am sure of it. If we could get to the moon we'd have better rail service.

ANN: The seventies was women's lib!

DELORES: The eighties was money and shoulder pads.

ANN: You remember the eighties?

HILDA: How old are you, Harry?

HARRY: I'm forty-six, and still my mother's child…

Nothing else ever matched that.
Until I saw the water rising.
It came so fast.
Haven't been so afraid since World War II.

(The silence is broken by HARRY crossing the stage on his walker. HARRY leaves the space.)

HILDA: *(Sings "The Ballad of the Pacifist Grandmother.")*
I HAD AN UNCLE IN THE WAR
WHICH WAR?
A BIG WAR
THE KRAUTS DIDN'T GET HIM
INFLUENZA DID

I HAD A HUSBAND IN THE WAR
WHICH WAR?
A BIG WAR
THE JAPS DIDN'T GET HIM
HIS HEART CONDITION DID

I HAD A SON IN THE WAR
WHICH WAR?
A BIG WAR
THE GOOKS DIDN'T GET HIM
DRUG ADDICTION DID

I HAD A GRANDSON IN THE WAR
WHICH WAR?
A BIG WAR
THE ARABS DIDN'T GET HIM
FRIENDLY FIRE DID

ROSE: *(Enters and collects the menu cards. To ANN.)* Where are your glasses? Where is your hearing aid?

ANN: I appreciate it when my children come to visit.
I had so many of them.
I can't remember all the names.
They blend together.
Sometimes there is something I recognize.
A smell. A tooth. A look.
They all sound alike.

ROSE: Maw Maw, do you remember typing?

ANN: What about it?

ROSE: How hard it is to remember where the right key is?

ANN: Everything is hard to remember, and they took away my keys. Nothing locked can be opened now, and I can't make a getaway. No way out now.

ROSE: Want to see me tap dance?

(She does. EVERYONE laughs and claps.)

SCENE: THEY KEEP US ENTERTAINED.

MARIAN, an ancient lady with gold hoop earrings, fake golden hair, and sequins on her knit top toodles in on a walker. She has a bag of sheet music looped over the handles. Alternatively, NETTIE dresses up, perhaps in a feather boa and long gloves, and entertains the residents with a song.

NETTIE/MARIAN: SING-ALONG TIME! *(If someone other than the actress playing NETTIE plays MARIAN, add:)* Marian is going to play the piano for us!

(Excitement all around.)

NETTIE/MARIAN: How are we today? There you are. How are you, honey?

(HARRY brings her coffee.)

NETTIE/MARIAN: Thank you, sweetheart. You know just how I like it, don't you, sugar? I'm going to play your favorite today. Do you remember this one?

(She passes her hands over the keys really quickly and launches into a golden oldie. Everything is cocktail piano style. Very decorative, full of arpeggios. Her voice is full of vibrations, thin and reedy. In the most recent version, NETTIE, dolled up as the entertainer, sang "I'm Just Wild About Harry." Any old favorite tune will do; it changes with the performer. Various people sing along. ANN wheels her chair in the opposite direction and stares ahead vacantly. NETTIE/MARIAN wheels ANN's chair back around and tries to engage ANN and DELORES, who is cranky, with more patter.)

NETTIE/MARIAN: Whose birthday is it today?

(ANN raises her hand.)

NETTIE/MARIAN: Again? *(To DELORES.)* You holding up all right?

(To HILDA.) She's feeling poorly just now, isn't she?
What's new with you, honey?

HILDA: Vern works quite well, I think, and so does Harry. He does not live quite as I would have him live.

NETTIE/MARIAN: That's right, sweetheart, keep up your standards.

ANN: I work well, too.

NETTIE/MARIAN: That's right, dawlin'! Keep it up!

DELORES: I want to do as well as I can. We must know, and know that we know.
It takes time to learn to do this right.
We should make the mind reach for this.

NETTIE/MARIAN: You do that, sweetheart!

ANN: It takes time. It takes time to learn.

NETTIE/MARIAN: No one in a rush here!

HARRY: The man can find some good work to do in due time.

NETTIE/MARIAN: Just take your time. You do just that.

(The RESIDENTS sit back. They relax. They smile.)

NETTIE/MARIAN: That's it for today! I have to go now, but I'll be back! *(From offstage.)* Be good, and they'll give you ice cream tonight!

ALL: ICE IS NICE!

(They do a dance. It's an ice cream/appetite dance. It gradually peters out. NETTIE rolls in a food trolley or lowers the "table." In the production, it flew in from above.)

SCENE: WE LIKE TO EAT.

NETTIE: FOOD! Come stuff your faces!

(The RESIDENTS rearrange themselves for the meal.)

ANN: *(To ROSE.)* I'm going to make you some good food!

HARRY: At my age, I am not able to eat fried foods.

DELORES: I can't taste a thing.

(Perhaps NETTIE puts bibs on the RESIDENTS.)

HARRY: Once upon a time, in an old country that had already fought the war to end all wars, money was worthless and it took wheelbarrows of it to buy bread. If you remember this story, you know it wasn't a happy one. In America, schoolgirls soon collected toothpaste tubes to melt down to make warplanes.

ANN: Now everyone just wants to have white teeth.

HILDA: There is always the question of white might versus right.

DELORES: Where's lunch? Where's dinner? So what if I just ate, I wanna eat.
I was always hungry; never had enough; had to move out of our place, move away,
'cause I'd wake up the landlady's son with my crying from hunger,
not enough milk, not enough to eat,
We did window shopping in big hairbows
looking through the plate glass for good things to eat
on that stretched salary that didn't go far enough.

HILDA: Let us all lend a hand to all those in need of us.

It is right for us to do good to the ones in need.

ANN: *(To ROSE.)* I loved my job. I had an excellent job. Your daddy was going to Korea, but I had the best boss I ever had.

ROSE: During the war in Vietnam, she practiced her stenography during the evening news, because you never knew when it might come in handy. She took down every word Walter Cronkite said.

HARRY: *(As Walter Cronkite.)* Most of us can do much more work than is now done.
Most of us can do far more work in much less time.
It is right for all of us to do all the work well.

Wish me luck; then make me work so luck will come.

NETTIE: *(To HARRY.)* Remember, no one can do his best work when he does not possess good health.
(To ROSE.) Can you believe?
My fifty-five-year-old overweight dentist just got sent to Iraq. He joined the National Guard thirty years ago, and this is how he's thanked.

ROSE: God bless America!

DELORES: Say Aaahhhhhhhh…

ANN: So they turn you over and look for bruises. They turn you over and change your diaper. They turn you over and give you a suppository to stop the vomiting. They turn you over and let what's under crawl out. You're no body with feelings, you're a stone, something in storage, an object to be kept clean and dry, it's a countdown, a waiting for the stone to cease speech altogether and weep no more my baby there's a long sleep coming.

(Silence. Pause. Then…)

NETTIE: Here's your ice cream!

HILDA: Len is ill. He fought a hard fight.

HARRY: But has he killed an enemy? Has he beat the bad guys yet?

HILDA: He has lent a hand to those in need of us.

HARRY: What if the hand that feeds gets cut off?

HILDA: Isn't that like cutting your nose to spite your face?

(HILDA tries to feed HARRY.)

HILDA: Here, Harry, here's the good stuff. Come on. Open up.

(ROSE tries to feed ANN.)

NETTIE: They grapple with it, but the journey from plate to mouth is perilous. The cake falls off the fork, into the lap. Every bite is effort-full. It takes all the concentration there is.

ANN: I don't need you to feed me. I want to do it myself.

ROSE: I understand. I try to be independent, too.
Even babies strive to be independent.

NETTIE: *(To ROSE, as they move upstage to the food cart.)* You have to make some old people feed themselves. Some of them just want everything done for them.

HILDA: We can learn to like to do all that we need to do.

(DELORES, a thin, frail lady in a limp sweater, sings. EVERYONE ELSE joins in on the chorus.)

DELORES: *(Sings "The Eating Song.")*
WE LIKE TO EAT
BECAUSE WE STILL CAN
EVEN WHEN WE CAN'T THINK OR SPEAK
WE LIKE TO EAT

LIVING THINGS NEED NOURISHMENT
AND WE'RE STILL ALIVE
LIVING THINGS REPRODUCE
AND MOST OF US HAVE
BUT NOT ME

WE LIKE TO EAT
BECAUSE WE STILL CAN
EVEN WHEN WE CAN'T THINK OR SPEAK
WE LIKE TO EAT

I WAS A NURSE ALL MY GROWN LIFE
I WAS A NURSE IN THE GREAT BIG WAR
LATER, I TOOK CARE OF MY FATHER
NOW I CAN'T TAKE CARE OF MYSELF

WE LIKE TO EAT
BECAUSE WE STILL CAN
EVEN WHEN WE CAN'T THINK OR SPEAK
WE LIKE TO EAT

I DIDN'T EXPECT TO SEE THIS DAY
I WATCH. I WAIT
THEY KEEP US ENTERTAINED

WE LIKE TO EAT
BECAUSE WE STILL CAN
EVEN WHEN WE CAN'T THINK OR SPEAK
WE LIKE TO EAT

BUT I'M TIRED OF EATING
FOOD DOESN'T TASTE GOOD ANYMORE
IT'S THE FIRST APPETITE WE DEVELOP
AND THE LAST TO GO

(Pause. Silence. Then…)

HARRY: A boy who is fifteen or sixteen thinks of a man of twenty-nine or thirty as an old man; but when the boy gets to be twenty-one, he has had a change in his point of view and thirty is no longer old. Today men at fifty-nine to sixty and many at seventy or eighty are young in heart and mind. *(He cries out.)* Please, shine my riding boots!

HILDA: My, we're an interesting bunch!

SCENE: WATERY SPOUT.

ROSE: Maw Maw, want to go outside before I have to leave?

(ROSE wheels her GRANDMOTHER outdoors, where there is a fountain playing and cars passing by in the distance. ROSE sits at ANN's feet. They watch the water and the traffic. Music, projections.)

ANN: Watery…spout. Look at that watery spout.

ROSE: Do you wonder where the cars are going?

ANN: That's not the thinking I'm doing now.
I'm not figuring things like that.

ROSE: Can you still do shorthand?

ANN: Noooo…

ROSE: You said you cried when you got to the town where you and Paw Paw would live and saw cows in the middle of the streets and no sidewalks.

ANN: How now?

ROSE: Brown cow. *(She laughs.)*

ANN: I'm not asking questions like that.

ROSE: Someone tried to throw herself in the bayou.
They fished her out.

ANN: Who?

ROSE: The fishermen.
She was soggy already

But they pressed the water out
Breathed the air in.
She's living still.

ANN: No fish in that watery spout.
But a lot of dishes. Yes, I have a lot of dishes.

ROSE: Well, we better go in so you can do them! *(She wheels her GRAND-MOTHER in.)* Goodbye, Maw Maw. *(To EVERYONE.)* I'll see you soon. *(ROSE leaves, but forgets her sweater on the wheelchair.)*

SCENE: NIGHTFALL.

NETTIE: BEDTIME!

HILDA: No! I'm not sleepy!

NETTIE: You know you need your rest!

HILDA: No! Don't take me back there!

NETTIE: Come on, Hilda, you know you enjoy your nap!

HILDA: Don't tell me what I like!
I do not want to lie down!

I want to stay awake!

When I close my eyes,
I see things!

Bands of yellow!

Strange shapes!

Blood on the walls!

NETTIE: Now, now, don't worry! We'll wash it right off! We'll clean it right up! You'll feel fresh when you wake up!

HILDA: I will never feel fresh again in my life! It stinks in here! I am not going to sleep!

HARRY: When I close my eyes
I see flashes of light

The torch of freedom
Burning things down.

Ruined flesh
Me trapped inside
Me trapped inside
While young people shop.

The living have to work
They have to keep active
From my perspective
Being busy builds time.

My days are endless
An endless vacant waiting
What I remember is my mother.
When will she come to see me? *(Shuffles off on his walker.)*

(ANN and DELORES, alone. DELORES is asleep in her chair; she startles awake.)

DELORES: Do you remember?

ANN: No…

DELORES: Has he changed your sawdust?

ANN: It isn't sawdust.

DELORES: Your sand, then…

ANN: It was sawdust once.

DELORES: Once!

ANN: And now it's sand.

DELORES: Now it's sand.

ANN: Watery spout…

Drowning in brown water, brackish, slimy, snakes in there
Clung to her lungs and wished for light and sight
Fights for air and rescue
Anyone will do
Bring out and up through dark drowning to light and sense.
Give clarity, O Lord.

I want words to swim and save me,
to reach land where I can stand,
solid, sure-footed, free.
(Pause.)
Quiet. It's quiet at last.

(NETTIE enters.)

ANN: I can hear people outside, but the drama is inside my head. My eyes surprise me, and I watch colors that others can't see. When I try to tell someone about it, they don't listen, so I stop trying.

DELORES: *(Waking suddenly.)* A plane is coming. Watch out!

NETTIE: A plane is a form of locomotion. It gets you from here to there in little time.

ANN: I have too much time. A day lasts forever.

NETTIE: I have no time for myself. I care for my child, I care for you old people.

ANN: Do you care?

NETTIE: I'm here, aren't I.

DELORES *(Calls out.)* A busload of soldiers just drove off. Perhaps they're on a recreational outing?

NETTIE: *(Confiding in DELORES.)* I'm unhappy with my body. The thickening middle, the thinning hair, the tricky teeth and eyes.

DELORES: That's nothing. Just wait. Everything hurts. I'm losing out.

NETTIE: This is only the beginning. *(She looks at the women.)*
Is this how I'm going to end up?
I'm an adult. I should really be able to cope with this. *(Doing stretches and exercises.)*
I am losing flexibility. Must do more to prevent a physical and mental slide.

I want to stay healthy and mentally alert all the days of my life.

(ROSE walks in, startling NETTIE.)

ROSE: I forgot my sweater.

ANN: Someone said something about perspective once, but I forget who, or where.

ROSE: *(To ANN.)* I got your prize, remember?—a red Chinese box, full of meaning for me, if not for anyone else. The prize you won for writing the best short story in seventh grade.

ANN: Something about breaking your nose to spite your foe.
But I don't have it, and I don't remember the details.

NETTIE: If we are what we remember, then who are we when we forget?

ROSE: In the space between time and after, she got stuck.

(Music. EVERYONE looks toward a pink ball of light. HILDA and HARRY return to watch the light. As it rises, the actors follow it with their eyes, until it disappears from view.)

PART III.
LAZARUS RISES

ROSE wheels ANN downstage and steps back into the group. CLAIRE walks in with shopping bag and goes to her MOTHER.

CLAIRE: Hello, Mother.

(ANN doesn't budge.)

CLAIRE: How are you today?

(No response.)

CLAIRE: I brought you these. *(She takes black socks from the bag.)* Shall we try them on?

(CLAIRE gives the socks to ANN. ANN puts one on her hand. Then she puts the other one on her other hand.)

CLAIRE: How are they, Mom?

(ANN raises her socked hands and looks at them. Then she looks at CLAIRE.)

ANN: I am very satisfied.

(End of play.)

NOWHERE ON THE BORDER

Carlos Lacámara

CARLOS LACÁMARA is an actor and playwright. He was born in Havana, Cuba, on November 11, 1958, and raised in Washington, D.C., Puerto Rico, and Los Angeles. He earned a degree in theatre from UCLA and studied playwriting with Simon Levy and Leon Martel at the UCLA Extension. He is the author of *Becoming Cuban* (The Hudson Theatres, Los Angeles, 2002) and *Havana Bourgeois* (Reverie Productions, New York, 2006; The Hayworth Theatre, Los Angeles, 2007). He has also been a professional actor for nearly three decades. He was a regular on the Nickelodeon series *The Brothers Garcia* and the NBC series *Nurses*, and has appeared in over a hundred films and television shows including *The World's Fastest Indian*, *The Mexican*, *Curb Your Enthusiasm*, *The Unit*, *Justice*, *Bones*, and *Close to Home*. He won the 2007 Met Life Playwriting Award and the 2008 HOLA Award for Best New Play for *Nowhere on the Border*. He has just finished the third in a trilogy of plays about Cuba called *Exiles*, which deals with the Mariel Boatlift of 1980. He lives in Los Angeles with his wife, television writer/producer Carol Barbee, and two sons, Lucas and Diego.

Nowhere on the Border was first presented by The Hayworth (Danna Hyams and Gary Blumsack, Producing Directors) and Fixed Mark Productions (Carol Barbee, Artistic Director) on June 10, 2006, at the Hayworth Theatre, Los Angeles, with the following cast and credits:

Gary .... Patrick Rowe
Roberto .... Carlos Lacámara
Pilar .... Cheryl Umaña
Don Rey .... Javier Grajeda
Montoya .... Mark Adair-Rios
Jesus .... David Michie

Director: Bert Rosario
Stage Manager: Mark Bate
Lighting: Kathi O'Donohue
Sets and Costumes: Miguel Montalvo

The New York premiere of *Nowhere on the Border* was presented by Repertorio Español (René Buch, Artistic Director) on September 13, 2007, at Repertorio Español, with the following cast and credits:

Gary .... Ed Trucco
Roberto .... Ernesto De Villa-Bejjani
Pilar .... Elka Rodríguez
Don Rey .... Frank Robles
Montoya .... Gabriel Gutiérrez
Jesus .... Carlos Valencia

Director: José Zayas
Stage Manager: Fernando Then
Design: Robert Weber Federico
Spanish Translation: Alejandra Orozco

SCENE 1

The Cabeza Prieta Wildlife Refuge, Arizona, ten a.m. The severe morning sun bakes the gray dirt and sickly vegetation of the Sonoran desert. Partially hidden under a paloverde tree and a large straw hat rests a man. He does not move. Only the scratching drone of insects offers any hint of life. After a long moment, we hear the jangling of metal. It grows louder until GARY DOBBS enters. GARY is a fit, fifty-year-old man. He carries a backpack, a video camera, binoculars, and a utility belt sporting a cell phone, a GPS tracking device, a large metal flashlight, a can of mace, and a 9mm Beretta. He stops and scans the landscape with his binoculars. As he lowers them, he winces and covers his nose with his sleeve. He inspects his immediate surroundings. He spots the man under the tree.

GARY: Jesus Christ. *(He steps closer, but the smell repels him. He pulls out his cell phone and his GPS. Into phone.)* Ranger One? HP five here. I got a dead Tonk at…North thirty-two, thirteen, sixteen. West one thirteen, nineteen, fifty-one. Advise…I can't tell… *(Takes a step toward THE MAN, crouches, and peers at him.)* I'd rather not…'Cause he smells like shit, Kenny. Just call BORSTAR or whoever…I'm going to set up on a ridge about two miles south of 25 E…

(THE MAN under the tree raises his head.)

GARY: Jesus Christ! He's alive…The god damn Tonk.

(THE MAN, ROBERTO CASTILLO, is a darkly tanned Mexican in his late forties. He stands and stretches.)

GARY: He's on the move…Yeah, yeah, I know the drill… *(Steps back as he fumbles to turn on his video camera. He points the camera at ROBERTO while holding the* cell phone with his shoulder. He lays his other hand on his pistol.)*

ROBERTO: Buenos días.

GARY: *(Still into phone.)* Call the Border Patrol.

ROBERTO: ¿No eres la migra?

GARY: He's talkin' Mexican at me.

ROBERTO: ¿No hablas español? Eh— Spanish?

GARY: He wants to know if I speak Spanish…Okay. *(To ROBERTO.)* No. *(Back to phone.)* Don't worry. I'm giving him a wide berth…Okay…Just get here as quick as you can…Roger. Out. *(Hangs up the phone and continues videotaping.)*

ROBERTO: *(Heavy accent.)* You are not Border Patrol. La migra, they speak Spanish. Who is Roger?

(GARY continues taping in silence.)

ROBERTO: I am Roberto Castillo.

(ROBERTO takes a step closer to GARY. GARY backs up.)

GARY: The Border Patrol is on its way.

ROBERTO: Good. You work for them?

(No response.)

ROBERTO: What is a "Tonk"?

(No response.)

ROBERTO: You are making a movie?

GARY: I'm not supposed to talk to you.

ROBERTO: Then why you wake me up?

GARY: I thought you were dead.

ROBERTO: Me? Why?

GARY: The smell.

ROBERTO: Ah si. I here so long. I get used to it. Is not me. Is her.

(He points to a small rock formation close to GARY. GARY looks down.)

GARY: Jesus Christ. *(He swivels his camera to the corpse.)*

ROBERTO: Yes. She has been dead a long time. Three, four weeks maybe.

GARY: Jesus.

ROBERTO: I call the Border Patrol, but they don't like it when I find a body. Is more paperwork for them. But they always come and take it, and try to find who it is…if they can.

GARY: You've found other bodies?

ROBERTO: Si. A lot of dead people in this desert.

GARY: What are you doing out here?

ROBERTO: I am—do you have to keep pointing the camera?

GARY: It's for your own protection.

ROBERTO: If I am not in your movie, I will die?

GARY: Just makin' sure everything's on the up and up.

ROBERTO: I don't know what that means.

GARY: You walk here from Mexico? Lookin' for work?

ROBERTO: No I come from the Highway 8.

GARY: You walking south? Trying to get back into Mexico?

ROBERTO: No. I am looking for my daughter. She walked through this desert last month from Mexico. She wanted to join her husband. He's in Albuquerque. But she did not arrive. I have been looking for her two weeks. I find a lot of dead people, but not her. I have a map. See? *(Takes out a worn piece of paper.)* The boy who was walking with her, he draw it. It is where he left her. She could not walk anymore. He stayed with her a little, but then he had to go. *(Holding up map.)* You know where this is?

GARY: No. I'm new to these parts.

ROBERTO: Nobody knows. It all look the same. Maybe you could make a movie of the desert around here? I could show Jesus, the boy who drew the map. Maybe he say yes or no?

GARY: *(Lowers the camera and speed dials his phone.)* Hold on a minute, José—

ROBERTO: Roberto.

GARY: Roberto. I'm going to…Ranger One? HP five. What's your ETA…? You call the Border Patrol yet…?

(ROBERTO steps to the side and begins to lower his fly to pee. GARY points his camera at him.)

GARY: Found a real body here. Definitely deceased. This guy says he's found lots of them. Says he's called the Border Patrol…

(ROBERTO notices the camera pointing at him and moves to another spot. GARY follows him with his camera.)

GARY: No, he talked to me…

(ROBERTO tries to wave GARY off, but GARY keeps the camera pointed at him.)

GARY: Just get here ASAP…Jesus, Kevin I gave you the coordinates…Okay…I see…

(ROBERTO gives up and zips up his fly.)

GARY: You think this Tonk might be one...? Okay...I'll give it a shot. Don't worry. I can take care of myself. Call me when you're close. *(Puts phone away.)*

ROBERTO: *(Frustrated.)* Who will want to see this movie of me doing pee-pee?

GARY: My people want to rendezvous with us back on the road. So why don't we—

ROBERTO: What is that? Rondeboo?

GARY: Meet. They want to meet us—

ROBERTO: Who? What people? What is a Tonk?

GARY: We're The Homeland Patriot Project, a volunteer organization providing support to the Border Patrol and other law enforcement agencies. My commander—

ROBERTO: Roger or Kenny?

GARY: There is no Roger. That's code for— Look, my people asked me to invite you to accompany me back to the road where they dropped me off. It's two miles that way. When they come, they'll have water and snacks—

ROBERTO: I have water.

GARY: Okay, then we can help you—

ROBERTO: And potato chips. You want?

GARY: No, thank you. Just please take a walk with me, so we can meet them and sort this whole thing out. What do you say?

ROBERTO: No, thank you. I should stay here. Until the Border Patrol come.

GARY: The Border Patrol will find us quicker on the road.

ROBERTO: No, I watch out for her. *(He motions to the corpse.)*

GARY: This isn't your daughter, right?

ROBERTO: No. But is somebody's daughter. And if somebody found my daughter...like this...I would like them to watch out for her until somebody come and take her home. You understand?

GARY: That's very noble, but they know where she is. I gave the coordinates.

ROBERTO: *(Sits.)* I make sure.

GARY: Look, my people got some DEA intel about a group of drug smugglers in this area. I think you'd be safer coming with me.

ROBERTO: *(Studies GARY for a beat.)* You think I am a drug smuggler?

GARY: I didn't say that.

ROBERTO: Oye, do I look like a drug smuggler?

GARY: I don't know.

ROBERTO: You think I make up story about my daughter?

GARY: That's for the Border Patrol to decide.

ROBERTO: Okay. The Border Patrol will know. I wait.

(GARY is about to say more, but stops himself. He checks his watch and then sits on a rock opposite. ROBERTO gobbles down some potato chips. GARY points the video camera at him. ROBERTO sneaks a peek at the camera and then begins chewing in a slower, more polite manner.)

SCENE 2

DON REY, a husky, forty-year-old man wearing a crisp guayabera shirt and gold jewelry, enters with PILAR. PILAR is twenty-five. She covers her full-bodied figure with an oversized T-shirt. Don Rey rests a jewel-encrusted hand on PILAR's shoulder as he leads her through the area where ROBERTO and GARY sit. The two men take no notice of the intruders. PILAR and DON REY's conversation takes place in another time and place.

PILAR: I cleared out the shed in the back, and I bought a new mattress. I made curtains…

DON REY: Very nice.

PILAR: It's been three years since he was home. I bought pork, and mami was helping me with the tamales, and then he calls the day before Christmas and says he's not coming.

DON REY: Oh, no.

PILAR: We had been planning this for six months.

(DON REY snaps his fingers and a stage-hand sets two chairs on stage. PILAR and DON REY sit.)

PILAR: He said he couldn't get away now that he was the foreman. He said they were building a bridge or a football stadium or something. And he said these days it's harder to get back into the United States once you leave.

DON REY: That's true.

PILAR: So then I call him on Christmas, and his roommate picks up the phone. And you know what he tells me? He says that Naldo isn't making bridges. He's not a foreman. He's cleaning chicken guts in some factory. He hadn't gotten any raises or anything. So what else is he lying about? Maybe he has a new wife…

DON REY: No, no, Pilar. Relax. Let me tell you something about men. And I know this because I was a man once.

(He chuckles, but she doesn't.)

DON REY: It's a joke because obviously I'm still a man.

PILAR: Yes, I understand.

DON REY: Well…a man—now listen carefully—a man must fight other men every day of his life.

PILAR: Naldo doesn't fight. He's small, and he has allergies.

DON REY: I don't mean just with the fists, a man will fight with his brain, his charm, a gun. Anything. And what does he fight for? Land? Money? Power? Of course, but these are merely more weapons to use against other men, because…a man is only as good as he is better than the man next to him.

PILAR: I don't agree. I think—

DON REY: I am not talking about you. I am talking about men. Rank is everything for a man. Is that good or bad? Doesn't matter. It's primal. And no laws or religion or happy thinking will ever change it. A man must triumph over his comrade. Why? For you. So you will love him.

PILAR: That's ridiculous. I already love him. I want him to come home—

DON REY: It's not ridiculous because it's not rational. It is driven by the animal inside the man. The beast that will fight until he can place his foot on the neck of his rival and shout, I have conquered. She is mine! And that is why he lied to you about plucking chickens. Metaphorically speaking, of course.

PILAR: You mean, he feels like a failure?

DON REY: *(Shrugs, "obviously.")* You want some coffee? *(He signals to an unseen waiter.)*

PILAR: You don't think he's found another woman?

DON REY: Working in a chicken factory?

PILAR: He needs me there.

DON REY: Yes, he does.

PILAR: I have to go.

DON REY: I know.

PILAR: Can you help me get to the North?

DON REY: I help people every day.

PILAR: When can I leave?

DON REY: That depends. It's not cheap.

PILAR: How much?

DON REY: Well, I could arrange transportation, hotels, food, and personally accompany you to Tucson, Arizona, for three thousand dollars.

PILAR: Three thousand? I don't have that much money. I've never even seen that much money. Nobody I know has—

DON REY: There are other ways, if you don't mind walking. I can take you to the border, set you up with a guide. You take a short walk through the desert. A day, day and a half, maybe. Then we pick you up across the border and take you somewhere safe...all for one thousand, five hundred.

PILAR: I can raise, maybe, three hundred dollars.

DON REY: Pilar, there are many expenses. Buses and hotels and people to pay.

PILAR: Maybe four hundred if I save for another year.

DON REY: *(Stands.)* I'm sorry.

PILAR: Please, Don Rey. I'm going to the other side. One way or another...I'm going.

DON REY: *(Studies PILAR for a beat.)* Maybe...No, I can't take any more risks.

PILAR: What? Please.

DON REY: You are willing to work hard?

PILAR: I've worked hard all my life.

DON REY: And I can trust you?

PILAR: You can.

DON REY: I might be able to arrange a loan.

PILAR: Really? I'll pay you back. I promise.

DON REY: Three hundred now. Twelve hundred at fifteen percent. Your husband pays half when he picks you up in the United States. The rest you pay me out of future salary.

PILAR: Of course.

DON REY: *(Coldly.)* Do not let me down, Pilar.

PILAR: Of course not. Thank you, Don Rey. Thank you.

DON REY: Don't thank me. My reward is helping good people like you.

(PILAR and DON REY exit.)

SCENE 3

GARY and ROBERTO have been sitting in silence for an hour. GARY has stopped videotaping. It's hot. ROBERTO stands. GARY springs up and resumes taping. Keeping his eyes glued to GARY, ROBERTO cautiously walks over to the paloverde tree. GARY mirrors his movements. ROBERTO sits. GARY sits.

ROBERTO: You really hate Mexican people, don't you?

GARY: I don't hate anybody.

ROBERTO: But if you hated somebody, Mexicans would be at the top of your list, right?

GARY: Nope.

ROBERTO: Then who? The black people?

GARY: I'm no racist.

ROBERTO: But you say you are volunteer. Nobody pay you, so you are here for fun.

GARY: Yeah, I'm havin' a great time. How 'bout you?

ROBERTO: No. I am not.

GARY: I'm here to help the authorities uphold the law.

ROBERTO: For no money.

GARY: For no money.

ROBERTO: Because you are such a good person?

GARY: Because I love my country.

ROBERTO: You don't find that in Mexico. I mean, we love our country, but not for free.

GARY: Maybe that's one of the differences between our cultures.

ROBERTO: Yes. You are rich enough to spend a day with me for no money.

GARY: I ain't rich. *(Points his camera at ROBERTO.)* So who's paying you to be here?

ROBERTO: *(To himself.)* Hijo la chingada. *(To GARY.)* You love your country, so you come to this desert to kill Mexicans.

GARY: I ain't killed anybody.

ROBERTO: But if I run away, you will shoot me.

GARY: Why would you want to run away?

ROBERTO: To get away from your pinché movie.

GARY: You don't want to be seen on tape?

ROBERTO: Now I wish I was a drug smuggler. Then I could shoot you and your camera.

(GARY lowers the camera.)

ROBERTO: Thank you.

GARY: Battery's dead. I got enough.

ROBERTO: Yes, I am sure it will be a big hit.

(GARY puts his camera away. ROBERTO studies him for a beat.)

ROBERTO: You hate Mexicans so much you will come to this horrible place from— where you from?

GARY: Kentucky.

ROBERTO: You will come from Kentucky just to keep Mexican people from getting a job in your country?

GARY: You're breaking the law.

ROBERTO: So if somebody in your village in Kentucky he drive through a red light, you make movie about him?

GARY: Look, Pedro—

ROBERTO: ROBERTO.

GARY: Roberto. I don't know if you keep up with current events, but my country is at war. On 9/11, three thousand Americans were murdered because we didn't keep our borders secure. Now I don't blame some Mexican peasant for wantin' to come to America. From what I understand, your country's pretty fucked up. But if you're gonna come here, you better do it legally, or we're gonna catch your ass and kick it back to Mexico or Arabia or wherever.

ROBERTO: So it is Arabs you hate?

GARY: I hate criminals. And when you step across our border without papers, you're a criminal.

ROBERTO: I don't know any Arab people. And I don't know anybody who wants to be a criminal—well, my mother's cousin—but I never met anybody who come here so he can be a criminal. I don't even know anyone who really wants to come to America. You think we want to leave our home and our family? To walk through this terrible desert—?

GARY: Then don't.

ROBERTO: That is easy to say for you. You are rich, with your spyglasses and your movie camera—

GARY: I ain't rich.

ROBERTO: What do you know about having no work? About trying to find food for your children and protect them, and you can't, so they leave, and you don't know where they are? What do you know about the sacrifice—?

GARY: Don't talk to me about sacrifice. My son is in Iraq right now risking his life for this country. He's fighting terrorism over there; I'm fighting it here. *(Pulls out his cell phone.)*

ROBERTO: Your son is in Iraq?

GARY: *(Into phone.)* Ranger One…? Hello?

ROBERTO: That's no good.

GARY: Ranger One…? Kevin…? *(No response.)* Shit. *(Puts phone away.)*

ROBERTO: *(Steps toward him.)* When did he—?

(GARY reaches for his gun. ROBERTO stops.)

GARY: They should be here any minute.

(The lights change abruptly.)

SCENE 4

A Mexican rap song kicks in. PILAR enters. She refers to a small piece of paper as she searches for an address. From another part of the stage, a twenty-year-old cowboy, JESUS ORTIZ, appears with his own piece of paper. Facing the audience, PILAR knocks on whatever part of the stage is handy. JESUS joins her. A shaft of harsh light reveals that a door has opened.

PILAR: *(Shouting over the music.)* We're looking for Montoya.

(Marijuana smoke billows out. PILAR brushes it away from her face. JESUS winces. From the opposite part of the stage, a wiry eighteen-year-old, MONTOYA, struts on. He wears black jeans and a sleeveless T-shirt with the word "Molotov" on it. A single lock of red hair hangs over his face. He drinks a beer and faces the audience.)

MONTOYA: *(Yelling over the music.)* You my little chickens? Wait, I got your names here somewhere… *(Searching his pockets, but quickly giving up.)* Que la chingada, who else would you be? *(Over his shoulder.)* Turn down the music! I got business!

(The music stays loud.)

MONTOYA: *(To himself.)* Pendejos. *(Back to PILAR and JESUS.)* Welcome to Sonoita. You guys are staying in the back room tonight. Tomorrow morning, not too early, I'll come get you and—

(The music volume is lowered.)

MONTOYA: *(To himself.)* Thank you, Putos. *(To PILAR and JESUS.)* Tomorrow, we drive to where we cross the border—

JESUS: Where's that?

MONTOYA: Hey, slow your roll, snoop dog. That's privileged information. We walk at night, just a couple hours, three hours max…maybe eight. You're each responsible for your own water. A gallon at least. Two if you can carry it. When we're over the border, we meet up with a couple of other groups, then a few hours walking, and we get picked up by our people in the United States. Everything's under control. I done this lots of times, and I always keep my little chickens safe.

(The music volume soars as the song hits the chorus.)

MUSIC: California, who stole it?

MONTOYA: *(Sings the response.)* "Fucking Gabachos!"

MUSIC: Arizona, who stole it?

MONTOYA: "Fucking Gabachos!" *(To PILAR and JESUS.)* Oldie but goodie, uh?

MUSIC: Texas, who stole it?

MONTOYA: "Fucking Gabachos!" *(To PILAR and JESUS.)* Get to the store and buy some food.

MUSIC: Nuevo Mexico, who stole it?

MONTOYA: "Fucking Gabachos!"

(PILAR and JESUS look around confused.)

MONTOYA: *(Pointing.)* That way. And don't look lost.

MUSIC: Hey, fucking Gabachos…

(JESUS and PILAR exit.)

MONTOYA: *(Calling after them.)* Don't catch anyone's eye!

MUSIC: We're gonna take it back!

MONTOYA: *(Singing.)* "We're gonna take it back!"

(The music and lights abruptly shut off.)

SCENE 5

In the blackout, we hear whistling. Bad whistling. Lights fade up. ROBERTO sits and whistles. He and GARY have been sitting a long time.

GARY: Could you please stop that?

ROBERTO: What?

GARY: The whistling.

ROBERTO: I was whistling?

GARY: For the last hour.

ROBERTO: I not notice.

GARY: For the last half hour, I've been trying to figure out the melody, but there's no melody, just… *(He imitates ROBERTO.)*

ROBERTO: Oye, I'm a good whistler.

GARY: No, no. This is whistling… *(Whistles "The Yellow Rose of Texas.")*

ROBERTO: And what is this?

GARY: "The Yellow Rose of Texas." Anybody walkin' by would say, hey that guy's whistling "The Yellow Rose of Texas." Somebody hears you whistlin' they say, oh dear god, my brain. I must flee before it starts bleeding.

ROBERTO: You are a very tense man.

GARY: You can't carry a tune. *(Gulps down some water.)* God damn this heat.

ROBERTO: It is a habit to whistle. I work hard all my life. It passes time.

GARY: I know. *(Half singing.)* "Whistle while you work."

ROBERTO: Stop the mocking me, please.

GARY: I wasn't mocking you. It's the song: "Whistle while you work…" *(He whistles the next refrain.)*

ROBERTO: I don't know that.

GARY: It's from *Snow White*…

(ROBERTO shows no recognition.)

GARY: You don't know *Snow White and the Seven Dwarfs*?

ROBERTO: It never snow where I live, and I only know one dwarf. A cousin. Actually, is the same cousin that wanted to be a criminal. But a criminal dwarf…is a sad thing.

GARY: *Snow White*'s a cartoon. Walt Disney…?

(ROBERTO shrugs, "Don't know.")

GARY: Don't you got movies where you come from?

ROBERTO: No.

GARY: Snow White is this beautiful princess, and an evil queen orders a hunter to cut out her heart. But he can't do it, so he cuts out a pig's heart instead, and Snow White runs away and finds this house in the woods. She goes to sleep, and when she wakes up there's seven dwarfs starin' at her—

ROBERTO: This queen, she was arrested?

GARY: It's a bedtime story, you know, for kids.

ROBERTO: You tell this horrible thing to children before they are supposed to sleep? That is very cruel.

GARY: Kids love it.

ROBERTO: My children would have cried. The woman wants to cut out the girl's heart, and she wakes up and seven dwarfs are growling at her—

GARY: They're not growling. They're friendly—

ROBERTO: The last thing I would like to see when I wake up is dwarfs. I don't care if they are smiling. I would scream.

GARY: What kind of bedtime stories do you people tell in Mexico?

ROBERTO: I don't know about all Mexico. Is a big place. But where I am from, we do not tell bedtime stories. We work. No time for stories.

GARY: You don't read stories to your kids?

ROBERTO: *(Amused derision.)* I don't have books. I don't read so good anyway. My mother could not read at all. No, we don't read stories.

GARY: So after a hard day's work, what do you do?

ROBERTO: Sleep.

GARY: And the kids, they don't play?

ROBERTO: Of course they play. All children play.

GARY: What kind of games do they play?

ROBERTO: Games? Uh…La Cebollita.

GARY: La cebo—?

ROBERTO: The little onion.

GARY: They play with onions?

ROBERTO: No, mocking guy. The game is called The Little Onion. One child holds onto a tree and the next child holds onto him then another and another until five, six children are holding on like a chain. Then another child tries to pull them off one by one like pulling an onion out of the ground.

GARY: So you pretend to be an onion that's being pulled out of the dirt.

ROBERTO: Yes.

GARY: No wonder y'all want to come to America.

ROBERTO: Is a fun game.

GARY: Sounds magical.

ROBERTO: And there is another game where children hold hands and make a circle. And one child gets in the middle of the circle, and they call her Doña Blanca. And one kid outside the circle is the wolf, and the kids holding hands try to keep the wolf from getting Doña Blanca. The kids in the circle, they are called Pilares…

GARY: Pilares? What that?

ROBERTO: Pilar… *(Growing morose.)* A pilar means…column.

GARY: Column. Like in a building?

ROBERTO: Yes.

GARY: So, onions and columns. Fun for the whole family.

ROBERTO: Only children.

GARY: Don't get bent out of shape. I'm just teasin' you, man.

ROBERTO: No, is…Pilar is my daughter's name.

GARY: The one that's missing?

(ROBERTO nods. GARY studies him for a beat.)

GARY: You called her "column?"

ROBERTO: *(Defensively.)* Is a pretty name. In Mexico many girls—

GARY: Okay, okay. Look, she'll probably turn up. She could be in the U.S. somewhere and just hasn't called.

ROBERTO: She would have called her husband. She was very in love with him.

GARY: Maybe she got arrested. She did break the law.

ROBERTO: No, I talk to the Border Patrol.

GARY: You did, huh? And they didn't arrest you?

ROBERTO: No, I have visa. You want to see?

(He reaches for his pocket. GARY reaches for his gun.)

GARY: No. I don't know what a visa looks like. We'll just wait for my people to come. They'll know.

(Pause.)

ROBERTO: Is all the husband's fault. Pendejo.

GARY: Her husband's name's Pendejo?

ROBERTO: No Pendejo, it means…moron. He say he go to the north six months. Three years, he's not back. And Pilar, she was going to have his baby, and still he left. Then she lose it before is born. He sends a little money sometimes, but she make more money selling the vegetables. She grow vegetables when I could not work anymore, and she make a store—like you would say a…a stand—to sell vegetables. And she get so busy, I start to work for her. She's smart, but the husband? Pendejo.

GARY: What did you use to do? Before.

ROBERTO: I work in the copper mines.

GARY: A miner?

ROBERTO: Twenty-eight years. Until I hurt my back, and they retire me.

GARY: You seem alright.

ROBERTO: I am alright. They didn't want to wait for me to get better. A lot of people need jobs.

GARY: My daddy was a coal miner. And his daddy, and his.

ROBERTO: And you?

GARY: I'm a steel worker.

ROBERTO: You are lucky. To me they say, you are hurt? Goodbye. I even work in Arizona for two years. That's where I learned the English. I talk good, no?

GARY: Good enough.

ROBERTO: You betcha. I go to class at night. The other workers, they go to the bars and find the prostitutes, but not me. Prostitutes are expensive, and one time I get a rash. No more. I have family. I go home. Pilar, she has a family, but no baby. One day she tells me she is going to the north. I say, no. Is dangerous, and she is soft, you know? She is not used to walking many miles. But once she decide something, she is…like a rock.

GARY: Stubborn.

ROBERTO: Stubborn.

GARY: Looks like she gets it honest.

ROBERTO: What does that mean?

GARY: She gets it from you.

ROBERTO: I not stubborn.

GARY: Then let's head up the road.

ROBERTO: No, I stay here.

GARY: There you go.

ROBERTO: I beg her not to go, but what could I do? I had nothing for her. No money. No nice house. My wife and I we work hard but for what? We can't keep our children happy…and safe. You understand. Your boy is in Iraq. You must have tried to stop him from going—

GARY: I did not. I'm proud of my boy.

ROBERTO: Yes, but—

GARY: He's a god damn hero.

ROBERTO: *(Mulls this over for a moment.)* Pilar is no hero. She is lonely.

(Night falls suddenly.)

SCENE 6

In the moonlight, MONTOYA marches on stage. He stops, looks, and listens.

Nothing. He pulls out a vial of cocaine and takes a snort. With a new spring in his step, he exits. PILAR slogs on, following MONTOYA's path. She carries a heavy canvas rucksack. Her foot catches on a cactus. She doubles over.

PILAR: Hijo tu puta madre.

(She sits to examine her foot as JESUS trots on.)

JESUS: Are we resting?

PILAR: Even the plants are out to kill you in this chingado desert.

JESUS: *(Bends down to take a look.)* That cholla spiked you good. *(He reaches for her leg.)*

PILAR: Don't touch it.

JESUS: You got to take it out.

PILAR: I'll do it.

JESUS: *(Surveys the trail ahead.)* Montoya! Oye! We have to stop for a minute!

(PILAR winces as she fails to pull the barb out of her ankle. JESUS takes out his bandana and grabs her foot.)

JESUS: Look away. *(He gets a hold of the spike using the bandana.)* Ready? One…Two— *(He pulls the spike out.)*

PILAR: Bésame el culillo!

JESUS: You sure can cuss, Señora.

PILAR: It's my new hobby.

(He ties his bandana around her ankle.)

PILAR: Thank you.

JESUS: *(Turns back to the trail.)* Montoya!

MONTOYA: *(Enters.)* Shut the fuck up! You think it would be fun to meet a real live Border Patrol agent? Let me

tell you something, baboso: La migra loves to kick wetback ass. It gives them a hard-on.

JESUS: Can you please watch your mouth around the lady?

PILAR: I don't give a fuck.

JESUS: Well, I do. She's hurt. I didn't want you to walk off without us.

MONTOYA: Why the hell would I do that? If I don't get you little chickens across this desert, I don't get paid. You can trust me…I want to get paid. I was climbing up the ridge looking for my partner. His group should have met us by now.

JESUS: When do we cross the border?

MONTOYA: Hijo le, we crossed it hours ago.

JESUS: Where? I didn't see.

MONTOYA: There's not a line in the sand. Not out here.

JESUS: So this is The United States?

MONTOYA: For now, maybe. But the invasion is on, 'mano. It's like the wagon trains in the old West. But this time the settlers are going north. This here is the wild frontier. We're nowhere. *(Turning to PILAR.)* Can she walk?

PILAR: You bet your culo. *(She starts getting up.)*

MONTOYA: Órale. Rest a minute and keep quiet. I'm going to look around. I'll be right back.

(PILAR sits back down. JESUS surveys the area. He gazes up.)

JESUS: Look at the stars.

PILAR: *(Glances up, but quickly looks away.)* Too many.

JESUS: They're beautiful.

PILAR: Too beautiful.

JESUS: What do you mean?

PILAR: Nothing. I've seen stars all my life.

JESUS: You can see a lot more here than where I come from. Where are you from?

PILAR: Sinaloa.

JESUS: I'm from Durango. We're neighbors. What are you going to do in the North?

PILAR: Pluck chickens.

JESUS: There's good money in that?

PILAR: No.

JESUS: You should try one of the ranches in Texas. I hear they got a lot of work. Especially if you're good with horses. You ever work with horses?

PILAR: No.

JESUS: Well, I'm sure they got other jobs. Me? I break horses. I have a place back in Durango. Nice little ranch. Got about a dozen mares. I'm going to make money, get myself a good stud, maybe breed some racehorses. Build a big house for my family. *(He pulls out his wallet.)* See? Here's my wife, Araceli. That's my little baby, Perla.

(PILAR takes the photo.)

JESUS: I miss them already. But four months in the North, and we're set for life.

PILAR: Four months?

JESUS: Four, five, whatever it takes.

PILAR: My husband's been gone for three years, and it's always, "Just a couple

more months, mi amor. I'm about to hit it big. Next Christmas, I promise." And you know the worst part? The money. What you need is your husband, instead you get a check in mail. Here's a few pesos. Stop bitching. I hate those fucking checks.

JESUS: I know a guy where I live, he went to the United States for six months. He came back in a big car, bought a new house, and sent his kid to private school.

PILAR: I know ten guys who never came back. You know what I would do if I were you? I'd march right back to Durango and ask your family to forgive you. I'd eat every one of them chingado horses before I'd leave this.

(She holds up the photo. He takes it back. MONTOYA returns.)

MONTOYA: Okay, here's the deal. My partner didn't make it. He probably got busted. I don't know. So it's just the three of us. Which means I'm doing this job for almost nothing. So here are the new rules. We walk all night and tomorrow morning, rest a couple of hours, and walk the afternoon and the next night—

JESUS: Shouldn't we be there by tomorrow afternoon?

MONTOYA: Depends how fast we walk. Just follow orders and don't give me any shit. Okay my little chickens? Ándale.

(MONTOYA strides off. JESUS follows. PILAR limps after them.)

SCENE 7

GARY tries his cell phone again. Nothing.

GARY: They must be out of range. *(Tries to take a swig from his canteen, but it's empty.)*

ROBERTO: The Border Patrol will come. They always do. You need more water?

GARY: I'm fine. How many dead bodies have you found?

ROBERTO: Six.

GARY: And they always take this long getting there?

ROBERTO: Seven— Sometimes longer.

GARY: How long you been out here?

ROBERTO: Two weeks.

GARY: Where do you sleep?

ROBERTO: I borrow my cousin's car. I sleep there.

GARY: Your dwarf cousin?

ROBERTO: I wish. The dwarf, he has a big car. No, is another cousin.

GARY: You just been roaming around aimlessly?

ROBERTO: No, I have map. *(He shows GARY the map.)*

GARY: *(Recalling.)* That's right.

ROBERTO: *(Referring to map.)* See? Jesus said he left her in a ravine like this—

GARY: That's a ravine?

ROBERTO: Yes. Then he went north—

GARY: Looks like a squiggle.

ROBERTO: Is not a squiggle. He did not leave her in a squiggle.

GARY: You know what I mean.

ROBERTO: No I don't. Stop talking. He went north five, ten miles until he come to a very smooth dirt road.

GARY: A drag.

ROBERTO: Drag?

GARY: Yeah. The Border Patrol drags tires tied to the back of their trucks with chains. Makes a smooth dirt road. Any Tonks—migrants walk over it, they leave footprints.

ROBERTO: Why don't the Tonks just wipe away the footprints with a bush?

GARY: They do, but the Border Patrol can spot that, too.

ROBERTO: What's a Tonk?

GARY: *(Examines the landscape.)* This here's a ravine. You sure this isn't your daughter?

ROBERTO: Yes, I am.

GARY: How could you tell? This body's all black and rotted and…

ROBERTO: Pilar did not have a turquoise ring.

GARY: I don't see no ring.

ROBERTO: Is over there.

(He points behind GARY who turns to look.)

ROBERTO: With her arm.

GARY: Jesus Christ.

ROBERTO: The animals, they drag her from down there. See the marks? Here…and here. All the bodies are eaten up like this. This desert…is a hungry monster.

GARY: She could have bought the ring and not shown it to you.

ROBERTO: Why would she do that?

GARY: I don't know. Maybe she didn't want you to know that she spent money on jewelry.

ROBERTO: No, Pilar, she would not waste money. She was saving for her trip. She is a…how you say? She counts the money and guards it…

GARY: A penny-pincher.

ROBERTO: That's good. Yes. She is a penny-pincher.

GARY: I'm just saying, it wouldn't be the first time a daughter kept a secret from her father.

ROBERTO: *(Getting testy.)* I know my own daughter.

GARY: Okay, okay.

ROBERTO: And, Jesus said he put a blue and white striped towel over her face when he left. You know, to keep the sun away. There is no blue and white towel.

GARY: *(Looks around and nods. He focuses back on the dead woman and shakes his head.)* They should take all these dead bodies and lay them right on the border. One look at this and a good whiff, y'all would think twice about coming over here.

ROBERTO: You think we do not know the danger?

GARY: It's one thing to hear about it. It's another to see it.

ROBERTO: That is true.

GARY: I mean look at that. That says it all. There's your prize for trying to sneak into America. And I'm not blamin' her. It's the American businessmen who give her a job, they're the real criminals.

They lured her here. And they got the politicians in their pockets. Why do you think they don't build a wall or bring in the National Guard? Campaign contributions—bribes. So what if I lose my job to some foreigner making fifty cents a day? What have I got to complain about? At least now I can get a taco at any strip mall in town.

ROBERTO: You lost your job?

GARY: I'm fine. Don't worry about me.

ROBERTO: I'm not. I am just making conversation.

GARY: Let me tell you something, Alberto—

ROBERTO: Roberto.

GARY: Whatever. I know you've heard of the American Dream. That's why you people come here, right?

ROBERTO: If the dream is making money, yes.

GARY: It was once about more than money. The American Dream was a promise made to every boy born in this country. It said, if you work hard, you can be whatever you want. And for a long time, America kept that promise. You could go to a good school for free, where you'd be safe and pledge allegiance to one nation under God, and everyone spoke English, and Columbus was a good guy, and your mom would be there when you got home, and your dad was your hero, because he worked hard all week, and then on Saturday he'd teach you to throw a curve ball, and on Sunday you'd all go to church, and everyone prayed the same and then had a picnic and ate hamburgers and hotdogs, not burritos. And you knew, as sure as the sun rises in the morning, that your life would be better than your father's, and your son's life, even better than yours. And now that promise…it's not only broken, it's been pissed on and flushed down the toilet.

ROBERTO: You really hate Mexican food, don't you?

GARY: You don't get it. How could you? Our cultures…they just don't mix. My sister, she lives in a real nice neighborhood. Married, two kids. One night, she's sleepin' in her bed when she hears all this screamin' and loud music. She looks out the window, and the house next door is full of Mexicans drinking and shoutin'. They'd rented the place out to a bunch of illegal aliens. All of a sudden, she's livin' next door to a boardin' house. My sister's got two little girls, for Christ's sake. They shouldn't have to see strange men passed out drunk in the driveway and pissin' on their lawn. That might be okay where you come from—

ROBERTO: I don't like to see men pee. You're the one with the camera—

GARY: I'm talkin' about forty guys living in one house, partying and drinkin'—

ROBERTO: These are young men, no? When you were a young man, you did not drink and have parties?

GARY: Not next door to my sister's kids.

ROBERTO: She should ask them to be quiet.

GARY: Hell, she got them arrested and sent back to Mexico.

ROBERTO: So what is the problem?

GARY: The problem is it's happenin' all over. You know what that can do to your property value? No, of course not. Look, I know things are tough in your

country, but that ain't our fault. We got problems of our own, and we can't have you people comin' here and makin' them worse. You understand?

ROBERTO: Yes, I understand. You lost your job, and you are angry.

GARY: It's not just that.

ROBERTO: I don't blame you. I know what that is like to work many years in one thing and then…Did a Mexican take your job?

GARY: Gates Rubber moved the whole damn plant to Mexico.

ROBERTO: Una maquiladora.

GARY: What?

ROBERTO: That is what we call it in Mexico. Maquiladora is a foreign factory. Mostly American. Many people want to work there. Now a lot of them are moving to China.

GARY: Well, turnaround is fair play, isn't it?

ROBERTO: I don't know. How you can be here?

GARY: I'm here to protect my country—

ROBERTO: I mean for no money. The volunteer.

GARY: I'm only here for a week at a time.

ROBERTO: You find another job?

GARY: Yeah, I'm working. You think I am a freeloader?

ROBERTO: Where you work?

GARY: *(Considers whether to answer.)* My wife manages a Hallmark store at the mall. I work there.

ROBERTO: You work for your wife?

(GARY does not respond.)

ROBERTO: What is Hole-mark?

GARY: It's a store that sells greeting cards. You know, happy birthday, happy anniversary…and Christmas ornaments. We got a Santa Claus, about yea big, you press a button, it says ho-ho-ho.

ROBERTO: A little statue that talks?

GARY: Yeah.

ROBERTO: That's clever.

GARY: And wrapping paper…ribbons and bows.

ROBERTO: Sounds pretty.

GARY: Very pretty.

(They remain silent for a moment.)

GARY: Working for your wife's a bitch. I mean for a man…to be living off your wife.

ROBERTO: Or your daughter.

GARY: It's hard.

ROBERTO: Very hard.

(They drift off into their own thoughts. Together.)

SCENE 8

Night falls. MONTOYA strides in, followed by JESUS. MONTOYA stops and studies the horizon and drinks some water. JESUS joins him.

MONTOYA: The sun's coming up. We have about four more hours before it gets too hot. We gotta move.

JESUS: Wouldn't it be easier to walk down there?

MONTOYA: And easier for la migra to bust us. Where the hell is that Quedada?

JESUS: She's coming.

MONTOYA: She better move her culo if she doesn't want to end up coyote food.

JESUS: She's doing the best she can. How much farther?

MONTOYA: A couple hours. We're almost through the first desert. Then we pass the second desert, through the low pass until we see the lights of Ajo. That's another reason we got to keep to the high ground. We want to spot those lights.

JESUS: Ajo's the town we stop at?

MONTOYA: No my little chicken, we go around Ajo to meet our contact. It's under control. No worries.

(PILAR trudges on.)

MONTOYA: Oye, what are you doing? Sightseeing?

PILAR: *(Plops down on a rock.)* Chingate, mula. *(She gulps down water.)*

MONTOYA: If you walked as good as you cursed, we'd be there by now. Let's go.

PILAR: In a minute.

MONTOYA: No. No minute. You think you're tired now? Wait 'til that sun hits you. You don't know what it's like. The sun here wants you dead. This whole place does. There's a lot of spooky shit in this desert. Spirits, demons. And they don't come out at night. It's the sun lets them loose. There's tiny men, the Yaqui call them Surem, they live in the red shadows. And La Cabeza Prieta. A friend of mine saw it. A Dark Head, it came right out of the ground. Black like coal with white teeth. And it laughed at him. My friend's never been the same.

JESUS: *(Sarcastically.)* What about Chupa cabras?

MONTOYA: It's here, too.

JESUS: You can't scare her into moving faster.

PILAR: Actually, it's working.

(She starts to rise. JESUS gently pushes her back down.)

JESUS: Give us five minutes. We'll move faster after we catch our breath.

MONTOYA: *(Glares at JESUS for a beat.)* Okay, five minutes, but I want you to take something. Give you a little energy. *(He produces a small vial with white powder. He takes a sniff and passes it to PILAR.)*

JESUS: No, Señora—

(She takes a sniff and hands it back to MONTOYA. MONTOYA pulls out a cell phone.)

MONTOYA: I'm going to go up there and try to get a signal. Five minutes.

(MONTOYA exits. JESUS sits beside PILAR. She downs more water.)

JESUS: Take it slow. It's got to last.

PILAR: Thanks for the help.

JESUS: That guy's an idiot.

PILAR: As long as he knows where he's going.

JESUS: *(Points to the sky.)* Well, that's the North Star, you see?

PILAR: I don't want to look at the stars.

JESUS: But if you just look—

PILAR: You look.

JESUS: You don't like stars?

PILAR: I wasted a lot of time gaping at the stars. It only brought heartache.

JESUS: Okay…We're going north. Then west…at some point.

PILAR: Thank you.

(Pause.)

JESUS: You must be looking forward to seeing your husband?

PILAR: I'm scared to death. Three years.

JESUS: It'll be great. You have kids?

(PILAR shakes her head, "No.")

JESUS: And the rest of your family? They back in Sinaloa?

(PILAR nods.)

JESUS: What does your father do?

PILAR: Nothing. Yours?

JESUS: My father's the best horseman in Durango. He's got the palsy now, you know, he shakes—

PILAR: That's too bad.

JESUS: Yeah, but once he's on a horse… His chin is high, back straight. It's like the horse becomes his body, and he's pure spirit. I think he learned to ride to pick up women.

PILAR: Did he?

JESUS: In his day…He's okay. He still works hard.

PILAR: I wish my father did. He just sits around telling stupid stories about his life in the mines.

JESUS: Sounds interesting.

PILAR: It's not. I try to get him to help me with the store—I run a vegetable stand. I tell him to clean the carrots or stack the onions. I come back a few minutes later, and he's talking shit to a customer.

(Lights focus on ROBERTO.)

ROBERTO: When Pilar was a little girl, she had a friend from Oaxaca. A tiny Indian girl. Very dark. Her name was…uh…I don't remember. We called her La Negrita. She would come over to the house and sit, very proper, hands in her lap, and she would talk with Pilar for hours. But, the thing is, she didn't speak Spanish. She only spoke Indian, and Pilar, she couldn't speak Indian. So La Negrita would talk and talk her Indian, and Pilar would answer in gibberish. Machaha saca wicky boochoo. *(Laughing.)* The tiny Indian must have thought she was retarded. But they were good friends even though they could not speak. When La Negrita left—her family went to the North—Pilar cried a lot. She wrote her many letters. I pretended to mail them, but I didn't know where her friend went. I still have those letters. Pilar…she loved that little black Indian very much.

(Lights back to PILAR and JESUS.)

PILAR: Ever since he lost his job, it's like he's shriveling into his own little world. Not that he ever gave much of a damn about me and my mother. Now that he's home, he expects service twenty-four hours a day.

JESUS: What did he say about your leaving?

PILAR: He hates Naldo, my husband. He didn't want to lose his servant…

(Indicating herself.) …so he insulted Naldo.

(Lights on ROBERTO.)

ROBERTO: My little angel, I have nothing against Naldo. I'm just pointing out the fact that he is a homosexual.

PILAR: Shut up.

ROBERTO: Why are you angry? I thought it was common knowledge. He sits like this. *(Demonstrates.)* And when he's happy he giggles, and he tells me that I have a beautiful shirt. What man tells another man that he has beautiful clothing? I don't hate him because he's homosexual. I'm just saying that he probably went to the North to find other homosexuals and pretty clothing and…accessories—

PILAR: You want to hear about our sex? How hard he got when—?

ROBERTO: *(Covers his ears.)* How dare you talk like that to your father? *(Turns away.)*

(Lights back to PILAR and JESUS.)

PILAR: I'll bet he hasn't even noticed I'm gone.

(MONTOYA bounds in.)

MONTOYA: Okay, let's move.

JESUS: Did you get a signal?

MONTOYA: It's under control. No worries.

(A spotlight flashes over them.)

MONTOYA: Border Patrol. *(Dives to the ground.)* Get down, pendejos!

(JESUS and PILAR crouch low. They all wait in silence until they hear a helicopter engine in the distance.)

MONTOYA: Fuck! Move!

(MONTOYA flies off. JESUS and PILAR scramble after him as best they can.)

SCENE 9

Day. GARY and ROBERTO sit. ROBERTO takes a drink from his water jug.

GARY: …A nice hot meal waitin' for you when you got home.

ROBERTO: Oh, that was nice.

(ROBERTO passes his water to GARY who takes a swig.)

GARY: Your wife don't cook for you no more?

ROBERTO: Christmas maybe. She found a job at a maquiladora putting together radios or something. The money helps, but me and my sons we have to find our own food.

GARY: Yeah. I got sick of mall food. So I bought myself a cookbook.

ROBERTO: No.

GARY: Yes. Real simple stuff. But good. 'Course I add my personal touch. Give 'em a little punch. There's this quesadilla I make when I'm in a rush. You get two tortillas—

ROBERTO: Tortillas? I thought you hate Mexican food.

GARY: I never said that. I just hate what it represents.

ROBERTO: Too many restaurant choices?

GARY: Quiet. Now, take two tortillas and toss them on a frying pan with plenty of butter. Throw in a mound of grated cheddar cheese, some green chiles,

ham, and a little garlic powder—that's my touch—and in two minutes, you got a meal.

ROBERTO: I don't know cheddar cheese or garlic powder…

GARY: You could improvise with what you have.

ROBERTO: I learned how to make beans.

GARY: From scratch?

ROBERTO: You betcha. You take a pound of brown beans, wash them, and soak them overnight in seven cups of water.

GARY: Overnight? That's a real commitment.

ROBERTO: All good things are worth sacrifice. The next day, you add salt, a little manteca…

GARY: Man-tay—?

ROBERTO: Manteca…How you say the fat from a pig?

GARY: Lard?

ROBERTO: A little lard.

GARY: I miss lard.

ROBERTO: Then a lot of lard. And here's the secret thing, a glass of tequila.

GARY: Oooh…

ROBERTO: Riquisimos.

GARY: Wait, wait. Let me write this down. *(Searches for a pen and paper.)*

SCENE 10

White-hot sunlight consumes the desert. MONTOYA plods in, burned and exhausted. JESUS follows.

JESUS: *(Scorched voice.)* I thought you said west.

(MONTOYA continues. Oblivious. JESUS grabs his arm and turns him around.)

JESUS: Ajo is west, right?

MONTOYA: *(Also sounding parched.)* We're going west.

JESUS: No, we're going east. Look at the sun.

MONTOYA: Why the fuck would I want to do that?

(PILAR stumbles on. Feverish, dazed.)

MONTOYA: Those are the Growler Mountains. We got to go over those, then it's just a couple of hours.

PILAR: *(Falls to the ground. Gravelly, weak.)* More mountains?

JESUS: You've been saying a couple more hours for two days.

MONTOYA: Don't forget, I saved you from the Border Patrol. That cost us some time.

JESUS: We're lost, aren't we?

MONTOYA: No, pendejo. I know exactly where I am. Those mountains, then a couple of hours. No worries, okay? Mira, find some shade. Rest a little. And then…zoom-zoom, we meet our contact. Okay?

(MONTOYA nabs the best shade under the paloverde tree. PILAR stays where she is.)

JESUS: We should find some shade.

PILAR: Where?

(She's right. There's no shade. Fuck it. He sits beside her. She pulls out her plastic gallon jug. Only a quarter of the water remains. She takes a sip.)

PILAR: *(Wincing.)* It's hot like coffee. *(She drinks more.)* Aren't you going to drink?

JESUS: I dropped my water yesterday, running away from those lights.

PILAR: Hijo le. *(Hands him her jug.)*

JESUS: No, you need it.

PILAR: If you die, I'm stuck alone with Punk Ass over there. Drink.

(He does. He takes off his hat and puts it on her head.)

PILAR: *(A little chuckle.)* I had to come to this chingado desert to find a gentleman. Why did your wife let you go? Why didn't she make you sell one of those horses and buy her some nice clothes? What more could she want? Or better yet, why didn't you bring one of those pinché horses with you? We could have ridden north in style.

JESUS: That would have been nice. Don't worry, you'll see your husband soon.

PILAR: *(Nods. After a moment…)* I've forgotten what he sounds like. I have some photographs, so I can see how he looks. But I can't hear his voice in my head. *(Closing her eyes.)* I try…real hard…I try…but when I do…

ROBERTO: *(Faces forward.)* Cookooru! *(Uses his hand like a puppet.)* Cookooru! I'm Pepe the Chicken. You want a big treat?

PILAR: *(Faces forward.)* I'm not in the mood, Papa.

ROBERTO: Cookooru! Just say the magic word. Cookooru!

PILAR: I got a lot of work to do.

ROBERTO: You think you're too old for Pepe the Chicken?

PILAR: Yes, I'm twenty-two years old. I'm not going to say "Cookooru."

ROBERTO: Ha! You said it. Cookooru! The magic word. Cookooru! Here's your treat. *(He makes kissing noises while Pepe the Chicken reaches out to kiss Pilar.)*

PILAR: I'm about to have my period. These cramps are killing me—

ROBERTO: *(Quickly covers his ears.)* What the hell has happened to you? *(Turns away.)*

PILAR: Chingado, hijo de tu puta madre, cabrón chocho! *(Sighs.)* God damn it, I love to cuss. It's better than sex. At least from what I can remember. It's been so long. You know, I just discovered the joy of cursing recently. Before that… *(With a chuckle.)* I wanted to be a saint. Not to be like a saint, to actually be one. When I was a girl, I would go through a checklist every night: Am I guilty of gluttony? No—back then I was skinny. Lust? Hardly. Sloth, greed, anger? No. Pride? No, I was very proud of not being prideful. Envy…? That was a hard one. When I watched my father and my brothers together…With me? My father would toss me a smile here and there, call me his little angel, but with my brothers, he fought and argued and laughed…I think envy was my downfall. So if I couldn't be a saint, I figured…what the fuck?

(PILAR squints at JESUS, tired and confused.)

PILAR: You have a baby?

JESUS: Yeah. I showed you the picture, remember?

PILAR: Is it a girl?

JESUS: Yes.

PILAR: You love her?

JESUS: Very much.

PILAR: *(Lays down. A weak laugh.)* It's strange. You're killing yourself to escape what I'm killing myself to find.

JESUS: I'm not trying to escape—

PILAR: I know. You're going to breed horses.

JESUS: You don't understand.

PILAR: You love baby horses more than your own. *(She closes her eyes.)*

JESUS: No, I… *(Pause.)* Look, I don't have any horses. No big surprise, eh? But we did. Once. We had a little ranch. My family lived there a long time, but we had no papers. One day somebody showed up with papers…Araceli and I came to Sonoita two years ago to get across the Border, but we didn't have enough money…We live in a dump. *(Laughs.)* I've said that all my life, now it's really true. "El Dompe." You don't come from a big town, so maybe you've never seen one. I hadn't. It's a city, within a city, but it's made of trash. It has mountains and valleys and buildings. It has rich and poor, all living off garbage. There is even police—they are drug addicts—they sniff glue and collect taxes. If you don't pay, they bust down your shed or worse. They work for somebody. I don't know who. The good places are higher on the trash mountain. Only well-connected people can live there. These people know the missionaries that come to help, so they control who gets what. Their houses are made of garage doors and boards. Some even have carpet. Higher is better because the rain won't flood you out. I was smart, I built our shed on a slope so the rain, when it comes, flows through the house, under the bed. The outcasts—Indians, Central Americans—they sleep below in "pig village" with the pigs that are about to be slaughtered. For two years Araceli and I worked and picked trash, all so I could come here. *(He laughs and takes a small sip of water.)* Leaving them...there...I'm almost grateful for the heat and the pain of this place. You understand...? Pilar?

(PILAR has been asleep. JESUS lays down beside her.)

JESUS: You understand. *(Closes his eyes.)*

SCENE 11

GARY whistles "The Yellow Rose of Texas." ROBERTO tries to follow along.

GARY: No, listen.

(GARY whistles more and stops. ROBERTO tries to imitate him.)

GARY: You're hopeless.

ROBERTO: Let's whistle something good like... *(Whistles.)*

GARY: That's not even a song. It's a criminal misuse of air.

ROBERTO: That is "Adiós Amor." *(Starts singing.)* Adiós amor. Te vengo a despedir. Hoy que te vas. Adiós amor. Yo se que nunca—

GARY: Oh, dear God, no. Okay, okay...I believe you. Jesus Christ.

(GARY's phone rings. He scrambles to answer it as ROBERTO keeps singing.)

GARY: Kenny...? Where the hell are you? *(To ROBERTO.)* Shut up.

(ROBERTO stops singing.)

GARY: Nobody...It's Rober—The Tonk...I'm alright. Why...? No shit...Jesus Christ...

ROBERTO: What's happening?

GARY: Is he going to be okay...?

ROBERTO: Who?

GARY: *(To ROBERTO.)* Shut up. *(Inspects ROBERTO.)* Late forties. Straw cowboy hat. Brown shirt, blue jeans...Okay...Okay... *(Puts his hand on his holster.)*

ROBERTO: Why do you call me a Tonk? What is a Tonk...?

GARY: *(Pulls out his pistol and points it at Roberto.)* Shut up!

(ROBERTO does.)

SCENE 12

MONTOYA wakes up with a gasp. He scrambles away from an invisible desert demon. When he realizes the creature came from his dream, he squints up at the sun.

MONTOYA: Fuck you.

(He stumbles over to the others and kicks JESUS.)

MONTOYA: Up, chickens. Up.

(JESUS stirs.)

MONTOYA: Come on. It wants to kill us. We gotta move.

(JESUS staggers to his feet. MONTOYA starts off.)

JESUS: Hold it. Señora...Pilar.

(He tries to pull her up by her arm, but she lays there, limp and burnt.)

JESUS: Help me.

(MONTOYA shuffles over to PILAR and gives her a kick.)

JESUS: Hey!

(PILAR does not move.)

MONTOYA: She's not going nowhere.

JESUS: Help me.

(JESUS grabs one arm and pulls.)

MONTOYA: Puta madre.

(MONTOYA grabs the other. They raise her to a sitting position, but she falls back.)

MONTOYA: We gotta go.

(The fall arouses PILAR somewhat.)

PILAR: *(Delirious.)* Okay... good... good... *(She slowly raises herself to her hands and knees.)*

JESUS: Come on, Señora.

(JESUS gently touches her arm, but she jerks it away in pain.)

PILAR: Ah! Don't scratch me.

JESUS: I'm sorry. Stand up.

PILAR: Don't scratch. *(Wincing and writhing, she begins to crawl.)*

JESUS: Señora?

PILAR: *(Starts taking off her clothes.)* Don't scratch.

(JESUS tries to stop her. She fights him off and tears at her clothes.)

JESUS: Pilar, please.

(He grabs her in a bear hug. She wails in pain.)

PILAR: Naldo!

JESUS: You have to go.

ROBERTO: *(Turns forward.)* No.

JESUS: You can't stay here.

ROBERTO: This is your home.

MONTOYA: Come on.

ROBERTO: I forbid it. End of discussion.

(PILAR shakes her head, "No.")

ROBERTO: It will kill your mother.

(PILAR continues shaking her head.)

ROBERTO: *(Pleading.)* My little angel, you can't do it. You're too fat.

PILAR: *(A hoarse cry.)* Shut up.

ROBERTO: Fat in a nice way. Pretty fat...like a doll...like a baby.

JESUS: If you stay, you'll die.

(PILAR starts to rise.)

ROBERTO: Please, Pilar. I'll find money somehow, and I'll buy you a pretty dress, and I'll take you to the dances. There are a lot of nice boys who would love you.

(JESUS lifts her.)

JESUS: That's it.

(She takes a step and crumbles to the ground.)

ROBERTO: *(Soothing.)* My poor little angel. *(Turns away.)*

(JESUS bends down to her, but PILAR does not stir.)

MONTOYA: She's toast, 'mano.

JESUS: She's just tired. Thirsty. Help me get her by the shade.

MONTOYA: We're wasting time—

(With an unexpected burst of fury, JESUS grabs MONTOYA by the shirt and throws him toward PILAR.)

JESUS: Help me.

(Cursing, MONTOYA helps drag PILAR under the spindly tree.)

MONTOYA: *(Trying to catch his breath.)* A little exercise. Just what we needed. Let's go.

JESUS: In a minute.

MONTOYA: We're in a race here, 'mano. Against that fucker. *(Pointing at the sun.)* He's bigger and stronger than us. We gotta be faster.

JESUS: We're not leaving her.

MONTOYA: She's dead, man. Look at her. The sun beat her. It's sad, but what can we do? It happens a lot out here. You want to end up like that?

JESUS: *(Retrieves her water.)* She just needs a drink.

MONTOYA: Don't waste that on her.

JESUS: We're not going to let her die.

(He tries to give her water, but she's incoherent, and it spills.)

MONTOYA: The only chance she has—any of us have—is for us to get out of here and bring back help.

JESUS: You don't even know where the hell we are.

MONTOYA: Sure I do. That way—north—is Highway 8.

JESUS: What about Ajo, west?

MONTOYA: Fuck that. North is the highway. North is the way out of this desert.

JESUS: By the time we got back, she'd be dead.

MONTOYA: No, buey. A couple of hours there and back. She'll be fine.

JESUS: What if she wakes up, and we're gone? She could wander off. We'd never find her.

MONTOYA: She's not waking up, 'mano.

JESUS: No. We stay.

MONTOYA: *(Glances around, thinking.)* Okay. Here's the plan. I'll go and bring back water and food.

JESUS: And save yourself.

MONTOYA: Save us all, 'mano. It's the only way. Three hours, I'll be back.

JESUS: Whatever. Go.

MONTOYA: Thing is…I'm gonna need some money. To buy water and food.

JESUS: I paid you one thousand dollars to get me—

MONTOYA: Oye, I didn't see any of that. The Coyote and the Syndicate gets it. They only pay me a hundred dollars for each little chicken I get through.

JESUS: Don't you have money on you?

MONTOYA: No, man. If the Border Patrol catches me with a wad of cash, they'll know I'm the guide, and then I'm fucked. You get caught, they just dump you back over the border. Me, they throw in prison. Come on 'mano, I need the money to save you. And I gotta save you to get paid.

(JESUS reaches into his pocket and pulls out some neatly folded bills. MONTOYA quickly rifles through them and throws some back.)

MONTOYA: No pesos. Just dollars. Okay, I'll be back in three or four hours. Five max. *(Scurries off.)*

(JESUS sits beside PILAR and puts her head in his lap. He takes a small sip of the boiling hot water. PILAR opens her eyes slightly.)

PILAR: Naldo?

(JESUS strokes her hair. PILAR falls back to sleep.)

SCENE 13

GARY still speaks on the phone, pistol at the ready, pointed toward the sky. ROBERTO stands frozen.

GARY: *(Into phone.)* I got it covered… *(Getting testy.)* I know what I'm doing. Out. *(Puts his phone away and faces ROBERTO.)*

GARY: Tonk is the sound a metal flashlight makes when it hits a human head.

ROBERTO: Oh…Now I wish I did not know that.

GARY: Let's go. We're heading up the road.

ROBERTO: Why? What is happening?

GARY: A Border Patrol agent got shot a few hours ago. That's why nobody's come.

ROBERTO: Shot? Where?

GARY: Not far from here. Apparently, he stopped a couple of illegals who told him a story about looking for their sister who was lost in the desert. They begged him for water, and when he went to get some from his truck, they shot him.

ROBERTO: He is dead?

GARY: Not yet. They caught one of the shooters. They were drug smugglers who got separated from their pals last night. They were heading into this canyon to meet their associate from the U.S. He described the guy as fortyish, dark, slender. Wore blue jeans. *(Pauses awaiting a response.)*

ROBERTO: Does he also have two hands? Because, hijo le, then it has to be me.

GARY: He also said the guy spoke fluent English. How come you speak so good?

ROBERTO: I told you already. I think the sun is making you crazy. If I was a criminal, why would I stay here all day with you?

GARY: Maybe because I was watching you.

ROBERTO: Gary, you are a stupid man. You know that I am not a bad guy. When the Border Patrol come—

GARY: The Border Patrol don't know a thing about you. My people checked.

ROBERTO: Then your people are more stupid than you. Did they talk to Stewart? Or Bradley? They know me.

GARY: Roberto, I'm going up the road now, and you're coming with me.

ROBERTO: Or what will you do? Shoot me? You will shoot me because I will not leave this poor woman, and you are too stupid to know what a drug dealer look like, so you will shoot this Mexican? Then you will feel like a big man?

GARY: No, I won't shoot you.

ROBERTO: Then how can you make me go? You cannot, you stupid gabacho pendejo—

(In one graceful move, GARY maces ROBERTO in the face.)

ROBERTO: Ahh! *(Falls to his knees.)*

GARY: Who's stupid? Huh? You could have just taken a little walk with me, gotten some food, maybe a beer, and cleared this whole thing up. But no. You want to stay here by a fucking corpse that you don't even know. *(Crouches down to gather his belongings.)* Now that's stupid. Only maybe you're not so stupid. Maybe you've just been waiting for a chance to make your move. Maybe you don't give a shit about this pile of bones— *(He freezes. There's something by the tree…He approaches it carefully.)* Jesus Christ. *(Picks up a blue and white striped towel.)*

SCENE 14

The full moon blankets JESUS and PILAR with cold, blue light. A coyote howls in the distance. JESUS smiles. He tries to answer with a howl of his own, but his voice cracks.

JESUS: *(Voice like sandpaper.)* This is a night for riding. When the women in our ranch would make piloncillo, from sugarcane, my father would take me into town with him to sell it. He'd wake me up at three in the morning, and we'd ride in the moonlight…I love the world like this…Only white and black. You can't see what's in the shadow. All you see is silver. Shining. *(Pause.)* He's not coming back. *(Examines the water jug. It's almost empty. He gently shakes PILAR.)*

JESUS: Señora? Señora…I have to go. I have to. Pilar?

ROBERTO: *(Turns forward.)* Pilar?

JESUS: Pilar?

(PILAR opens her eyes. She stares up, past JESUS, to the night sky.)

ROBERTO: The stars are beautiful, aren't they? Almost too beautiful. You want to reach out and grab them. But you can't. They're too far away. And the more you want them, the more their beauty hurts, because you can never keep it for yourself. But when I watch you looking up at the sky, I can see that it's not the stars that are beautiful. It is you looking at the stars. That is the real beauty. Without you to watch them, my little angel, stars are cold and meaningless.

JESUS: I'll leave you the water. Okay? Pilar? Okay.

(He starts to rise. PILAR reaches up and grabs him.)

JESUS: Señora?

(She tries to speak, but no sound comes.)

JESUS: *(Leans in close.)* Pilar, I have to bring back help. You rest.

(He starts to stand, but she holds him.)

JESUS: I'll be back. I promise.

(She shakes her head and holds on, still trying to speak.)

JESUS: Here. *(Pulls a ring off his finger.)* This was my father's. He won it when he was a young man. It's the only thing, beside my wife and baby, that I care about. *(Puts it on her finger.)* I'm coming back.

(But she does not let go. She rasps out a sound. JESUS puts his ear to her lips.)

JESUS: "Coo…kuroo"? I don't understand.

(ROBERTO smiles and turns away. PILAR relaxes and lays back down. JESUS searches through his bag. He pulls out a blue and white striped towel and gently places it over her eyes.)

JESUS: Rest. *(Forces himself to stand.)* I'll be back. *(Exits.)*

SCENE 15

ROBERTO kneels by the corpse holding the towel. GARY stares. After a very long silence...

GARY: When he told me he wanted to join up, I thought it was an April Fool's joke. *(Pause.)* He never even liked toy guns as a kid. He liked to draw. Comics mostly. Monsters, superheroes. On Father's Day, he'd draw me and him like a superhero team. Kid had talent. But he didn't have the grades for no scholarship...His mother went nuts, but I said the army'd make a man of him, and he'd be serving his country and...and all that. *(Pause.)* When I drove him to enlist, he was calm, listening to the radio, but I was shakin'. I thought it was 'cause I was afraid he might get hurt, but when I looked at him sittin' there bobbin' his head to the music, I realized what I was really scared of was who he'd become once he got over there. He was still a boy. In that car, at that moment, he was still my little boy. I didn't want to let that go. So I pulled off the highway, and right there in the parking lot of Food Lion, I begged him not to do it. I told him I'd find a way to pay for college or a trainin' school. I'd help him get a good job somewhere, but he knew I couldn't do nothin'. I work at a god damn Hallmark Store...I couldn't do nothin'.

(Silence. ROBERTO gently places the towel on the ground and crosses himself. In the distance, the sound of a helicopter engine grows louder.)

GARY: Border Patrol.

(The helicopter passes overhead and its engine grows faint. ROBERTO pulls himself to his feet. He picks up a large rock, carries it center stage, and sets it down. He crosses back for another rock, which he places beside the first.)

GARY: What are you doin'?

ROBERTO: I need to remember this place. Her mother...she will want to see.

(ROBERTO continues. After a moment, GARY begins to help. ROBERTO stops. When GARY notices ROBERTO staring at him, he freezes. The two fathers look at each other for a long moment, then, silently, ROBERTO accepts GARY's help. As the two men gather stones, the helicopter returns and the sun grows brighter. The helicopter's roar grows deafening and the sunlight blinding, until...)

(Blackout.)

(THE END.)

AMERICAN BADASS

or 12 Characters in Search of a National Identity

Chris Harcum

CHRIS HARCUM is an actor and playwright. He was born on September 6, 1970, in Wilmington, Delaware, and raised in High Point, North Carolina. He received a BFA in acting from the University of North Carolina at Greensboro and an MFA in acting from the University of Virginia; he also trained at the North Carolina School of the Arts. Harcum is the author of the plays *I Don't Know, Hermetic Intervention, Instant Gratification, Trading Lunches, Rabbit Island, Milk & Shelter,* and *The Devil in Ms. Spelvin.* His short plays include *The Perfect Set, Vulnerability Assessment, An Inconvenient Holiday,* and *The Tree in the Yard.* He is the creator of the solo performances *The Monster and the City, Some Kind of Pink Breakfast, Gotham Standards, Anhedonia Road, Mahamudra (or Postconsumer Waste Recycled Paper), Things You Don't Know, Weight and Weightlessness,* and the forthcoming *Green.* As an actor, his credits include *Toys in the Attic, Amadeus, My Thing of Love,* sub*Urbia, Six Characters in Search of an Author, The Miser,* and *Romeo and Juliet.* His teaching artist work includes the Neighborhood Playhouse Junior School, Queens Theatre in the Park, The Leadership Program, and the University of Virginia; he also conducts private solo performance workshops. Harcum is the Artistic Director of Virgodog Theatre; the Associate Artistic Director and Resident Playwright for Core Theatre Co.; a Master Mason of the Brick Theater; and a member of Transport Group, New Jersey Repertory Company, Actors' Equity Association, and the Dramatists Guild of America. He lives in Brooklyn, New York, where he runs many circles around Prospect Park and makes weird noises on his Fender Strat.

American Badass, or 12 Characters in Search of a National Identity was first presented by Virgodog Theatre and Fevvers Productions as part of the New York FRIGID Festival (Erez Ziv, Managing Director) on February 28, 2008, at the Kraine Theater with the following cast and credits:

Performed by: Chris Harcum
Directed by: Bricken Sparacino
Lighting Design: Maryvel Bergen
Costumes: Chris Foster
Multimedia and Animation: Daniel McKleinfeld
Graphic Design: Carolyn Raship
Original Music/Sound Design: Debby Schwartz
Film Segment: Evan Stulberger

www.chrisharcum.com

Dear Reader,

This was my stab at peeling the big onion of the Bush Administration and its effect on people. What I thought America should be versus what it actually was and the scary places it was going. Being overwhelmed gave me a bad case of playwright's block that only the deadline of an opening night cured. When I wrote this between December 2007 and February 2008, I had no idea both major parties would eventually sweep George W. Bush under the rug by the time the conventions happened in August. I'm sure many years from now theorists, historians, critics, and artists will have other conclusions about his reign. Hopefully, this time capsule will be more of a reminder than a reality.

As I look at this piece again, I think it is the beginning of a dialogue. Equal weight to the left and right is attempted but of course not everything is included. Were I to write this piece again, there would be other characters and concerns addressed. If I were to write this for performers other than myself, I'd include more gender and race issues. I encourage creative casting if this is done with more than one actor. Also, it can be produced minimally or with multimedia to connect the play with current events I can't possibly know about now. From my experience, the characters play best with honest performances instead of easy caricatures.

I write this note only two days away from the 2008 presidential election. We are currently in two wars and a new financial crisis on top of being bombarded with politics straight from Crazytown. There is the potential of change so it's hard to say how this piece will be regarded down the road. Hopefully, the artist and the citizen will each have a more integral role in our government. If not, please use this as a springboard to make that happen.

Your friendly neighborhood,

Chris Harcum

NOTE

The introduction and all the transitions are prerecorded to help the actor shift from one character to another. Those recorded parts can be done simply as audio or with an added visual/multimedia element. Using brief bits of music as intros to or underneath certain passages in the main monologues is encouraged. I use the word "beat" throughout in place of "pause" to signify a shift in the character's thoughts or to represent a response by the unseen characters on stage.

INTRO: VERY BIG BROTHER

Pre-show announcement with exciting music.

What's up America?! Lemme hear you say, "yeah!" If your candy's unwrapped, lemme hear you say, "oh, yeah!" If all your devices are silenced, lemme hear you say, "Hell yeah!" If you can find the exits, lemme hear you scream!!

Alright, alright, alright. The Department of Homeland Security wants you to have a good time but any talking or heckling during the show will get your ass worked over with enhanced techniques. Ladies and gentleman make some noise for **AMERICAN BADASS**!

1. ANTI-POST-HIPSTER

JEFF is a thirty-year-old who isn't from Brooklyn but proudly lives there now.

AMERICAN. BADASS. Now that's a title. Like who's the badass? Is it that we're the badass? Or is it that *America*'s the badass? 'Coz we're not. Not anymore. Not really. We were. I think we were. I don't know.

Piece of friendly advice? Don't mess it up. I mean don't make it *meta*. You know, META. Like you talk about the thing while you're doing the thing. Or you talk about yourself without really talking about yourself. Because that's what people think solo performance is. That crap. I'm not saying *you* do that; just, you know, *don't* do it.

Anyway, make sure you make it fun for the audience. You know, like don't be too morose or talk about stuff people avoid thinking about. 'Coz we're just out enough from 9/11 to be okay but not enough to really be doing things

about something yet. I mean, you don't have to be fluffy like we had to be right after but you can't, like, do anything that's really about 9/11 because that's so…so…Because right after 9/11 we were all about how we're like each other and all human and shit. But now, NOW, we can say we don't like people so much. New York is back in business. You can tell by all the assholes on the subway and…and…God I hate them!

And, for the love of good taste, don't try to stand up for some injustice no one'll really do anything about. You couldn't pull that off and, besides, no one cares! *(Beat.)* If *I* were doing a show called *American Badass*, I'd make it about how we used to be number one but now we're becoming a joke and how we'll be speaking some other language and asking people to please not laugh at our soft dollar and how much I want to go live in some other country and pretend to not be from America because it's such a fucking embarrassment, you know? But the trick is to do all this without totally offending everybody. Because people take their religion and politics so seriously.

Have you written it yet? Nah, you probably just say the first thing that comes off the top of your head. 'Coz that would be easier. Oh, oh, oh. You could do a thing where you're twelve different George Bushes, you know: asshole, puppet, Jesus freak, asshole again. How did he get to stay president with an approval rating so low? If he were a specialty burger at McDonald's he would've been dropped from the dollar menu by now. "No one's buying the McBush!"

But what you reeeally ought to do is a show where part of you represents how things are and then another part represents how things should be and then you get in a wrestling match like this... *(He begins to wrestle himself. It builds into a bit from a karate movie until he throws himself all over the stage.)* No one's ever done a one-man stage combat show before. I could hook you up with my friend, Qui. He could choreograph it for you in a jiffy. That would be cool. See, you have to give the audience enough of what they expected to see for them to like it. Then, every now and then, you can put in the stuff you actually care about. That's the secret—not too much!—just enough to not feel like you're selling out. *American Badass* just screams one-man action comedy.

Ugh, I can only imagine what it's like if you're out there by yourself and they fucking hate you. 'Coz you know, right, if they're having a bad day and they're not there, you can feel that, right? It's like when you're in the subway and there's that guy taking up three seats giving off that gangrenous-pea-soup-and-entrails smell and you can't move to the next car because it's locked. You're that guy! And, man, if you're off, then the whole audience has to suffer. For a looong time. Because of you. Sucking. Heh, heh, heh, haaaaaa-uhhhh. Well, send me an email and if I'm not doing anything...you know...I'll try to come out but I'm probably busy. Well, good luck.

TRANSITION: UNCLE SAM JR.

A slide show of hand-drawn images, including a picture of a six-year-old dressed as Uncle Sam.

"O beautiful for spacious skies, for amber waves of grain, for purple mountain majesties, above the fruited plain! America! America! God shed His grace on thee, and crown thy good with brotherhood from sea to shining sea!"

Good morning Oak View Elementary. My name is *(name of performer)* and I am in Ms. Vertolli's first grade class. I am dressed today as Uncle Sam to celebrate the anniversary of the signing of the Declaration of Independence on July 4, 1776. This stated that the Thirteen Colonies in North America were "Free and Independent States" and that "all political connection between them and the State of Great Britain, is and ought to be totally dissolved." President Lincoln later explained the importance of this document by saying, "Four score and seven years ago our fathers brought forth on this continent, a new nation, conceived in liberty, and dedicated to the proposition that all men are created equal." Benjamin Franklin wrote, "Those who would give up essential liberty to purchase a little temporary safety deserve neither liberty nor safety." God bless America!

2. ARTICLE 88 (RAPTURE IS COMING)

EDWIN is an eighty-year-old man working the snack bar in a New England train station near the Canadian border. He is constantly busy cleaning and restocking, even though there is little work to do. He only stops occasionally when making a point.

How are you, young man? That's good. Help yourself to the coffee there. There should be plenty of milk...unless you prefer a splash of coffee in your milk, in which case there should be more of it back here in the fridge. That's a joke. We give those away for free. That's right. *(Beat.)* No, just make your change in the dish there. We do things the old-fashioned way here. *(Beat.)* Or you can leave your passport. That's another joke.

You're headin' north on the Maple Leaf. I know all the schedules. Your train breaks here for twenty minutes in our little town before headin' on. We get the Empire stopping by later followed by the Adirondack. You do what I do long enough, you get a sense for what's comin'. You don't need a schedule. *(Pause.)*

Are you doin' somethin' Big today? *(Beat.)* You don't have to actually answer that. I like to ask that and see what goes on behind the eyes. Most people don't have anythin' big. They just have that Evil Little Thing that is eating them alive. Most people I know do Nothin'. They spent their lives workin' to finish the Evil Little Thing so they could finally do Nothin'. So now they do Nothin' and they're three hundred times more miserable than before.

(He sees a regular commuter walk by.) Hello Mr. Mike. How are you today, sir? Your Patriots are looking unstoppable this year. It's better to have a good offense than a good defense but they got both, don't they? *(Beat.)* That's right. That's right. Alright. *(He pauses until the commuter goes out of earshot.)* That fool gambles everything away.

I paced the floors for three months before I finally decided either the devil was going to get me or the TV was so I got this job. It's a good thing. It gives me a chance to meet people. Martha passed on a few years ago. Between Thomas and Alexander. You can let that sort of thing crumble you. I know a fella, his wife died on him, he just shriveled up. Couldn't cook. Couldn't figure out what to do with himself. I didn't expect to find myself here but you have to shore up and do the best with what you're dealt. Not

that I gamble because I don't. *(He speaks to himself as he wipes the counter more vigorously.)* Why do people want to throw away their good money like that? Those fools get what they deserve. If I had that kind of money, I wouldn't…

Sorry. I'm doing it again. I talk out loud a lot, especially at home. I had two sons. Thomas was in finance. He was on the seventy-sixth floor of the first tower. Then Martha passed because of the embolism. Alexander was a Reservist who wound up in Iraq. So I find myself in the middle of this whole conversation and remember there's no one there. I'm not crazy or losing it. Not yet anyway. I'm usually talking to Martha out of habit. Makes me miss her less and I'm sure, in a way, she *is* there. We snap at each other a lot less now. Mostly I talk about how crazy people are with their crackpot ideas.

I served this country in Korea. If there's one thing I learned it's respect. Article 88. Don't use contemptuous words against the President or any higher ups or it's the court martial for you. All those countercultureniks and beatniks trying to cause trouble. Leave well enough alone. Now they're telling you there's problems with the environment and the ozone. Questioning whether the war is…Why bother making yourself miserable over that? If the chiefs thought things were bad for us, they'd tell us. You have to have faith in the people in office. You may not always agree with them but they have a tough job and they deal with things you don't want to know about.

No one has to worry about that anyway. I go to the new big church down the road. They call it one of those megachurches. Never thought an old Anglican like myself would wind up at an Evangelical church but they took me in after I lost my home from those bills. You have to hand it to them, they take care of people. Makes you have faith in something rather than sitting around worrying. Last week we read Revelations. "Fear none of those things which thou shalt suffer." Armageddon will come. Some people think it may already be here. I think, "not yet, Lord, I'm not done yet." But that's selfish. There's something bigger than what I want. Jesus will come down and we good Christians will get our Rapture bodies and be taken to a better place. I'll see Martha and the boys there and I hope I see you there too. Oh, looks like the Maple Leaf is ready to take you up to Ontario. Well, carry on and try to do somethin' Big today.

TRANSITION: QUALITY OF LIFE
Phone call.

OUTGOING MESSAGE: Thank you for calling the *New York Times*. Leave your story idea after the tone.

CALLER: Yes, here's what you should be reporting at the *Times*. I have the answer. It's very simple. You can solve the world's problems in one word: manners. If people chewed with their mouths closed and learned how to say please and thank you. If people could drive without road rage or know that people aren't video games. If there was some value to other people just because they happen to be people. Men don't know how to shake hands like men anymore. Forty-year-olds are dressed like adolescents. A woman practically spit on me because I held the door open for her. Everywhere you look, adults walk around with their underwear hanging out. We can't begin to address equality if people don't know how to interact with one another. The media rewards celebrities for vomiting their mental illness all over and then we want to emulate them because we don't have any real leaders teaching us right from wrong anymore. How can we have any kind of civil discourse over serious issues if we can't show basic respect for each other? How do we get down to fixing real problems if we can't hear over all this childishness and distraction?

3. DO AS I SAY…

JUAN is a forty-year-old in the South Bronx leaning out the door of a classroom.

Okay, thank you Mr. Bohlke. I'll take it from here. Yeah, we'll stop by your office and say goodbye on the way out.

(He closes the door and waits a bit to let the principal get down the hall. He turns toward his son, Livan.)

What the fuck are you thinking, you stupid piece of shit? Huh? I asked you a question, Livan. Look at me. Don't look at the floor. You go to school. Don't they teach you answers aren't on the floor? Or are you too stupid? That was rhetorical. Rhe-tor-i-cal. Why don't you march your tough ass over there and look it up. Oh, wait, I forgot, you're in third grade. That word's too big for your dictionary. When I grew up in the last century we didn't do shit like this in third grade. Or in high school. Unless we were psycho. Are you psycho? I'm not psycho. You must've gotten this from your bitch mother.

No. You don't get to get angry with me. You understand? I'm the adult here. You're the child. Adult. Child. Adult. Child. I'll knock your attitude across this dirty ass floor, you forget who you're talking to again. See if I don't. Try me.

So Mr. Big Third Grader, you're planning on blowing up the school, huh? Don't. Talk. And if you're man enough to blow up the school then you're man enough to hold in those tears. No wonder there's gotta be cops in the schools here. How you going to blow this place up? You can't even figure out how to make cereal in the morning or put on your jacket.

Why? Huh? Why would you do this? *(Beat.)* Initiation. Initiation? To what, the Cabbage Patch Kids? The Sesame Street Gang? So which gang then? *(Beat.)* The Crips. No shit. The. Crips. *(Beat.)*

Good work. Now you're a terrorist. Yes you are. You're so smart you should be reading the *Post*. Then you'd know. They prosecute gangs just like terrorists. Those lawyers will get you. Put you in juvie, if you're lucky. They might throw your worthless ass in Riker's. Yeah, then you'll come out lookin' like your Uncle Rico all tattooed and old and fucked up. No, no, no, you want to do man things, they'll put you in with the men and then you'll be writing me sad letters about the cell you share with some guy named Shitty Cent or whatever. Oh, yes you will.

Who put you up to this? Because I'm going to get you out of it. You have no idea, Livan, no. You look at me and see a good-for-nothin' who does odd jobs. You forget the fact that I lived twenty lives before your worthless ass came around and do the shit people don't wanna do. Pop. Pop. I clear the shit up. I'm good at that. Except with your mother. *(Beat.)* No, she's not coming back. Because I messed up!!

Listen to me. Look at your father when he's talking to you. Bring your mind back here. I'm sorry. We're gonna do it different now. I'm sorry. For everything.

For yelling at you. For the times I hit you. I just get angry. You understand. Everybody else … fuck 'em. Unless they're suckin' your dick, they ain't doin' you no favors. And even then you never know. If I could, I'd get you the hell out of here. These fuckin' people.

I don't know why you gotta go to school anyway. Computers do all the hard figurin' out of stuff. The world still needs people like me to take care of their shit. If I wasn't so busy doin' that, I'd teach you. I'd teach you for real. I'd teach you the important stuff. Like what you do when someone looks at you the wrong way. You sucker punch 'em right in the face before they get a chance to do nothin'. *(Beat.)* Alright, let's get out of here. We'll say goodbye to that asshole principal of yours. Don't ever listen to that douche, you understand me? Good. You ain't half bad when you aren't fuckin' up. Let's go, you little fart squeezer.

TRANSITION: THE NEXT TOP COMMANDER-IN-CHIEF #1

BLUE BOY is on a reality show vying for the heart of America.

I think I will come ahead in tonight's final three to become America's Next Top Commander-in-Chief. America is indeed more beautiful than ever in my eyes but she's a little hesitant because she's been through a lot of abuse. I think America is ready for a change and I'm the one who can bring about that change. She doesn't want the same bad things happening again and again. I'm not going to lie like Big Red or Indy. I think America wants a guy who's going to tell the truth and I'm that guy. She wants someone who is going to tell the truth no matter what. Now I'm not the richest one here but when you have real character and a vision for the future…let's just say I think America will make the right decision and I'll be the Next Top Commander-in-Chief.

4. MY BUSH'S GOAT

GEORGE W. BUSH in the flesh.

RECORDED VOICEOVER: And now it's time for another edition of Where Are They Now: Presidential Edition. This week we're catching up with former President George W. Bush at the opening of his Presidential library.

BUSH: Defining moment? I thought maybe it was a practical joke. Maybe Ari or Turd Blossom was playing a funny on me. That was our first year so we were still horse-sassing around a bit. You know we were down in Florida. I was going to hear some kids read before giving a talk about No Child Left Behind. I always liked that title. Good title. Good title.

I was sitting outside the classroom waiting to go in, and I saw an airplane hit the tower—the TV was obviously on. And I used to fly myself and I said, "Well, there's one terrible pilot." I said, "It must have been a horrible accident." But I was whisked off there; I didn't have much time to think about it.

I was concentrating on the program at this point, thinking about what I was going to say about the plane crash. Obviously, I felt it was an accident. I was concerned about it, but there were no alarm bells. Then Andrew comes over and says, "A second plane hit the second tower. America is under attack."

I am very aware of the cameras. I'm trying to absorb that knowledge. I have nobody to talk to. I'm sitting in the midst of a classroom with little kids, listening to a children's story and I realize I'm the Commander-in-Chief and America's just come under attack. *(He points and winks at one of the interviewers.)*

We're at war and somebody has dared attack us and we're going to do something about it. I realized I was in a unique setting to receive a message that somebody attacked us. It became evident that we were, you know, that the world had changed.

Ari had "DON'T SAY ANYTHING YET" written on it in big block letters in the back. I thought I have people and they're doing what they need to do. Because that's what you do when you have people.

(The lights change to indicate a flashback. He has a blank look.)

"Really good readers, whew! These must be sixth graders! Hoo! These are great readers. Very impressive! Thank you all so much for showing me your reading skills. I bet they practice too. Don't you? Reading more than they watch TV? Anybody do that? Read more than you watch TV? Oh that's great! Very good. Very important to practice! Thanks for having me. Very impressed."

(The lights restore.)

To this day people ask me what was going on in my head at that moment. *(Beat.)* I always appreciate that question. But I'm the commander—see, I don't need to explain—I do not need to explain why I say things. That's the interesting thing about being president. I'm also not very analytical. You know I don't spend a lot of time thinking about myself, about why I do things. *(Beat.)* There's an old poster out West, as I recall, that said,

"Wanted: Dead or Alive." *(He points to someone in the audience.)* Go ahead.

(The lights change again.)

RECORDED FEMALE STUDENT: Thank you Mr. President. It's an honor to have you here.

BUSH: Thanks.

RECORDED FEMALE STUDENT: I'm a first-year student in South Asia studies. My question is in regard to private military contractors. The uniform code of military justice does not apply to these contractors in Iraq. I asked your Secretary of Defense a couple months ago, what law governs their actions. Mr. Rumsfeld—

BUSH: I was gonna ask him. Go ahead. *(Beat. Chuckles.)* Help.

RECORDED FEMALE STUDENT: *(Laughs.)* Well, I was hoping your answer might be a little more specific.

BUSH: Well, I guess you came to the wrong place.

(He chuckles. The lights change again to indicate another reality. He points to a different reporter.)

BUSH: Shoot.

RECORDED OLDER WOMAN: How do you respond to critics who say you are a silver-spoon Yankee who went to both Harvard and Yale and that you are only pretending to be a good ol' boy?

BUSH: Look at me. Americans know what I really am. *(He makes some silly faces and chuckles. He points to another reporter.)* You. No, him.

RECORDED MALE: Mr. President. Home foreclosures are rising at astronomical rates. How do you intend—

BUSH: —Yes. I know people are concerned about pocketbook issues. You must be disappointed in this Democratic Congress. I wish I could do something about that. But our stimulus packages have done plenty. If I could, I would give one of those every day but… *(He points to another reporter.)* Yes.

RECORDED WOMAN #2: It is well documented that your wife's favorite book is *The Brothers Karamazov*. In lieu of the severe problems in our education system and the failure of No Child Left Behind, do you worry that your association with the children's book *My Pet Goat* tarnishes your image as an education reformer? Some say it is the only book on public record you have read.

BUSH: Just a second ago I was going to Harvard and Yale. Look, good people across our country know I've worn my Bible out reading important passages that have kept my faith going. *(He points to another reporter.)* You.

RECORDED MALE #2: In a recent behind-the-scenes account, it seems Dick Cheney made more of the important decisions on bigger issues. Do you feel—

BUSH: —Well, he was the A student. I was the C student. But we had an understanding. I was still The Decider. He might be smarter but I'm the President. *(He points to another reporter.)* Yes.

RECORDED MALE #3: Ralph Nader has said you put us in an illegal war with Iraq just to prove to your father, President George H. W. Bush, you could take care of Saddam Hussein.

BUSH: And I did. *(He points to another reporter.)* Next.

ALL RECORDED VOICES: WHERE IS OSAMA BIN LADEN?

BUSH: I can't…I'm not…If I could go out there after him myself I'd…I'd…I don't know. *(He points to another reporter.)* Please. I thought this was going to be…whew. Yes.

RECORDED FEMALE STUDENT: *(Laughs.)* Well, back to justice in regards to the private military contractors. Mr. Rumsfeld answered that Iraq has its own domestic laws, which, he assumed, applied to those private military contractors. However, um, Iraq is clearly not currently capable of enforcing its laws much less against, you know, over our American military contractors. Um, I would submit to you that in this case, uh, this is one case that privatization is not a solution.

BUSH: Mmm.

RECORDED FEMALE STUDENT: Mr. President, how do you propose to bring private military contractors under a system of law?

BUSH: Yeah, I appreciate that very much. I wudn't kidding. *(Beat. Chuckles.)* I was gonna—I pick up the phone and say, "Mr. Secretary, I got an interesting question." This is what delegation—I don't mean to be dodging the question, although it's kinda convenient in this case, but never… *(Chuckles.)* …I really will, I'm gonna call the Secretary and say you brought up a valid question and, "what are we doing about it?" Because that's how I work. I'm a…a…Thanks.

(The lights restore.)

BUSH: Yes. I was tested on a regular basis. But it gave me political currency that I used. There were times where I found it hard to stay the course. But in my mind I thought, "So long as I'm the President, my measure of success is victory—and

success." Like the time I flew onto the deck of the USS *Abraham Lincoln* and gave the speech in the flight suit. "Major combat operations in Iraq have ended. In the battle of Iraq, the United States and our allies have prevailed." People had to give me a hard time for the banner that said, "Mission Accomplished." I knew what it meant and they knew too. So my defining moments for myself might not be the same as others' were of me. So be it. I don't particularly like it when people put words in my mouth, either, by the way, unless I say it. For those who try I say, "Fool me once, shame on—shame on you. Fool me—you can't get fooled again."

TRANSITION: GIANT O REAL ESTATE

Radio commercial.

NARRATOR: Are you tired of renting? Tired of being broke? Would you describe yourself as sad and lonely? Well, Giant O Real Estate Training Centers can put you in charge of your life. You can be a proud homeowner, landowner, property owner, and have MASSIVE multiple orgasms!! Yes, you heard right. Bad credit, no credit, hostile credit—you can OWN your own property and have mind-blowing releases all day long. Just listen to this testimonial.

NERD: I lived in my parents' basement for forty-two years. Now I have my own building and people *(Shivers with orgasm.)* pay rent to me. Thanks Giant O!

NARRATOR: But, wait, that's not all. Call today or log onto our website and you can get two for the price of one.

OLD MAN: My wife and I were going down the road to a nasty divorce. Oh, oh, oh yeah. But now, we have multiple property ownerships. It's like getting the key to your dreeeeeeeeams!

NARRATOR: Our weekend seminars include: Adjustable-Rate Mortgages and Alternating Thrust Techniques, Delaying Ejaculation and Escrow Analysis, Multidwelling Units, and Transfer of Ownership. Act now and you'll also get a free once-in-a-lifetime workshop on World Dominance and Geo Pleasure Principle Positioning. The market is good. The orgasms are bountiful. Call now!

5. MY OWN PRIVATE GUANTANAMO

GLENN lives in a big city where anything can be delivered.

Yeah, they're pretty good views but this whole section is going to get covered up when they develop this area. God knows what that'll do to my property value. I'll probably have to move again. But it's all a game. Just like anything else.

You come highly recommended. I said I needed someone who is really good at what she does but also I need discretion. *(Beat.)* Oh, good. You know what they say about discretion. It's the better part of indiscretion. I'm looking for some stress relief. My doctor recommends I find a way to let out a lot of these pent-up things. He suggested racket ball or some other exercise. I thought, "Fine but I want something more…interactive."

But, here's the thing, I need something that goes beyond the usual role-play, spanking, bad names, make me crawl situation. And I'm not just talking about shoving something up my ass or making me lick the toilet. I don't just need to be

restrained or have my dick stepped on. I don't just need to get off. I need to go to a place that's pure bliss. To forget.

I had a job that's similar to yours. I went to this place and did stuff. "Stuff happens."

Maybe you've heard about stress positions? The idea is that you don't leave any scarring. Physically or psychologically. I think most of my work was on a more spiritual or soul level. You rattle them until they think they're going to be leaving this world and then you bring them back. And repeat. And repeat. And repeeeeeat. Sometimes boredom or fatigue will set in. I'll think, "My God, if I'm getting worn out, this poor bastard has to be." Then I get angry and really get into it. That's when I know I'm cooking. You too? Niiiice.

I'm sure you've heard about waterboarding by now. That's when you…oh you have. Oh good. I find the whole debate over it ridiculous. Of course it's fucking torture. The moment you begin to play God you're torturing someone. Then again no cop, no foul. And even if there is a cop, you still say no foul or you fuck the cop up by any means necessary. I love that phrase. It opens up so much creativity.

It wasn't easy work defending freedom against enemy combatants. Sometimes to relieve some stress after a hard day of "violating habeas corpus"…oh yes, we'd make jokes about that. It wasn't like we weren't aware. "Who's going to practice extraordinary rendition today?" "Not me, I'm too busy abusing human rights." We'd practice things on each other. There were some kinky bastards there. I loved it.

The problem is human nature. The Army threw out the only conviction of the one officer who was court marshaled for Abu Graib. Lt. Col. Jordan is scot-free. That's right. All of us are. They say it's human nature to confess. I don't need to confess. I need to be punished. I need someone to do things to me. I need you to turn this into my own private Guantanamo. I need you to give me sensory deprivation until I hallucinate and crave your attention. I need you to make me not be able to think systematically. Starve me. Make me eat my own shit. I need you to ruin me. Ruin me. Ruin me!

You like that? Fuck. Let's go. Ruin me!! Come on. Ruin me!! That's right. RUIN ME!!!

TRANSITION: BE ALL THAT YOU CAN…

College station announcement.

You're tuned in to 90.1. The best ten-watt station on your Internet dial. So, I just got this in from our local recruiter. If you're done with selling plasma for beer money, they're sayin' to go down to the quad from ten a.m. to six p.m. to talk with them about getting into the Army or the Army Reserves. They'll be giving away lots of free prizes, school supplies, and pizza. The GI Bill will pay up to seventy-one thousand dollars towards your college tuition. So I guess if you like pizza and free stuff, um, go there.

Also on Thursday your local chapter of the American Civil Liberties Union will be holding a membership drive where they'll be telling you about their history as an offshoot of the American Union Against Militarism and how the GI Bill only pays twenty-two hundred dollars on average for college tuition. They'll have coffee, stickers, and other cool schwag. That's also ten to six Thursday

outside the cafeteria. So be sure to check that out.

Finally, I'll be having my annual I Just Wanna Go to College and Get Laid Charity Event. That's in Madison Dorm, room 318, North Campus. That will begin once this shift is over and go until the end of the year. Ladies, be sure to call here for details or shoot me an email anytime at havepity@getlaid.edu.

Next up we have a nonstop set starting with "Liberty's a Welcome Mat" by High Fructose Corn Syrup and "Cheney's a Dick" by Damaged Amygdala. Keep your devices tuned in here.

6. COMPASSIONATE CONSERVATIVE

TED is a completely sincere preacher at a large church.

Let us pray. Dear Lord, we thank you for giving us this time together. Please watch over our brave men and women fighting to preserve our way of life. Deliver them to safety and give them the strength necessary to carry out their duties. We ask that Your Will and their missions work together. Amen.

(He opens his eyes and spreads open his arms to engulf the congregation.) In a way we are all soldiers for the Lord, aren't we? We make sacrifices. Put ourselves in harm's way for our loved ones. We have to trudge through dark times. *(Beat.)* For the familiar faces gathered before me, you know I have a tendency to take the long way around the barn but I do get to the point eventually. Today, I'm going to cut straight to the other side of the valley.

First, the good news is that we have received a healthy portion of federal money for our faith-based initiatives for Responsible Fatherhood and Sexual Abstinence. But that's only for those programs so we will need to match those funds this year at our annual picnic and car wash. Or if you can see to it in your hearts to give what you can when we make the offering today it will make a welcome difference.

But to go back to what I said earlier, I've been thinking a lot about the soldiers who have so generously given of themselves so we could be here today. Some of them, I know and you know, came from this church. And, not because I'm a good Christian, but because I'm a good Southerner, I want to say a few words about the God-fearing people who made the contribution to our initiatives. *(Pause.)* Those of you who've pored over your Bibles know there are plenty of examples of Christians being persecuted throughout history. So as a Christian soldier I want to defend the folks in our White House this week for attacks they have received.

(He points out one woman in the congregation.) Letty, you're one of my faithful who come every Sunday. You know I always mention my beautiful wife, Sarah, and my two bundles of joy, Matthew and Mark, with whom the Lord has blessed me. I don't know about the rest of you but the care and the maintenance of the outside of the home has fallen to me. I mow the lawn, get my knees dirty digging weeds out of the garden, and I get up on the roof once in a while to make sure everything is in good repair. On certain days, this is difficult. I have sermons to write or I need to wrangle the boys to go to practice or Sarah needs for me to make the dinner. In those times I do my best to see why the Lord is testing me

and I ask Him for help because I know I can't do it all.

Lately, I've been thinking about our President and the tough job he must do. But I know his unwavering faith makes his job easier for him. This congregation came together to help after Katrina ravaged New Orleans. The Good Lord doesn't like bragging but I read churches like this one did more, in fact, than FEMA did. And, in that spirit of generosity, I think we should gather the troops—the Christian soldiers—at this time when it feels faith across our beautiful country the Lord has blessed us with is sagging. Earlier this morning, I heard two grown men on the television fighting like little children over the FISA bill. This is the—let me look at my notes, I want to say it correctly—the Foreign Intelligence Surveillance Act. Now, you might wonder why anyone would have a problem with that, especially after some of the tragedies we have witnessed. But, like in so many ways, people get upset when they are asked to have the same kind of rules put on them that are put on others.

And it simply comes down to this. If you have asked the Lord to come into your heart to give you forgiveness then you don't have anything to hide. All your sins have been taken away. It's the sinners who need to worry about FISA because they have something to hide. It's the people who have given up their faith who think we need to have a separation of church and state. It's the ones who DO NOT believe in creationism who have trouble accepting the opportunities God is giving us during this dark time.

As a father, a husband, and a man of God, I'm glad we have someone who has the determination and consistency to make the decisions I wouldn't want to make. Homeland Security begins with him and I want us to remember that as we think about events. Anyone here who has children will know that there are times, for their own good, you need to go, as a parent and as that Christian soldier, into their room and do a little, shall we say, reconnaissance mission.

"But Dad! This is my room!" That's my Matthew, my eldest son. That's when I remind him of Proverbs 1:33, "But whoever listens to me will dwell safely, and will be secure, without fear of evil." Just as fathers provide security, the Lord has offered us security, and it has been reinforced by the man we have been blessed to have in the White House. So let us take this moment to pray in silence to thank the Lord for bringing us this man who provides our security, Mr. George W. Bush.

(He closes his eyes and clasps his hands. Long pause as he prays.)

Amen.

TRANSITION: LIBERAL ELITE

CONSERVATIVE RADIO PROGRAM HOST with a barking voice.

No, listen caller, you shouldn't blame yourself for being misled. It's not your fault! The liberal media would have you believe if you don't recycle every piece of paper or those plastic things that hold your beer together, that we're going to go to hell in a hand basket. They perpetuate the global warming myth by showing you pictures of polar bears swimming near the North Pole. But you never see in those pictures how much ice is actually up there. Then—and here's what you have to be careful of—then they turn it

into an economic issue. But the truth is it costs double to recycle than it does to put a landfill someplace and, look, you can cover it over and make a football field or whatever you want and no one will ever know they're on top of garbage. Watch out! They'll do a magic bullet connecting the environment to the economy and then the economy to the war. I know you're laughing at home listening to this but they pull out the bogeyman and then they blame the conservatives of being fear-mongerers. Who the hell do they think they are?

7. PATRIOT DAY

BOB is addressing a boardroom in Chicago.

Alright, alright, alright, alright. Who wants to make some money? Come on, who wants to make some money? I can't hear you. Who wants to make BIG MONEY? Now we're talking. So let's get down to business. I am pleased to announce we will be moving into a new era in the greeting card industry. As you know, we've been looking for something to become the Mother of all holidays. Christmas without religious connotations. But what? Valentine's Day had its heyday. Mother's Day is good but limited. People never really got behind Independence Day. Finally, it dawned on me. Take the worst thing and make it the best thing ever. Patriot Day. That's right. We're gonna make September 11th a real national holiday. It's perfect. It's already on the calendars.

Originally it was called the National Day of Prayer and Remembrance for the Victims of the Terrorist Attacks on September 11, 2001. What a terrible title. You can't make money off that. Then it became 9/11. We kicked that around awhile but it's too close to 7-Eleven. And you can't rhyme it with too many good words. Heaven, Blevin, and basically you're done.

At first we were worried about backlash. That people might be offended. But have you been to Ground Zero lately? Those buildings are going back up, there's no doubt about that now. And if you go on an anniversary, forget about it. I went this last time as a research trip. Boy, no one's mourning. Okay, yeah, maybe a little bit around 8:46. Then it's all these angry groups trying to get a piece of something. Screaming about how Bush planned it and how no one is telling the truth about Tower 7.

Has your head been in the desert? 7 World Trade Center. It's the building adjacent to the twin towers. It went down after five p.m. on September 11th. There was all this back and forth about whether it was the fires or if it was a controlled demolition as part of the plan to make a lot of money. It doesn't really matter. It's been back up again for years now. They made it a green building and it's being touted as the Safest Skyscraper in the World. Progress!

Now the Freedom Tower is following suit. Do you see where we're going with this? Why can't we turn the nation's frown upside-down? That day can be seen as our real rite of passage. We should celebrate it as a birthday for every Patriot in the country.

Plus I think the good folks in the White House might look kindly on this. This way when people hear Patriot, they think, "Oh Jeez, I need to put in more overtime. I've gotta buy all those Patriot Day presents for my family and friends

and coworkers." They're not thinking about the Uniting and Strengthening America by Providing Appropriate Tools Required to Intercept and Obstruct Terrorism…or USA Patriot Act. This way we can pump more 527 money into elections to do other important things. It's a win-win-win. We're talking about creating a revolution, a true revolution, through multiple streams of calculated marketing strategies. Show the first slide please!

Tasteless? How dare you? Lights up! Lights up! Up yours, Ted. You haven't had a decent idea for this company in years. You don't recognize a good thing when you see it. This is to make people feel better about being an American and to stimulate the economy one more time in the year. That's why we're here, isn't it? I don't know about you but I certainly didn't drive in today to do my charity work.

Lemme put this another way. We've got to keep this ship from sinking. Global industry is taking all of it Over There. Halliburton going to Dubai was just the tip. Have you seen it Over There? I don't want to go Over There. I want to stay here with my wife and my kids and have the kind of life that makes my parents proud. That means I have my house and my neighbors and my kids go to their sweet little school.

Yes, we lost three thousand that day but we have over three hundred million in this country. How is making Patriot Day a time we exchange gifts worse than Easter? Hmm? On Easter they killed Christ but people still buy chocolates and eggs. Tell me how it's worse, Ted, because I'm baffled. Tell me this is in bad taste. Well, Ted, if you look around this room, you'll see you're in the minority here. Tell you what, Ted, there's the door. You walk out it, you'll be looking for your next job in Saudi Arabia. It's your choice. Okay, fine. See ya, Ted. Anybody else? *(Beat.)* Good. Let's roll up our sleeves here and do something Big today.

TRANSITION: THE NEXT TOP COMMANDER-IN-CHIEF #2

INDY, with a fat cat voice, is on a reality show vying for the heart of America.

Tonight is final eliminations. Here I am. Everybody underestimated me the whole way and that's been my strength. America is tired of guys like Big Red or Blue Boy. I may not be the most attractive candidate but I know I can buy my way into America's heart, give her what she wants, and become the Next Top Commander-in-Chief. America knows I'll take her to places she's never been. God. Bless. ME!!!

8. THE UNDERGROUND CITY

AASIF is a twenty-eight-year-old Asian American in Montreal.

I like being here in Montreal a lot. The culture is so vibrant. My girlfriend and I went to the Musée d'art contemporain. Con-tempor-ain. Is that right? I'm still working on it. And I really like being in The Underground City. It's got everything you could want and it's like being in a big warm womb. That sounded weird. *(He gets up to leave.)* Well, thank you for your time. Good luck. Thank you. Take care.

(He stops at the door and returns.) Wait. I'm sorry. I know I didn't get this job. You know what? Tear that resume up. That's not what I am. Um, here's why I want to work at this antique store. I'm…okay,

I went to Harvard and I studied something fairly useless. Blah, blah, blah, a few years go by and I see this opportunity overseas. I go over as a civilian. An unarmed civilian. Brilliant, right?

We were put in the palaces because that's sort of the nexus for a lot of activity in giving the place a big makeover. One day I was up in Najaf and I saw this graveyard, a big, beautiful graveyard with these ornate structures. This graveyard is really important in the Shia Islam religion. And they're tearing out chunks of it to expand a bus station that's next to it. Insanity everywhere. No one knows why we're there or what anyone is supposed to be doing. I joked a lot with the guys about how our real mission was to *make* the missing WMDs. They'd howl every single time.

One day things are going along and my name gets confused with this spy's name. My parents named me Aasif to bring out more of that part of our heritage. So I'm detained. I don't know why. They put you somewhere that's devoid of time and place. You don't know if it's day or night. If you're in Basra or Boise. They drove me around a lot so who knows. Maybe I made too many missing WMD jokes.

(He gets up and moves into another reality.) I was in a room that was all metal. Had a mattress and a bucket. I was handcuffed and naked for a couple of weeks. The lights were always on, except for when they had me in blackout goggles and stuffed my ears to confuse me more. Loud noise going all day all night. I started going out of my mind. They starve your body but feed your head this crazy shit you don't know whether to believe or not. Guys in masks saying I'm a terrorist over and over again. Gave me this whole fake history. I stopped eating

or sleeping. You get to a certain point and you find yourself lost. I couldn't make myself eat so they shoved a feeding tube in me to keep me alive.

"I'm an American!" I shouted over and over. They said it didn't matter. Anyone could be a terrorist. They said they had my girlfriend and my mom. I heard their voices but I couldn't tell if it was real or not. They said they'd rape them if I didn't confess. It got to a point where I felt like I was this little twig and soon I was going to snap and be no more. God, I wanted to die so badly but I wouldn't confess to something I didn't do.

Then they just came in. "Oops, it was a mistake. So sorry. Here are some fresh clothes and a severance package. Have a safe trip home."

(He returns to his seat and the job interview reality.) I read up about things after what happened to me. Do you know Project for a New American Century? They made the core of the Bush White House and they wanted to privatize the military. Eisenhower warned us about this. They presented their big plan in September of 2000. It was revolutionary but it needed TIME unless…unless some terrible event like Pearl Harbor happened. Look at how Bush reacted when the planes hit. He let those kids read and then he stood up and yawned before getting photo ops. They cranked things up with Blackwater but couldn't cool down after Afghanistan so they forged on to Iraq. How do we make peace with a Big Lie?

I went over because it was a job and I saw dollar signs. I bought them telling me I'd be protected the whole time. Like I'd be exempt from danger. I wondered if it was karma for stuff I'd done but I really think it was the WMD jokes.

The cover-ups are incredible. Here's the biggest violation: there's nothing I can do about it. It never happened. I know the truth but can't do anything about it. I have this dream where I go to D.C. and I stand in front of the White House and yell, "Just give us the truth!!" The front walls open up and the truth flows out like rivers of light and the layers of all the deceptions and betrayals and wrong-headed reasoning smooth out and it all makes sense and it can all stop.

I think about living in a free country and what that means. I can understand giving up a little privacy but if you have to give up your sense of humor to fight the War on Terror then stop the world and let me off. So that's why I'm here in Montreal with my odd resume asking for a job in a noncorporate environment that feels very well protected. I'll let you think about me a bit more. Keep the part of the resume with my name and contact info. The rest of it's bullshit.

TRANSITION: STANDARDIZED ACHIEVEMENT GAP

Phone call to a news talk show.

I've been watching your program for a long time and you're missing the point. The number one endangered species in this country is the American citizen. It was a good experiment but now it's done. What's killing us is our education system. Just hear me out. I've been in the trenches. The Department of Ed. gave out report cards and I was at the fifth worst school in the city. Plus—and you won't believe this—plus it was built on top of a toxic waste site and the material for the playground was made of recycled truck tires. So all these kids have asthma and other stuff. They can't run around like regular kids, not for too long. The food's inedible so the ice cream man and the hot dog vendor at the front door make a killing.

On top of this, they aren't learning anything because it's all this top-down "teach to the test" nonsense. They're performing better on standardized tests but we're creating a generation of consumer prisoners. It's not surprising then that elementary school kids join gangs. No one talks about this or does anything about it and that's unconscionable.

But the kids in affluent areas have their own set of problems. They don't know how to think critically or creatively. They don't have the adaptability to collaborate across networks. They don't know how to ask good questions. And they expect to have everything given to them. This entitled lethargy leaves them unprepared for college so they take extra remedial classes. Less than half of eighteen- to twenty-four-year-olds vote.

And globally we're losing. They come over here to take our menial jobs. We ship off our manufacturing and tech support jobs. Then what? Our white-collar jobs start going to India and China where researchers and paralegals work cheaper. Soon it'll be our CEOs and CFOs. If we aren't making better Americans, what will we be excelling at? How will we show the world we're still the best?

9. COMPETITIVE EATER

JIMMY, who speaks like a professional wrestler, is doing a remote interview on a late-night talk show. Occasionally he puts his fingers to his ear to hear the host's responses from his earpiece.

I'm sorry. I'm having a little trouble picking up the satellite feed. Oh, there you are. Well, I'm here in front of Nathan's on Surf Avenue in Coney Island where I'm sure your viewers, Dave, will remember what a heartbreak it was to see Kobayashi lose to Joey Chestnut. But, even so, you have to admit it was great to have the yellow belt come back to America last July 4th. With Kobayashi's arthritic jaw, Chestnut is the man for me to beat. I know I might be a long shot since I just began Competitive Eating last summer. Oh yeah, that very day in fact. I was standing right over there next to a guy whose entire head was tattooed and felt like I received a calling. What's more American than shoveling huge amounts of food in a short amount of time?

Since then, I've been going through a strict training regimen and I've actually lost quite a bit of weight. Ironic, isn't it? Who doesn't want to be me? So I'll be putting out my special diet book after the competition when the world knows who Jimmy "Slaughterhouse" Dillon is.

(Beat.) I take my inspiration from the work of two great eaters. Eric "Badlands" Booker ate fourteen pounds of cabbage a day to prepare. And he downed fifteen Burritoville Burritos in eight minutes. Then there's Sonya "the Black Widow" Thomas. Remember *Cool Hand Luke* eating fifty hardboiled eggs in an hour? She did sixty-five in under seven minutes. She's only one hundred and five pounds and eats one big meal a day. I've been also running, biking, swimming, and taking ballet classes. Laugh all you want then feel how tight my ass is. I am a machine.

(Beat.) I've been working with different techniques. I played with Kobayashi's "Japanesing," which is breaking a dog in half and putting both ends in. Usually,

you use water. I have a new thing where I've been training my gag reflex and larynx so I can do a whole dog gulp every fifth dog or so. Chestnut did sixty-six dogs in twelve minutes and, even though they dropped two minutes from the time of the competition, I'm gunning for eighty dogs to take the Superbowl of Competitive Eating to a whole new level. After that and the book rollout, I'm going after Kobayashi's cow brain record of seventeen-point-seven pounds in eight minutes.

I think I should make it clear for the kids watching that the International Federation of Competitive Eating strongly discourages any training at home or in an unsafe environment. I always have a spotter. All sorts of things can go wrong, the least of which is a "Roman Incident." *(Beat.)* Vomiting, Dave. That's automatic grounds for disqualification. Kobayashi upchucked in '02 and was almost tossed out but he held in most of the contents and the vomit in his mouth. There's still some fighting over this in certain circles but I say if you keep the puke in 'til the bell, you get to stay in the Big Chowdown.

I'm doing this because Nostradamus predicted I would dominate in this arena. He said, "After there is great trouble in mankind, a greater one is prepared." That's me, I'm the greater one. If there's one thing I want to leave behind for my children it's a sense that I went to places others wouldn't dare and achieved something unbelievable. That's the whole idea of being an American, isn't it? There's no place for number two. I'm doing this to show the world we are indeed the number one biggest, badass consumers in the world. USA! USA! USA! Everyone say it with me! USA! USA! USA!

TRANSITION: DISAMBIGUATION

Late night infomercial.

Chances are if you're up at this hour, you're not getting the sleep you need. Why? Because you look older and heavier than you did yesterday. And it isn't going to get any better. All the stress and toxins lead to intestinal buildup, excess fat, and wrinkles. This can lead to a bad sex life and being ostracized at work.

Like you, I was thirty pounds overweight, ugly, and miserable. Diets didn't work. Exercise was unfulfilling. I was running out of answers. Then I found the ultimate medical breakthrough right in my own kitchen. A gluten-free combination of acai berries, fiber, soy, green tea, and spinach.

The Superfood Miracle Pill is an antitoxic, wrinkle-reducing, craving remover that is also a fast-acting internal and external enema for your entire body. That's right. It flushes away everything that's bad for you and bad about you.

Some of the pleasant side effects include a loss of guilt and shame. It erases embarrassing moments you've experienced from the memories of other people who witnessed them. It takes back seven or eight things you shouldn't have said every day and it gives you an aura that shimmers with brilliance.

Call in the next three minutes and you'll receive your first shipment of this amazing product absolutely free. Just pay the shipping and handling and it's yours in three to five business days. Act fast. Supplies are going quickly.

You don't have to live forever but wouldn't you like to have the option?

10. RED ROVER

KARL, an upper middle-aged neocon, addresses conservative scholars off the record.

Before I start, I want to thank my hosts for their graciousness. It's always a pleasure visiting Jerry Falwell's Liberty University and especially getting to talk here at Jesse Helms School of Government. It's like getting a home-cooked meal. "Some are born great, some achieve greatness, some have greatness thrust upon them." You're all college students. Who said that? Yes, the great William Shakespeare. Bonus points who can tell me where that's from. That's Malvolio in *Twelfth Night* Act Two Scene Five.

And some people wait for history to happen to them. I don't buy into that. I say go out and grab the pig by the tail. I'm going to let you in on a little something. Actually, a whole bunch of little somethings but this is all strictly off the record. I never said it. You never heard it. That's how things work in what I do. You scratch my back and I won't cut you. You see this? This is the smile I use when I say things like that. Do you have one? Let me see it. Good. How about you? This is a sharp bunch. I bet you Jesse and Jerry are smiling down on us right now.

Okay. I'm sure the fine people at this university assign lots of good books to read. History and theory. That's good. That's important but it's not as important as one thing. Winning. I've been called a lot of things in my time. Most of which can't be put in print. I've also been called Kingmaker, Brain, Architect…Turd Blossom. Now that was a term of affection, don't get too upset about that. Some people want to know how I do what I do. Others want to

know why. As I look around this room of bright conservative scholars, I know I don't need to address why. Why is for the weak-minded on the other side. The media doesn't go running up to an Olympic athlete who wins the gold after suffering through lots of pain and ask, "Why?" If you ask me that three-letter question, you're not worthy of me as a colleague or opponent.

No, I look around here at your eager faces and know you want to get down to the How. *(Pause.)* By any means necessary. You know who said that?

Nope, it was Jean Paul Sartre. Act Five of his play *Dirty Hands.* "It is not by refusing to lie that we will abolish lies: it is by eradicating class by any means necessary." The rest of that quote might be garbage but those last four words are important. Then Mr. X took it and you saw how that turned out.

Negative campaigning. Good or bad? That's right, good. One, it brings more people out to vote. Oh, and let me say, you don't have to believe anything I'm saying. I have the factual and statistical evidence. You can go behind me and do the research if you want. But I know odds are you won't. Two, negative campaigning is unethical and ineffective. *(Shakes his head "no.")* Three, it's only recently we've started going negative and it's beginning to get ugly. *(Shakes his head "no.")* What we do now is softballs compared to way back when. Read the Declaration of Independence. They basically wipe their behinds with the Brits, taxation without representation, and on and on.

We happen to live in a wonderful time. An era of enlightenment the world has never seen. We have focus groups, research, polls. We know what they think and feel about things. You just have to know what to do with that information. Fortunately for us, we do and they don't. They come up with all these theories, they push forward issues, and rally around vague ideas like hope. *(Shakes his head "no.")*

You go out, hit them hard, and put them on the defensive. You get the dirt on them. Make things up. Hammer away at them until they are reeling and spinning. Then you take their message so you leave them with nothing. And you do it with this. *(He points at his smile.)* Because a good American trusts in us. Because we align ourselves with God. What's it say on your money? "In God We Trust." Francis Scott Key put that in the "Star-Spangled Banner" and it was mandatory—MANDATORY!—to put it on all our coins in 1908. Otherwise you are a Liberal, Hippy, Dipwad, Socialist, Traitor who coddles terrorists, cheats on his wife, and pisses away our money. Our money that says…? "In God We Trust." Amen. *(He pats his pocket.)* That's the change I believe in. The kind in my pocket.

They whine, "they don't fight fair." Politics is dirty but then so is football, working for a living, and getting baked beans down your shirt at a family picnic. Of course it's dirty. You don't have to be a better person to be the better candidate. We have to win it… "by any means necessary." Even if you reverse, smear, distract, confuse, mislead, or draw blood. In fact, it's only good television if you do that and that's how you keep the liberal media eating out of the palm of your hand.

This is strictly off the books but, most people I work with, I wouldn't trust them

if my life depended on it. They're evil, manipulative bastards who would sell their parents and children in a heartbeat. They sold their souls years ago to fit in. And I love them for it. Because they win.

Now, I never said any of that. Who said that? *(He pinpoints someone in the audience.)* Did you say that? You ought to be ashamed. They are good people. You show me one bit of evidence connecting me to ever having said anything like that. That is outrageous that you accuse me of that. I would never say such a thing because it simply isn't true. That is slanderous, sir, and I take personal offense at it. What they have been through deserves our respect and I would hope we could rise above this sort of pettiness and, frankly, stupidity that is bringing down politics. *(He pauses and then he points at his smile.)* Your homework, if you haven't already, go read *The Book of Five Rings* and Machiavelli. Class dismissed.

TRANSITION: HISTORICAL REENACTMENT FANTASY CAMP

Radio or TV advertisement.

VOICE 1: What are you doing this vacation?

VOICE 2: We were thinking about going on a cruise or taking the kids to a theme park. Maybe drive around and see parts of the country they haven't seen yet. What about you?

VOICE 1: We're reasserting our Patriotism by participating in the All-American Historical Reenactment Fantasy Camp.

VOICE 2: The All-American Historical Reenactment Fantasy Camp! What's that?

VOICE 1: Only the best thing since sliced bread. Usually if you go to a historical place they only have boring markers or cheesy actors who are "in character" telling you what they do there. With the All-American Historical Reenactment Fantasy Camp, history comes alive and YOU get to be a part of it.

VOICE 2: Sounds incredible.

VOICE 1: It is and there's three different camps across the country: Up North, Down South, and Out West. For example, Up North, you get to protest the Stamp Act with the Boston Tea Party.

VOICE 2: Wow.

VOICE 1: Down South you can fire muskets under the command of Nathaniel Greene at the Battle of Guilford Courthouse.

VOICE 2: My boys would love that!

VOICE 1: And Out West—

VOICE 2: —We can live out the Japanese internment camps?!

VOICE 1: Whatever you want, pal. It's the U.S. of A.

VOICE 2: I'm there!

VOICE 1: Being American. Don't just dream about it. Live it!

11. SUPER MAN

ERIC, a Blackwater contractor from North Carolina, is in a bar near where they're building Blackwater North in Illinois. He is drunk.

It's almost you-don't-have-to-go-home-but-you-can't-stay-here time. Damn baby, you lookin' fine tonight. Heaven must be missin' an angel…'cuz he's off jerkin' it hard, thinkin' 'bout you. That

seem forward? I don't care 'cuz I've seen the action baby and I know this one brief muthafucka we got. So you better grab those reigns tight if you're gonna stay on. And if there's one gal in this saloon who looks like she can stay on top of a buckin' steer, it's you.

Who am I? Why don't you just call me what all my friends do *(Reveals his belt buckle with a big red "s.")* Superman. Except I'm Superman all the time. Why hide the fact that bullets bounce off you and you're impervious to all the shit that'd kill a regular man. How else could I have gone to Iraq several times and lived to tell about it?

That's right, hot stuff. *(Beat.)* Shit no, I wasn't in the Army. I wasn't in the Marines or any of that shit. I saw those planes go into the towers and I was half-done calling my recruiter when my buddy said to call down to Blackwater. That's right baby. Smartest call I ever made. I'll say this. If the government had its head out of its ass from the get-go, it would've left the regular military bitches at home and let the big boys do it right from the start. The regs go over to fight for their country so they don't make dick and then they come back with PTSD. Then if they go back over they get complex PTSD, which stands for Batshit Fuckin' Crazy.

I don't have any of that shit. I went 'cuz it's a job and I made bank. They took me out 'cuz we got drunk celebratin' one night and I accidentally shot this Iraqi police guard. No big deal 'cept he was guardin' some public official who got "elected in" there. So they got me on the first plane out to avoid getting prosecuted by Iraqi law. At least I got my shit straight. I can channel my anger so it don't fuck me up. I heard most guys don't like to talk about what goes on.

Me? Shit, just ask, I'll tell you whatever. *(Beat.)* It's a rush! I love it! I don't care what anybody thinks. When you're over there and the adrenaline's pumpin' and it's you or this insurgent lightin' one or the other of you up. Yes!! I'm alive!!! You see all these faces of people going around here and they have no idea what it means to be living.

I'm back now doing skydiving demos and helping set up Blackwater North in Mount Carroll, fifty miles left of here. It's not as good as being over there 'cuz I'm an adrenaline junkie. What you see over there is like this action film. Only it's different 'cuz it's real. Try as much as they can, they'll never get it right. I mean, when you got human teeth in your hand or you're wiping brains off your NVGs just so you can see, it's different than when you're sitting in a movie theatre smelling popcorn.

I seen a hell of a lot of stuff. But I ain't fucked up. Not all of it's like, you know, "a rocket blew up by my head and fucked my buddy up." I did see that. But this guy'd play this joke. Oh God, it was funny. He'd tell new contractors it's the Arab custom to shake with their left hands. "Don't ever shake with your right hand. You'll just offend them and then they might behead you right there." 'Course the left is what they use to wipe their asses with. Diesel fuel and one-hundred-twenty-degree Third World shit smell is all you smell over there. They shit in the sand and cover it up with their foot. We had to use burn shitters, which is a diesel drum with fuel in it and once a day, a low-totem Army reg'd have to set it on fire and stir it with a stick. Sorry. Shouldn't talk about shit so much in front of a lady. I'm still gettin' used to bein' back here.

The dogs over there are fucking crazy. You know how pit bulls freak out here. Well those little bastards are starved over there so they started eating dead people and there's a lot 'cuz anyone with a gun is an insurgent. Or if they're near one. Light 'em up. But you see these dogs going around with fuckin' human legs and shit in their mouths. It's food but fuck, you know? So at nineteen hundred, that's seven at night, we'd do Operation Scooby-Doo and shoot all the dogs we could see 'cuz you don't want to wake up with one of those fuckers making a Scooby snack out of you.

You'd see all the dumb-ass things the regs and the Iraqi police'd be doing. I mean I'd feel like Robocop going around in my full Battle Rattle and my Kevlar helmet. Plus I'm Superman. But regs would be running around like it's World War I. They put scrap metal, we call it Hillbilly Armor, on the sides of their Humvees 'cuz they were given vehicles that were made to pick up the kids in the suburbs but they ain't made to take insurgent attacks in Najaf.

Then they're out training the Iraqis to take over. What a joke. Over there, women are for making babies and men are for everything else. So if you want to have sex with a woman you have to be married. To do that, you have to buy them off the dad. So, in the meantime, the men fuck around with each other. So regs are out there going, "fall into formation" and the Iraqis are holding hands and kissing. The men! They'll Never Be Ready To Take Care Of Themselves. They don't want to be. They want America to bring America without all the American shit. Like they want the conveniences but not our way of life. It's the least we can do since we went in without a plan and fucked it all up there.

Imagine if China came here and fucked up the infrastructure to put in "democracy" but they're really here for the corn so nobody's taking out the garbage or dealing with the sewage so our kids are playing in rivers of shit on the side of the road, you'd be pissed off too. Look at New Orleans or Mississippi. That's Iraq on our home turf. Blackwater was there. Wish I got in on that action. Nine hundred and fifty bucks a day. Tax free. There'll be other stuff. Fires in Cali. Riots and shit. Gonna be like thirteen hundred a day.

Shitheads over here don't know their history. My granddaddy's granddaddy was an old scalawag during Reconstruction in Tennessee. They were the Republicans who sided with the freed slaves. They went through hell dealing with the Klan and other assholes but they got the Fourteenth Amendment done and the Fifteenth Amendment done. It could be the same over there. But they don't want to do it themselves. Yeah, we could pull out and they could fight it but that's fuckin' stupid. People who say, "we had our civil war, they should too" don't know dick. We're up to our chins over there and need to do it right. The end. Period.

Blackwater's smart. The government using them is smart. They got all the international law and American law figured out. Like play-the-stock-market-real-good smart. They have guys from all over the world working as contractors like me. Shit, Iraqis are even working for us under Blackwater. That blew my mind but you get used to it. Guys from Honduras are pretty tough but the guys who trained under Pinochet are hardcore motherfuckers. Real mercenaries. You gotta step your game around them.

Don't worry, we all swore allegiance to the American Constitution.

(He points at a television screen.) Here everybody's freaking out over the baseball players using steroids. "Our heroes aren't heroes." Who gives a shit? Worry about some real shit for a change. I know guys who are using steroids and you should be thankful. Beats what the Syrians do. When you fight up north in Iraq it's like the fuckin' O.K. Corral. Down south they get all covert and hide in shit but up top they stand in the fucking road and it's face to face. Syrian fighters, man, they load up on you name it: Valium, codeine, horse tranqs. Light 'em up with forty shells, they'll still be standin' shootin' back at ya, they're so drugged out. Man that was fun!

I'd go back in a heartbeat if they'd let me. Shit, after I saw Scotty burned and hanging in Fallujah, I'd go back 'til it's done. It's done when I feel like it's done 'coz no one else knows when it's gonna be done. I guess when they have Disneyland.

(He looks over at the bartender who has announced it is time to leave the bar.) Alright, we'll get out of here. *(Beat.)* What you say, hot stuff? Wanna hop on my back and fly to my hotel?

TRANSITION: THE NEXT TOP COMMANDER-IN-CHIEF #3

REPUBLICAN CANDIDATE with an Austrian accent is on a reality show vying for the heart of America.

So tonight is final eliminations. We've gotten down to the final three: Indy, Blue Boy, and yours truly, Big Red. And tonight is the final decision. There can be only one and America's going to pick me. Indy is too much of an outsider. Blue is too weird. My plan is to tell America right to her face that she knows I will stay the course. She can count on me for a future of strength and prosperity. Once I win her over, I'm going to do things to her I shouldn't tell you on TV. I will be the Next Top Commander-in-Chief!!

12. ACTIVIST

THOMAS is on a street corner.

Excuse me, do you have seventy-six seconds for your country? I understand. *(He see the next person.)* How's it going? Do you have a minute for your country? That's cool. *(He tries another person.)* You look like a Patriot. Have a minute, man, for your country?

Great! *(He is caught off guard.)* Uh…uh… sorry. I don't really have a spiel. No, no, no. I'm not asking for any money. I don't need any money. I'm just…uh…doing a grassroots-effort thing. Not for a candidate or cause. I'm not with any "cause." I'm here to create a groundswell of dialogue. Or discourse. Or I don't know which but, you know, something to get people talking.

(Beat.) True, I could reach a lot more people on the Internet. But aren't you sick of your inbox being glutted with urgent message after urgent message after contribution request?

(Beat.) I stop sometimes and think I'm now of an age where I could run for President. You know the old "you don't like it, change it." But I don't know what I'd do. *(Pause.)* What's wrong with saying, "I'm an American"? A lot, it seems. I mean, can you say that without having to run around with "These Colors Don't Run" stickers and look for a fight? All this eye-for-an-eye stuff until everyone is scared enough of us so we can turn

into a benevolent father or something. "We're number one! We're number one! We're number…" What does that mean? Is that important? It's like our national identity has low self-esteem.

You hear how we're hated around the world. Some say it's because we're the best and they're jealous. Others because we're stupid and lazy and obnoxious. "They want to take away our way of life!" Or some because we consume and consume and we expect MORE. I know most people don't give a shit. I didn't give a shit until a minute ago. I guess I wonder whether we're drones doing the bidding of the higher ups. Or are we citizens involved in this civilization or are we Patriots sitting on the porch with a shotgun? Or do we even care because we just expect a bigger slice of the apple pie to be handed to us? The more I become an adult, the more it's clear we haven't grown up.

(He acknowledges another person who has stopped to listen.) I don't know about you but I'm kind of scared. But I wonder if that's more out of wanting things to go the way I want them to go. So as part of this dialogue, I thought we could come up with a question. A good question. What's the thing that puts everything else into perspective? Everybody's got both barrels blazing: stop this, start that, more of something, less of another…give that to this because it's never happened before. But what should we really be doing? If I take my needs out of the equation or my family's or whatever and pull back to the big picture, what's the thing that puts it all back in order? Past the spin and the noise and the lunacy?

(Beat.) I sometimes think I can wrap my mind around it but it's never quite it. People say, "well, things were built on this or that but now it's all changed."

"It's not the war, it's the economy." "It's not the economy, it's the environment." "It's the left." "It's the right." But it's all missing something and I want to figure out what it is. Right now.

(A third person stops to listen.) Maybe it's hate or selfishness. But that's stuff that's hard-wired into us as human beings. So you figure what can we do, except keep plugging away? I think I understood things better when I was a kid. My friend Andy had flag duty during safety patrols in sixth grade. Andy and this girl would carefully unfold the big flag each morning and run it thirty feet up the pole. Then they'd carefully fold it back up each night. That seemed like such a big job because I was told in Cub Scouts if the flag touched the ground, you had to burn it. And you put it in a triangle to look like Paul Revere's hat.

During the burial ceremony for fallen soldiers, they fold the flag into a tight triangle with just the stars and the blue background showing. No red or white stripes. That's put over the heart on the casket and after the eulogy and gun salute, it's presented to the next of kin with the points going towards the presenting officer. While the officer and the kin are both holding it, the officer says, "On behalf of the president of the United States of America, the commandant of the Marine Corps, and a grateful nation, please accept this flag as a symbol of our appreciation for your loved one's service to God, country, and corps. Semper fidelis and may God bless you." Then they salute them.

Where did all the day-to-day flags go? A few years ago there were flags a couple inches apart everywhere you looked. Now I only see them at the post office. Those "Never Forget" signs everywhere. When the flags went away, people stopped being as…I guess people remember the pain but I think we've already forgotten something really important.

(More people have gathered.) To me, being an American doesn't mean going out there and being the biggest bully. It's not whipping everybody up into some nationalistic fervor. It sure as hell isn't about protecting some kind of red, white, and blue lifestyle. To me, it's about Liberty. Real Liberty. The Declaration of Independence. The Constitution. The Bill of Rights. Not interpretations or readings of this stuff. The real thing. Today. Of the people, for the people, by the people. Not God, King, Victim, Veteran, Profiteer, Vacuous Waste of Space. We are the government and the government is us. That's how we're supposed to be different. We should know those documents one hundred percent, not just quote the famous parts for our own use.

How do we get back to having those be the foundation, inside us day-to-day as we negotiate this crap shoot? We the people in order to form a more perfect union and the rest of it are essential to us being together at our best. How do we get back to striving to improve who we are? That was the point, right? Where we all get a chance? I don't think Americans are lazy people or lazy workers. I think most Americans are lazy citizens. I think I'm standing here because I want to turn that around. I think we can do that. I used to think having a revolution meant rioting and fighting and blood. But I think this is the start of one. A quieter one. *(Pause.)* Wow, I've said a lot. I'll shut up now. What do you think?

(The End.)

A FIRE AS BRIGHT AS HEAVEN

A One-Man Show

Tim Collins

TIM COLLINS is a writer and an actor. He was born in Oneida, New York, and raised in Sherrill, New York. He graduated from Marlboro College with a BA in theatre and solo performance. He also trained at Arts Education Schools London. His solo shows include *Dateline* (2003 15 Minute Playwriting Festival, Belfast, Maine), *Puzzles* (2004 15 Minute Playwriting Festival; 24th Annual National Storytelling Conference, Boston, 2005), and *The Power Play* (2005 15 Minute Playwriting Festival; 1st Annual Festival of Cultural Exchange, Portland, Maine, 2005). His acting credits include a co-starring role in the independent feature film *Redbelly*. He is the recipient of Marlboro College's Sally and Valerio Montanari Theatre Prize, a Wallis Foundation Grant, and a commission from the Center for Cultural Exchange. He is a three-time winner at the 15 Minute Playwriting Festival, and was team captain for the St. Louis Slam Poetry Team in 2006. Collins is currently working on a sequel to *A Fire as Bright as Heaven*, which explores American life after the 2008 presidential election, as well as two other solo shows: *Conventions*, which explores niche consumer groups in the United States, and *The Script*, which addresses dating violence and sexual assault. The latter, created in conjunction with the St. Louis Regional Sexual Assault Center, will tour high schools and colleges in 2009. He writes, produces, and tours his solo work nationally, and lives in St. Louis, Missouri, with his fiancée.

A Fire as Bright as Heaven was first presented as part of the New York International Fringe Festival (Elena K. Holy, Producing Artistic Director) on August 13, 2008, at the Cherry Lane Studio Theatre with the following cast and credits:

Performed by: Tim Collins
Company Rep: Trevor Savage
Tech/Lights: Marika Kent
Stage Manager: Kimberly Bower

www.timcollinsonline.com

A Fire as Bright as Heaven is a composite of four one-hour solo shows and one fifteen-minute monologue that I created and toured with over a seven-year period (2001–2008). Each one-hour show has been distilled into approximately twenty minutes, and these twenty-minute segments make up the chapters of *A Fire as Bright as Heaven*.

I never intended to combine the individual shows into a sort of mega-show—I was, instead, creating a show a year addressing what was, to me, the current major political anxiety aggravating the American consciousness. As 2008 staggered towards the presidential elections, I realized I had a series of material that spanned the past seven years of American history, a sort of one-man chronicle of events and opinions. I started honing down the scripts and came up with a story of American emotion as told by people who seem to have little influence on national events, yet who are hugely influenced and affected by those events.

Chapter 1 is a distilled version of *Eleventh & Love*, a solo show that I began writing while I was studying acting in London in the fall of 2001. I arrived in England a few days before September 11th, and when the attack occurred, I was filled with a surreal sense of isolation from the tragedy, and my shock and grief had a muddled, alienated quality about it. Endless television coverage and sympathy from strangers was all I had to go on for four months, so I started writing *Eleventh & Love* as a means to comprehend events that still to me now seem mostly incomprehensible.

Chapter 2 is a version of *Puzzles*, a show written while I was employed part time at an educational toy store in coastal New England. The beginning of my employment coincided with the U.S. invasion of Iraq. I started writing the show in the midst of a chaos of customers shopping for toys (both war-themed toys and the more pacifistic variety), vociferous antiwar and pro-troop protestors marching in the streets, and incessant NPR news reports coming in on the toy store's sound system.

Chapter 3 is a version of *The Power Play*, a show I was commissioned to create by the Center for Cultural Exchange in Portland, Maine. *The Power Play* was based on interviews with people I approached on the street—at random, I accosted people for their opinions about the dominant concern at the time, terrorism (*The Power Play* was created in 2005).

Chapter 4 is a version of *Gun Shy*, a show about my experience of going "undercover" to the 2007 NRA National Convention that was held at the America Center in St. Louis, Missouri. The original show ran about an hour—the orignal script I wrote, if performed in full, would easily have run three hours—the NRA Convention was one of the most staggering displays of human effort I have ever seen. Go check one out and see for yourself.

Chapter 5 is a version of *Door To Door*, a fifteen-minute, single-character monologue. This is the only chapter in *A Fire as Bright as Heaven* that was not honed down from a larger piece. It is in this chapter that the narrator comes to the end of his journey, meeting a character who, in the course of the show, best expresses the particular agony of life as a anxious American.

I perform *A Fire as Bright as Heaven* by attempting to establish the integrity of each character in turn, one after the other, in hopes of creating a living conversation between individual entities on stage. Transitions between characters are quick, with an effort to solidly land each personality before embarking on the dialogue. There are occasional props, a baseball hat or hooded sweat jacket, but the emphasis is always on gripping the character with the whole body, working to become this other person, then to fully depart from that personality and move on to the next—fast, simple transitions with character delineations made clear via physical embodiment.

CHAPTER 1
LONDON, ENGLAND, 2001

Stage is set with four chairs in a half circle; the actor will occupy each of these chairs as he assumes the characters of, from left to right, TIM, BRUCE, LUCINDA, and LES. Lights up on TIM, holding two bulky suitcases.

TIM: I flew from New York City to London on September 10th, 2001

(Bags drop to the floor, loudly.)

(Second chair.)

BRUCE: Welcome. My name is Bruce Doppler, I'm Professor of American Studies here, you can call me Professor Doppler, but I also act as unofficial advisor to American students studying abroad—you guys— So—in light of the recent attack on the World Trade Center, I thought to circle the wagons, so to speak, and create a space to talk, process, ask, and hopefully, to understand. So. Anything goes. Hit me. Yeah—

(First chair.)

TIM: … I just can't believe it. It's like … they attacked a—symbol of—America—

(Second chair.)

BRUCE: Okay, great, let me cut you off right there, not to tell you that you're—*wrong*, per se, but instead to—*make you aware*—of information you may not possess. The World Trade Center was constructed in *1953*. Were you aware of that? That's what I thought. So, right there, strictly in terms of time frame, no way the WTC could qualify as a "symbol" of American anything—it simply wasn't in existence long enough. So, in that way, your symbol theory goes—right out the window. So to speak. But I want to acknowledge, that while it wasn't intentional, you did bring up a good point. Yes, you did. Now we've negated the World Trade Center as a symbol, but the terrorists—and I'm going to ask you to indulge me on this point because I think it might lead to something—interesting—the terrorists may have done themselves—one better—if they had selected a target with more—symbolic impactfulness? For example, just off the top of my head—the Statue of Liberty. That would have been a pretty clear message sent. What I'm really asking is—what would have been a more effective target for the terrorists,? A less ambiguous target for the terrorists? Anyone? *(Turns to TIM.)* How about you?

TIM: *(Pause, speechless. Looks to audience, then shaking his head "no," turns back to BRUCE.)*

BRUCE: No? The Washington Monument...that would have been a good one—a pretty clear statement there. Don't let me dominate the conversation, anything goes. Anyone? A better, more effective target for the terrorists? *(Turns to his left, to LUCINDA.)*

(Third chair.)

LUCINDA: *(A female student. She stares at BRUCE, pauses, then responds with an exhalation, half-startled, half-contemptuous.)*

BRUCE: I'll take that as a "no." Uh... Mount Rushmore—would have been— almost *too* non-ambiguous, though, then again, the terrorists may not have had the petrol to make it that far, and I think the

amount of petrol was part of the point. A more effective target for the terrorists? How about you?

(Fourth chair.)

LES: *(A male student, wears a Yankees baseball cap. He sits silent for a moment, then breaks into a wide awkward grin, laughing to fill the space, turns to audience, then back to BRUCE, and the grin and laughter cease instantly and he only shakes his head "no.")*

BRUCE: No? ... The Vietnam Memorial—that would have been— memorable. Though, come to think of it, they would have risked blurring ideologies, with Islam, presumably, on the side of the terrorists, and Communism on the side of the Vietnamese, so...that could have gotten...messy...So, yeah... *(Turns to TIM.)* Did I—answer your question?

TIM: No. *(Rises, speaks to audience.)* I was studying in London for three months, studying theatre. But I spent most of my time walking, outside.

(Sound cue: jet plane passing overhead.)

TIM: I spent most of my time sitting, inside. *(Sits downstage left.)* Londoners approached me:

LONDONER: Are you from America? I'm sorry.

TIM: You're sorry that I'm an American? Oh...it's okay. It's not that bad...

LONDONER: No, no, I mean about the World Trade Center...Try not to take it personally.

TIM: *(Pause.)* Thank you.

MURRAY: Welcome to Acting for the Stage, I'm Murray, your professor for the semester. Sad news, of course, about New York. It may help you to hear what the British might say in times like these, we might say: "Oh, shit." *(Pause.)* A bit of a joke…if there's anything at all that I can do…in the interim, we've got a tremendous amount of exciting work to dive into, and let's do so… *(Distracted.)* after we field a question from the back…yes?

(First chair.)

TIM: Sorry—do you mind if we cancel or reschedule class today? Considering—the news.

MURRAY: Ah! Well, as I said, we have a tremendous amount of work, and a very limited amount of time in the term, so, no. Sorry. Although, I do understand how you all must feel—

(Third chair.)

LUCINDA: Uh…not to be rude, but—I *don't* think you know how we feel.

MURRAY: Ah. No, obviously I don't know your *direct experience*, but, of course, the British have been living with the very real threat of terrorism for—decades, and take my word for it, you simply cannot let it derail you—you simply have to—get on with things.

(Fourth chair.)

LES: Uh…not to be rude, but, you're talking about the IRA, right? Well, not to be rude, but you can't really compare the World Trade Center and the IRA, I mean, not to be rude, but the IRA's mostly blown up like—pubs and mailboxes, and the World Trade Center—that's—that's a *building*. That's—*real.*

MURRAY: Ah—I would be loathe to deduce what you mean by *real*, and, I think, to compare *this* terrorism with *that* terrorism is—rather, missing the point. You see, the British have—

(Third chair.)

LUCINDA: No, the point is that thousands of people are dead, which is nothing like the IRA. It's like—a *War.* What would you or any British person understand about that?

MURRAY: …What would the British understand about *war*…? I'm amazed at the question…That you're upset is understandable—

LUCINDA: *(She rises.)* We'd just appreciate some sympathy.

MURRAY: …Of course. We'll just pick up next week, then.

LUCINDA: Thank you. As Americans, we appreciate you trying to understand.

MURRAY: …Well. We foreigners do what we can. *(Moves away, downstage left. Gestures to TIM, calling him over.)* Tim, is it? Try not to worry. Give it some time—these things tend to get a bit easier to understand, after a while.

TIM: Really?

MURRAY: *(Pause.)* No. No…See you next week, then.

(LUCINDA stands downstage center, holding an unlit candle. Speaks directly to audience.)

LUCINDA: Okay, listen up everyone, this is Lucinda talking—we need to keep this candle ceremony short because, since it's raining outside, we have to have it here in the dorm foyer, which means we can't actually light the candles. Because we'd set off the smoke alarms, so what we're going to do, it's stupid, but we're just going to hold the candles like they're lit, and we're going to go around, and say something about remembrance, and then we'll have a moment of silence, and, I'll start. The attacks on the World Trade Center reminded me of a time when I was eleven, when I jumped into a swimming pool and landed on my head. I remember—there was a moment like a silver flash, where I could have chosen to die. But I didn't, I chose to live. Obviously.

Science confirms that there are multiple lifetimes happening around us all the time—it's physics—and in one reality, I died, and in another reality, I was crippled, but I chose *this* reality, because I knew I could help the world more by not being injured or dead. We choose, is the point. And I know, in another life, those people chose to oversleep, and miss their flights. And, I know, in another life, the terrorists chose not to fly the planes into the buildings, but to change their minds, and land safe, and apologize. Or never to be a terrorist at all, in another life, they chose to be something else—pediatricians. And in another life, people in the building chose not to jump and fall, but to jump and survive somehow, to fly away, somehow. In another life, it was different, but in this life, they chose to die, and they did it—for us, to help us—to help teach us a lesson that we needed to learn. I don't know what that lesson is, yet, but we choose, we choose everything, it's up to us. I think so. Don't you think? Every little thing—is up to us?

If this candle were burning right now, it would be burning my hand, so I propose we have our moment of silence in the dark— *(She reaches out, as if turning off a light switch.)*

(Blackout.)

(First chair.)

TIM: It's just so sad. All those innocent people—

(Second chair.)

BRUCE: Okay, not to cut you off, but, if we're going to swallow the conceit that the people killed were *innocent*—well—you're going to have to ask yourself some tough questions about what it means to be an economic consumer moving currency within the suprastructure of the largest military superpower in the history of the world. By some estimates, each American citizen is a very legitimate target. But I want to get back to a point I made earlier which I think was—interesting, about the irony overshadowing the 9/11 attacks and how most Americans are unaware of that irony: If you really consider the nature of the corporations housed in the towers—and not to oversimplify things, but, I get a sense, that's what you need—the primary focus of those corporations in the towers was to—outsource American jobs. So, in that way, the terrorists, by destroying the World Trade Center, were actually *defending Americans*. And I think that is both very ironic, and very interesting. Comments?

(First chair, TIM rises, walks downstage center.)

TIM: A conversation with Shinya, student of sports medicine, from Japan.

SHINYA: Hey, man, that's some wild stuff happening in America, yeah? Terrorists, anthrax…it's wild, right?

TIM: Yeah…it's…yeah.

SHINYA: Listen, if you want, I could help you, to move you and your family, to Japan.

TIM: ...What?

SHINYA: You know Kyoto? My father owns a company there, and I could get you all jobs. I mean, I just thought, it would be difficult to live in America right now, you know?

TIM: ...No, not really. What do you mean?

SHINYA: Oh, I was thinking, it is similar to Japan, when Japan lost the War. You know, World War II? It was difficult. My grandparents talk about it all the time—

TIM: Well, yeah, but, you can't really compare the World Trade Center and World War II—it's not really the same thing—

SHINYA: Well—no, it's not exactly the same thing—no—I know it's not exactly the same thing—

TIM: I mean, I appreciate you trying to understand—

SHINYA: Well, no, it is, uh—loss. It takes time to get over—and I just thought—if you wanted to be out of the country for a while—with your family—

TIM: Wait, wait. What do you mean by—what do you mean by "loss"?

SHINYA: Hmm? What do I mean by— Oh—no—I don't mean to be insensitive. You know. World Trade Center. Pride. I think is similar to Japan, when Japan lost the War—

TIM: Look, I understand what you're saying, America was attacked, and Japan was attacked, but, Japan *surrendered*, you know? America didn't *surrender*. Right?

SHINYA: *(Pause.)* No—you're right.

TIM: I'm sorry, I didn't mean to—

SHINYA: No, no. Forgive me. I just assumed that I, perhaps, knew what you Americans might be feeling—but now that I think about it— I'm sure I have no idea.

(Fourth chair.)

LES: So do you think America will go to war now?

(Second chair.)

BRUCE: It's interesting, what I hear, the sort of—*meta-assumption* under which you operate, coming from, presumably, your caucasian, middle-class, public school background—you see the world, not as it is—no, you see a *version* of the world, that you've been *trained* to see. Which is not your fault...well. I could make a pretty substantial argument proving that it is your fault, but I don't want to talk about that right now, instead, I want to get back to a point I made earlier that I thought was—interesting—about Americans qualifying as legitimate targets—

(Third chair.)

LUCINDA: I don't understand what you're talking about. What does this have to do with the people who died. Who fell. Who were in the planes.

(Second chair.)

BRUCE: Yes, people died. And that was sad—but it was sad in a *particular context. (He stands suddenly, shouting.)* I'm going to ask you to remain seated until I'm finished speaking— *(Sits, resumes speaking, calmly.)* You have no idea— you're in the ideal position, outside of the United States—you're free to see this event from the best perspective—free of American sentimentality—

I moved away from the United States nearly nine years ago, and made my home here. And when I go back, I see a country sick—blind, a nation blinded by itself and its sense of specialness, American specialness

It's only by being away from the United States that you can see it for what it really is— Not that you have any historical perspective to assist you—you hardly remember—*Reagan*—you have no idea how many times "our country" has betrayed the people who've attempted to love something about it—

And so 9/11 happens...and you think, yes. Yes, America *deserves* this, paybacks are a *bitch*

And 9/11 happens, and you see—that it wasn't payback that you wanted, you were, instead, waiting for an event that would change things. And you think, if I could have *been there*, and been part of that experience, part of that loss, then maybe I could—reset something in myself, and life in America would make some kind of *sense* to me, I could be a part of it again, I could find a way to make a home there, again. But you miss it. I miss it. Because—I'm far away...

(As if waking up, turning his attention to the STUDENTS and audience.) You're going to go back there, but it's different now—everything's changed—and you're going to look for the home you once knew—you're going to search—and you won't find it. *(Rises as STUDENTS leave.)* Where are you going? Where are you going? Where will you go?

(Moves downstage center, becomes JESSICA. The conversation is hushed, almost whispered.)

JESSICA: Hi.

TIM: ...Hello.

JESSICA: I'm Jessica.

TIM: ...I'm Tim.

JESSICA: Fancy a good time?

TIM: ...Are you a prostitute?

JESSICA: ...Yes.

TIM: Oh...cool...um—so how much do you—charge?

JESSICA: Twenty quid.

TIM: Oh, yeah, twenty quid...for what?

JESSICA: ...For sex. For intercourse?

TIM: Oh right. Well, I better not.

JESSICA: Why, are you gay?

TIM: ...Not that I'm aware of.

JESSICA: Why not give it a go, then? Be a daredevil.

TIM: ...Ha! Oh, no, no, thank you, I better not, thank you, though, thanks.

JESSICA: ...Alright. Come back if you change your mind.

TIM: Okay...Hey, sorry, do you mind if I ask you—do you—*like* this job? I mean, you probably get to meet different people—which is the point, I guess, but I imagine you do a lot of waiting around—not that you're not busy—I mean, obviously, you're busy—well, not *obviously*, I'm just saying, you're a professional—anyway, uh—

You know, I've been here awhile, and am going back—*home* in a few days, and—I've been doing a lot of waiting around, waiting. And yesterday I was walking off of High Street, down this side street, and I heard someone yelling in this thick accent: "Please, please help myself,"—and I looked, and there was this man who had fallen down a staircase off the street and the whole side of his head was—blood— So I ran down the steps, and he was actually this huge guy, and he was trying to sit up, and I was like, "don't move," because I could see that he was hurt really bad and I thought, for a second, in a small way, it must have been like this—in New York.

It must have been like this, there.

And someone must have called the ambulance, because they take him away on a stretcher, and his hand pulls away from mine and I've got his—blood all over me, so I walk, I don't know where, exactly, and get on the subway, ride for a couple of hours, and I get off at some tube stop north of London, and I walk out of the tube stop there is the most— the sunset—it's like the sky has exploded and all the tall chimneys are smokeless and up, and the television antennas are catching the light just right and orange-blazing, and the sky above the sun was this sort of molten gold, cut through with lavender, and it was—the prettiest thing. And—I'm waiting—

JESSICA: …Are you saying that…you're lonely?

TIM: …Yes.

JESSICA: Well…I can help.

(TIM stares for a moment, then, slowly, reaches his hand out for hers, so slowly. Blackout.)

CHAPTER 2
New England 2003

Lights up. TIM stands center stage, arms flung wide.

TIM: New England, 2003. *(Starts spinning.)* A small blond boy in blue shoes spins by the train table. He holds a tiny, two-propeller passenger plane. *(Stops spinning.)* On Wednesdays, I work in a toy store.

MALE CUSTOMER: Excuse me—you sell little plastic Army soldiers in here?

TIM: Army soldiers…uh…no. No.

MALE CUSTOMER: *(Pause.)* How about G.I. Joe men?

TIM: G.I. Joe…no, no, we really only carry educational kinds of toys. Trains… tops…firemen. Do you want firemen?

MALE CUSTOMER: Educational toys?

TIM: Yeah.

MALE CUSTOMER: G.I. Joe *is* educational.

TIM: Yeah. Okay. Have a nice day— thanks.

On Wednesdays I work in a toy store, but on *this* Wednesday, America is forty-eight hours into the heart of the Iraqi Invasion and I am at the heart OF INFORMATION COMMAND— *(Moves as if opening a newspaper.)* The *Boston Globe*, Special Two-Page Spread, full-color high-res pics: *(He animates each photo through fast movement.)*

Blackhawk helicopter gunships in smothering Desert Storm liftoff

And: Iraqi matriarchs wrapped in black weeping and clenched over garland-draped casket

And: Rumsfeld—Cheney—Tony Blair in straight gray suit and tie, perched at podium looking—constipated. Constipated with power—!

I am informed, so fully and efficiently informed, I feel so close Persian dust chokes my throat. I—

CUSTOMER: Excuse me—do you sell little plastic fighter jets here? Little F-16s or—little Stealth Bombers or—little Apache attack helicopters? Do you have any of those here?

TIM: *(Pulled from his reverie.)* No—we're an educational toy store. We don't sell war toys.

CUSTOMER: Okay, but, strictly speaking? An F-16—that's educational.

TIM: Yes. Okay. Have a nice day, thanks.

Audio, I need audio—To keep up with the latest breaking events, I slalom the radio dial back and forth between WNPR and the local public access community radio station:

The Local Public Access Community Radio Station:

PUBLIC ACCESS RADIO STATION DJ: Okay, you've just heard two hours of—World Music—which is, of course, music from all over the World. No kidding. Tune in next week, when I'll be joined by Steve and AJ—well, not AJ, because—AJ's a *tool*... but—me and Steve, and we'll play more World Music, which is, of course, music from all over the World...which I already said, because...I'm an *idiot.* So, anyway, here's the news. On Iraq. *(Moves as if hitting appropriate buttons. Awkward pause as he realizes the news is, in fact, not playing. Looking around the booth frantically, then, back on the air.)* —Sorry about that dead air! Big surprise, community radio, real professional around here—so, we'll be back with the news, as soon as

we find it—in the meantime—here's a little more *reggae.*

(TIM moves as if retuning the radio dial.)

NPR DJ: *(Slow monotone.)* You're listening to NPR—National Public Radio. Support for NPR comes from Magnolia Pictures. From the Lending Tree, providing you quality, low-interest loans, Lending Tree. com. From Wal-Mart. And from listeners like you. This is NPR, National. Public. Radio.

SECOND NPR DJ: Welcome back. We are at the epicenter of the excitement—you can hear the telephones ringing in the background, as we enter the thirtieth hour of Maine Public Radio's Spring Pledge Drive—

(TIM moves as if rapidly retuning the radio.)

PUBLIC ACCESS RADIO DJ: *(Singing clumsily.)* Buffalo Soldier, in the heart of America. Ay Yi Yi, Yida Yi Yi, Ay Yi Yi Di Yi Di Yi Yi—

(TIM moves as if rapidly switching off radio.)

TIM: Outside, an antiwar protest. And the drums—

(The following segment is dancelike, TIM embodying each PROTESTER in turn as he describes them.)

DRUM DRUM DRUM DRUM and the Ranks of the Earnestly Bearded bear signs upon the sidewalk, ponytails snapping like hemp whips

Standing shoulder to shoulder with:

Soccer moms daubed in essential oils, diminutive children dangling at their kneecaps, howling like Luddite zealots, chipping at the concrete with chewed-through tofu wieners keeping time with the Drum Drum Drum Drum—

And here's:

Long aligned lines of Hatha Yoga Practitioners, breathing deeply in Wide-Awake-Warrior-Pose, stretching out arms and auras all the way to the Persian Gulf, knocking chakras clean from every U.S. Marine they gleam upon—

And here's:

A hippie visionary, tripping on herbal popcorn.

And here's:

Stout-armed leftist grandmothers bearing subversive handbags

And here's:

Co-op checkout checked-out boys in black battered hoodies getting ironic about Anarchy, smoking herbal cigarettes, and flicking stiff singular digits at the MAN

And here's:

Gangly organic artists influencing violins through violence to whine whirling siren sonics, while contra-dancing coffee house divas clog lustily to Reveille played on one tarnished bugling bugle bleating betwixt the breathing beats blundering DRUM DRUM DRUM and the steady Strum Strum Strum and the heady Hum Hum Hum of pseudo-toned mantras rising up from the ranks:

NO ATTACK ON THE PEOPLE OF IRAQ!! DRUM DRUM

NO ATTACK ON THE PEOPLE OF IRAQ!! DRUM DRUM

NO ATTACK ON THE PEOPLE OF IRAQ!! DRUM DRUM

BUSH! PULL OUT!! WE WISH YOUR FATHER HAD!!

DRUM DRUM

TIM: A man walks in

ANTIWAR PROTESTER: *(Smoking a cigarette.)* You know, protesting is okay. COUGH!! It makes us feel better. But the only thing that really makes a difference— are the American corpses. COUGH!! Not to be morbid about it, but— COUGH!! COUGH!! Fucking allergies. *(He takes a drag on his cigarette)* Don't tell anybody, right—COUGH!! but when I'm out there, and everyone's— you know—visualizing World Peace? You know what I'm visualizing? *(He places his index finger to his temple.)* Shoot straight. Shoot fast. Aim for the head. Aim for the face. Sniper them from alleyways and rooftops. Throw Molotov cocktails and nail bombs. Dig pit traps, set tripwires. Strap bombs to your bodies, and kill as many American soldiers as you can. COUGH Look—protesting isn't going to stop the War. Reading Noam Chomsky isn't going to stop the War. Emailing the White House isn't going to stop the War. I mean…what's going to stop the War? What is going to stop the War? What's going to stop the War? Voting? *(He slowly begins laughing.)* Look, American corpses are the only thing that's going to stop…COUGH American corpses—COUGH fucking allergies—COUGH!! American— COUGH wait a second COUGH COUGH!! I'll be back—COUGH *(He turns away.)*

TIM: A woman walks in

WOMAN: Puzzles. Do you have any puzzles? *(Pause.)* These protesters, the way they go on…I support them, you know—but it's not that simple—It's easy enough to go and complain. But I read, in *Newsweek*, that Saddam Hussein put his enemies in *Acid Baths*. Acid Baths. What kind of mind—could even *conceive* of— It said it took them *eight hours* to die…And then I think—even if you're not *for* the war, you could at least support the troops, because they are *over there* and they are in *danger*, right?— how old are you? *(Nodding.)* My son is twenty-one— he could be over there. Boys his age, and your age, *are* over there—and younger— Let me tell you something: Everything is different when you have children. And you think—if *my son* was over there, I'd want him to do—whatever he had to do—to come home alive. And if that means—shooting, killing—to—defend himself—well— *(Pause.)* But I suppose Iraqi mothers are saying the same things, aren't they? *(She stares, overwhelmed, then waves it away.)* Puzzles—do you have any puzzles? Big, solid puzzles? For my little ones—I teach little ones—they love puzzles—trying to figure out how they all fit together. *(pause)* Maybe they can figure them out. Because I can't! I know I can't!

(TIM begins spinning, arms thrown wide.)

TIM: A small blond boy in blue shoes spins by the train table the shadow of a white foam airplane drapes a black cross upon his body he holds a tiny two-propeller passenger plane, and as he spins, as he spins, he speaks:

BOY: *(Spinning.)* Help. Help I can't land…Help. Help I can't land…Help. Help, I can't land…I'm going out of control…

TIM: Yeah, kid—I know how you feel.

(Blackout.)

CHAPTER 3
NEW ENGLAND 2005

TIM: New England, 2005

(Lights up on TIM, holding a tape recorder and speaking to the audience.)

TIM: Hi, excuse me? Hi. I'm going around, working on a project, asking people questions about current events, homeland security, that kind of thing. Do you mind if I ask you a couple of quick questions? Great. I guess my first question is: Do you ever worry about terrorism?

MAN: *(Sixty, pumping gas.)* First I'll ask you to stand back right now because I do not want to blow up. They spark. Tape recorders, electronic devices can throw off sparks, and gasoline— *(Gestures as if to nearby gas pump and vehicle.)* filling up the *Yukon* here, a project that oftentimes can take upwards of an entire afternoon. *(Sets gas nozzle to pump hands free and moves downstage.)* Alright now—fire away.

(Listening to a question from TIM.) Terrorism. What about it? No, I don't worry about it. Why? Why should I? Because, young man, at our defense is the finest antiterrorism organization in the world—the United States Armed Forces. You have heard of the United States Armed Forces? They have single-handedly been defeating what you call *terrorism* around the globe for the past two hundred and fifty—plus—years! With a few…*unfortunate* exceptions *(Gives himself sign of the cross.)* that have been given an…*undue* amount of attention from a *liberal* media—

(He stops, eyeing TIM, and perhaps the audience.) I notice your eyes are glazing over. Maybe you can't handle my little

discourse. You want me to continue? You sure? Alright! I'm going to give it to you—both barrels!

A *liberal* media, poised to *sap* the credibility of our nation's government—and at the same time pursue their own agenda, which is to—what? *(Waits about two seconds for an answer.)* Incorrect! To *demoralize* the American People! Who, in their need for—some kind of—hope, turn to the same media that sold them that story of the death of the spirit of their own nation. The People turn to that Media, and lo and behold, they are welcomed by that Media, yes, and are offered in return—TV shows, movies, TiVo, Internet… *distractions* for a lifetime. And don't forget—here's the evening news where you can be reminded that your leaders are *liars* and crooks and criminals and *thieves*, and by the way there's nothing you can really *do about it*. But don't worry—don't worry, because at ten p.m., on *HBO*, there's a little TV show make you forget about all your problems—make you forget everything, just—clean the slate—it's about—about *(With great difficulty and disgust.)* …*lesbians*…oh, and the great *time* the lesbian ladies are having, and the great—*sex* they're having… right there on the TV—and for Chrissake while you're at it, why don't you let my *grandchildren* watch, I'm sure that'd be *wonderful* for them, just *positive growth* for their developing young minds, not that I have any say in that in the first place—in the first place!

And now—if you'll excuse me, my gas tank is full up and I'm sure that little tape recorder of yours is too— *(Turns and checks gas pump.)* Ah—not quite full yet. Now stand back with yourself young man, stand back. You've got yourself

some hot opinions there—now we don't want them to *spark* on us—and blow ourselves up. Do we?

MAN: *(Forty-one, drinking from a bottle wrapped in a paper bag.)* Ah…yeah, I think there's a terrorist organization out there, gunning for America…but I think—there's terrorist organizations, out there, gunning for America who *are Americans*, you know what I mean? Like, I can't even stand on the corner anymore smoke a joint, I got fifty FBI guys up my ass!! You know what I mean? *(To an audience member.)* You definitely know what I mean…But as far as like standing around in a building, getting blown up by a terrorist bomb or an airplane—no, I'm not too worried about that. *(Drinks from bottle.)*

What *am* I worried about? Well— yeah, here it is, it's the thought of the FBI, Police Department, and Security, interfering with innocent people's lives. I think that right there is the real threat to the average American. Yeah. I mean, it's crazy. I was just down in Cambridge, Harvard Square, you know, real high-security area, standing on the corner, drinking a Bud Light, okay? Cops are gonna walk right up to you and be like: "Hey—what are you doing?" What?! Bud Light, what?! Especially, you know, especially if you don't look the part. You know, you're not dressed like a student, or wearing a—business suit, or—you know. *(He pulls the bottle out of the bag, revealing a nonalcoholic sports drink. He pauses.)* What? I'm trying to stay hydrated. Don't tell anyone, alright? I'm trying to keep down appearances.

So. John Kerry, right? I think Kerry could have done the job. I'm not saying he's the greatest person in the world or anything—definitely not, definitely not—I'm saying, he was *egotistical* enough to get the job done right, maybe. No, because, I mean, because like, if it's written down, in some *book*, fifty years from now, that John Kerry was *the guy* who like—saved the United States of America? John Kerry's gonna be like: "Yeeeah, baby!! That's right!! That's right!! What's up, that's right, John Kerry woot-woot!" You know what I mean? *(To audience member, again.)* You definitely know what I mean— So, I think, anyone in that position, wanting to be President, has got to be a crazy egomaniac—but, I think, John Kerry can do it— *(Pause.)* What am I saying? *Could've done it.* Maybe he could have done it. In the right way.

GIRL: *(Sixteen, holding a notebook)* What do I think we can do about terrorism? *(Pause.)* That's hard. Well, I guess I could organize the people of this city together…and we could all shout at Washington? But that's not really going to *change* anything? And I could do—artwork, or, make a movie, or—write a play? But—probably the only people who'd come see it probably already *agree* with what I'm saying, so—why bother? And I could *vote*, I guess…but no one really takes voting too *seriously* anymore? What do I think we can do about terrorism? I don't know. I guess I wonder—is that even a relevant question? I mean— I can *imagine* a world—how I'd *like* it to be—where there's no war, and torture and killing and stuff, but— I don't know how to make that happen. Like, I don't understand a way—I mean, I don't even have a way to—begin.

MAN: *(Thirty-five, holding a latte.)* Terrorism? Are you a Liberal? Geez, you Liberals! What is this, some kind of poll, some kind of Liberal poll? No, that's

fine, that's fine, that's fine…Put this in your poll—George Bush *won*. Get over it. *(Holds up hand for a high-five.)* No, I'm just messing with you, I'm just messing with you. Gimme some of that. Look, I understand where you Liberals are coming from. I am surrounded in my life by Liberals. My whole *family* is Liberal. I understand where you're coming from, and I respect it— Okay, I *don't* respect it—but I understand. But I also understand *what a Liberal is.* You can put this in your poll— A Liberal is someone who *wants* things to be one way, doesn't like how things *are not* that way, and is unwilling to come to terms with the fact that things *can't* be any other way. The way things are *is* the way. Okay?

You know, every Sunday, I have the same conversation with my dad. Now my dad, the man is as liberal as you can possibly imagine—Okay? I mean, he was going to vote for *Howard Dean*. And I say, Dad, look, there's no difference between you and me, there's no difference between Liberals and Republicans, except for one key thing: I, Republican, am happy, while you, Liberal, are miserable. Okay? You understand, everybody here understands, that the United States needs to make hard choices to be in the position it's in. Our leaders cannot be "nice," because if they were "nice," then our lives wouldn't be so nice. We got safe cities, safe roads, cheap gasoline—relatively speaking— *(To an audience member.)* Compare us to Germany, sweetheart, there you're going to pay fifty Deutsche marks per Hitler-liter, okay? Lattes, whenever you want them, *whenever* you want them, God Bless America. Hybrid cars … organic flaxseed … enemas—whatever you're into, I'm not judging you…okay, yes I am…We have these things because our country is powerful, because our country makes the hard choices internationally. And this is the reason, this is the reason, why I'm happy and you Liberals are miserable, see, I wake up in the morning, open up my curtains on my country and its hard choices, and I say: "yes." And you, Liberal, wake up in the morning, do downward dog, *(Does feeble impression of this yoga move.)* have a little green tea, a little NPR…you open up your curtains on your country and its hard choices, and you say: "No." You say "No!"

You say no to George Bush—you know you do. No to Iraq. No to Afghanistan. No to Free Trade—and that kills me, because, what do you do—you get up, leave your *oil-heated* home, drive your *gasoline-powered* car, hello? And what do you do? I'll tell you what you do: You get yourself a latte. Just like me. Only I say "Yes." And *you* say: "Miserable." That's the difference.

Well, plus, I make a lot more money than you. I mean, a lot. But, that's a choice. It's a free country. You want to be a rebel, go right ahead. Stay poor. *(Holds up hand for a high-five.)* Nah, I'm just messin' with you. Gimme some of that. Don't leave me hanging. Don't leave a brother hangin.' It's all good.

You know, you remind me of my parents—they said "No"—but they took it a step further—they went "back to the land." You know what that is? Yeah. I've always said, I don't begrudge my parents their leftist politics, I begrudge them raising me in a *yert*. You know what a yert is? Yeah, it's like a hippie tepee. So, my parents tried the yert-thing, and then, I grew up, and then—eventually—*they* grew up, and they gave up their Little

House On The Prairie fantasy, and now, they express their resentment mostly in the form of—bumper stickers. *(He take a moment to enjoy this.)* But that's their prerogative—they endured the use of an outhouse for over a decade, I think they've earned the right to *bumper stick.* But you—you young Liberals, you pretty much jumped right to the bumper stickers, didn't you! I mean, hear me out. This is the reason why the left is dead and buried, because you next generation types aren't saying anything fresh or relevant! No, no, no, no, no *(He begins to spin in a circle, covering his ears with his hands, loudly singing to the tune of "Ode to Joy." He stops and steps forward to drive his point home.)*

I'm through listening to you Liberals— every single one of you, from age two to ninety-two, is ramping on the same kind of—outdated humanist Green Party—sub-ivy league, pseudo-intellectual, hippie-nouveau-riche—ex-Gen X, New Age dropout—antiauthoritarian B.S., which isn't even your original philosophy! No! My parents were saying the same thing at *Woodstock* and they had the benefit of *better drugs,* so what's your excuse? *(Pause.)*

(Holds up hand for a high-five.) Nah, I'm just messing with you. Gimme some of that. It's all good. It's all good. Don't leave me hangin'. Come to the dark side. You know you want to. It's all good.

(In the course of the high-five, he seizes TIM's hand and pulls him close.) All I'm saying is, the difference between you and me, is that you are outraged, and I am accepting. That's it. My parents tired to change things, tried to change the world, guess what, didn't work. They caved in to reality after a while. And you're not going to change anything either.

Okay? Sorry. Harsh. Harshing your gig. You can't change anything. Now I've accepted that, and you haven't—and that's the reason, right there, that is the reason, why you are miserable, and me— *(Pause.)* …I'm happy.

MAN: *(Twenty-one, hooded sweat jacket.)* Everybody dies, man! Big bad American Army!! The Beasts of the West—over there, killing them all for oil. *(He approaches a chair on stage, pretending to hold a variety of weapons, which he uses on an imaginary prisoner.)* WELCOME TO ABU GRAVE PRISON! WE WILL NOW INTERROGATE THE PRISONER! (He utilizes a handgun, machine gun, chain saw, rabid dog.)* You may now release the prisoner…

I know there's some kids over there, man, in the military, who think they're doing the right thing and all, and that's all good and grand, but they don't understand, they're just over there fighting so that some rich fat fuck sitting behind a desk over here suckin' on a big brown cigar, can like—make more money! Or people can get cheaper gas! Makes me sick—we started a fucking *holy war*…We are going to be fighting this thing for a hundred and fifty motherfucking years.

Why? I'll tell you why— BECAUSE WE HAVE NO FUCKING CLUE!

I don't mean to sound cold or anything, dude, but I've seen this coming for a good ten years or so. We are headed for some serious *hurt*. Society is going to start to collapse, and when it does, it's not gonna be any harder for me to suffer or survive than it is now. No, dude, I get stared at, spit on, fucking treated like I'm homeless—I'm not homeless! I just…hang out a lot! And I get treated

like spit! By these people who don't even do anything—they just *shop* and *drive* and *eat* and *spawn children!* They don't think about things, ask *questions*, never think about ways we could actually *change things for the better*—

They spit on *me?!* These sheltered people man, when these buildings along Main Street are *burning*, and the terrorists *really* start fucking putting hurtin' on us like you wouldn't believe LIKE YOU WOULDN'T FUCKING BELIEVE! DUDE! These SUV-driving motherfuckers are going to go crazy, man THEY'RE NOT GONNA KNOW WHAT TO DO!

They're gonna go crazy, man—start talking to themselves: "Hi, how are you, hi how are you, hi how are you hi how are YOU?!" And then—you know what's going to happen, dude, the funny punch line? These SUV-driving motherfuckers are going to start come crawling, crawling in the street, begging for food, begging for a blanket, crawling up to me, up to me and my friends, dude…You know what I'm going to be like!

Here's your blanket! *(Spits noisily.)* Here's your food! *(Kicks.)* Why don't you crawl back to the suburbs? Oh, I forgot, you can't, the suburbs *HAVE BEEN CLUSTER BOMBED*

And you, and all the *rich fat fucks* who bought and sold us into this shit— I think YOU created the terrorists, YOU made them hate us, YOU created a society where there's nothing to do except drive to *the grocery store*, then drive to work, and drive to your little cubicle-home *prison*— pay your Verizon bill pay your T-Mobile bill then drive back to *work*— a boring, boring boring BORING BORING

BORING BORING BORING
BORING BORING BORING
SOCIETY WHERE THERE'S NO
ROOM IN IT FOR *ME*

—you deserve everything—you deserve
everything—*And I'm never going to have
any sympathy for you*, EVER *(Long pause.)*
…Not to sound like a crazy person or
anything.

The World Trade Center, man, it's
all about the fucking World Trade
Center…It hurts me, it still hurts me
to think about that shit…does it still
hurt you? But—the thing is—the funny
punch line is—that's *nothing* compared
to what they're going to do to us,
dude…they're going to burn us down,
with a fire, a fire as bright as heaven

I'm not 100 percent—don't quote me on
it—but when it happens, you're going
to remember me—and you're going to
remember—this conversation

TIM: *Holding tape recorder)* Hi— Excuse
me—I'm going around, working on a
project where I'm asking people questions… *(As if he, himself is asked a
question.)* What kind of questions? Oh,
well, mostly about terrorism—

What do *I* think about terrorism? Oh—
well—uh—actually, it's interesting that
you asked, because I was just talking to
this guy and he was saying how he didn't
think we'd be any safer from terrorism
even if John Kerry had gotten elected,
because he said he remembered hearing
how Osama bin Laden was making plans
to attack America sometime during *Bill
Clinton's* presidency…and I thought:
That's interesting. Does that mean we
can't even blame George Bush?

But then, I was talking to this woman,
and she was saying how terrorism is

just "an unavoidable by-product of our
expanding Global Economy." And I
thought: Okay, maybe.

But then I was talking to this *other*
woman, and she was saying how terrorism is actually a symptom of our own
spiritual deficiencies. And I thought:
Is that *true?*

But then I was talking to this *guy*, and
this guy talked my ear off, he nearly filled
up half a tape by himself, he was saying
how there can't be any substantial change
in the world until the people of the world
can *unify*. And I was like: Okay, but how
does that happen? And I asked him and
he just looked at me and went: "Hah." So
I made a point to ask everyone I talked
to: How would the people of the world
unify? And no one could tell me. So I
thought…that's interesting. *(The pace
builds, becoming frantic.)*

But then I was talking to this woman and
she was saying that the *real* problem is
that we have to stop supporting Israel,
because, she said, Israel polarizes the
Islamic community against *us*.

But then I was talking to this *guy*, and
this guy was saying that the *real, real*
problem is the means by which we pursue the terrorists—because he said the
means by which we pursue the terrorists
actually helps to create *more terrorism*.
And I thought: that's confusing…

But then I was talking to this other
woman, and she was saying that the *real*
problem, the *real, real, real* problem, is
that America is losing its focus. That it's
getting harder and harder to focus on
the solutions, because there's so many
questions. Too many questions. And I
thought: that's interesting!

But then this other guy, he was saying, the
real, real, real, real, real problem is that

Americans can't ever reasonably expect to ever feel safe again. *(Pause.)* And I thought: That's interesting...Is he right? Is that *true*? How do you know? How do you know? How do you ever really know if what anyone ever says is really true?

(Pause, then, with growing urgency.) But then I talked to this other guy...Oh, but before that...I talked to this woman, and she said...no, but before that, I talked to this guy, from Europe, Eastern Europe, and he said...wait, but before *that* I talked to these kids in a park—and they were saying...wait! Before that, this woman, this woman, you *have* to hear what she was saying...you should hear it...I can play it for you, I have the tape right here, I can play it for you, if you'll just give me another second of your time—you just—there's a lot of opinions here, and you can't understand any of it until you've heard all of it—I don't know if this is the right tape—but I can get it, if you'll just give me one more second of your time...just another second of your time—just one more second of your time...

(Blackout.)

CHAPTER 4
ST. LOUIS 2007

TIM: St. Louis, 2007. I went to the NRA National Convention because I wanted—to understand

I'm sorry, is this the line to get into the main part of the gun show?

MAN IN LINE: *(Slightly hostile.)* No. This line's for Ted Nugent.

TIM: Oh right! Ted Nugent is here, cool, I saw his posters...

MAN IN LINE: ...*Yeah.*

TIM: Is he giving a concert now—?

MAN IN LINE: ...*No.*

TIM: He write a book or something? Is he signing autographs?

MAN IN LINE: *(Turning, confronting.)* ...*YEAH.*

(TIM backs away.)

TIM: I looked the part, it was my *attitude* I needed to disguise—too much eye contact, I was playing it too curious.

Yes, I went in disguise. I felt that to be the right choice. I needed to be undercover, to see. My first impulse was to go with the mud boots and ball cap, to try and capture that steadfast deer hunter look. Then I thought, no, instead, khakis and tech-force sunglasses, to portray an ex-special forces guy turned state trooper, lots of jaw tension, fists clenched. I really had no idea what these people were like, so, in the end, I went with a sort of standard Uni-bomber meets Idaho militia member thing: military surplus sweater, frayed at the edges, lots of ambiguous pockets, shoes with no shine—playing a character, maybe, someone with desperation stockpiling, someone on the edge. *(Pause.)* I'm not on the edge, it's just an *act.*

NRA DJ: WELCOME TO THE BIGGEST CELEBRATION OF FREEDOM IN NRA HISTORY! You're listening to *Patriot Radio*, and we are back, *live*, at the National Convention. With more than three-hundred and fifty exhibitors and sixty thousand visitors over the course of two days, this really is the best opportunity to meet with like-minded folks interested in charting the future of the Second Amendment. And don't forget, after today's special breakout session, "Shooting Skills For Life & Fun," we'll hear from the convention's keynote speaker, retired Marine Lieutenant Colonel Oliver L. North!

TIM: For weeks beforehand, the billboards loomed over the St. Louis interstate:

COME SEE ACRES OF GUNS, GEAR, AND OUTFITTERS

I've long written off gun-culture people as backwards, at best, but the billboards, they made me anxious.

I'd been anxious anyway. Driving past gas stations: three eighteen a gallon…three-twenty seven a gallon…three eighty-five a gallon…and I can't help but think: when is it going to say five dollars a gallon? Or thirteen dollars, or twenty-six—they can make it any price they want

GUN SALESMAN: Seeing anything you like, or liking everything you see? These are the classic .357 magnums, just like Dirty Harry. 'Course, when Dirty Harry said the .357 was: (Does a Dirty Harry impression.) "The most powerful handgun in the world"—sorry, I admit, I'm a bit of an actor—he helped make the .357 the most popular handgun in the world. Now, of course, it's the Glock that gets the most screen time, and you can see the effect it's had on sales of that particular weapon, but, truth be told, it's the Magnum that's the real shooter's choice—

You know, it's a funny thing, Hollywood. George Clooney…Sean Penn… Tim Robbins…the amount that they bemoan our President and the War, and the state of the world, but truth be told, it's always been Hollywood that has done more for the sale of guns than any advertising campaign the NRA or a gun company

could ever come up with, ever. Ever. (Whispers.) Ever.

'Course, real-live guns are always better than some crummy movie—why, I'll tell you why, truth be told, you don't have to sit back and watch, you get to get right in there and shoot them yourself!

TIM: I'd been anxious anyway— It's the conversations I'd been getting into with friends, half-serious, half-drunk, over the third bottle of wine, where people are throwing around expressions like:

MALE FRIEND: It's the decline of the American Empire.

FEMALE FRIEND: (Smoking a cigarette.) It's just like Ancient Rome.

HI-TECH HOLSTER SALESMAN: One-fifth of all murder victims are killed by their own guns. Now that's scary. (Gestures to his shoulder holster.) These hi-tech but technically simple holsters will prevent your gun being seized and used upon you in the midst of a situation. (Goes up to audience member.) Pull on that weapon. You're sooner likely to pull me over, if that were possible, than to take that weapon away. But, for me: (Click—takes gun out of holster.) it's that easy. (Click—puts gun back in holster.) Now, let's imagine a scenario—(To same audience member.) what's your name? (Before he can answer.) Bob. Okay, Bob, let's say you—and that guy over there, you've just broken into my house—didn't think you were going to commit a crime today, did you, Bob?

Maybe you did.

Bob, that guy over there, he's got a knife. A knife, now, that's scary. I fend him off, Bob, you go for my weapon, you don't get it, I fend you off, and (Click—takes *gun out of holster.)* I shoot you, Bob. I kill you. Then I pacify that guy with the knife.

Didn't think you were going to die today, did you Bob? Maybe you did…You're a good man, Bob. Bad burglar, good man…

I keep one of these attached to the headboard of my bed—my wife, she's vacuuming, she worries that she'll "set it off." I say, "That's impossible—if that gun, in that holster, goes off, I'll—vacuum the house—for a *year*." Vacuuming, now that's scary. *(Click—puts gun back in holster.)*

HIDDEN HOLSTER SALES-WOMAN: These are our Hidden Holsters, providing you quick access to your concealed firearm. This is the QwikClip, which is fine, except you'd have to leave your shirt or blouse untucked to cover it, which is not fine. Now this is the SuperTuck, it's really the superior model, perfect for us ladies, as it allows you to leave your shirt or blouse tucked in, so you can continue to look put together. I wear mine all the time. It's peace of mind knowing that protection is there, and best part, I can stay tucked in, so I don't look a terrible mess…

TIM: Massive banners hung overhead in the main hall, sixty feet long, depicting an image of a U.S. Marine. The banners read:

IF YOU CAN WRITE ENGLISH, THANK A TEACHER.

IF YOU CAN SPEAK ENGLISH, THANK A SOLDIER.

The main hall was a labyrinth of kiosks, booths, display cases, divider walls lined

with guns, and thousands and thousands and thousands of people. To the left, a kiosk with assault rifles on display, and you could pick them up. A kid in a Hawaiian T-shirt, probably twelve years old, picked up a rifle and called to a man across the kiosk, leaning over a selection of infrared scopes.

KID WITH RIFLE: Dad! Hey Dad. Dad, look! *(He holds the gun Rambo-style.)* Dad! Hey Dad! *(Holds gun as if shooting, spraying bullets.)* Dad. Hey, Dad! *(Swings gun around awkwardly, looks down barrel. Suddenly, BOY responds, surprised, as if reprimanded by his father. Slowly puts gun down, turns away.)*

TIM: I crossed the kiosk to talk to a salesman.

Can I hold that?

SALESMAN: Sure.

TIM: Wow, it's really light.

SALESMAN: Polymers, mostly plastic.

TIM: Hey…what do you shoot with this thing? Elephants?

SALESMAN: No. Well, yeah, I mean, I guess you could hunt with it—

TIM: *(To audience.)* As if on cue, a small man with large glasses and a plaid shirt raced past—

MAN WITH GLASSES: Actually, you shoot turkeys with it!! Ka-pow! Ka-pow! Ka-pow!

TIM: *(To audience.)* and was gone.

SALESMAN: We designed these mostly for foreign militaries, but there was enough civilian interest to bring it over to the United States.

TIM: Civilian interest? Like who?

SALESMAN: Hobbyists. Gun clubs. Citizens. Like you. *(Takes the gun back.)* Have a nice day.

TIM: *(To audience.)* At the back of the hall, next to the Gold Rush Café, which sold both Freedom Fries and Freedom Burgers—a booth that read: "Fellowship Of Christian Investors." They had an image of the World Trade Center, on fire, overhead, a cross. I had to see what these guys were selling.

CHRISTIAN INVESTOR: Pardon me friend, would you like a bracelet? Each color represents one of God's commandments.

TIM: No thanks, maybe later—What do you guys do, exactly?

CHRISTIAN INVESTOR: My heart is to—reach the unreached. Every day, more than eighty thousand people die who never heard the teachings. That is more than twenty-five World Trade Centers, every single day. The media can and will not comprehend people going to their grave in a Christ-less state as a sorrow greater than 9/11, but you and I, you and I can. Now, let me ask you a question—are you aware—it's no secret, but are you aware—there are now more Muslims in our country than there are Jewish individuals? That is a fact. We are encouraging people to bear a compassionate witness on the Muslim population in this country. *(Moving in on TIM.)* Friend, in these Last Days, there is a wondrous scheme awaiting each one of us. We must, with all our hearts, reach out for it—!

TIM: …Last Days? Last Days of what?

CHRISTIAN INVESTOR: Friend, are you a Christian?

TIM: Uh, no—

CHRISTIAN INVESTOR: Well… Never mind. *(Turns away. To audience member.)* Excuse me friend, would you like a bracelet?

TIM: *(To audience.)* I passed by the Glock booth: dozens and dozens of pistols on display, blocky, streamlined. Men and women, kids, whole families, pointing pistols up, aiming—click click click

There were Glock T-shirts on display:

THIS IS MY GLOCK. THERE ARE MANY LIKE IT BUT THIS ONE IS MINE.

and:

CHANGING THE WORLD, ONE GLOCK AT A TIME

and:

SUCK MY GLOCK

Exiting the main hall, the last stop: The NRA Store. Fifteen aisles of merchandise—a pyramid of books, *The Courage To Be Free*, by Charleston Heston. NRA blue jeans, with built-in concealed handgun pouch . And on display, NRA artwork…

NRA MARKETING DIRECTOR: I notice you're looking at our *Founder's Flag* painting, which is the newest item in our catalogue. I'm the Marketing Director for the NRA,—I get to decide what goes in our catalog, and I just think this is *great art*. Now, this picture has "Hidden Images of Hope" in it—let me lead you through, because I'm sure you can't see properly—Here we have a kneeling man, representing faith in troubled times…see that? And here we have an angry, demonic face representing the 9/11 tragedy—

TIM: Oh, that's funny, I thought that was supposed to be George Bush—

NRA MARKETING DIRECTOR: …No. Uh-uh. *(Pause).* Nope. And you'll see here a tattered "Old Glory," which represents all the American people who've turned their backs on their own country in this troubled time.

TIM: …Can I ask you something?

NRA MARKETING DIRECTOR: It sells for $159.99, framed.

TIM: What? Oh, no, not the painting—it's just that—I look around here and I really get a sense of people—preparing—for something…

NRA MARKETING DIRECTOR: That's right—you're likely to find here everything you need to be at your highest level of preparedness—for example, in our catalogue, *(Picks up catalogue, begins leafing through it.)* you'll find—let's see—yes, here's our newest flashlight—it's exciting, the beam actually shines brighter than your car headlight—

TIM: Uh-huh.

NRA MARKETING DIRECTOR: Perfect for lighting up dark environments, or blinding would-be intruders—

TIM: Uh-huh.

NRA MARKETING DIRECTOR: And here's our complete line of conceal and carry apparel—

TIM: Uh-huh—

NRA MARKETING DIRECTOR: Enough room in there to cover whatever you're wearing underneath—

TIM: Huh.

NRA MARKETING DIRECTOR: Here you have our selection of top-quality survival knives—

TIM: Hm

NRA MARKETING DIRECTOR: Pretty much everything you need to keep you and your family safe, to get ready, to prepare—

TIM: How about a gun? Can I buy a gun in there? Hadn't really planned on it, sort of an impulse buy, just so I could feel safe—ready, ready, so I could feel ready. Would I buy one here with you, or out there, or—how do—how do I get a—how do I get a gun?

NRA MARKETING DIRECTOR: *(Pause. He closes the catalogue.)* You're not a member, are you? This is a gun *show.* You can't *buy* guns here.

TIM: …Sorry… *(Turns to leave, then recovers himself.)* No, that's not what I mean…Look, while some people here—preparing—with guns—maybe to use on human beings, but, not to sound stupid, but wouldn't they rather want to prepare by—enabling their own sense of *humanity*? You know, if they're going to stockpile something, why not stockpile—the arsenal of the human heart? I mean, not to sound stupid, but come on, really, what's more powerful, some—gun—or the human—the human heart?

NRA MARKETING DIRECTOR: *(He uses his hands to wordlessly demonstrate—one hand, a fist, simulates a heart. The other hand simulates a gun. Pause. He fires at the heart, and the heart is destroyed. Pause.)* I think you better find your way out.

TIM: The long ascent out, I took the stairs. The parking garage stairwell, steps climbed along wide windows. Outside, a gray dusk fell, the lights from the radio tower dim and red. Families, men, trudged upwards, towards cars. But the steps ended abruptly, roped off with construction tape… People hesitantly spilled onto an unfamiliar level, and it seemed that no one knew where they were, in relation to where they had arrived. We trudged together, a mob in the artificial night, in the gathering dark, pressed around asphalt roundabouts, unable to locate the means to leave, grumbling and cursing, everything unfamiliar. Wandering towards the way—and not finding it. Trekking the ramp winding up and up and up and up and up and up and up, until the press of bodies was so thick with backtracking, muttered curses, collisions, families in mute confusion—that

there was nowhere left to move to

there was nowhere else to go

(Blackout.)

CHAPTER 5
2008

TIM moves to center stage, holding clipboard, upon which there is affixed an OBAMA bumper sticker.

TIM: 2008.

(TIM moves as if knocking on a door, downstage center.)

TIM: Hello! I'm going door to door with the Obama campaign—

(The door slams in his face. He is stunned, momentarily. Moves downstage right, towards a new door. Knocks.)

TIM: Hello! I'm going door to door with the Obama campaign—

(He hesitates, briefly, anticipating a second slammed door. He is relieved that it does not happen again.)

Oh, good. I'm going door to door, checking in with people in this pre-election time, checking in to see what people are thinking about, talking about, maybe even what people might be worried about—for example—the economy…I mean, what do they expect us to do about that? But anyway…I think the idea of discussing, listening—that's a process that—uh— *(He has forgotten, momentarily. He steals a glance at the Obama sticker.)* —Obama—would support. So. What do you think?

TAYLOR: *(Thirty-four, is groggy, as if pulled from sleep. He is wearing a bathrobe.)* Obama? Come in, come in, come in. I thought you were the Mormons. *(Allows TIM to enter, shuts the door.)* Obama—yeah. I'm sorry, I'm trying to quit coffee today, so I'm a little PTSD. *(He spends a moment slapping his pockets, searching for glasses. At last, he finds them.)*

Obama…yeah. Of course. And I know he's going to win. He has to— if he doesn't, I'm going to kill myself, so…There's a lot at stake. To tell you the truth I'm not even ready yet for the Olympics—uh—the *Election*—even at this point. To tell you the truth, I was pretty heavily involved with the *Nader* campaign? Ralph Nader? I know, I know, but I was going to college in *Vermont*. So—That was sort of the peak of my career as a political activist. I'm not really ready to get back on the horse just yet.

I *worry*. I feel *guilty*. Does that qualify as political action? I'm really *pro* guilty and worry, I think they're powerful forces of good. It's like, when you're driving along a highway, and you see a car broken down on the side of the road? And your first thought is: *I need to pull over and help them.* And your second thought is: *No, wait. This is a setup. If I pull over, they are going to rape and murder me.* So, you don't pull over, you keep driving, and you feel guilty, and worry, and, I think, that guilt and worry go out of the car, into the world, and help...Maybe not the driver of that broken-down car *directly*, but it's an energetic contribution, like prayer, just more...American.

I've been sending my guilt and worry to Iraq in regular monthly installments. I hope one day to kick that up a notch and lead like an Elite American Apology Squad? Armed with baked goods. We'll parachute into the Baghdad suburbs, and walk up to Iraqis saying: *"Hey, remember that invasion thing? Sorry about that. We feel really bad. Really bad, you have no idea. Scone?"*

Since you asked, I've been feeling really bad about pretty much everything lately. I sit down to read the *New York Times* and forget who I am. NPR—NPR! NPR, NPR, NPR! I wouldn't have a political opinion at all unless NPR gave me one, and still—*All-Things Considered-This-American-News-From-Washington* gives me a hemorrhage.

I mean, it's all about *oil.* I'm glad prices have stabilized, sort of, in the past couple of months, but the idea is we're running out, right? But then I read recently that in Venezuala, they pay nineteen cents a gallon, so I'm not exactly sure where the *shortages* are happening. But then I read on the *Drudge Report*, some economist was saying that four dollars a gallon or whatever we're paying is relatively cheap—that relatively speaking, we should be paying a lot more. Okay, maybe four dollars a gallon isn't a big

deal, maybe we should get over it, but it's not the price—it's the *implication* of unlimited price *increase* that really gets me, you know?

And I blame China! I have nothing against China, I like China, I buy their stuff, but, according to NPR, China is the up and coming world power, China needs oil, China's where the money's going, and—I started to think about it. This refocus of global financial attention really...hurts my feelings. I mean—come on, what does *China* have that we don't?

...a billion more people, granted.

I'm just trying to come to terms with the fact that soon, America will *no longer be in charge.* We've peaked as a society, Tom Brokow or whoever saying our "Greatest Generation" was like—eighty years ago, World War II, making our generation—what—the "Half-Priced Sale Generation?" We're fading, and in a way, in my leftist-sentimental-Rage-Against-The-Machine kind of way, I'm fine with that, we deserve this, America's foreign policy has been so gross, America's been so gross...But. In every other way, I'm like: Woah Woah Woah Woah WOAH WOAH WOAH. We're *America.* Somebody needs to *do something about this.*

But hasn't something already *been done?* Wasn't this whole Bush-Cheney thing the orchestration of an evil, Neo-Con, military supremacy New World Order? Yeah? Well, if this is the American New World Order— why are we paying four dollars a gallon for gasoline? I mean, didn't we *win* over there in Iraq?

...I'm sorry, I don't mean to sound like a prick—I've just had a very demeaning eight years, politically speaking, we all have, and I would like a little compensation. More than just my Economic Stimulus Check—which, by the way, I do not even feel *remotely* stimulated. *(He turns to get something, then stops abruptly.)* I was just going to offer you some coffee, but, since I'm quitting…*shit.* I don't know what you're supposed to offer people once coffee is out of your life. Tea? Methadone? Emptiness?

Since you asked, I'm as hopeful as anybody that Obama's going to save this country, but this oil thing is really freaking my shit out.

Do you ever read *Harper's*? I don't recommend it. I read this stupid article in *Harper's*, about Peak Oil, like, two years ago, and I have been *insane* since then. Talked about the death of the suburbs, food shortages, bread lines…it was just a stupid article, but that term "bread line" really has a way of haunting the imagination. It's just that I have spent a lot of time contributing energetically to this country, and I deserve to be saved.

…Do you ever watch *Oprah*? I don't recommend that, either. I was at my mom's, I watched an episode by accident…it was about this positive thinking movement—have you heard of this? You can buy the instruction manual at Target. Basically, you use your mind to draw things into your life through the power of attraction—like, "I now have prosperity, I now have a new car." Whatever—you basically think it and you get it, and that may sound stupid if you've ever, say, gone to college, but I was like, I'm just going to suspend cynicism and try it—but I'm going to *include America* in the equation so we can all benefit…so it was like: "I—*we*—now have…cheap gasoline. We now have…Obama." I know, it's stupid…"We now have *hope.*"

That one stuck. "We now have hope, we now have hope, we now have hope." And I did it really intensely, for almost—two weeks—and something happened. I woke up in the middle of the night, drenched in sweat, total spiritual breakthrough, this mantra-thought echoing through my mind, and this was it:

This. Is. Total. BULLSHIT.

It doesn't work! Positive thinking doesn't work. I want it to, and it doesn't. Oprah wanted me to lie to myself, and I'm not going to do it.

So I reinvested in hatred…and that didn't work either. Not in a *Beatles* kind of way, but simply because the people you're trying to affect with your hatred are too powerful. For example—okay. Not that I've wished George Bush to come to any real harm. Not really. Not *really.* But I've been hating that guy SO intensely for like—*eight years*—me and millions. Everybody. Billions—me, Oprah, all of China has been hating this guy, and I'm thinking: What? Is he magically protected by *Valdemort*, or something? Seriously, he must be surrounded by a ring of psychic warlocks, blocking all the hate-beams, because, how else could someone withstand all that *global loathing* and not just—burst into flames?! Or…choke on pretzels a little more often? Or, I don't know, maybe, *lose an election. Once or twice?*

Does human thought accomplish anything?! Yes, if it's used properly, and guilt and worry are the true path. They happen automatically, they apply to all circumstances, and I don't need an instruction manual—they are my energetic contribution to the planet!

…I really need a cup of coffee…

Because I watch an HBO special on Abu Ghraib and feel like puking for a year. What do you do about it? Well, I worry. I feel guilty. I'm working hard. The War goes on and on and on, and I'm trying really hard not to compare myself to those good, complacent Nazi citizens living around the corner from Auschwitz during World War II—what do you do about it? I worry, I feel guilty, I'm working hard. Gasoline goes up—I worry. I can't afford to buy a *Prius*, I feel guilty: I'm working hard! I'm waiting in line to get a cup of coffee, or waiting to fill up my gas tank, and I'm thinking stupid thoughts like: *When the shortages come, these are the people who are going to be trampling my broken body.* I mean, I see people broken down on the side of the road all the time, I don't help them. If I were broken down—I hope someone would help me.

I worry, I feel guilty…but I'm not an idiot, I understand that doesn't really do anything either. The only thing that seems to change is the price of gasoline— that keeps going up and up, having nothing at all to do with *ME*. What I might want! What I might be feeling! BUT WHO GIVES A SHIT ABOUT WHAT I'M FEELING

Who cares what I think about oil and China and Iran and the dollar. About invasions and Guatanamo and torture. About Condoleeza, inflation, Afghanistan, and the housing market. Who cares what I think about the *Drudge Report*, MSN dot com, the *New York Times* Week In Review, and NPR for SIX HOURS A DAY—which, by the way, is a toxic amount of symphony music—but it's also a lot of news, and who cares that I'm trying to stay informed when it only makes

me feel STUPID and USELESS and DOOMED

I'll just stop worrying! I'll just stop feeling guilty! I'll just stop caring!

And then…I hope the Mayans are on schedule. I hope the Christians are right. Why did I ever bother caring in the first place? Who cares when it feels like, all you can do, all you can productively do, all you can productively do in this country is feel afraid, and wait for the worst, and even that doesn't change anything! Doesn't change anything! Doesn't change anything! …who cares? Who cares…

…I do. I care. I fucking care, I'm an idiot, I care. I don't want things to change, I don't want people to be hurt, I don't want to be hurt, I want to help. How do I do that? How do I do that? What do I need to do?

…*I really need a cup of coffee*…man, give me your Obama bumper sticker, and get out. *(Pause.)* You don't have any bumper stickers? *(Pause.)* What, do you want me to sign something? You don't want me to sign anything? Do you even *work* for Obama?

(TIM, holding clipboard, stands in shock. He attempts to show the bumper sticker to TAYLOR as if that were proof of his legitimacy as a canvasser. Then—

TIM: …No…but I'm going to vote for him—that's kind of like working for him— *(He scrambles to explain.)* Sorry about the deception, it's just that you asked "who cares," but, see, I care, because—the things you were saying, that's how I feel, and I think that Obama would support the idea of people talking, and other people listening and saying "Yes, that's how I feel," and that's, I think, the start of something important—

What? Get out?

Okay... *(He steps outside.)* So, anyway, I was saying, the idea of people saying things and other people hearing those things, and letting the person who said them know that they feel the same way is the basis for community and really starting something—

(Door slams shut. He stands there for a long moment. Then, knocks urgently on the door.)

Sorry, if you can hear me, I wanted to say one last thing, something you said made me think of it, and I wanted to share it, because I think I feel the same way you do, and this has helped me—

When I was a kid I was vacationing with my family in Upstate New York—it was out in the country—I had been there a bunch of times before, but never this time of year, it was late in the fall, and it had been so cold, the leaves had already fallen off the trees. Anyway, I was outside, playing, alone, and it was dusk, the sky was red, and I heard this sound, like a—howling from the bottom of the Earth. And I thought it was the end of the world.

Turns out it was a train. The whistle was louder because the leaves were already off the trees. But at the time I ran into the house to try and find someone to tell me what it was. And I couldn't find anyone—it seemed like everyone was asleep or away. So. What I did was, I went to the back of the house, into a dark room, and I sat down, and I waited, and I told myself that I would try to sleep, and if I woke up in the morning and I was still alive, everything was going to be okay. And in the morning, I woke up...and things were okay. So, the next night, I tried it again...and things were still okay.

I think of that story. Especially lately. At night. When it's late. And I can't sleep.

(He waits. Waits. And the door does not open. Slowly moves away, downstage right. He finds another door. Knocks. Knocks again. No one there. He moves slowly across the stage, to downstage left, to another door. Knocks. Knocks again. No one. He moves slowly to downstage center. Pause, fist poised before the door. Knocks. Blackout. Knocks again.)

(End.)

CONVERSATION STORM

Rick Burkhardt

RICK BURKHARDT is a composer, playwright, actor, director, and musician. He was born in 1970 in Cambridge, Massachusetts, and grew up in Urbana, Illinois. He attended Harvard University and the University of Illinois, where he studied with Herbert Brün, and earned a PhD in music composition from the University of California, San Diego, where he studied with Chaya Czernowin. He composes, writes, acts, and directs for The Nonsense Company, a touring experimental music theatre trio. Since 2003, they have performed their original work in over forty cities in both the United States and Europe. Burkhardt is also a singer-songwriter and accordionist for The Prince Myshkins, a touring satirical political cabaret duo. His chamber music compositions have been commissioned and performed by chamber groups, soloists, and orchestras in Europe, Canada, Mexico, and the United States and at international festivals such as Darmstadt and Donaueschingen. In 2005–06, The Nonsense Company toured his historical collage play, *The Climb Up Mount Chimborazo*, a meditation on the education of Simón Bolívar, and his deeply reverent neoliberal translation/adaptation of *The Threepenny Opera*. Burkhardt is currently writing the book for Nicholas DeMaison's opera, *Ursularia*, which will be staged by The Nonsense Company in collaboration with Chicago's Opera Cabal. He lives with The Nonsense Company in a big, old house in Madison, Wisconsin.

Conversation Storm was first presented by The Nonsense Company on September 7, 2006, at Theatre de la Jeune Lune, Minneapolis, with the following cast and credits:

Hugh.. Ryan Higgins
Godfrey.. Andy Gricevich
Alec ....Rick Burkhardt

Directed by Rick Burkhardt and Andy Gricevich

Conversation Storm was subsequently presented by The Nonsense Company as part of the New York FRIGID Festival (Erez Ziv, Managing Director) on February 28, 2008, at the Kraine Theater with the following cast and credits:

Hugh.. Ryan Higgins
Godfrey.. Andy Gricevich
Alec ....Rick Burkhardt

Directed by Rick Burkhardt and Andy Gricevich

The play has since toured, with the same cast, to over two dozen U.S. cities, including San Francisco; Austin, Texas; St. Louis; Missoula, Montana; New Orleans; Bellingham, Washington; and Baltimore.

www.nonsensecompany.com

NOTE

The three characters, Godfrey, Hugh, and Alec, are all in their mid-thirties.

The character of Godfrey sometimes plays the waiter. This should be shown as simply as possible: when he is Godfrey, he wears a baseball cap; when he is the waiter, he drapes a cloth napkin over his arm.

Sometimes, scenes begin or end in the middle of a word one of the characters is speaking. This is shown in the script by placing the unspoken portion of the word in brackets:

HUGH: [O]kay look, I am not going to play the tor[turer]

Letters in brackets are only given as a guide to the actor—they are NEVER to be made audible. The effect should be more extreme than one character being interrupted by another—it should sound like a TV channel being flipped in mid-word.

A café table. Three characters standing.

HUGH: Donald Rumsfeld says

ALEC: "People are fungible."

GODFREY: *(Delivers the following like a lecturer, with a pointer and signs, or perhaps slides?)* "Fungible" meaning interchangeable, or exchangeable for equal quantities of equal worth. A playwright has given me thirty minutes to refute Rumsfeld's statement.

Three characters: Godfrey, Hugh, and Alec, rendered in a fading gray twilight filtered through November clouds.

Three forms of insomnia: transient, idiopathic, and psychophysiological—not to be confused with sleep apnea, the sudden loss of breath during sleep known to cause heart attacks, or with "sleep deprivation," referred to in CIA manuals as "sleep management." Recently, benzodiazepine receptor agonists such as zolpidem and zaleplon have replaced barbiturates as the leading pharmaceutical treatments for insomnia. *(Displays a pill bottle.)* Their only side effect is that patients may form dependencies, unable to sleep without the pills; no sleep in turn may cause hallucinations, anxiety attacks, existential loneliness and depression, tissue failure, oral ulcers, protracted agony, admittedly short of that described in Bybee's memo as sufficient to constitute torture. No coffee, ever.

If I may be permitted a tangent: Jay S. Bybee *(Picture of Jay S. Bybee.)*, assistant attorney general under John Ashcroft in 2002, father of four, member, Church of Jesus Christ of Latter Day Saints, owner of large kazoo collection, now superior judge on the Ninth Circuit Court of Appeals. Co-author with John Yoo *(Picture of John Yoo.)* of the so-called "torture memo," which instructed the Bush administration that acts of torture can only be prosecuted as torture if they rise to the level of pain associated with quote organ failure, impairment of bodily function, or even death unquote; also that the president may order torture, and that torture can be legally justified as self-defense.

End of tangent. Scene One: The onset of Hugh's insomnia.

(GODFREY hands off the pill bottle to HUGH, sits at the table.)

HUGH: Interior. Restaurant. Midwinter. Evening upon us, night stretches out before…etc. Hugh's and Godfrey's reminiscence: their friendship in high school, their lovers throughout the '90s, their one-night stand in Manchester in 1992, where Godfrey was studying to become a prison psychiatrist (this may not have occurred).

GODFREY: That reminds me. I'll tell you a recurring dream one of my patients has—

HUGH: —and so on— *(Sits at the table with GODFREY.)*

GODFREY: —Based upon Shakespeare's *Henry Six Part Two*, act two scene one—which also was the inspiration for this play! The peasant Saunder Simpcox claims he cannot walk, he must be carried like a monarch in his chair. Stop me if you've heard this one. Gloucester—the duke of Gloucester—snaps "Well sirrah, we must have you find your legs. Fetch me a beadle and whips." Simpcox once whipped leaps from his chair and flees the stage. A miracle!

ALEC: Scene Two—Alec enters.

HUGH: Oh shit—don't look!

GODFREY: I cannot fucking believe—

ALEC: Hey guys. How bizarre that I haven't seen you since high school!

HUGH: Scene Three. An empty chair. No real excuse. We have to let him sit with us. We have to talk.

GODFREY: Scene Four.

HUGH: So, what have you been doing since 1988, when the Reagan Youth disbanded?

ALEC: Scene Two—Donald Rumsfeld enters.

HUGH: Oh shit—don't look!

GODFREY: I cannot fucking believe—

(Note: whenever fragments of dialogue repeat, the actors also repeat the actions they performed the first time the dialogue was spoken—as if the play has gone back in time.)

ALEC: The restaurant bursts into flame and is then plunged into blackness.

GODFREY: Scene Five.

HUGH: Alec—

ALEC: *(To the audience.)* I'd rather tell this one myself: My sister, younger than me, depressed since childhood, goes to visit a therapist in Montana in 1996. She is placed under hypnosis, and urged to recover memories which may be the cause of her depression. This is one of those instances where the mind, already under duress, reaches for fantasy in its most readily available forms, forms which I fear are not its best: Led by the therapist's questions, my sister recalls that she and I as children were forced by our parents and grandparents to take part in Satanic rituals, including incest, human sacrifice, and being closed into coffins with dead bodies. She remembers that I raped her during the rituals, and that the bodies are buried beneath a gazebo in our parents' backyard, where there is no gazebo and never has been. She then disappears, her car found fifty miles outside of Billings. She has been told to cut off all ties to the people in her memories, lest we dispute their accuracy. Certain objects left in the car imply a suicide, but something contrived about their placement convinces the police detectives otherwise. Years pass. I sink into a deep depression. Not only have I been accused of an atrocious crime with no opportunity to confront my accuser, no jury, no evidence, but worse, my childhood memories have been erased and replaced with terrifying caricatures. In the play I plan to write, the sister's brother's depression deepens, leading him ultimately to suicide. The father, a broken, subjugated man, in the final scene receives a phone call from his estranged and penitent daughter, during which he reveals to her and to the audience the tragic fate of his son.

HUGH: Alec, I...I didn't know you wrote plays!

GODFREY: Alec could at this point burst into tears.

ALEC: I don't. My sister does call, eight years later, during the Thanksgiving holiday. She speaks to my mother, who has been instructed not to confront her about the memories or her disappearance—so, their conversation consists entirely of pleasantries: a remarkable performance.

GODFREY: This is taking too long.

ALEC: I imagine my play traveling to church groups like the one I've joined, or perhaps to college campuses—

GODFREY: Scene Six.

(ALEC freezes.)

HUGH: A mist blows through the open door of the restaurant, brushing Alec's face. It's been a strangely balmy winter. The machines for making coffee are humming like ships on the ocean, occasionally releasing blasts of steam.

ALEC: Scene Seven.

GODFREY: Hey, could we get some water over here?

HUGH: Outside, the leafless trees hem in the sky, jagged-black branches rattling.

ALEC: Can you say it more like a bad, bad customer who thinks he's being funny?

GODFREY: *(Trying the instruction.)* Hey, could we get some water over here?

ALEC: Can you say it like you're trying to be funny and like eighty percent succeeding?

GODFREY: Hey, could we get some water over here?

ALEC: Can you say it like you're actually furious, but being funny to cover that up?

GODFREY: Hey, could we get some water over here?

ALEC: Say it so that the people you're sitting with think you're being funny, but the waiter can hear that you're actually acutely pissed off—?

GODFREY: Can you do it?

ALEC: Hey, could we get some water over here?

GODFREY: Hey, could we get some water over here?

ALEC: Hey, could we get some water o—

GODFREY: I don't know what you're looking for. *Is* it funny, or, is it

ALEC: It's funny to everyone except the waiter.

GODFREY: But it's not a comedy, right?

ALEC: No, right, you're aiming for one surgically funny moment, but no long-term comic effects.

GODFREY: Hey, could we get some water o—

HUGH: Scene Twelve

ALEC: *(Suddenly seated at the table, in mid-conversation.)* But listen, while we're talking about torture, let's imagine that a nuclear bomb has been planted in Manhattan.

HUGH: Oh no.

ALEC: And you've got the guy who planted the bomb in a cell, for questioning. And the bomb will go off in half an hour.

HUGH: Stop!

ALEC: And the guy won't talk.

HUGH: STOP!

ALEC: Would you use tor[ture]

GODFREY: Scene Eight.

HUGH: Completely predictable argument about the number of casualties in Fallujah.

ALEC: Scene Twelve.

| HUGH: [O]kay, look, I am not going to play the tor[turer] | ALEC: [e]very time you hear about—it's a comple[tely] |

GODFREY: Scene Nine.

ALEC: *(Suddenly standing, oblivious.)* Try it,

HUGH: Alec, wait—

ALEC: okay, like starting very harsh, aggressive, and then mysteriously the harshness is gone and it's just good-natured, joking…

GODFREY: Hey, could we get some water over here?

HUGH: Since when is Alec directing this play?

ALEC: yeah…I think that's effective, and I think we should try it in reverse.

GODFREY: What's my motivation?

HUGH: You did not say that.

GODFREY: I'm trying to achieve…?

ALEC: Water.

HUGH: Alec.

ALEC: Just try it, just start out just joking around, then just inexplicably turn into a…monster.

GODFREY: Is the waiter a real person?

ALEC: That depends how you address him.

GODFREY: "Hey, could w[e]

ALEC: Scene Twelve.

| HUGH: I am not going to play the torturer in your story, Alec, or in any other sto— | ALEC: [hea]r about—it's a completely hypothetical scena[rio] |

HUGH: Scene Nine.

GODFREY: [w]e get some water over here?"

HUGH: An intense, incredible wind whips through the restaurant.

ALEC: Yeah...I think I liked it better the first way...

GODFREY: Starting with the angry...

ALEC: Right. Starting angry and moving toward

GODFREY: Scene Twelve.

HUGH: You're kidding right? This is a joke? One of the major achievements of the twentieth century is that torture is illegal. You want to reverse that because of some story you read in a comic book?

ALEC: But listen, while we're talking about torture, let's imagine that a nuclear bomb has been planted in Manhattan.

HUGH: Oh no.

ALEC: And you've got the guy who planted the bomb in a cell, for questioning. And the bomb will go off in half an hour.

HUGH: Of course!!

ALEC: And the guy won't talk.

HUGH: Scene Ten.

GODFREY: Totally rote conversation about whether Hiroshima was justified.

HUGH: The same conversation we had twenty years ago!

ALEC: Scene Twelve.

HUGH: Noooo o o o o o o o o o *(Through ALEC's line.)* | ALEC: Or let's say you could go back in time and kill Hitler—would you kill

GODFREY: Scene Ten.

ALEC: —would have died.

(Five-second pause.)

HUGH: But

GODFREY: Scene Twelve.

HUGH: That you would even *think* of using—

ALEC: Now you're telling me what I can and can't think, that's—

HUGH: No, just, I can't believe we're even talking about this! When the Geneva Convention—

ALEC: Okay so is that what liberals want? They want to cut off all debate on a controversial issue that—

HUGH: Torture, Alec, torture, torture...is, is *bad,* and *controversy* arises when—

ALEC: I agree the word has negative connotations. That's why it's an ethical dilemma whether or not you would use—

HUGH: Scene Eleven.

GODFREY: Why isn't the waiter bringing us water?

ALEC: Scene Twelve.

HUGH: I am not going to play

GODFREY: Scene Eleven.

ALEC: Because no one's playing the waiter.

HUGH: So Godfrey must play the waiter.

GODFREY: And Alec must say

ALEC: "Hey, can we get some water over here?"

HUGH: Scene Twelve.

ALEC: *(Spoken exactly as he spoke his previous line.)* So, you're saying you'd let the bomb blow up New York?

HUGH: There's no bomb in New York Alec!

ALEC: You don't know that.

HUGH: You said I knew it! You said I was one hundred percent certain, no possibility of error! If I don't know for sure, forget it—bet's off.

ALEC: So you're saying you would use torture if you did know?

HUGH: Oh God. What do I do?

GODFREY: *(As the WAITER, pouring water.)* It's a trap. If you say you'll use torture, Manhattan is saved and he wins. If you say you won't use torture, Manhattan is destroyed and he wins. All you can do by arguing is to bolster his case that the hesitant liberals with their ethical qualms are unable to rescue Manhattan.

HUGH: My desire to end torture is not a qualm, it is a moral imperative.

ALEC: Saving New York is a moral imperative.

HUGH: There's no bomb in New York Alec!

ALEC: You don't know that.

HUGH: You said I knew it! You said I was one hundred percent certain, no poss— Oh, shit. How can I stop this conversation from happening?

GODFREY: Don't say anything.

HUGH: You mean I just have to let him—

GODFREY: You don't have to talk.

HUGH: Yeah, but then *he'll* ta[lk]

GODFREY: Scene Eleven. Sorry guys, I'll bring you a pitcher. Just so you know, the kitchen closes in about five minutes.

ALEC: I thought the kitchen closed at midnight.

GODFREY: It's about five to midnight.

HUGH: That's amazing.

ALEC: Scene Thirteen.

(Loud music blares forth. HUGH suffers. GODFREY sits, puts on hat, ceases to be the WAITER.)

HUGH: *(Shouting over music.)* I am not go[ing]

(Music stops.)

GODFREY: Scenes Fourteen through Eighteen—Hugh demolishes Alec's argument!

HUGH: [wh]ere you're a heroic and incorruptible CIA agent sent to save a helpless innocent public from an incorrigibly evil villain—this is your idea of an ethical dilemma? This is a fairy tale ripped o[ff]

GODFREY: Scene Fifteen.

HUGH: [doe]sn't have the ethical complexity of a story problem on the SAT! And even if you cou[ld]

GODFREY: Scene Sixteen.

HUGH: [po]ssible to know for certain the exact time it'll go off, the exact identity of the guy who planted it, the exa[ct]

GODFREY: Scene Seventeen.

HUGH: [i]s it always New York?— let's say the bomb's in Tegucigalpa Honduras—do you use torture then? Or what about Havana Cuba, a city you've been threatening with nukes for over fifty year[s]

GODFREY: Scene Eighteen.

HUGH: [t]alk if you torture him, but let's say he will talk if you torture his son. Would you torture hi[s]

ALEC: Scene Nineteen.

GODFREY: [h]ave the worst trouble with joint pain, I used to play racquetball every day and I can't anymore. Just the body's way of saying sorry, you're thirty-five now!

ALEC: Yeah well remember all those all-nighters we used to pull all the time in high school—!

GODFREY: Uff! no more!

ALEC: I gotta get eight hours or I'm a wreck.

GODFREY: Hugh can't sleep at all without his pills.

HUGH: Godfrey…

GODFREY: And he can't drink coffee or—

HUGH: Godfrey!

ALEC: Recently I can no longer distinguish between certain colors. Some of them are no problem, but blue and gray, for example, just seem like one color to m[e]

GODFREY: Scene Twenty.

(GODFREY and ALEC continue their conversation from Scene Nineteen silently in the background.)

HUGH: The night stretches out like an autopsy, its hours pulled like organs from a corpse. Each living, twisted, disfigured organ carrying a secret which can be bruised or pinched, or even killed, or made to disappear, but can only be revealed after death.

ALEC: *(To HUGH.)* Can we at least discuss this in a civilized way?

HUGH: We cannot discuss which torture techniques we're going to use and when in a civilized way, no.

GODFREY: This is taking too long. *(Becomes WAITER.)*

HUGH: Incredibly predictable argument about the effects of free trade policies on third world econo[mies]

GODFREY: Scene Twenty-One. Okay, here's your order: Pancetta-Wrapped Loin of New Zealand Venison with a Huckleberry Zinfandel Sauce Accompanied by Herb Spatzle Served with Caramelized Brunoise of Butternut Squash and Fennel in a Champagne Saffron Vanilla Bean Verjus, and for you the Grilled Thyme-Infused Swordfish On Top of a Brunoise of Very Red Ratatouille Complemented with a Duo of Sweet Potato and Parsnip Puree in a Shiitake Mushroom Glacage Garnished with Crispy Shallot Rings, Sunburst Pearl Onions, and a Lime Dill Creme Fraîche Sevruga Caviar Filling with a Hint of Currant. And you both looked hungry so I brought you some complementary Timbale Roti of Free-Range Quail and Squab with an Essence of Coconut, Lime, and Yogurt On a Bed of Couscous with Pine Nuts, Ginger, and Apricots Surrounded by a Tarragon Artichoke Ragout Wrapped in a Katafi-Crispy Shredded Phyllo with a Rosemary Pinot Noir Glaze, on the house. Oh, and it turns out we're out of Seared Farm-Raised Ostrich Fan Filet Accompanied by Yam Flan and Merlot Cassis Sauce over Madjool Date Risotto in an Arugula and Rosemary Pesto Garnish Served with Baby Field Greens and a Pear Cider Coulis, so I brought you some Roasted

326326326326326 RICK BURKHARDT

and Braised Wild Rabbit Jus à La Natural Served with Mushroom-Potato Gnocchi and Savory Medallions of Muscovy Duck Carnitas Stuffed with a Compote of Braised Sweet Applewood Bacon and Toasted Hazelnut with Smoked Salmon Pinwheels in a Watercress Sauce and a Medley of Crushed—Scene Twenty-Two—in a Cabernet Sauvignon-Sauteed Strawberry Creme Anglais Sauce with a Black Licorice Pomegranate Parfait Gelato Assortment in a Mascarpone Drizzle. Is there anything else you'd like?

ALEC: Can we get some water over here?

GODFREY: Oh, sorry guys, I'll bring you a pitcher. Just so you know, the kitchen's closing in about five minutes.

ALEC: I thought the kitchen closed at midnight.

GODFREY: It's about five to midnight. Also, I thought you'd like to know that Otto Doerr-Zegers, a psychotherapist who studied torture victims in Chile, described torture as a kind of total theatre, including a set, with special lighting, sound effects, props, and backdrop, whose victims are both audience and actor, subject and object.

(Lights out. Sound of conversation continuing on tape, too soft to be intelligible.)

HUGH: *(In darkness, over the sound of the tape.)* What happened?

(ALEC's voice on the tape: "I thought the kitchen closed at midnight" played backwards.)

HUGH: What?

GODFREY: *(Enters with flashlight.)* Sorry guys, I didn't realize you were still

here. The restaurant's been closed for hours. Can I get you something? *(Pause.)* More water? Coffee?

HUGH: *No* coffee, ever.

ALEC: I'll have some coffee.

GODFREY: I'll bring you a pitcher. Just so you know the ki[tchen] *(Flashlight flickers out.)*

ALEC: or kill	HUGH: [y]eah
Mussolini? would	well what about
you go back in	Henry Ford? can
time and kill	I go back in time
Mussolini? or	and kill Henry
Joseph	For[d]

(Flashlight illuminates ALEC just as he smacks a file folder on the table. Flashlight moves to illuminate HUGH.)

HUGH: What is that?

(Flashlight moves to illuminate ALEC.)

ALEC: Proof.

(Flashlight moves to illuminate HUGH.)

HUGH: Of what?

(Flashlight moves to illuminate ALEC.)

ALEC: We know there's a bomb in Manhattan. We know

(Flashlight moves to illuminate HUGH just as he smacks a larger file folder on the table. Pause. Flashlight moves to illuminate ALEC, who smacks an even larger file folder on the table. Flashlight out. Sound of more folders smacking on table continues through:)

ALEC: *(On tape, very quiet but somewhat intelligible.)* [wh]en they get older have trouble with joint pain, with breath support, with being able to sing. Some are unable to stand without shifting their weight from side to side, causing extreme complications in the arches of the feet. Others' hands freeze into clawlike mitts, men's especially. All this can be solved via the free market. I read a book which proved that poverty in the third world doesn't exist anymo[re]

(Gunshot. Flashlights swirl around ALEC, who is holding a gun against GODFREY's empty hat. After one and a half seconds, flashlights off. Long pause. Music fades up very slow and quiet—if possible, Beethoven String Quartet Opus 132, Movement 3, played at half tempo. Sound of HUGH weeping. GODFREY enters with flashlight, water pitcher. Music stops suddenly.)

GODFREY: Okay, here's your order. We've got, dead bird, looks like pigeon, just beginning to fester, and one sewer rat, they just killed it, and I think, yeah, they left the bullet in there so, you know, just be careful. Oh, and you know we're out of maggots. I'll bring you some assorted live bugs. Let's see…is there anything el[se]

(Flashlight out, pause. The same music up again, very slow and even quieter.)

HUGH: Now what?

(The water pitcher is filled with a strange substance, which GODFREY, still as the WAITER, smears on HUGH's face during the next lines, while slowly, a different light illuminates HUGH's face.)

GODFREY: First the blackness will relax into a few gray streaks, followed by strips of blue or red. It's called dawn. It happens all the time.

HUGH: Are we still going to do the scene we talked about doing, where the prisoner is stripped naked and forced to dance with the American Soldier?

GODFREY: No, we're just going to imagine it. Dim lights, soft music. A few bad apples making an aesthetic choice. No wonder the Army banned cameras.

HUGH: Why damage the body?

GODFREY: Because they'd never be beautiful enough for it. Beauty requires too much of people.

HUGH: How do you make cruelty beautiful?

GODFREY: Simple—by imagining it. Imagined cruelty is always beautiful.

HUGH: What is this?

GODFREY: Menstrual blood.

HUGH: Godfrey?

GODFREY: If you become the torturer in his scenario, even for a few minutes, even just to prove him wrong, you betray every torture victim who ever lived on this earth.

HUGH: But what choice do I have?

GODFREY: I'll bring you a pitcher. Just so you know, the kitchen's closing in about five minutes.

HUGH: Then morning breaks. Trees too drenched to snap at the root go flaccid, smacking the ground over and over in gale-force wind. Drab black graying clouds, their dingy distended bellies bloated with sky filth pressed up against the windows, pour their guts out with each slit.

ALEC: I thought the kitchen closed at midnight.

GODFREY: It's about five to midnight.

HUGH: You said that already!

GODFREY: That was yesterday. You've been here all night.

HUGH: Where's Godfrey?

GODFREY: Who? *(He is gone.)*

(Lights up. Music off. HUGH standing. ALEC seated at table.)

HUGH: I'm going back in time and changing the play. I'm going back in time and killing the play. Yes, Alec, I will use torture. What techniques are available to me according to the most recently declassified CIA training manuals?

ALEC: Stress positions.

HUGH: *(Lecturing, similar to GODFREY's first monologue.)* Stress positions: quote likelier to sap his resistance unquote simply by holding the body in one awkward place, skin becomes taut, excruciating, ankles double in size, blisters erupt, kidneys shut down, quote pain which he feels he is inflicting upon himself unquote. Doesn't work in thirty minutes though. What else?

ALEC: Sensory deprivation.

HUGH: Sensory deprivation: the mind caves in on itself, leading to psychoses, delusions and powerful hallucinations, anxiety attacks, persistent amnesia, superstition, permanent mental disorders such as prosopagnosia, the inability to distinguish faces or common objects. Also doesn't work in thirty minutes. Next.

ALEC: Sleep deprivation.

HUGH: Sleep management? For thirty minutes? Come on—we have to get the information now!

ALEC: Waterboarding.

HUGH: Waterboarding! Now you're talking. Submerging the victim's head in water to "induce the misperception

of drowning," elegant phrase, the water in the lungs, the vomit in the water, and the poor foolish victim suffers from a "misperception"! But anyway, we do it. Four minutes. Vomit in the water. Five more minutes. By the book. *(HUGH sits opposite ALEC.)* Scene Thirty. Do you talk?

ALEC: *(Pause.)* Me?

HUGH: Yes you! I'm the torturer! Someone has to be the victim. Otherwise the scenario doesn't work! Do you talk?

ALEC: What's my motivation?

HUGH: I'm asking the questions! You have no motivation, or any other human qualities aside from a vast capacity for evil twenty minutes away from full realization! Do you talk?

ALEC: No!

HUGH: Ha! Well done. We wasted ten minutes on the waterboarding. Scene Thirty-One. What next?

ALEC: Electric shocks?

HUGH: Electric shocks can cause a heart attack! If we kill you, we'll never find the bomb! Hurry up and strip.

ALEC: Now?

HUGH: Yes, now—when do you think? The bomb goes off in nineteen minutes!

GODFREY: *(From offstage.)* We said we weren't going to do that.

HUGH: Shut up Godfrey.

GODFREY: I said, we're not going to—

HUGH: You're not helping, Godfrey!

ALEC: No, he's right. This is just a thought experiment.

HUGH: "Just"—! So, *think!* We strip you naked and slam your penis in the door of the bathroom stall.

ALEC: In the restaurant bathroom?

HUGH: What, you were picturing a gleaming aseptic chamber with state-of-the-art techn—

ALEC: You have to at least take me in to the preci—

HUGH: In New York traffic? We're twenty minutes to the inferno—this is taking too long! Do you talk?

ALEC: How do you hold me down if you're holding both the stall door and my penis—

HUGH: Oh, you think there's only one of us? You think this is a "clash of dueling wills"—one torturer, one victim? Come on! There's at least five of us and one of you! This isn't *fair.* Do you talk?

ALEC: I don't know.

HUGH: You don't know—not good enough! Scene Thirty-Two. Agent Godfrey suggests crushing one of your testicles.

GODFREY: *(From offstage.)* I do not!

HUGH: Godfrey, you imbecile, we can't do that! He might black out! We need him conscious! Scene Thirty-Three. We grab a steak knife from the kitchen and pry off a fingernail.

ALEC: Stop it.

HUGH: According to Jay Bybee it's okay!

ALEC: I said stop it!

HUGH: I'll stop it when we've got the nuclear bomb!

ALEC: It's in Columbus Circle.

HUGH: No, say that with more dripping bitterness—you've just

ALEC: Shut up.

HUGH: Perfect. A pair of choppers to Columbus Circle. Scene Thirty-Four. Were you telling us the truth?

ALEC: *(Smiling.)* Of course not.

HUGH: Of course not, that's what we think too. We have no choice but to bring in your son.

ALEC: What?

HUGH: Your son.

ALEC: *(Standing, almost leaving the stage.)* Come on!

HUGH: What?

ALEC: No!

HUGH: To save Manhattan? You wouldn't torture one ten-year-old boy?

ALEC: *(Returning, but not sitting.)* I think you're enjoying yourself too much.

HUGH: Oops! I forgot—torture is fine as long as we don't enjoy it too much. Great! Scene Thirty-Five. You're my superior officer. I'm enjoying myself too much. What do you do?

ALEC: You're fired!

HUGH: I'm free!

ALEC: In your dreams, buddy! You're under arrest.

HUGH: Ohhhh, sweet justice. Good, so you've arrested the torturer for enjoying himself too much fifteen minutes before the inferno. Scene Thirty-Six. Now what?

ALEC: There's at least five of you you said.

HUGH: So true! We just keep coming. So, you be one of them and tell me what you do.

ALEC: Am I torturing myself now?

HUGH: No, that *really* won't work. I'll be the prisoner.

ALEC: Do you talk?

HUGH: You haven't even done anything to me!

ALEC: Imagine that I have!

HUGH: No, no—This is your nightmare, not mine! In fifteen minutes I'll be glowing dust, along with millions of New York Democrats who'll vote against you in the next election even if you do save their lives! My screams are music! You can do anything to me!

ALEC: But you're saying you'll talk if I torture your son?

HUGH: There's only one way to find out, you liberal wimp.

GODFREY: *(Enters as WAITER.)* Guys, just so you know, the kitchen closes in about five—

ALEC: *(Puts GODFREY in headlock.)* Okay, let's say I torture your son.

HUGH: Right. Scene Thirty-Seven. How?

ALEC: Waterboarding!

HUGH: Please be serious—waterboarding's a fear technique, you're trying to scare *me,* not him! Besides it takes too long. You've only got—

ALEC: The bathroom stall.

HUGH: Say it.

ALEC: I'll— no.

HUGH: You don't even have the guts to say it, you expect me to believe—

ALEC: I'll slam his penis in the door of the—

HUGH: You've stripped a ten-year-old boy naked?

ALEC: Yes.

HUGH: In a public bathroom?

ALEC: Yes!

HUGH: Pervert!

ALEC: You did it to me!

HUGH: No! Pshaha—he still thinks he's the victim! *You* did it to *me*—remember? Infidel! *(Viciously.)* You with your *Baywatch* and *Sex in the City* and bachelorette reality shows—can you even imagine how revolting you appear to those of us who had erotic art three thousand years before you did?!? Do you seriously think anyone is going to miss New York?

ALEC: *(Dropping GODFREY, who slumps on the table.)* So you just let your son be—

HUGH: I've already planned to have my son blown up, moron! Like you and me, he has nine minutes to live! You think a big macho ethnic stereotype like me is scared of a little blood—you dipshit! You're running out of time! You'll have to play on my famous sexual inhibitions. Scene Thirty-Eight.

ALEC: Oh, no…

HUGH: Go ahead, rape him.

ALEC: Stop!

HUGH: You have almost nine minutes.

ALEC: Scene Thirty-Nine—

HUGH: Scene Thirty-Eight. Come on.

ALEC: I won't do it.

HUGH: You won't?

ALEC: You're playing a game with me.

HUGH: You proposed this game!

ALEC: I said I won't do it.

HUGH: You mean you can't.

ALEC: I mean I wouldn't if I could, and I happen to be proud of the fact that I can't under these particular circumstances, all right?

HUGH: That was impressive. But since when do you have to get it up? Force him to suck me.

ALEC: Are you insane?

HUGH: I have just set a nuclear bomb to go off in Manhattan. You have just pulverized a ten-year-old boy's penis. The words "sane" and "insane" no longer— Scene Thirty-Nine.

ALEC: How much time's left?

HUGH: Eight minutes.

ALEC: He's sucking you.

HUGH: Why?

ALEC: We're making him.

HUGH: How are you making him?

ALEC: What?

HUGH: You heard me.

ALEC: I'm holding a gun at his head, and—

HUGH: If you shoot him, I'll tell you nothing.

ALEC: He doesn't know that.

HUGH: Of course he does.

ALEC: I have a gun, you know, I'm going to use it. Let's see what your son does.

HUGH: Okay, he kneels before me and takes my bruised, bleeding penis into his mouth. Do you photograph this, American soldier?

ALEC: No. Sure. Whatever.

HUGH: It is horrible, humiliating. I am enraged, chained, in a hood. He weeps. For a long still moment you observe the scene, an embarrassingly beautiful, tender moment of total degradation. You become furious at the sight of such fragility and grab the back of his head, grinding his face into my crotch. One of you is yelling "tell us where the bomb is hidden" over his screams and cries. Another one of you holds me from behind, grabbing my ass and shoving my pubis over and over into the face of my weeping, naked, ten-year-old son.

ALEC: Okay. You've made your point. *(Pause.)* So, do you talk?

HUGH: Scene Forty. I talk. I tell you the bomb is in the A-line station on 110th Street. It will go off in six minutes. Just then the radio report comes in that there was no bomb at Columbus Circle.

ALEC: So you're saying I don't believe you this time either?

HUGH: That's up to you. The choppers speed off to 110th. You can either believe me, or you can fuck my son.

ALEC: I would never do that.

HUGH: You're a beacon of humanity. Scene Forty-One. After the bomb goes off in Washington Square Park, they'll replace you with someone who will.

ALEC: *(Sits.)* Unlike me, you have a sick imagination.

HUGH: Unlike you, I have an imagination. *(Drinks, splutters.)* This is coffee!

ALEC: Are you sure?

HUGH: I was drinking—oh God—hot chocolate—

ALEC: Sometimes hot chocolate tastes like coffee.

HUGH: —where's my pill bottle—shit—oh shit! *(Searches frantically for the pill bottle.)*

ALEC: *(Producing the pill bottle, holds it out at arm's length away from HUGH.)* Scene Fifty. Tell us where the bomb is hidden.

HUGH: What?

ALEC: Pervert. Scene Fifty. Tell us where the bomb is hidden.

HUGH: There's no bomb.

ALEC: We know there's a bomb. We know you planted it. Our intelligence is accurate, timely, and consistent. We never perform torture except under the most extreme circumstances, with an assurance of success, and in any case all of our techniques for information extraction are not only legal and effective, but morally clear and justified.

HUGH: *(Convulsing in pain.)* Okay!

ALEC: Occasionally a few bad apples unable to handle the pressures of combat may abuse—

HUGH: Yes, you're right—

ALEC: The U.S. Army bends over backwards to avoid civilian casualties—

HUGH: —I know they do—

ALEC: —with a nearly 100 percent success rate,—

HUGH: —that's excellent—

ALEC: —and as a result of our efforts, democracy has spread throughout Iraq and the Middle East, and for the first time in history millions around the globe are being lifted out of poverty by the free marke—

HUGH: *(Controlling the pain.)* We have your sister.

ALEC: What?

HUGH: Scene Fifty-One. We have your sister.

ALEC: You have—

HUGH: Yes.

ALEC: Where?

HUGH: *(Transparently faking it.)* You'd like to know, wouldn't you.

ALEC: Yes, yes, yes—

HUGH: Give me the pills.

ALEC: Where is she?

HUGH: Admit that torture doesn't work. *(Pause.)* Admit it.

(HUGH and ALEC are frozen. GODFREY rises from his slumped position on the table.)

GODFREY: Scene Twenty-Four. Hey, wow, what are you guys doing here? Haha! I never thought I'd run into you two together!

ALEC: *(Still frozen, but speaking naturally.)* He's explaining how the terrorists will go away if we just treat them with love and kindness, like old friends.

HUGH: *(Still frozen, but speaking naturally.)* That's just what I was saying,

Alec, that's exactly what I was saying. How did you manage to unerringly extract that clear populist message from my convoluted cloud of elitist intellectualizing?

(Over the course of GODFREY's next speech, HUGH and ALEC slowly, undramatically unfreeze into ordinary sitting positions.)

GODFREY: Haha! Just like old times! You guys! Life really is just a rerun of high school isn't it? Remember that great big argument you had all senior year about nuclear war? That was *so funny!* Scene Twenty-Five! Wow, high school—what a humpfest! You wanna talk about the body falling apart as you get older—I used to be able to come so many times in one day—Jesus! I mean, one minute you're just going through the motions, hoping your half-a-hard-on will stay erect for long enough to get the condom on, the next minute all this stuff is squirting out of you—holy shit! Who knew? 'Course, as I don't have to tell you, Mr. Happy doesn't work *that* shift anymore! Haha! Oh God, senior year—It was so boring! Scene Twenty-Six. Remember Mrs. Clytempaulie? Whoa—*who doesn't?*—I mean this lady couldn't teach Shop to save her life! Fifty minutes of interminable droning lectures—twice a week!—I thought I'd faint! It was as if all the oxygen had left the room! I'd be stiff as a board, rubbing my penis against the bottom side of the desk—by the end of each class, my undershorts would be caked with the sperm from four or even five ejaculations! I could hardly peel myself from the desk! The fragrance was so strong—it drew comments from everyone—even Principal Jordache! But you know, it kept me awake!

(HUGH and ALEC are by now seated normally. GODFREY continues, oblivious.)

GODFREY: That reminds me. I'll tell you a recurring dream one of my patients has. *(During the following, GODFREY reprises the gestures he used during his speech about Saunder Simpcox at the beginning of the play.)* Scene Twenty-Seven. Godfrey will be killed in the prison riots that sweep across this country, and the U.S. prisons in other countries, six years from now, unreported in the news. So I wanted to give him that speech. Scene Twenty-Eight. That's it.

HUGH: And then the patient wakes up.

GODFREY: Can you say that more casually, like it's no big deal?

HUGH: *(More casually.)* And then the patient wakes up.

GODFREY: Maybe. Legally, you know, I shouldn't be telling you this.

ALEC: Anyway it wasn't Mrs. Clytempaulie who taught Shop. It was Mr. Mannakachru.

GODFREY: You're kidding me! Oh boy, that's funny—Ha ha ha! Wow. All the little details go first! Scene Sixty. The only other customers at the restaurant are a Japanese family at a table in the corner. The young girl from the family is playing with a SuperBall. One false bounce and the SuperBall goes skipping across the floor of the restaurant.

ALEC: Well, it's been great seeing you guys. *(Puts down the pill bottle, leaves his seat, starts walking offstage. He does not act out the following narration.)*

GODFREY: The little girl leaps from her seat, scampering after her ball. As she passes by our table I see she is no more than eight years old. Alec reaches out and in a sudden movement breaks her neck.

(ALEC freezes.)

HUGH: The girl falls to the ground—her red dress hangs behind in Alec's hand. I hear the waiter speaking Japanese while Alec folds the dress and sets it gently on the table, rising from his seat and taking down his pants. I'm about to say something important to Alec—I'm leaning forward to begin my sentence. My head moves low—the screams I hear come from further and further away. I sink into a heavy sleep. *(HUGH, slumping forward, falls asleep on the table.)*

GODFREY: Scene Sixty-One. *(While speaking, GODFREY becomes the WAITER.)* When I wake up the restaurant is dark, rain pounding the walls on all sides; with each gust of wind, another frenzy of giant raindrops beats down hard and blunt against the windows. Shakespeare's complete works lie open in front of me. I hear the sound of glass cracking, but looking up in fear I see the glass intact and Godfrey outside. Rain ricochets off his skin, his useless clothes disposed of by himself or others. At first I think he sees me, but he's asleep, shivering curled on the ground, his mouth open, the rain fills him drop by drop.

Scene Sixty-Five. When I wake up again, people pour me holiday drinks and ask me how I've been. I ask about the decorations and the baby girl. They ask about Godfrey. I ask about the movie they've rented for their son, in which a poor mouse from the country pretends to be a rich mouse from the city, terrified the whole time that the rich mice will see through his masquerade, until—Scene Sixty-Six—a fairy godmother reveals that the poor mouse is actually the heir to a forgotten fortune worth millions. So, happy end. *(Pause.)*

Scene Twenty-Nine. Everybody talks about the storm.

(Lights fade slowly to black.)

KRAPP, 39

Michael Laurence

MICHAEL LAURENCE is a theatre artist and filmmaker. He graduated with a BFA in theatre in 1992 from New York University's Tisch School of the Arts, where he studied at the Experimental Theater Wing with Kevin Kuhlke, Mary Overlie, and Ryscard Cieslak and at the Classical Studio with Louis Scheeder and Deloss Brown. After college, he studied directing with Anne Bogart, and worked with theatre legends Judith Malina and Joe Chaiken. He is the author of the plays *The Escape Artist* (Tribeca Lab, 1994), *The Escape Artist: Virgil's Cauldron* (Phil Bosakowski Theatre, 1999), and the co-creator (with playwright-performer Edgar Oliver) of *Chop Off Your Ear* (Angel Orensanz Foundation, 2000). He also wrote and directed the independent feature film *Escape Artists* (Anthology Film Archives' 2005 New Filmmakers Series). He is a founding member of The Cliplight Theater, for which he has directed Jesse McKinley's *Quick Bright Things* (HERE Arts Center, 1995), Edgar Oliver's *Master of Monstrosities* (La MaMa, 1996), *I Am a Coffin* (La MaMa, 1997), *My Green Hades* (Phil Bosakowski Theatre, 1999), *The Drowning Pages* (La MaMa, 2000), and *Maverick* by George Demas (Culture Project, 2003). As an actor, Laurence has performed extensively in New York and regional theatre, film, and television. His most recent credits include the Broadway revival of Eric Bogosian's *Talk Radio* (2007), the New York premiere of Michael Hollinger's *Opus* (Primary Stages, 2007), and the off-Broadway revival of *Two Rooms* by Lee Blessing (Platform Group, 2008). *Krapp, 39* won the award for Outstanding Solo Show at the 2008 New York International Fringe Festival. He lives in Manhattan with his wife, Sherri, their dog, Penelope, and a colony of "rescue" cats.

Krapp, 39 was first presented by The Cliplight Theater (George Demas, Artistic Director) as part of the New York International Fringe Festival (Elena K. Holy, Producing Artistic Director) on August 10, 2008, at the Schaeberle Studio Theatre with the following cast and credits:

Performed by: Michael Laurence
Directed by: George Demas
Creative Collaborators: Jon Dichter, Alyssa Bresnahan
Lighting Design by: Sonia Baidya
Stage Manager: Regina Betancourt

Krapp, 39 subsequently opened at The SoHo Playhouse (Darren Lee Cole, Producer) on January 13, 2009, with the following cast and credits:

Performed by: Michael Laurence
Directed by: George Demas
Creative Collaborators: Jon Dichter, Alyssa Bresnahan
Lighting Design by: Sonia Baidya
Sound Design by: Bernard Fox
Stage Manager: Dan DaSilva
Production Manager: Jon Johnson

www.cliplighttheater.com
www.krapp39.com

ACKNOWLEDGMENTS

My deep gratitude goes to:

My friend Jon Dichter for his artistic collaboration, invaluable to the development of this project. Jon is a brilliant writer, theatre artist, and filmmaker, currently living in Seattle, and the seeds of the project were sown in a series of tape-recorded long distance phone calls with him. Our invigorating, probative, ongoing dialogue started with transparent discussions about the concept of the piece, character analysis, structure, and my process in preparing for the role, and moved into frank and intimate discussions of creative process, personal and artistic failure, the psychology of solitude, loss of romantic love, the mysteries of aging. Really, we covered it all: life, love, death, and art. "Echo-locating" is the way Jon once described the process of always finding our way back to Krapp in these big conversations; I find the term to be beautiful and apt.

Jon played many roles in that process: friend and foil, maestro and muse, sage and scold, contrarian and confidante.

The snippets of our dialogue used in the various productions were edited from many of these conversations.

My friend and frequent collaborator George Demas. George is a superb and savvy director and producer, and I'm proud to have worked in the trenches of downtown theatre with him for over fifteen years. George shepherded and shaped this play through all of its incarnations with patience and wisdom. The journey from the initial birthday presentation (only a few hours to rehearse, no real "script") to festival staging (limited resources, lots of adrenaline), to fully staged production could not have happened without his inspired stagecraft and leadership. His collaboration in the development of ideas, and especially his shaping of performance and the visual landscape of the show, including the use of video, was inestimable. Though we've developed shorthand in working together all these years, we wanted to shatter the mold of our familiar process with *Krapp, 39*, and I think we joyfully did.

As with Jon, snippets of our many recorded conversations were used in the various productions of the play.

Alyssa Bresnahan, one of the finest actors I know, for bringing my mother's voice to life.

My friend Marc Palmieri, for his genius for self-deprecation, and for his thoughtful feedback and suggestions.

Michael Wiener and Neke Carson, curators of the performance series at the Gershwin Hotel, NYC, who graciously presented an early version of the piece in February 2008.

Elena Holy, producer of The New York International Fringe Festival, for believing in the play from the beginning.

Darren Lee Cole and Scott Morfee, producers extraordinaire, for taking it to the next level.

Sherri Laurence for her love and encouragement.

The inimitable Samuel Beckett

The late Jason Bauer
Who will forever be
The original Krapp for me.

NOTES ON THE DEVELOPMENT OF THE PIECE (OR NOTES ON FAILURE)

Krapp, 39 started out as a birthday party. I was about to turn thirty-nine, and looking back over my life-so-far, I was haunted by my failures, both personal and artistic.

Maybe it's no wonder Samuel Beckett's *Krapp's Last Tape* was on my mind.

I had studied the play as an acting student in college, seen several productions over the years, and now, as a professional actor coming into the middle age of my career, hoped for the opportunity to one day play the role. (Coincidentally, 2008 marked the fiftieth anniversary of the first production of the play, with anniversary productions happening around the world.)

All around me I saw theatre and film tapping the vein of American triumphalism, but from my vantage point, perched on the edge of forty, alienated and adrift, I felt a perverse affinity with Beckett's strange and shambling antihero.

I found myself becoming deeply introspective around the themes of the play—specifically fear of aging, loss of love, the death of a parent (which resonated particularly since the recent death of my mother), and, of course, *failure*.

That much of Beckett's play involves the sixty-nine-year-old Krapp ruefully listening to an older, autobiographical tape—one that he made on *his own* thirty-ninth birthday—only deepened my identification.

Now, in most (if not all) productions of the play, the fact of this older recording requires the creation of a "dummy" tape, recorded by the actor playing Krapp, putting on the voice of his younger self. I thought about this as an interesting problem for every production of the play and for any sixty-nine-year-old actor. And then a possible solution occurred to me: what if the tape was an authentic one, recorded by the selfsame actor thirty years before?

Wishful thinking, maybe, but I wanted to create the artifact that could be used in my hoped-for production of *Krapp's Last Tape* in 2038.

On February 12, 2008, my actual thirty-ninth birthday, I performed an early sketch of *Krapp, 39*. It had a few of the elements of the current version, and culminated in the recording of that tape. The invited (captive) audience was made up of friends and colleagues who were expecting a birthday party, but instead of balloons and cake they got a blast of Beckett. It seemed like a fun idea, and after all, your birthday is the one day of the year when your friends are happy to indulge your foibles. And I think I had some notion that I could alleviate my sense of failure by going public with it, as channeled through Krapp. Performance art as emotional exorcism.

Nursing my obsession, I decided to pursue the project throughout my thirty-ninth year. I cobbled together a script (basically transcribed from the video document of the birthday performance) and submitted it to The New York International Fringe Festival. I was surprised and grateful when it was accepted, but there was a stumbling block: I suspected I would not be able to use any of Beckett's copyrighted text. Without that text, the piece would lose its reason for being.

I fretted for weeks trying on increasingly absurd ways of getting around the problem—could I project a video of me reading the text, for example? Or could I induce someone in the audience to read it and I remain an "innocent" bystander? Could the reading of it happen offstage like an inciting event in Greek drama? Could I read it inaudibly? I threw out each new ridiculous idea. Time was running out and I was failing. But then the Eureka: *Failure!* It's the place I started from, after all, the governing principle! My quixotic desire to record the text, and my inability to do so, would be the starting point for a newly structured version of the piece. *Krapp, 39* would be a "documentary" play in which I would explore the themes of *Krapp's Last Tape*, but in very personal terms. It would be a marker for my own "end of youth," and at the same time would shadow and pay homage to Beckett's masterpiece.

And it would finish in *failure*. Or *might*. (I don't want to give away the ending here.)

Even my attempts to obtain the rights, my "Search for Beckett," so to speak, would become part of the story, and email exchanges with the Beckett estate could be woven in as narrative threads. If nothing else, my appeals would keep the narrative of failure alive. Actually, the more I was rejected, the better it would be. (Here I should mention that the agents for the Beckett estate were, in fact, very gracious to me.)

Since I wanted the structure to mirror *Krapp's Last Tape*, I kept the excuse of a thirty-ninth birthday party as the frame. This meant pretending that every night I performed the piece would be my actual birthday, but that seemed to be a fair and amiable fiction.

In terms of design, I also took my cue from Beckett: a tape recorder and desk would be center. But in a sort of transposition of technology, instead of using a reel-to-reel device, I would use modern digital playback/recording devices. And to add yet another layer of recording, I would capture the action of the piece as it was happening with digital video cameras.

Contemplating haunted Krapp and his tapes, I began to think about personal archivism of all sorts—journals, diaries, letters, audio and videotapes—and raided my own keepsakes, letters, and notebooks for material that could be relevant to the piece.

I had tapes of my own: All the way back to the conception of the project, I had been having phone conversations with two friends and colleagues around the themes of the play; first with Jon Dichter, a brilliant writer currently living on the West Coast, and then with George Demas, my director. (See Acknowledgments.) I had recorded all of these conversations onto cassette tapes using a flimsy little device I bought at Radio Shack. I edited the tapes on my computer, pulling sequences that could be incorporated as elements into the production.

As for the journal entries, they are all connected to my own actual journals, but sometimes I invented scenarios, or created alternate versions of my past. Names were changed, of course. The process of shaping the entries and juxtaposing them with the recorded phone call sequences involved a lot of trial and error; process dancing with content, the past dancing with the present.

Though they are the lynchpins of the play, the journal entries were the final elements to fall into place. In fact, I was still shaping them up until the day of the first performance at the FringeNYC

Festival, and continued adding and rewriting as the run went on. Sometimes my tinkering would unbalance the play, and I had to circle back, but I tried to keep in mind that there could never be a final version of the play, only a *next* version.

That mindset was the key to the project. For a play about process, I had to stay *in process*. And for a play about failure, I never wanted to be too *afraid to fail*.

CHARACTERS

MICHAEL, a thirty-nine-year-old actor

Recorded Voices:
> GEORGE, a friend
> JON, a friend
> MICHAEL'S MOTHER

TIME

October 28, 2008. Michael's thirty-ninth birthday. Evening.

SPACE

A dark room. The space is ambiguous. Or maybe dualistic. Or even a contradiction. In one sense, it is a "personalized" space, sort of an actor's rehearsal space, or laboratory. In another sense, it is "neutral." A stage in this very theater. Wherever "this very theater" is. Video cameras on tripods downstage left and right pointed toward the center of the room. Downstage center, a simple black desk. Upstage center, a six-foot black "tech" table. Between them a black swivel-backed, rolling office chair. Left of the desk is a large flat-screen monitor on a pedestal draped in black cloth. The desk is bare except for a microphone and a laptop computer that glows in the darkness. The tech table is covered with objects—the flotsam and jetsam of a self-archivist's life. In the center stands a camcorder on a quick-release tripod.

NOTE

Periodically throughout the performance, Michael takes the camcorder and films various objects on the tech table, sometimes scanning them briefly, sometimes lingering and zooming in closer and closer. His live-cam images appear on the large flat-screen monitor. The objects include

- A dog-eared copy of Samuel Beckett's *Krapp's Last Tape*
- A program from a 1998 production of *Krapp's Last Tape*

- A sealed letter from the literary agency for the Beckett estate
- An "Irish Accent Training Manual"
- A large, beat-up, red dictionary
- A paperback copy of Fontane's *Effie Briest*
- Samuel Beckett's novella, *First Love*
- Stanislavski's *Building a Character*
- Shakespeare's *King Lear*
- An anthology of solo performance texts
- *Collected Works of T. S. Eliot*
- A St. James Bible (red)
- Numerous open journals and composition notebooks
- A stack of printed emails relating to discussions of *Krapp*
- A bundle of love letters tied with a ribbon
- Birthday cards
- A large candle in a glass bowl
- A black metal lockbox
- An antique pocket watch
- A reel-to-reel tape recorder
- A cassette tape recorder
- A phone-call recording device
- VHS and digital videocassette tapes
- A skull
- A plaster gargoyle
- A porcelain Buddha
- A miniature telephone from a charm bracelet
- A round makeup mirror
- A furry Daniel Boone coonskin cap
- A framed photo of Michael and Jon
- A framed photo of Michael and George
- Numerous photos of Michael as a choirboy, his mother, and Samuel Beckett
- A folder with his mother's newspaper columns
- Various playbills of Michael's plays
- A bottle of vodka
- A pack of cigarettes
- A bottle of prescription pills
- A miniature audio mixing board

Lights fade to black. The machines hum and glow in the darkness. A phone rings in the dark, amplified through the stage speakers.

GEORGE: Yeah, Mike?

MICHAEL: Hey, George, sorry, we got disconnected—this recording apparatus is a pain in my neck...

(As the audio continues, it becomes clear it is a recorded phone conversation.)

MICHAEL: ...So as I was saying, Beckett's play *Krapp's Last Tape* is about a sixty-nine-year-old man who makes an archival recording of his thoughts and impressions on his sixty-ninth birthday, as he does every year on that day. But to prime the pump, so to speak, he first listens to an older tape. He chooses one at random from a box, and it happens to be the tape he recorded on his thirty-ninth birthday...

GEORGE: *(Doubtfully.)* Uh-huh. And it'll be your thirty-ninth birthday.

MICHAEL: Exactly! And here's the thing—whenever anyone does a production of *Krapp*, they have an old man playing the part, and they have to create a dummy tape of him as a thirty-nine-year-old man, he has to use a fake voice...

GEORGE: Uh-huh.

MICHAEL: So, this is my concept—on my own thirty-ninth birthday, I want to build a theatre piece around this...I don't know...thirty-year theatrical foresight. I want to record...in front of a live audience...the thirty-nine-year-old Krapp soliloquy that I will use in a conventional production of *Krapp's Last Tape* thirty years from now, in the year 2038, when I'm sixty-nine years old.

GEORGE: *(Trying to understand)* Um... and so what? Okay, so you're...you're recording the Beckett text...um...is there something beyond that? I mean, are you writing something...*beyond* that...?

MICHAEL: *(With mounting enthusiasm.)* I don't know...now that you mention it...there could be something more...I suppose...it could be expanded...the soliloquy could be just the jumping-off point...the *convening event* of the piece, the central event of the piece. But I could blow up this clown from the inside! I could build a piece that mirrors the structure of Beckett's play. I could have archival tapes of my own, journal entries, recorded conversations just like this one...that speak to the same themes as Beckett's play—love, loss, failure, aging...that I listen to...before I record Beckett's text...

GEORGE: *(Sarcastically.)* Yeah...and you don't think that's just a touch *heavy* for a birthday party?

MICHAEL: *(Laughing.)* George, why are you being so dubious? This is *my* birthday...!

GEORGE: *(Trying to muster enthusiasm.)* Well, alright...

(Music: The opening chords of the Beatles' "Birthday" morph into Schubert's achingly beautiful "String Quintet in C Major." Lights up: MICHAEL stands downstage center, absentmindedly eating a banana and staring into the darkness. He looks like a guttersnipe phantom—wild, unkempt hair, unshaven, dirty three-piece gray suit. He takes another bite, scrutinizes the banana, and gently tucks it into the shallow pocket of his waistcoat. It protrudes from the pocket, peeled and half-eaten. He crosses to the downstage left and right video

cameras, and takes a moment with each, framing them on the desk. He crosses to the flat-screen monitor and powers it on. He sits in the rolling chair and scoots into the tech table, his back to the audience, and turns on the video camera. He aims it at his face and adjusts it so that he is framed in a closeup. He rotates the flip-out screen so he can see himself in it, and pushes "record." The camcorder whirrs to action, and the closeup image of himself jumps to life on the live-feed flat-screen monitor. He pulls a letter from his breast pocket, and puts on a pair of reading glasses. As the Schubert fades, he tentatively leans into the microphone which is cabled into the laptop, and adjusts the volume on the mixer.)

MICHAEL: Testing… *(His voice jumps from the speakers. He reads the letter into the camera.)*

"To the Literary Agent for the Samuel Beckett Estate:

"My name is Michael Laurence, and I've developed a solo performance work called *Krapp, 39*. It is not a play in the conventional sense, but might be best characterized as an autobiographical documentary theatre piece. An investigation of myself, of the famous character Krapp, and the psychological intersection of the two. It is an original work, though obviously inspired by Mr. Beckett's *Krapp's Last Tape*, and I am respectfully seeking the permission of the Beckett Estate to include a section of text from his play.

"Please note the enclosed material for specifics.

"Thank you for your help in this matter. I've included all my contact info in the hope of hearing from you at your earliest convenience.

"Respectfully,

Michael Laurence
AKA Krapp, 39"

(He pockets the letter and speaks to the camera.)

October 28, 2008

Thirty-nine today.

Haven't slept for three nights in a row because of my old ailment.

"Restless Leg Syndrome."

Three bananas before bed didn't help.

Today is the day I record my tape.

Today I'm Krapp.

I've prepped my journals. Birthday entries going back to twenty-nine. Tedious work. But it helps me…get at the…*connection*. To Krapp.

Krapp.

Who is Krapp?

Who am I?

(He swivels his chair around and scoots into the desk. Types into the laptop. Leans into the microphone and narrates.)

(Note: The laptop holds all of MICHAEL's birthday journal entries in a scrollable format. During all the "journal" sections, the actor may occasionally refer to text on the laptop, but mostly his focus is forward and "out." He does not address the audience, however. In fact, he seems unaware of it. Rather, like an obsessive self-archivist, he is self-consciously narrating for the cameras placed around the stage.)

October 28,1998
New York City
"Michael Sees Krapp"

(He reconsiders this entry title. Deletes and retypes.)

October 28,1998
New York City
"Krapp Sees *Himself*"

Twenty-nine years old today. I'm writing on my new laptop computer that Mama sent me for my birthday. It's great. I'll have to go back and transfer all my old journals onto it.

Went to my friend Jason's show last night in the basement theater he owns on St. Mark's Place. Mary was supposed to go with me. We were supposed to go to the play and then go to my party at E.'s house, but we got in a fight over a dream.

I had a terrible dream, she said. *You were cheating on me. On a boat with a girl in a red dress,* she said. She was shaking.

Wait a minute, I blustered. *You're kicking me out because of a dream? On my birthday?*

I'm a very intuitive person, she said.

And then she threw a vase at my head.

(A beat.)

The fact is she *is* very intuitive.

(A beat.)

Anyway, Jason performed a one-man show—Samuel Beckett's *Krapp's Last Tape.* Jason always talked a lot about Beckett. I'd never read the play, never seen it, was dreading it, actually. Don't like Beckett. Don't know why. I'm a philistine, so sue me.

I was in for a surprise. It was a birthday play.

An old man on *his* sixty-ninth birthday, wolfing down bananas and booze,

listening to audio diaries in the dark. Stalking his memories. There is no story. Just a voice, a ghost in the machine. The old man rails at his thirty-nine-year-old self. And bit by bit it adds up to a life about to be a death.

Jason was brilliant. He's brave and unpredictable as a knife in the dark. Classical singer, actor, director, reader, writer, world traveler, dreamer, drug addict, drunk. He once called me the Virgil to his Dante in hell. That's too much—let's just say I feel *suburban* in his presence. I love him and envy him. It's complicated.

I was jealous. I couldn't play that role now, not at twenty-nine, couldn't pull it off, not like him. *But* I had an idea: when I'm thirty-nine, a decade from today, I'll record that thirty-nine-year-old Krapp's monologue. I'll seal it up in a box, and some day I will play the role, and the voice that will haunt me will be me. Really me!

(A beat.)

(Self-loathing.) God, Michael, you're such a narcissist, give it a rest.

(Music: The song "It's My Party (and I'll Cry If I Want To)" morphs into a soundscape of children's voices on a playground. MICHAEL pulls a manila envelope addressed to him off the tech table, opens it, puts on his reading glasses, and reads into the mic.)

"Dear Mr. Laurence,

"Thank you for your dramatic reading of *Krapp's Last Tape* for our fifth grade class here at Sawmill Elementary. We are especially proud of our "Visiting Artists" program, and having you participate was a privilege. I hope you weren't too discouraged by the Q&A session following the reading. Generally speaking this a relatively shy group of fifth graders, but the children told me later that they liked the reading very much, and thought that you were "interesting" and "nice."

"As you know, after your reading, the fifth graders were asked to write a short essay on *Krapp's Last Tape*. I'm sending along a few of them that I thought you might enjoy reading. Toby, the introverted boy who shared his lunch with you in the cafeteria, refused to write an essay on the grounds that his "reaction to your reading could not be expressed in words." He made a drawing instead, which I've also sent along.

"Thanks again, and we all send along our best wishes for your solipsistic performance at the Fringe Festival.

"Fondly,

Kristin Palmieri
Homeroom 3
Sawmill Elementary School"

(He pulls the essays from the envelope, chooses one, and reads into the recording mic.)

MICHAEL: Essay (Amy, age eleven, homeroom 3):

"The story *Krapp's Last Tape* by Samuel Beckett was about a boring, old man named Krapp who loves to be lonely. Since he is so bored, he always drinks and eats bananas. One time, he took out a dictionary and looked up a stupid word.

"He also listens to a tape which he recorded when he was thirty-nine. It brought back lots of memories.

"Krapp thinks that drinking and sexual life took too much of his waking time, so he's going to cut it out.

"Also he is sad because his mother died and he didn't talk to her enough. He knows she died because he watched her hospital window and the blinds went down and in Ireland that means you are dead.

"*Krapp's Last Tape* is trying to tell us that each one of us is just like Krapp in the story. Some people just like isolations. They never think of the communication in between people. This is why many people feel so lonely."

(He picks up a second essay, reads into the recording mic.)

Essay (Keith, age ten, homeroom 3):

"Samuel Beckett's *Krapp's Last Tape* shows a person who has a dream to become a famous writer, but instead he fails.

"Along with his problems as an old man, he can't go to the bathroom and he is also an alcoholic. He is just bored and plays his tapes from thirty years ago, trying to figure out what he should do with his life.

"Krapp is a typical person because he only cares about his own self.

"When he was younger he loved a girlfriend, but he believes she was a distraction to his success. He finally breaks up with her at a romantic place in a boat. Bam! He just closed his doors to what was most important to his life.

"The old man regrets what he did in the past, but he wouldn't change one thing about it because what was then, was then, and what is now, is now."

(MICHAEL pulls out another sheet of paper from the envelope. It is Toby's drawing: A grotesque crayon rendering of a banana and a man's red-eyed, weeping

face. MICHAEL *is disturbed by the draw-*
ing. He spins his chair around to face the
camcorder on the upstage table and holds
the drawing up to it, scooting in closer
and closer like a human camera dolly. The
drawing jumps up on the live-feed monitor.
He takes a roll of Scotch Tape from the tech
table, and carefully tapes the drawing to the
front of the desk: "exhibit A." He leans back
in his chair, broods. He lurches to the tech
table, seizes the tattered red dictionary, flips
to an entry, and reads into the mic.)

"Solipsistic. From sol·ip·sism [sol-ip-
siz-*uh*m]

"1. *Philosophy.* The theory that only the
self exists, or can be proved to exist.

"2. Extreme preoccupation with and
indulgence of one's feelings, desires, etc.;
egoistic self-absorption."

(He considers this a moment, then slams the
dictionary shut. Lights cross fade down on
the desk and up on the tech table. RING!
RING! Over the speakers we hear another
recorded phone conversation.)

JON: …But forty is a *flaccid* number,
and yet it's sort of huge in people's
lives. Because forty is the official end
of youth. We can tell ourselves all kind
of stories, but at forty you ain't *young*
anymore. So…

MICHAEL: Right…

(As the conversation unreels, MICHAEL
crosses to the upstage table, detaches the
camcorder from the tripod, and starts to
film various objects on the table. The im-
ages appear on the flat-screen monitor:

• *A framed photo of MICHAEL and*
  JON

• *A framed photo of MICHAEL and*
  GEORGE

• *A dog-eared copy of Samuel Beckett's*
  Krapp's Last Tape

• *A program from a 1998 production of*
  Krapp's Last Tape

• *An anthology of solo performance texts*

• *A miniature telephone from a charm*
  bracelet

• *A phone-call recording device*

• *VHS and digital videocassette tapes*

• *A reel-to-reel tape recorder*

• *A cassette tape recorder*

• *A porcelain Buddha)*

JON: …And at thirty-nine, well, there's
the iconic bridge to middle age…this is
all stuff that you know, because, you're
turning thirty-nine, and it's all alive and
real for you in ways that it once was
for me…

MICHAEL: …Right…

JON: …But Beckett is also picking up
on that same thing because he has this
guy Krapp looking back not at thirty, or
thirty-six, or twenty-eight…and not at
forty…but at *thirty-nine*…

MICHAEL: …Right…

JON: …He has him looking back at the
last moment of a certain kind of possibility in a life…

MICHAEL: …Well, I'll tell you *this*, I
was writing in my journal about turning
thirty-nine, and it has such *weight* for me.
I'm acting like I'm turning eighty. And
in so many ways I feel like I'm getting
so conservative in my life. I'm hedging
my bets. I'm frightened. I'm constantly
preoccupied with the future…with no-
tions of myself as a *failure*…not only as
an actor or artist…but as a *human*…

as a husband, son, brother, friend…it's bringing up all these huge questions around mortality, I guess…

JON: …Right…

MICHAEL: …And so I wonder if in some way this whole project isn't some kind of *wishful thinking*, or projected *wish fulfillment*…that by setting some artistic goal thirty years in the future, it represents some kind of *promise* that my life isn't about hedging bets…that my life isn't over in these important ways…because I *feel* like that right now…I'm not working…I'm an unemployed actor…I have all these thwarted dreams…my life as an artist is nothing like what I imagined it would be when I was eighteen…or even twenty-eight…

(BEEP. CLICK. MICHAEL returns to his desk and sets down the camcorder. The flat-screen monitor goes black. He leans in the recording mic, and narrates for the cameras.)

October 28, 1999
New York City
"Krapp in Three Minutes"

Thirty years old today. My birthday started badly. I woke up at a quarter to noon, the bed was empty where she had been, and somewhere around dawn my drunk had turned to a hangover in my sleep and my dreams had gone sour. But I couldn't remember them specifically, only that they were bad, and involved a woman's voice yelling at me and a terrible fire at sea.

Then I realized I needed to make an important phone call to explain why I wasn't at home and why I didn't call last night, but I needed to make it before noon and I couldn't possibly take a shower, brush my teeth, eat some toast,

invent an alibi, *and* find a pay phone in fifteen minutes!

So, I pulled on a dirty shirt and dashed out into the impossibly bright morning and located the little metal box on the wall—a pay phone to say where I was, but never *be* where I was. As I was dialing, I started to play that game that I like where you try to come up with the most ironic way you could die, and I pictured myself swinging from the metal cord of the pay phone like a noose.

The conversation wasn't a disaster but she was pretty distant sounding, and then just as she was getting to the critical part of her interrogation that mechanical voice chimed in with *Please deposit twenty-five cents for the next three minutes,* and I thought there is *no way* I just talked for three minutes!

But, of course, I didn't have any more quarters, so I said, *Baby, I'm out of quarters, I'll call you back in a while,* and she said *Don't bother,* and then the line went dead.

I started to panic, so I went into a bodega to get some more quarters, but the guy said *No change,* so I bought a tallboy for a dollar twenty-five and got the three quarters change, and downed the beer in thirteen gulps.

As I crossed 8th Ave, I saw a shoe shine stand and the sign said, *You Can't Close That Deal with a Dirty Heal!* (except "heel" was spelled H-E-A-L) and suddenly a shoe shine seemed to be just what the doctor ordered to calm my nerves.

I said, *How much?* and he said, *Speed shine, three dollars, three minutes.*

Now, when I was a kid on trips to New York I used to love it that the cabdrivers and shoe shine guys were so friendly and chatty.

(Low and ominously.) But now I'm thirty and I prefer quiet rides and quiet shines. When did that change? Why? Actually, come to think of it it's not just me, the whole city changed, the whole city sank into a solitary bad mood, and cabdrivers never chat with you anymore.

(Brightly.) But this shoe shine guy *was* chatty in the sweetest way. He told me about his three daughters, and how it's hard but *a man's gotta do what a man's gotta do*, and how he loves his job, the people he meets, what's the point if you don't? And the whole while I was watching the neon sign for the peepshow blinking across 8th Avenue.

And then somehow the conversation turned to me and he asked *Did I have kids?* and I said no, and he said *You better get busy then young man*, and I said I wasn't sure I was up for the *Inner Spiritual Revolution* that that would entail, and he laughed and asked me what did I do, which I always hate because I don't know why, but I'm embarrassed to say I'm an actor, so I said I was a writer. As if *that's* better. And we talked about my project, and that I was making progress and had gotten a couple of hours writing in this week, and he laughed and said *Two hours a week ain't a job, it's a chore.* And then with a thwap of his cloth the three minutes was up.

But the shoe shine really only alleviated my dread for a few minutes, so I stumbled across 8th Ave and into the neon blinking peepshow, feeling paranoid and dirty, but doing it anyway. I walked into the booth with the girl who knew me a little bit—it was a Tuesday—and slid my five-dollar bill into the three-minute

slot. The mechanical shade clicked and whirred as it went up, revealing her feet to knees to hair to head, framed in the rectangular window. I picked up the little white phone on the side of the booth and pictured myself swinging by the neck from its cord. She picked up her end and started to take off her clothes. I said, *No, don't, I just want to talk.* She said, *What do you want to talk about?* And I was thinking about what the woman I had been with last night had meant when she said, *I don't believe in unconditional love for a man. Who has time? I want to know what I'm getting*, so I asked the girl behind the glass did *she* believe in unconditional love? And she laughed and told me I was weird, so I said *No, really*, and she paused, and said, *I don't know, I guess so, doesn't everybody?*

Then there was an awkward silence, so she said, *How's the writing project coming?* And I said, *Well, it's more of a chore than a job.*

Then, I just stared at her and started thinking about the play I had seen in Jason's theatre last year on my birthday, *Krapp's Last Tape*, and how do you become an old man and alone, and a drunk, and how in the play, Krapp was a failed writer, and his only human contact was a weekly, perfunctory visit from a prostitute, and thinking that made me feel better, like what I was doing now was research, *dramaturgy*, and finally she said, *Window's gonna come down, don't you want a show?* So I snapped to and did what you do in the dark in that place, as the window shade slid down, erasing her head to hair to knees to feet, and as the light came on in my half of the booth I thought about Krapp and that old line, *You don't pay a prostitute to stay, you pay her to leave.*

Now I had that desultory feeling you get when you realize you've killed another day and it's barely begun, and I wanted a fresh start, so I just kept walking downtown, not quite knowing what I should do. Should I call "my girlfriend" back? Come up with a new set of lies? No, I should just get on a bus and disappear to Utah and work in a gas station. *(With bitter self-loathing.)* Yeah, work in a gas station. God, I hate myself. But I just kept heading downtown because at least there's good bookstores there while I make up my mind, and since I wanted to feel clean, when I passed that Catholic church on 10th Street, I didn't even think, but went right in, and I'm not even a Catholic, but Beckett was, wasn't he? Wasn't he!? No...was he?

Anyway, for the first time in my life I walked into a confessional booth, and clicked the door closed behind me, and laid my face against the rattan screen, and whispered those words I had seen in so many movies—*Forgive me Father for I have sinned. It's been thirty years since my last confession.* Then I confessed a few things and it felt *great*, actually. I confessed that I felt terrible for being a no-good, lying cad. I confessed to lust, lust run amok, and I confessed that I was consumed with envy of my friends and sometimes thought ill of them. I confessed that I was prideful and selfish and narcissistic, and that I hadn't called my mother in two and a half weeks. I even brought it up to the minute and confessed that I was drunk...well, not *drunk*, really, but a little buzzed...and that I'm not even Catholic and don't be mad at me, Father, but that I suspected that deep down inside I might even be a Buddhist.

I went on and on like this for about three minutes, and then a sneaking suspicion silenced me in my tracks.

(Low and ominously.) Was there anybody even in there? I peered through the rattan into the dark cubicle. Empty, sure enough. The father went to lunch, I thought, and I left the church. You could buy a candle at the exit, so I did, dropping a dollar into the copper box.

Now suddenly it's night, and I'm in bed, writing in my journal, thinking about threes, and my project, and three acts, and morning, noon, and night, and how you should structure things in threes, not twos or fours, like how if you say a line three times it's funny or spooky, or what you want it to be, but if you say it only twice it just seems random. And I think about how my every single human encounter of this day had lasted exactly *three minutes*. And how I had paid for each three-minute exchange—a quarter, three dollars, five dollars, a candle. And I think about time and children and love and work and that play, and how you have thirty-nine years to try to do something, forty-nine years to fail, fifty-nine years to love someone if you're lucky, and sixty-nine years to die.

(Lights cross fade down on MICHAEL and up on the upstage table. MICHAEL crosses to the tech table with the camcorder. RING! RING! Over the speakers we hear another recorded phone conversation.)

MICHAEL: Yeah, George, I've been working on the piece and something just occurred to me...if I'm going to do the Beckett speech at the end, then I kinda have to do it in an Irish accent...I mean that's how it's written...Irish idiom...

(As the conversation unreels, MICHAEL films an "Irish Accent Training Manual" and a dog-eared copy of Samuel Beckett's Krapp's Last Tape.*)*

GEORGE: Yeah, you could do that…but judging from what *you've* told *me*, an Irish accent is not your bag. I mean, I'm not being insulting, it's just…you're *bad* at it. There are actors who do accents, and actors who do *not*…and *you do not*…

MICHAEL: …So you think my Irish accent would suck…?

GEORGE: Listen…you told me you turned down four auditions for *The Lieutenant of Inishmore* because you didn't want to go in there and shit on their shoes…

(MICHAEL returns to his desk and prepares for a dialect practice session. He shakes out his jaw, does a few tongue exercises.)

MICHAEL: …But *Krapp's Last Tape* has Irish, you know…*cadences!* So, look, I'll *learn*. I mean how tough could it be? And if it sucks…then at least it will suck *honestly*…

GEORGE: *(Dismayed.)* Is there a difference? Between sucking and sucking *honestly*!?

MICHAEL: George! This whole piece is supposed to be about who I am *now!*

GEORGE: *(Doubtfully.)* Well, alright…

(BEEP. CLICK. MICHAEL puts on his reading glasses, opens the "Irish Accent Training Manual," and reads.)

MICHAEL: "Introduction to a Northern Ireland Dialect. Distinctive Sounds, Part One. Let's try 'a' as in

path. In this dialect, the 'a' vowel is unalloyed with absolutely no diphthong. American actors should avoid sliding into 'ae.' And British actors—let go of that customary 'ah' sound. Here are some practice words:

"fast, lass, ass, radical, bad, rascal, nasty, master, class, can't, prance, France, last laugh, rant, pant."

(MICHAEL does his best with the list of words, but his accent is dubious at best. He flips to a new page.)

"Now let's try 'a' as in *man*. Here the 'a' is slightly more rounded and is pronounced, 'aah.'"

"Here are some practice words:"

"matador, fallacy, phallus, phantom, California, slat, massive, irascible, fancy, rabbit, clap, trap."

(Triumphantly, MICHAEL adds his own word to the list:)

KRAPP!

(Encouraged by that last run, MICHAEL flips to a new page.)

"Now let's look at the post-vocalic 'r,' i.e., what happens when 'r' follows a vowel sound. In Northern Ireland, when 'r' comes after a vowel, it is quite pronounced. Here are some practice words:

"dark, lark, park, stark, fart, farm, fork, stork, yarn, market, dirty, pervert, murder, thirty-third, border, afford, lord, polar bear, solar flare, actor-for-hire, factor, Mother Hubbard."

(MICHAEL's having fun now. He flips to a new page.)

"Now, let's practice with some sentences.

"The master class was too fast and radical.

"The fat lass panted as she pranced through France.

"Matthew's cat had a talent for magic.

"The polar bear stared at the solar flare.

"She walked through the puddle with her whole kit and caboodle."

(MICHAEL is perplexed by this last sentence. What?)

Kit and caboodle?

(He dejectedly closes the manual. Quietly.)

Ah, well.

(His accent is ridiculous after all. FRUSTRATION! He tosses the manual, sits, broods. He looks at the glowing laptop. It exerts its inexorable pull, drawing him back. He leans into the mic.)

October 28, 2001
New York City
"Krapp Sings as a Boy"

Thirty-two years old today. Talked to Mama on the phone, she just got her test results back from the oncologist. Not good.

(A beat.)

S. bought me a cell phone for my birthday. So long to pay phones. Here's a new way to die, cancer from cell phone! That is, if the cigarettes don't get me first.

(A beat.)

(With glum sarcasm.) I'm at my job— polishing lamps in the antique store. Before that it was selling subscriptions on the phone. Before that it was handing out flyers in the bear suit. But I'm

still calling myself an actor. Yes, I got to play Hamlet at the Grand Canyon Shakespeare Festival, yes, a few out-of-towners, yes, I had that understudy gig, whoopee! I'm thirty-two years old, how long do I chase this chicken?

(A beat.)

The night is so quiet outside. I heard that old woman singing in the dark again, three buildings down. And I thought about that line in *Krapp* where he hears the old woman singing and he asks himself, *Did he ever sing as a boy?*

(Music: A single, haunting boy soprano voice fades in: "Once in Royal David's City." The hymn underscores the following.)

Memory:

I loved to sing as a boy! I was a boy soprano. My shining moment—

I had the solo at the Christmas Chorale at Concert Hall downtown. "Once in Royal David's City." Three thousand people in the audience. World-famous German conductor. The orchestra hushed. The conductor rested his baton. I started the solo. I was so proud; I was on top of the world. But then something terrible happened. At the height of the song, as I went up for the high "A," my voice broke in half. Cracked. I sounded like a foghorn. Puberty squawking through the crystalline "A." The conductor peered at me mercilessly from under his mantis brows. I went up again and squawked again. I started to cry. You could hear a pin drop. I finished the solo, barely, and slunk back to the anonymity of the boy choir.

(A beat.)

(MICHAEL listens, losing himself in the hymn. It fades out.)

Afterwards, the world-famous conductor appeared in my dressing room mirror.

(In a thick German accent.) He said, *Yah. You've had very good career. Now, is over.* The next night another boy took the solo, and I watched from the velvet seats. I never sang again. It was the first time I ever lost anything I cared about to age. I was eleven.

Thirty-two today. Maybe it's time to call it a day and join the real world.

October 28, 1988

New York City

"Krapp's Autobiographical Instinct"

Nineteen years old today. Mama sent me a birthday tape, a secret greeting, but I haven't listened to it yet because the batteries are dead in the tape recorder.

(A sudden realization.) That's where I get it! Mama! It's genetic, the autobiographical instinct. I picture her making her audio diaries, hunched over her tape recorder with a cat on her shoulder like a gargoyle, whispering her most secret self into the machine. Her long-ago dreams of being a writer thwarted long ago by being a mother.

(With an angry resolve.) I'll never do it. I'll never let my dreams be thwarted by someone else. If that means no family, so be it. If that means I end up alone, then…

(A beat.)

Mama also sent me a package of M&M's.

M & M for Michael and Mama.

And a check for a hundred dollars.

(A beat.)

Anyway, off to Shakespeare scene class. Can't believe the teacher is making me work on old man Lear. I'm only nineteen years old!

(Lights cross fade down on the desk and up on the tech table. MICHAEL picks up the camcorder. Audio: The voice of MICHAEL'S MOTHER on an old audiocassette recording.)

MAMA: Happy birthday, Michael. You're nineteen today. I know you don't like it when people sing "Happy Birthday," so I'll spare you that, but I'm thinking of you today. It's always been the biggest day of my life, too. It's 11:52 right now, which is the actual time you were born, even though I know you like to tell people that you were born at the stroke of midnight—that's a conspicuous fiction. Or maybe it's better to say that's an *amiable fiction.*

(As the tape unreels, MICHAEL films various objects on the tech table. The images appear on the flat-screen monitor:

- *Shakespeare's* King Lear
- *Birthday cards*
- *A plaster gargoyle*
- *Numerous photos of MICHAEL as a choirboy, his MOTHER, Samuel Beckett*
- *A folder with his mother's newspaper columns)*

MAMA: You're probably in rehearsal right now chewing those wonderful Shakespearean words—we're so proud of you. And I am so glad to hear you finished your book, what a great birthday present for yourself, and I can't wait to read it, even though it sounds like something maybe a mother shouldn't read…

Speaking of books, Tom and I were in the garage digging through old boxes from the Mississippi house, and I found a folder of my old columns that I wrote for that newspaper in Starkville. Some of them are a little embarrassing, and you were too young to remember, but most of the columns were about you as a little boy in the suburbs. I thought you might like to hear one of them on your birthday. Sort of a "from the archives."

So here it is:

"While I Should Be Keeping House"
By Judie Laurence
The Lowndes County Register
Starkville, Mississippi
August 1975

"A couple of years back, when he was four and a half, my Michael announced to me that he was going to be an author when he grew up. I was a little surprised because before that he had pretty squarely settled on a career as a street-duster.

"You can't talk Michael into anything about a career. Once, his father was admiring some houses he'd built with his blocks and suggested maybe he'd like to be an architect some day. 'I don't build these houses for myself,' Michael answered most emphatically. 'I build these houses to make Mama happy.'

"He ruled out teaching, too, on the basis that you'd have to spend too much time counting milk money if you were teacher.

"Once, when he was two or so, he told me he would never want to be a chicken, but that from time to time he might like to be a rooster.

"He's always had a kind of personal relationship with words, really. I remember

his telling me over lunch that he didn't like the word 'hypothesis.' He thought it might pinch him. And another time he ran into the house saying he had to know what 'plush' meant before it gave him the hives. Or there was the time, when he was three, when he asked for a Coke saying, 'I am so thirsty my throat is pushing the bone.' Or the time we were driving at the end of an all-night trip, and he peered out the passenger window at dawn and said, 'Look, Mama, the morning is boiling up with light.'

"We start every day with a game called 'What Kind of Animal Are You Today?' I rested assured the morning he said, 'Mama, today you are like a tree-toed sloth, but don't worry, tomorrow you'll be an otter.'

"He can express something he doesn't like, too. Recently, he spluttered out, 'This cough medicine tastes like Band-Aids.'

"Or: 'I like my bottom teeth better than my top ones. They are politer.'

"He *senses* things with words. When he was two and we were sitting on the porch swing on a very dark, very quiet night, he whispered, 'I think I hear a butterfly in my shoe.'

"Maybe his is a private destiny with language that started as soon as he could talk. I mean, any baby whose first real word was not Mama, or truck, or no, or even huggybear, but *smudgepot* must be going someplace interesting with words."

(MICHAEL zooms in very slowly on a photo of his MOTHER circa 1975. She is young and beautiful, seated at a typewriter with a cat on her shoulder.)

MAMA: "Anyway, soon after he announced he was going to be an author, he came to me and said, 'I have written my first short story. Will you spell it out for me, please?'

"Whereupon he dictated the following:

"'I want to tell you something. I had a magic boat. Then I fell off. Kerplunk. And I said, "I guess that that boat wasn't magic after all."'

"Admittedly, it could use some polishing, but it's got potential, if you ask me."

(MICHAEL seems disturbed, lost in memory. He puts down the camcorder, and the monitor goes to black. He returns to his desk.)

MAMA: *(Sweetly.)* So that's it. Enjoy your day. Call or write when you get a chance, and take good care of yourself. Minou sends you a Happy Birthday meow, too. Say bye-bye, Minou.

(The sound of a meow.)

MAMA: Bye, Bye.

(CLICK! MICHAEL leans into the mic.)

MICHAEL: October 28, 2004
Louisville
"Krapp's Dilemma Part 1"

Thirty-five years old today. I can't sleep. I've got these weird creepy-crawlies in my leg.

Didn't tell anybody it was my birthday this year. But E. remembered anyway and called to wish me "happy." He said he's walking around with a cane because he has the gout. I said I thought that was a nineteenth century affliction. He said, *Oh yes, I'd like to die in the nineteenth century.*

Day twenty-two of my sabbatical from booze. The cast went out to a bar last night, and I compulsively drank eleven tonic and limes, and then got vertigo and a ringing in my ears. The bartender said it was probably the quinine in the tonic.

(Triumphantly.) There's a nineteenth century way to die: death by quinine!

(A beat.)

Today is tech for this weird farm-disaster play. I'm sitting on the set on dinner break.

(A beat.)

Marriage? What to do…?

She said she could live without children, if that's what I'm afraid of. So, what am I afraid of?

After all these years of being a fuck-up…

I just have to make the leap into the void. That's what I tell myself, but then I flip. What am I doing? I never imagined myself *married!*

I want to be loved. I can admit that. I want to be accepted…and that makes me…what? Weak? So I'm weak. That's what I want.

(With mounting fervor.) But *marriage?* That's not *me.* I'm an *actor,* I'm an *artist.* I have this thing I do, that I scrape and claw, still, to get the chance to do, and that's all that matters. I have a religious devotion to these little black rooms, these tables, these pages of fantasy, these planks of wood, these cans of paint, and you know, I made a choice! And look at me now, I have no money, no fame, no family except these temporary families on the road…

I look around this theatre. I look around this set. There's a *house* for a set. Look at that…that house…it looks for all the world like a *house*. It's structurally sound, people go in and out…windows, doors…

But then, look, it's propped up by sandbags! Two-by-fours! I could *topple* it with a hard kick! And, you know, *that's* the house I live in. So! I made a choice…you want to be in the theatre…then *this* is where you live.

Permanence, marriage…don't even think about it. Months on the road, years on the road, and in between, staring at walls, years of staring at walls, and trying to get back on the road, trying to crawl back into some fantasy, some dream. And I don't mean dream like a *hope*, but a dream like a…*dream!*

(MICHAEL claws at the air, searching for words. A beat.)

(Quietly.) Bullshit. That's all bullshit. It's not about that.

Deep down inside I want to be alone.

So, really it's a *theological* question, isn't it?

Does my isolation mean a rejection of love?

Because that's what it meant for Krapp.

(He drops his forehead onto the mic with a thwump. A long, dejected pause as he examines his left hand. Suddenly, he grabs the camcorder, holds his hand up to the camera and films his wedding ring in closeup. Studies it in supersize on the flat-screen monitor. He returns to his journals.)

October 28, 2007
Washington, D.C.
"Krapp's Dilemma, Part 2"

Thirty-eight years old today. I lay down in the park in the dark with my wife. She told me she could no longer be happy without a child. I said *You told me you could*, she said *I've changed*, I said *I understand*, she said *I'm thirty-nine time is running out*, I said *I know*, she said *Where does that leave us?* I said *I don't know.*

She says *You don't know what you're missing.*

I say *But you have to want it, otherwise it's no good.*

She says *You'll want it once you have it, that's the way it works.*

I say *I know but I don't want to want it.*

She says *It's like an Inner Spiritual Revolution.*

I say *I don't want an Inner Spiritual Revolution. I'm barely hanging on!*

(With mounting desperation.) I'm almost forty. I have to make up my mind and God has me on a stopwatch. I'm not ready for me to be over, *my* story, me, me, me! What would a child be to me? I don't even like children, they make me feel exposed, I never wanted a child, I hated being a child, I would just fuck up a child and wait a minute, I *am* a child. There's only room for one child around here, and that's me! And what about my work? And what about the fact that I'm an *actor* for God's sake? I'm an *artist* for God's sake! I can't *afford* a child!

But then I think, no, maybe there's a *plan*, maybe God has a *plan*, a simple *plan*, and I can't see it, I'm in the way. Why do I take myself so seriously? Why can't I just let go? Like that guy on the TV show?

(A beat.)

(Quietly.) We lay there without moving. But I could feel the planet moving under us.

Then she got up, and wordlessly walked away.

She couldn't understand, I couldn't make her understand, it's a thought just around the corner from language. It is ineffable.

(A beat.)

After midnight. I might as well be the last man on earth.

(A beat.)

(With a low, dark self-loathing.) Solitude. I prefer it that way, I tell myself, I need it that way, I tell myself, it is my ineluctable destiny, I tell myself.

(A beat.)

Then I thought about a strange thing. I thought about an old man alone in a room with the mystery of his life. I thought about Krapp.

I thought about my work—the things I dreamed I'd do, and have never done, and maybe never will. And I wanted it all back.

(Lights cross fade down on the desk and up on the tech table. MICHAEL grabs the camcorder. RING! RING! Audio: Over the speakers we hear another recorded phone conversation.)

GEORGE: How's the writing coming? That's what I'm worried about...

MICHAEL: I can't sleep, George...the RLS. I haven't slept in three days...

GEORGE: What's "RLS"?

MICHAEL: I told you! "Restless Leg Syndrome!" I'm hallucinating from lack of sleep...I'm seeing ghosts in the windshield...I can't get *anything* done...

(As the conversation unreels, MICHAEL—still seated in the swivel chair—pans down his torso and films his shaking leg.)

GEORGE: Have you seen a doctor?

(MICHAEL films the prescription bottle, opens it with his free hand, zooms in close on the pills.)

MICHAEL: Yes, I went to the doctor and he gave me this Rx, but he warned me that the side effects are—get this—a propensity for gambling and extreme *sexual compulsivity!*

(GEORGE guffaws loudly. MICHAEL films the choice: pills, leg. Pills, leg. Back and forth.)

GEORGE: I'm sorry, I don't mean to laugh...I'm sorry. *(Sighing.)* Well, I don't know what to tell ya, Mike, you gotta finish the piece. Just take the damn pills and we'll pick up the pieces later...

(MICHAEL places a pill on his tongue, filming it in closeup.)

MICHAEL: *(Reluctantly.)* Alright. Here we go...

(BEEP. CLICK. MICHAEL swallows the pill. Music: the final measures of Handel's "Sarabande." As the music swells, MICHAEL films himself: his eyes as they go soft and blurry, his shaking leg as it comes to rest. Then back up to his face. He smiles wanly into the camera, and...Passes out! The stage becomes suffused in an eerie red led light. Audio: the click and whirr of an audiotape rewinding. Then, MAMA's voice from the earlier tape:)

MAMA: "I want to tell you something. I had a magic boat. Then I fell off. Kerplunk. And I said, 'I guess that that boat wasn't magic after all.'"

(Click. Whirr. Rewind.)

MAMA: "I had a magic boat. Then I fell off. Kerplunk. And I said, 'I guess that that boat wasn't magic after all.'"

(Click. Whirr. Rewind.)

MAMA: "I guess that that boat wasn't magic after all."

(Audio: smashing glass! MICHAEL bolts upright in the chair, stunned and disoriented. Audio: a heartbeat. Ka-thwump. Ka-thwump. MICHAEL picks up the camcorder from his lap, and trains it on his face. He looks tired, lost. He looks up and studies his own face on the flat-screen monitor. Listens to the heartbeat. Slowly he rolls back to the desk, zooming the camcorder in on the text on his laptop. He puts down the camcorder and the monitor goes black. He leans into the mic.)

MICHAEL: October 28, 2006
New York City
"Krapp Goes to School"

Thirty-seven years old today. I had a Hot Pocket and a cigarette for breakfast, walked the dog, and took the subway to my class. On the subway I opened the paper and read my horoscope and the obituaries. Then an elderly woman sat down next to me and started reading my paper over my shoulder. I glanced up at her. She said, "I love the obits. You meet the nicest people there."

Walking from the subway to my class, I caught a glimpse of my face in the tinted windshield of a parked limo. My reflection was distorted; I looked like an old man to myself. I looked like Krapp.

Anyway, Here's how the whole class thing happened:

Some weeks ago I told my wife that I felt like I thrived best in the role of a student, and it was sad to me that as you get older, you run out of opportunities to be a student. I'm thirty-seven. You're supposed to be battle-tempered and sage at thirty-seven. Thirty-seven is not an age for learning, thirty-seven is an age for *teaching*. Thirty-seven is an age for *doing*. *Producing*. What have I *produced*?

Anyway, I told her this, so she bought me a class at a continuing education center. As an early birthday present. *What a tender and thoughtful gift*, I thought. *My wife listens to me, my wife understands me.* Then she handed me something wrapped in pink tissue paper—a catalogue of courses, I guessed— and I thought about the august and intellectually rigorous class I might choose. Something like "Kierkegaard's Ambivalence: A Lutheran Perspective," or "Privacy and Surveillance: A Global Analysis." Or maybe just something *fun* like "The Vampire in Modernist Cinema and Literature." I *loved* this gift.

Where is it? I asked. *Columbia? NYU? The New School?*

And then she laughed and said, *Open it.*

It *was* a course catalogue. For The Open Center. In SoHo.

(A beat.)

I was confused. The Open Center is a new-agey kind of place—they do *meditation* workshops, and *chakra* workshops, and *progressive psychology* classes. Then my wife told me she had already picked a course and signed me up, and that I would love it, and *Here it is, see I highlighted it.* Whereupon I opened the catalogue to her selection.

"Act Your Age: Life Tools for the Eternal Adolescent."

Anyway, the instructor for "Act Your Age"—he's twenty-five by the way, his name is Burke—gave us a homework assignment today: to write about those areas of adulthood in which we felt challenged. I didn't understand the assignment, so I asked him to clarify. He said,

Well, Michael, why don't you just make a list of things you wish you could do at your age, but can't.

I said, *I battle depression and that sounds like a depressing assignment.*

He laughed and said he liked my self-deprecating sense of humor.

I said, *I'm not kidding.* And he laughed *again.*

Then he said, *Self-improvement starts with honesty.*

So, here it is. My list:

"Things I Don't Know How To Do But Should or Know Nothing About and Wish I Did."
By Michael Laurence, age Thirty-Seven.

I don't know how to:

Fold a shirt

Use an iron

Make the bed

Change a fuse

Use a drill

Boil spaghetti (is it seven minutes or fifteen ?)

Switch between the TV and the DVD

Send a text message

Retrieve a text message

Change the oil in the car

Open the *hood* of a car (it pops, but then that little latch, you can't…never mind.)

I don't know how to:

Not pay sticker price for everything

Not get scammed

Balance a checkbook

Do my taxes

Open an IRA

Find the place where I vote

Calculate the waitress's tip

I don't know how to:

Whistle

Play poker

Play the piano

Plant a tree

Pot a plant

Ride a horse

Tie a slip knot

Tie a bow tie

Read a roadmap

Pitch a tent

I'm frightened of the takeout delivery guy (okay, that's not really something "I Can't Do," but it *is* true…)

I don't know how to tell the truth when it might get me in trouble.

(He pauses, catching himself.)

What? "I don't know how to tell…?"

Did I write that? I don't remember that…

(A long beat as he struggles to remember. He doubtfully returns to the journals.)

October 28, 2005
Los Cruces, New Mexico
"Krapp Rewinds the Tape"

Thirty-six years old today.

Day ten of shooting on this Japanese indie film. I play a drifter named Nick who lives in the desert and can smell rain. He's the hypotenuse of a weird love triangle. Nick is stoic and self-reliant and can hotwire cars. Why do I always get these roles? *Stoic?* I'm about as stoic as a *hamster!*

Anyway, my wife flew out to be with me on set for a few days. When I got back to the motel, she brought out a surprise birthday cake that she had smuggled into the fridge while I was filming. She cut two slices and said, *Do you want the big piece, or the little piece?* and it really put the zap on my head.

The thing is, memories are so strange. There's that handful that stay with you your whole life, and you don't know why—a snippet of a conversation, something you saw out the car window as it flashed by, a smell, a dream. Decades later, these smallest of things loom in your heart with the most unlikely size.

And memories have a life of their own; they transform themselves with every revisitation, every time they spring up out of the dark of forgetting, alive, and triggered by this or that smell as you walk down Fourth Street, or that old man's voice you overhear on the stoop. The memory flickers to life, but like that child's game of "Telephone," where a story changes as it passes from ear to ear, so too can a memory change over time, but always re-presenting itself as the *absolute* truth of what *really* happened.

That's what happened to Krapp.

And sometimes a memory is just a ghost in the machine. You have a memory of a memory that never happened. Like that conversation that never happened, or that trip you never took, or that dress she never wore, but you're sure she did.

And what do you do with that memory now? If *that* didn't happen, if *that* never was, if *he* never said *that*, then who am I now? What else didn't happen? Who else didn't come? I trusted my self, I trusted the past, I can't be trusted with my past, I can't be trusted.

My wife held out two slices of birthday cake and said, *Do you want the big piece, or the little piece?*

And I went white in the face.

Memory:

Kendall was the daughter of the Baptist preacher next door, she was eleven and I was seven and I was impossibly in love with her. We used to play I was Daniel Boone and she was Mrs. Boone, and I would put on my coonskin cap and go on adventures around the neighborhood while she made mud pies under the house.

Anyway, it was my birthday and Mama had given us cake. Kendall held out two slices and said, *Do you want the big piece, or the little piece?*

Here's what I said. I was a pretentious little kid, I said, *I want the little piece now, and the big piece later.*

Kendall said, *You should have the big piece now, it's your birthday.*

I said, philosophically, *No. Always save the big piece. That way you'll have it for later.*

She said, *You'll never eat it if you're always saving it. You should eat the big piece now.*

I ate the little piece. And saved the big one for later. *Much* later. I'm *still* saving it. I'm thirty-six years old, and I'll *never* eat it.

Kendall grew up, traveled the world, wrote some books, won a Pulitzer, raised a family, and made millions of dollars. Kendall had her cake and ate it too.

I'm thirty-six, and can't fold a shirt.

That's what I told my wife as she held out the cake and asked me *What's wrong?*

(Lights cross fade down on the desk and up on the tech table. RING! RING! Audio: Over the speakers we hear another recorded phone conversation.)

JON: I look at *Krapp's Last Tape* and, for *me*, it's the moment when the lights go out. I mean the absolute horror...*the horror*...is that when the lights go out... for him...for Krapp...this is the moment of greatest light...

MICHAEL: Um-hmm...

(As the conversation unreels, MICHAEL crosses to the upstage table with the camcorder and films various objects on the table. The images appear on the flat-screen monitor:

- *A dog-eared copy of Samuel Beckett's* Krapp's Last Tape

- *Stanislavski's* Building a Character

- *Numerous open journals and composition notebooks*

- *A stack of printed emails relating to discussions of* Krapp

- *A bundle of love letters tied with a ribbon*

- *A large candle in a glass bowl*

- *A black metal lockbox*

- *An antique pocket watch*

- *A furry Daniel Boone coonskin cap*

- *Various playbills of MICHAEL's plays)*

JON: ...The moment when he gives up, when he's not interested in any of the things that human beings are usually interested in...

MICHAEL: Well, *love*...

JON: Excuse me?

MICHAEL: The moment that he gives up on *love*...

JON: ...Yeah, the moment that he gives up on love of *anything*...

MICHAEL: Well, yes, anything, but specifically on that tape Krapp is recording on his thirty-ninth birthday...I mean he's talking about a few things...he's condemning his past, assessing the present, talking about disappointment, artistic failure, the end of youth...but when it comes to *love*, he's talking very specifically about two things: first, the death of his mother...the loss of that *original* love...that original source of love is gone...extinguished in his thirty-ninth year...

JON: ...Right...

MICHAEL: And second, the loss of, or *forfeiture* of, *romantic* love. He talks about several different women, love miseries, but then finally a *breakup scene*...a breakup with a lover...final moments with a woman who he loves, and who loves him...in the boat on the lake. So, I'm just saying, I think, when you talk about what is extinguished, I think it's *love*...

(BEEP. CLICK. MICHAEL returns to the desk, having set the camcorder on the table

in auto-record mode. It films the plaster skull in closeup. The image hovers on the flat-screen monitor during the following.)

December 12, 2006
New York City

My old friend Jason's memorial today. A beautiful service at the Actors' Chapel. What a tragedy, thirty-nine years old, a life lived too close to the flame.

I sat in the pew and I thought of all the ways he cracked me open. I thought of his *Krapp's Last Tape*, in that basement theatre.

A. J.'s eulogy was crushingly beautiful.

E. read from *Endgame* and recalled asking Jason once what was the meaning of Art.

Art is about two things, Jason had replied. *Love. And Death.*

August 31, 2002
Cincinnati

Mama died today. Fifty-nine years old.

(A long beat.)

(Almost inaudibly.) I don't know what else to say.

(Lights cross fade down on the desk and up on the tech table. RING! RING! Audio: Over the speakers we hear another recorded phone conversation.)

JON: ...But inside of that...what was the *moment*, the *spark* that made you want to record thirty-nine-year-old Krapp's monologue when you're thirty-nine, and then revisit it in thirty years? I'm *guessing* here that there's something more than just a professional actor creating an interesting piece. There must be something in there that has to do with *you*, Michael, at thirty-nine...

(As the conversation unreels, MICHAEL wearily crosses to the upstage table with the camcorder and films various objects on the table. The images appear on the flat-screen monitor:

- A paperback copy of Fontane's Effie Briest
- *Samuel Beckett's novella,* First Love
- Collected Works of T. S. Eliot
- *A St. James Bible [red]*
- *Numerous open journals and composition notebooks*
- *A large candle in a glass bowl*
- *A black metal lockbox*
- *An antique pocket watch*
- *A round makeup mirror*
- *Numerous photos of Samuel Beckett*
- *A bottle of vodka*
- *A pack of cigarettes)*

MICHAEL: Well, I have a complicated set of reasons. One is my *mother*...my mother died before she was sixty...so then I think about the connection to Beckett's character, and central to Krapp's story is the fact that *his* mother died when he was thirty-nine. I've been thinking about my mother a lot as I think about this piece, and I don't want to sound maudlin, or go down a road here that I'm going to regret, you know, people hearing, but...I get scared every time I light up a cigarette these days, because my mother died of lung cancer, and *her* mother died of emphysema...

(MICHAEL films the pack of cigarettes.)

MICHAEL: ...But if I'm performing this piece in thirty years it means I'm still alive...I didn't die of cancer...AND...it means I'll still be an actor...at least in some capacity...I'll still be putting work out into the world in the face of, frankly, many failures…

(*MICHAEL films his reflection in the round makeup mirror, slowly zooming in to the iris of his eye.*)

MICHAEL: …And then I think again of parallels to Krapp, who is, after all, by conventional standards, a *failure*. He's a failed writer…

JON: Uh-huh…

(*MICHAEL sets the camera down on the table and zooms in close on a photograph of Samuel Beckett, his penetrating gaze. He returns to the desk. Beckett's inscrutable face hovers on the monitor for the rest of the performance.*)

MICHAEL: I don't know, Jon. Maybe this is just *hubristic*…this whole piece. Maybe it's just about my ego…how I want to be perceived by the world…*Krapp's Last Tape*…it's, you know, a *serious* play for a *serious* actor…and that's how I want to be *perceived*. And it's how I long to be perceived not only *now*, but *thirty years* from now…

(*BEEP. CLICK. MICHAEL leans into the mic. There is a manic gleam in his eye.*)

October 28, 2038
London

(*With relish, savoring the fantasy.*) Sixty-nine years old today. Moved from my suite at the Connaught Hotel in Mayfair to these more luxurious rooms at the Savoy overlooking the Thames and the West End theatre district—the scene of my resounding triumph!

It's three a.m. I have sent away the masseuse. Alone at last.

(*A beat.*)

A brilliant Opening Night for my *Krapp's Last Tape*. The New Royal Court Theatre is devastatingly beautiful and state of the art, and, of course, it was an honor to perform on the very stage where the play premiered eighty years ago today. I felt the ghost of Beckett hovering in the wings and smiling. And what to say of my old friend Jon? A brilliant soul—he's smiling somewhere.

At curtain call the audience jumped to their feet with a roar. Five calls, and still they thundered for more. Given my natural modesty, I was embarrassed to say the least. But I wept when, in the final deafening surge of applause my wife and daughter rushed the footlights with white roses. I pulled them both up on stage. *Daddy, I'm amazed*, she said. I am so grateful to them both. That meant more to me than anything—even the honorary knighthood bestowed upon me by King William.

I insisted that George, my director, join me for a bow as well, and he reluctantly obliged. He flies back to New York tomorrow for the Tonys, but at least he was here tonight.

To top it all off, the artistic director of the theatre brought a cake out on stage and the entire audience sang "Happy Birthday."

(*With mounting triumph*) Not bad, not bad, old man, after all those theatre festivals, all those basement performances, all that ignominy, and anonymity, and seemingly wasted potential. And then this play, *Krapp, 39*, and that recording which launched the "grand project," and a career that sprang into fame fully formed like Athena from Zeus's brain at age thirty-nine. Not bad. Not bad at all!

(A long beat.)

(MICHAEL's eyes fill up with doubt as he recoils from the fantasy, and reconsiders his future. He leans into the mic, and starts again.)

October 28, 2038 REDO
Florida

(Guttural and bitter.) Sixty-nine years old today. In my motel room at the Quality Inn in Sarasota. It's three a.m. I'm alone. Staring at a stain on the wall that looks like a nose. When I booked this joint they told me on the phone that it had the best view of all the motels. Now that I'm here, I see what they mean—I look out my window and it has a great view…of all the other motels!

Tonight was the Opening Night for my *Krapp's Last Tape.* At "The Sarasota Multimedia Festival for the Aged." The opening I planned thirty years ago. The audience seemed to like the show all right, all five of them, although one guy said I didn't sound like me on the *Krapp, 39* tape. I told him I recorded it thirty years ago. He said, *Yeah, that was a mistake.*

Financially, this was a bust, but at least I found a sub-letter for my basement studio back in Staten Island, so that's good.

After the show I found a bar where nobody would bother me. I had a few boilermakers in peace, and then this woman sidled up to the bar. She said *How 'bout we have a good time, sweetie?* I said, *I'm old, I'm tired, and I'm drunk, does that sound like a good time?* But she wouldn't leave me alone, she got all chatty, asked was I married, I said divorced, asked did I have any kids, I said leave me alone, and I mean that in the nicest way from the bottom of my very shallow heart.

I got back here to the motel and had another drink and about fifteen cigarettes and coughed what's left of my lung into my lap. I'm sure the motel will fine me a room cleaning fee.

I opened the dresser drawer and pulled out the ol' Gideon's, flipped it open to a passage at random. It said, "To him that hath shall be given, and to him that hath not shall be taken even that that he hath."

I closed the book and thought about Mama and my ex-wife and every woman that ever thought they loved me. And the children I never had. And the friends I drove away. And should I get another six-pack before the Economart closes. And then I thought about Krapp, and what George said that day in rehearsal thirty years ago, *Don't imagine you as Krapp, imagine Krapp is you.*

(A beat.)

Then I thought, fuck it.

Fuck Krapp!

I'm sixty-nine years old, I'm the right age to play *Lear!*

And then I thought about Lear's line, "The worst is not, so long as we can say this is the worst."

(Lights cross fade down on the desk and up on the tech table. RING! RING! Audio: Over the speakers we hear another recorded phone conversation. Disoriented, MICHAEL scans the stage and the lighting grid—where are those voices coming from?)

GEORGE: I think this *mania* you're going through has something to do with fretting about the past, parsing the future. But haven't we learned that the only thing you really have control over is *this moment*. Right now. In *this* room. With *this* audience.

(As the conversation unreels, MICHAEL crosses to the tech table and grabs a bottle of vodka and a glass. Takes a cigarette from a crumpled pack and dangles it from his lips. He picks up the letter from the literary agency for the Samuel Beckett estate, and crosses back to the desk. He sits at the desk, pours a drink, and lifts it to his lips. He stops, thinks better of it, and sets down the glass. He starts to light the cigarette, but thinks better of it, and breaks it in half. He picks up the letter again and fingers it, distractedly.)

GEORGE: It's like that T. S. Eliot quote I read you that says all *time past* and all *time future* is contained in *time present*. And as for the final Beckett speech, I think the only thing you're obliged to do is show us something *personal*. It's like a man seeing a great painting that he's admired all his life for the first time. We're seeing the *man* seeing the *painting*…

MICHAEL: Yeah, well, that is if they even give me permission to use the speech…

GEORGE: Well…you don't have control over *that*, either…!

(BEEP. CLICK. MICHAEL rips open the letter with a flourish and reads into the mic.)

MICHAEL: "Dear Michael,

"Thank you so much for your email. Your passion for the play is evident. However, we've now had a chance to peruse all of the material you sent us, and I'm afraid we cannot authorize any use of Mr. Beckett's copyrighted text in your project.

"I'm so sorry I couldn't be of help with this, but I must follow instructions from the Estate. Best of luck with *Krapp, 39*.

"Sincerely,

Jane Miller, Esq.
The Literary Agency
Samuel Beckett Estate"

(He crumples the letter. A long silence. Finally, he lifts his eyes and takes in the audience for the very first time. He scans their faces, making eye contact across the footlights. He smiles ruefully, leans into the mic, and addresses the audience with a quiet simplicity.)

MICHAEL: This isn't how I imagined this moment.

(A beat.)

Or maybe if I'm being honest, it *is*.

(A beat.)

Take the character away from the actor and what does he have?

(A beat.)

I wanted to be Krapp today.

To bring his memories to life. Of loss and love and death and art. And bananas.

I'll make the recording at home, I guess. By myself. There's still time. I have a year to be thirty-nine.

(A beat.)

Take the character away from the actor and what does he have?

(A beat.)

(And then, wordlessly, he seems to answer his own question: himself. He closes his laptop, putting it to sleep. He shrugs his shoulders and gestures ambiguously to the audience.)

October 28, 2008
New York City

Thirty-nine *today*.

Today I woke up, had a cigarette, walked my dog, was grumpy with my wife, apologized, fretted about the future, parsed the past, worried about my project, rewrote this speech to fit today, came to the theatre.

An ordinary day up until now.

And now I'm here.

Performing.

For a group of strangers. And a few friends.

It's what I do, although I don't always know why.

It's October 28, 2008.

(He looks at his watch.)

Ten forty at night.

My birthday.

(A beat.)

(He smiles into the microphone.)

(In an Irish accent.) I feel a *fire* in me now.

And anything could happen.

(Music: The Beatles' "Birthday" swells through the house as the lights fade to black.)

ABOUT THE EDITOR

MARTIN DENTON Martin Denton is the founder and Executive Director of The New York Theatre Experience, Inc. (NYTE), and editor and chief theatre reviewer for NYTE's website nytheatre.com. He has edited all the play anthologies published by NYTE Small Press featuring, to date, the work of 144 emerging playwrights. He is also the creator of the nytheatrecast (www.nytheatrecast.com), New York City's first regularly scheduled theatre podcast offering original content.

ABOUT THE PUBLISHER

THE NEW YORK THEATRE EXPERIENCE, INC. (NYTE), is a nonprofit New York State corporation. Its mission is to use traditional and new media to foster interest, engagement and participation in theatre and drama and to provide tangible support to theatre artists and dramatists, especially emerging artists and artists in the nonprofit sector. The principal activity of The New York Theatre Experience is the operation of a free website (www.nytheatre.com) that comprehensively covers the New York theatre scene – on, off-, and off-off-Broadway. An ongoing program is NYTE Small Press which publishes yearly anthologies of new plays by emerging playwrights. NYTE received the New York Innovative Theatre Foundation's Stewardship Award in 2008. Information about NYTE can be found on the Internet at www.nyte-inc.org.

Contact NYTE online at info@nyte.org or by mail at:

The New York Theatre Experience, Inc.
P.O. Box 1606, Murray Hill Station
New York, NY 10156

The PLAYS AND PLAYWRIGHTS Series
ISSN 1546-1319
Annual anthologies of new plays by emerging playwrights produced in New York City

Since 2000, The New York Theatre Experience, Inc. (NYTE), has published anthologies of plays which include complete scripts, biographical sketches, and a detailed introduction by the editor, Martin Denton. NYTE is a nonprofit corporation that utilizes its small press to promote the works of emerging playwrights so as to reach a wide audience to show the diverse spirit of contemporary theatre, in terms of genre, form, and subject matter. For complete information about these volumes, please visit www.nytesmallpress.com.

PLAYS AND PLAYWRIGHTS 2001
Edited by Martin Denton, Preface by Robert Simonson
ISBN 09670234-2-4 – Retail $15.00

Washington Square Dreams by Gorilla Repertory Theatre, *Fate* by Elizabeth Horsburgh, *Velvet Ropes* by Joshua Scher, *The Language of Kisses* by Edmund De Santis, *Word To Your Mama* by Julia Lee Barclay, *Cuban Operator Please...* by Adrian Rodriguez, *The Elephant Man –The Musical* by Jeff Hylton & Tim Werenko, *House of Trash* by Trav S.D., *Straight-Jacket* by Richard Day

PLAYS AND PLAYWRIGHTS 2002
Edited by Martin Denton, Foreword by Bill C. Davis
ISBN 09670234-3-2 – Retail $15.00

The Death of King Arthur by Matthew Freeman, *Match* by Marc Chun, *Woman Killer* by Chiori Miyagawa, *The Wild Ass's Skin* by J. Scott Reynolds, *Halo* by Ken Urban, *Shyness Is Nice* by Marc Spitz, *Reality* by Curtiss I' Cook, *The Resurrectionist* by Kate Chell, *Bunny's Last Night In Limbo* by Peter S. Petralia, *Summerland* by Brian Thorstenson

PLAYS AND PLAYWRIGHTS 2003
Edited by Martin Denton, Foreword by Mario Fratti
ISBN 09670234-4-0 – Retail $15.00

A Queer Carol by Joe Godfrey, *Pumpkins For Smallpox* by Catherine Gillet, *Looking For The Pony* by Andrea Lepcio, *Black Thang* by Ato Essandoh, *The Ninth Circle* by Edward Musto, *The Doctor of Rome* by Nat Colley, *Galaxy Video* by Marc Morales, *The Last Carburetor* by Leon Chase, *Out To Lunch* by Joseph Langham, *Ascending Bodily* by Maggie Cino, *Last Call* by Kelly McAllister

PLAYS AND PLAYWRIGHTS 2004
Edited by Martin Denton, Foreword by Kirk Wood Bromley
ISBN 09670234-5-9 – Retail $16.00

Sugarbaby by Frank Cwiklik; *WTC View* by Brian Sloan; *United States: Work and Progress* by Christy Meyer, Jon Schumacher and Ellen Shanman; *The Shady Maids of Haiti* by John Jahnke; *Cats Can See The Devil* by Tom X. Chao; *Survivor: Vietnam!* by Rob Reese; *Feed the Hole* by Michael Stock; *Auntie Mayhem* by David Pumo; *The Monster Tales* by Mary Jett Parsley; *Sun, Stand Thou Still* by Steven Gridley

PLAYS AND PLAYWRIGHTS 2005
Edited by Martin Denton, Foreword by Steven Drukman
ISBN 09670234-6-7 – Retail $16.00

Vampire Cowboy Trilogy by Qui Nguyen & Robert Ross Parker, *second.* by Neal Utterback, *Bull Spears* by Josh Chambers, *Animal* by Kevin Augustine, *Odysseus Died from AIDS* by Stephen Svoboda, *Maggie May* by Tom O'Brien, *Elephant* by Margie Stokley, *Walking to America* by Alberto Bonilla, *The 29 Questions Project* by Katie Bull & Hillary Rollins, *Honor* by TheDrillingCompaNY, *Kalighat* by Paul Knox, *Platonov! Platonov! Platonov! or the case of a very Angry Duck* by Eric Michael Kochmer

PLAYS AND PLAYWRIGHTS 2006
Edited by Martin Denton; Foreword by Trav S.D.
ISBN 09670234-7-5 – Retail $17.00

The Top Ten People of the Millennium Sing Their Favorite Schubert Lieder by Alec Duffy, *Burning the Old Man* by Kelly McAllister, *Self at Hand* by Jack Hanley, *The Expense of Spirit* by Josh Fox, *Paradise* by Glyn O'Malley, *Yit, Ngay (One, Two)* by Michael Lew, *Pulling the Lever* by Rising Circle Theater Collective, *The Position* by Kevin Doyle, *The Dirty Talk* by Michael Puzzo, *The First Time Out of Bounds* by P. Seth Bauer, *Aurolac Blues* by Saviana Stanescu, *The Whore of Sheridan Square* by Michael Baron, Appendix: New American Plays in New York City

PLAYS AND PLAYWRIGHTS 2007
Edited by Martin Denton; Foreword by John Clancy
ISBN 978-0-9670234-9-6 – Retail $18

lenz by bluemouth, inc.; *Office Sonata* by Andy Chmelko; *Kiss and Cry* by Tom Rowan; *They're Just Like Us* by Boo Killebrew; *Convergence* by Bryn Manion; *Red Tide Blooming* by Taylor Mac; *The Adventures of Nervous Boy* by James Comtois; *Another Brief Encounter* by Stan Richardson; *Corps Values* by Brendon Bates; *Diving Normal* by Ashlin Halfnight; *'nami* by Chad Beckim; Appendix: New American Plays in New York City

PLAYS AND PLAYWRIGHTS 2008
Edited by Martin Denton; Foreword by Mark Blankenship
ISBN 978-0-9794852-1-3 – Retail $18

The Telling Trilogy by Crystal Skillman; *What Happened When* by Daniel Talbott; *Antarctica* by Carolyn Raship; *Cleansed* by Thomas Bradshaw; *Linnea* by John Regis; *…and we all wore leather pants* by Robert Attenweiler; *Marvelous Shrine* by Leslie Bramm; *In Our Name* by Elena Hartwell; *Universal Robots* by Mac Rogers; *Fall Forward* by Daniel Reitz; Appendix: New American Plays in New York City

OTHER ANTHOLOGIES BY NYTE SMALL PRESS

PLAYING WITH CANONS: Explosive New Works from Great
Literature by America's Indie Playwrights
Edited by Martin Denton
ISBN 978-0-9670234-8-9 – Retail $26.00

Want's Unwisht Work by Kirk Wood Bromley; *La Tempestad* by Larry Loebell; *Titus X* by Shawn Northrip; *Genesis* by Matthew Freeman; *The Eumenides* by David Johnston; *Principia* by Michael Maiello & Andrew Recinos; *Uncle Jack* by Jeff Cohen; *Story of an Unknown Man* by Anthony P. Pennino; *The Brothers Karamazov Parts I and II* by Alexander Harrington; *Bel Canto* by Reneé Flemings; *Salem* by Alex Roe; *Bartleby the Scrivener* by R. L. Lane; *Frankenstein* by Rob Reese; *Northanger Abbey* by Lynn Marie Macy; *The Man Who Laughs* by Kiran Rikhye; *Bald Diva!: The Ionesco Parody Your Mother Warned You About* by David Koteles, Jason Jacobs & Jamee Freedus; *Fatboy* by John Clancy; *The Persians…a comedy about war with five songs* by Waterwell

UNPREDICTABLE PLAYS
by Mario Fratti
Edited and with a Preface by Martin Denton
ISBN 978-0-9794852-0-6 – Retail: $20.00

The Friday Bench; Suicide Club; Alessia; The Piggy Bank; The Fourth One; Dolls No More; Porno; Dina and Alba; The Bridge; Confessions; The Coffin; A.I.D.S.; Brothel (The Doorbell); The Letter; Mothers and Daughters; Beata, the Pope's Daughter; The Wish; Erotic Adventures in Venice (Promises); The Academy; Friends; Terrorist; The Return; The Seventy-fifth; Iraq (Blindness); "Che"; Anniversary; Missionaries; Sincerity